Saving Lives And Preventing Misery
The memoirs of Professor Sir John Wenman Crofton

Edited, abridged and annotated by David C. Kilpatrick

An environmentally friendly book printed and bound in England by
www.printondemand-worldwide.com

First published 2013 by
FASTPRINT PUBLISHING of Peterborough, England.

www.fast-print.net/store.php

SAVING LIVES AND PREVENTING MISERY
Copyright © David C. Kilpatrick 2013

ISBN 978-178035-541-2

The right of David C. Kilpatrick to be identified as the editor of this work has
been asserted by him in accordance with the Copyright, Designs and
Patents Act 1988 and any subsequent amendments thereto.
A catalogue record for this book is available from the British Library

Contents

Preface

John Wenman Crofton was one of the outstanding figures in twentieth century medicine. He was first and foremost a physician, but was also an academic and social reformer. He belonged to that great tradition of physician-scientists characterised by a rational and critical approach to medicine, to which René Laennec, Robert Koch, Ronald Ross and Richard Doll also belonged. His major contribution was to the treatment of pulmonary tuberculosis. This achievement was recognised by the bestowing of many honours, including a knighthood and the Edinburgh Medal.

After his "retirement" in 1977, he received a pension instead of a salary, but still kept himself very busy following his interest in public health. He and his wife, Eileen, also found time for regular holidays, often in Scotland with their Volkswagen camper van. It was during some of those holiday trips that John wrote a series of accounts of various stages of his life, mainly for his family, over a period of more than 20 years. These memoirs constitute a remarkable record of an extraordinarily long and productive life. They also contain important social history, describing the life of the prosperous Anglo-Irish before the First World War, military life during the Second World War, and the medical milieu of post-war Edinburgh.

Although ostensibly written for his family, I believe John wrote also because he felt impelled to leave a detailed record of his life and work. Shortly before his death, I suggested I should try to get this work published when I myself retired. Later, his widow expressed enthusiasm for the project, and I arranged for the original typescripts to be re-typed onto a modern computer. Unfortunately, Eileen also died before this was completed and before my own retirement. I have since edited and abridged the original texts totalling around 200,000 words to produce a revised version reduced by a quarter, forming twelve coherent chapters from which overlapping and repetitive material has been removed. In this task, I have been greatly assisted by two of John's daughters, my wife Alison and Dr Patricia Raemaekers. John was a co-founder of TB Alert in 1998, the only British charity working solely against tuberculosis, to which all royalties from the sale of this book will go.

John's own writings are preceded by an Introduction in two parts. In the first section, I give an account of the man and his work. In the second, I give a short history of tuberculosis in order to place John's most important work within an appropriate historical context.

As the rest of us grow older and die, memories of John will fade ultimately into nothingness. As he himself wrote, his life will be remembered simply as a footnote in the history of tuberculosis. Atheists can expect no more. Yet his work is estimated to have saved the lives of millions. It was a remarkable and outstanding achievement that few can equal and which deserves to be remembered as long as some form of human civilisation exists.

Introduction

Professor Sir John Crofton and the History of Tuberculosis

John Wenman Crofton (1912-2009)

John W. Crofton has been described as "one of the pre-eminent physicians of the twentieth century"[*] He left his mark most prominently in two fields. First, he was the leader of a pioneering medical team that established that pulmonary tuberculosis could be permanently cured by combination chemotherapy. The crucial insight was that monotherapy often led to bacterial resistance but this could be prevented by using a minimum of three drugs simultaneously. This principle remains at the present day, except the standard regimen involves four drugs. Second, he was a prominent public health campaigner who did much to change the public and political attitudes to smoking tobacco. Both those achievements were mediated by his profound drive and determination, and his ability to persuade others to act in a concerted manner. However, he was also unfailingly courteous, tolerant and kind. His approach was always positive, encouraging and gentlemanly.

John was born in Dublin (Baile Atha Cliath) to a well-to-do Anglo-Irish family. His mother was sweet and saintly, as all decent mothers are, at least as their sons remember them. His father, however, was brilliant, eccentric and domineering. His father's unreasonableness caused a deep rift between him and John's two sisters. It is tempting to conclude that John's humanitarian impulses were inherited from his Christian mother, and his drive and vigour from his father.

William Mervyn Crofton was evidently a very prominent citizen. When he was a student and felt unwell, he travelled to Oxford to consult the great Sir William Osler[#], no less. When he had thoughts about dealing with the Irish independence movement, he went over to London and obtained an

---

[*] Professor Neil Douglas, quoted in *The Scotsman* 4th November 2009; also *The Herald*, November 6th 2009.

[#] William Osler (1849-1919), physician, academic, educator and historian of medicine. Widely regarded as the father of modern medicine.

interview with David Lloyd George, the British Prime Minister. William Crofton was clearly no ordinary Dad.

John's schooling was unremarkable and apparently not unhappy. He was subjected to the standard scholastic experience of the affluent at that time, which involved boarding away from home. This inevitably caused some unhappiness and homesickness at first, as his account of his "prep" school at the age of nine reveals. Nevertheless, he adapted well and by the time he attended Tonbridge School in Kent, he was able to settle in and became a scholastic and sporting success. This was in part because he was a (self-confessed) conformist and one who took trouble to make friends and be accepted. His abilities on the rugby and hockey pitches probably won him much approval from fellow pupils and masters alike. But his relatively happy schooldays could also have been due to a benign regime at Tonbridge. John's recollection was of an enlightened establishment. This is consistent with Conrad Keating's speculation that Richard Doll's education was nurtured by an enlightened attitude at Westminster School at around the same time[*]. Yet it is hard to reconcile with the feudal customs of the exclusive private schools in England at that time. One might speculate that the tough upbringing away from his gentle home and family life provided the basis for some tenacity in his personality. One aim of such schools was to produce leaders of the Empire, and in that respect John was a successful product. He may have felt that he didn't learn "leadership" until he joined the army, but the basis was perhaps implanted in him much earlier along with a stiff upper lip.

Oddly enough, he considered that neither his school nor university education taught him how to learn effectively. This was responsible, in his view, for his relatively modest attainment at Cambridge and made him sympathetic to novel approaches in educational theory in later life. Yet his achievements at school and university were more than was expected of someone in his position; a medical degree was then, as now, a tough choice requiring much hard work and application. If he did not do as well as he himself thought he should, it may have been that so much of his focus was on holidays and latterly on climbing, in particular.

Certainly a substantial proportion of his account of his childhood, youth and student days describe holidays. These memories are vividly recalled and reported in remarkable detail. During his time as an undergraduate he became an enthusiastic and skilled rock climber, so at that time leisure may have been more important to him than his studies. Nevertheless, from an early age he was prepared to read widely and well outside the range of his

---

[*] Conrad Keating (2009). *Smoking Kills. The revolutionary life of Richard Doll.*

formal course requirements. He obviously had a lively and enquiring mind and he continued to read avidly and widely until his death.

By his mid-twenties he had done all that was expected of someone sent to a prestigious, expensive school by a forceful father, but (apart from climbing) he had not yet found himself. That changed when he became a junior physician and discovered his vocation:

> The outlook of the hospital over the Thames was delightful. I have memories of being hauled up to emergencies in the middle of the night and the peaceful atmosphere after the problem had been dealt with. The city lay silent about me save for the lights and faint engines of tugs and barges still moving romantically up and down the river. Somehow the feeling of that peace, against the background of at last doing such a wonderfully worthwhile job, mingled to give me much inner satisfaction and support.

From this point he could channel his drive and determination into his life's work. He was to combine his primary role as physician with his natural aptitude to be an academic and his third motivation to be a social reformer.

> Although medicine's immediate concerns are to save lives and prevent or ameliorate misery, I had to be aware of related longer term aims such as relieving poverty, more closely at home, more remotely internationally.

All this was interrupted by the War. Yet the War provided valuable medical experience, and the basis of an academic study of typhus[*]. Consequently, without the need for a period of supervised study, John was able to graduate with an M.D. degree and call himself "a proper doctor".

John's description of his student days is interesting. He worked hard at his studies, he played hard at hockey and he socialised extensively with a small group of male friends who called themselves "The Five Mile Club". They were unlikely to be true misogynists. It is more likely they were extremely shy with girls, and devised this "society" as a self-defence mechanism. John was a very late developer in forming romantic ideas about women. In later life, he held liberal views on sexual matters, but always retained a certain reticence at a personal level. These memoirs were written mainly for his family, and we must not forget that, according to Philip Larkin,[#] sexual intercourse began in 1963!

Politics was discussed amongst the friends, but it did not seem to have been of major importance to most of them. In his biography of Richard Doll, Conrad Keating lumps John together with Doll and Archie Cochrane as radical, left-wing young medics of the thirties. Nevertheless, there were

---

[*] An acute febrile disease from infection with *Rickettsia prowazekii*, intracellular gram-negative bacteria spread by body lice.

[#] Philip Larkin (1922-1985), poet and librarian.

significant political differences among the three. John was a lifelong and committed supporter of the British Labour Party. In contrast, Doll was a Soviet-supporting communist. Cochrane, a politically free-thinking anti-Fascist, interrupted his medical studies to join the British Ambulance Unit with the International Brigade in Spain, where he developed a mistrust of communist ideology. All three men served with the Royal Army Medical Corps (RAMC) during World War II.

John was already associated with the RAMC in 1939 and joined up at the outbreak of war. His war years were full of contradictions. There were times he faced great danger and was almost overwhelmed with medical work; there were risk-free periods with ample time for leisure. There were drunken, lazy, incompetent officers and ill-disciplined troops; there were effective, organised leaders and splendid, conscientious foot soldiers. There was generally poor communication from above and much moving on at short notice.

The Second World War made a profound impression on many (perhaps most) of the individuals who took part, whatever their backgrounds or attitudes. Although he would later observe that "war is hell", John considered that the war years converted him into a leader and also gave him the opportunity of foreign travel:

> I personally benefited from the war in several respects. As a young man I was very shy, especially with my seniors. The war gave me the opportunity of command and initiative. It greatly increased my self-confidence. I vastly increased my experiences of people, people of many different social backgrounds and indeed of many different nations. I served in thirteen different army units, often with considerable turnover of staff, so that I made many friends. After the war there was almost nowhere in the UK where I did not have a friend.

> I visited, at government expense, a number of different countries, serving in France, Germany, Egypt, Greece, Eritrea, Malta, and Northern Ireland, calling in at Cape Town and Durban on my way to the Middle East, and spending some leave in Palestine, Syria and Lebanon.

John's much younger brother, Dick, was killed while serving with the Royal Air Force (RAF). John hardly knew him, having been away at school and university while Dick was growing up. Whatever John's feelings about his brother, Dick's death seems to have affected John more through its effect on their mother who never quite got over her loss. Nevertheless, John wrote a moving poem after Dick's death.

John's general attitude to World War II was the conventional British (or Churchillian) viewpoint:

> By looking back more widely on the world scene, I am convinced how very essential it was to fight this war. Of course we knew that at the time, but the full horrors of the Nazis' arrogant, bestial and perverted cult of cruelty,

their anti-civilisation, was only revealed to most of us when the concentration camps were liberated and we had contact with those who had been so viciously racked and torn by the Gestapo and its minions. In ancient times Attila and Tamburlaine had butchered and tortured with the ruthless wildness of a savage barbarism. In our day Hitler had tragically debauched all the resources of a modern state to turn it from one of the most civilised nations of Europe into the very embodiment of evil …This must have been one of the few wars in history which had to be fought.

There is no mention in these memoirs of the cluster bombing of German civilians or unease about the Soviet Union as an ally. He felt that the atomic bombs dropped on civilians in Hiroshima and Nagasaki were necessary because such actions hastened the Japanese surrender. Nevertheless he took a compassionate view of the horror inflicted on Japanese civilians when he described a visit he made to Hiroshima after the war.

Another aspect of John's war is noteworthy in several ways. On some occasions, he acted as "Prisoner's Friend" or defence attorney at courts martial. His account of twice defending a Geordie miscreant reveals some satisfaction in using his intelligence to get an obviously guilty man off. It may have been this experience which prompted him to answer, when asked during a *Lancet Lifeline* interview, that he would have liked to have been a barrister if he had not been a physician. It also led him to conclude, "courts martial are remarkably fair", despite the absence of both qualified legal representation and a jury, and without the presence of either press or public. John was also a witness at another court martial which is remarkable for his attitude to the accused. A delinquent Sikh corporal had shot dead an officer at random, tried to escape by stealing a truck, then shot a policeman after he had been captured. Yet John has obvious sympathy for the criminal.

It was during the War that John first met Guy Scadding. They became friends and during the immediate post-war years Scadding became John's mentor and John, Scadding's protégé.

> I learned an enormous amount from Guy. We became lifelong friends.
> He gave me all my chances.

Scadding found John work at the Brompton Hospital in London, first unpaid, then in a registrar's post. Most importantly, Scadding asked John to act as local coordinator in the Medical Research Council's multi-centre trial of streptomycin. This was an introduction to randomised, controlled trials and John absorbed Bradford Hill's[*] concept readily. The experience of witnessing an apparent wonder drug lose its potency due to bacterial resistance was also not lost on him.

---

[*] Austin (Tony) Bradford Hill (1879-1991) was a medical statistician who advocated randomization in clinical trials.

By the time John had moved to Edinburgh he was aware of the importance of controls in clinical trials, the nature of drug resistance, and the diligence and tact required to prosecute a successful clinical trial. His insight into drug resistance and how to overcome it, his key medical insight in the 1950s, would not have been effective by itself. Equally, if not more important, was good organisation and administration. Patients had to be carefully monitored and nagged to do things properly, and that was also true of the medical and paramedical staff looking after them. All this required extremely hard work and the ability to inspire dedication in others. John seems to have had an exceptional ability to get the best out of colleagues and by then was used to working very long hours himself. Even then, this could not have been possible without the contribution of an exceptionally gifted and determined team.

One story from those days illustrates an endearing aspect of his personality. Although very well-read and erudite, John had a considerable ignorance of popular culture. There was one occasion when he claimed not to have heard of Mickey Mouse, but it is possible he was pulling our legs. Certainly he was genuinely astonished and uncomprehending when one of his patients attracted a lot of attention from newspapers and photographers. This was Lawrie Reilly, celebrated footballer, who, to this day is the holder of one of the best scoring records for the Scottish national team.[*]

The Edinburgh tuberculosis problem was solved in less than a decade but John spent several more decades travelling around the world spreading the word about combination chemotherapy and trying to improve treatment in countries where resources and organisation were poor. Back in Edinburgh he increasingly involved himself in academic administration. For several years he was vice-principal of Edinburgh University. This coincided with the period of student protest and unrest, yet John managed to contend with the revolting students without too much trouble. He had rather more difficulty with the staff - gifted, strong-minded, determined "angry men" - especially when he was Dean. He coped very well using charm and diplomacy and a liberal exploitation of social occasions. Nevertheless, he obviously found this period to have been extremely stressful, indeed his memoirs give the impression it was more demanding than the war years or the clinical struggle against tuberculosis.

It therefore came as something of a respite to act as president of the Edinburgh Royal College of Physicians. For the last few years of his formal

---

[*] Reilly scored 22 goals for Scotland in 38 matches between 1948 and 1957. In conversations, this editor attempted to keep John informed about Reilly. Shortly after John's death, his patient Reilly became the last survivor of the legendary Hibernian Famous Five forward line.

employment he happily spent time advancing the aims of the College at home and abroad. Later he was to expend considerable effort in successfully raising funds for a conference centre extension to the College. Today a seminar room in the College bears his name.

Retirement in 1977 brought about a change from salary to pension but not from work. He continued to travel the world and continued to campaign for better prevention and treatment of tuberculosis. Increasingly, social problems occupied his time and in particular the problem of tobacco smoking.

In that regard, John's contribution was the converse of Richard Doll's. Doll made the major medical advances involving tobacco but was reluctant to use his findings as propaganda. John made no medical advances in the field, but was a vigorous campaigner. He was instrumental in setting up the Scottish wing of the pressure group, Action on Smoking and Health, with his wife, Eileen, becoming its first director. He was one of many determined and effective agitators against the influence of the tobacco industry. In 2006, Scotland became the first country in the United Kingdom to ban smoking in public places, an outcome that must have seemed impossible when he retired from his university job in 1977.

Retirement also brought greater time for leisure. Travel was not just working trips with a holiday tagged on. John and Eileen had time for pure holidays, including visits to Corsica and further exploration of the Scottish Highlands.

John and Eileen had five children, three girls sandwiched between the older and the younger boys. Each sibling produced at least two offspring, a total of eleven grandchildren. A lunch to celebrate their golden wedding in 1995 was a remarkable spectacle. John and Eileen hosted the lunch in a spacious room in an inn in Haddington, surrounded by their direct descendants plus spouses.

John was generally very healthy throughout most of his active "retirement". Apart from hip replacements as a result of osteoarthritis, there were no serious medical problems until he reached his nineties. As part of his 90th birthday celebrations, John expressed a wish to climb a Munro[*] and Ben Vorlich was chosen as the location for a small family outing. Although a date was agreed, the hill walk never took place because John damaged his artificial hip. Sadly, he never walked freely again, getting around valiantly with a pronounced limp. In his mid-nineties, he collapsed after attending a function at the College of Physicians. This led to a diagnosis of aortic valve

---

[*] A Scottish mountain over 3000 feet high, named after Sir Hugh T. Munro who was the first to tabulate them in 1891.

stenosis. Other episodes of cardiogenic pulmonary oedema followed over the next year or so and in the summer of 2009, a bout of pneumonia. At this point, he realised he was dying and prepared for his end. It happened a few months later, at home with his wife beside him.

At John's request, his funeral service was conducted by Kenneth Boyd, a friend who was part of a philosophical debating circle. The main appreciation was given by Colin Currie, geriatrician, novelist[*] and former student representative all those years before when John was vice-principal. John's children all gave brief tributes. The main chapel of Mortonhall Crematorium was full − unusual for a man so old, one who had outlived most of his contemporaries. In attendance were not only former colleagues and friends, but also a few former patients.

John had a wide circle of friends throughout the world with whom he strove to keep in touch. Those who survive him will remember a warm personality, a life-long supporter of the National Health Service and its founding principles, and a compassionate advocate of social justice.

Tuberculosis

Tuberculosis (TB) is defined as tissue infection by the intracellular bacterium, *Mycobacterium tuberculosis*. The host cells infected by the tubercle bacilli are macrophages[#] and therefore any part of the body can be affected. Renal TB and TB meningitis are potentially fatal as acute illnesses, but mortality from the much commoner lung infection is usually preceded by a long period of chronic illness.

Pulmonary tuberculosis or "consumption" is the classic respiratory disorder of tragic heroines, like Violetta in Verdi's *La Traviata* and Mimi in Puccini's *La Bohème*. Equally moving, and a lot closer to home, is the description of the death of Margo Roberts from tuberculous meningitis and its effect on an ordinary Edinburgh family in Colin Currie's novel, *Sickness and Health[*]*. That kind of family tragedy, of a young girl dying amongst a loving family desperate but totally unable to help, was not rare in the Scottish capital in the 1950s.

Today, tuberculosis is estimated to cause 1.5 to 2 million deaths a year globally. Yet in most normal, healthy people it is a self-limiting infection that does little harm. The bacteria provoke a vigorous cellular response

---

[*] Colin Currie wrote under the *nom de plume* of Colin Douglas.

[#] Phagocytic cells, part of the innate immune system, widely distributed in body tissues..

critically mediated by interferon-γ and activated macrophages*. Usually, this immune response results in life-long containment (latent tuberculosis) that is asymptomatic. Sometimes the response is only partial or quite inadequate. Although individuals with a rare inherited immune deficiency[#] are particularly vulnerable, secondary immune deficiency associated with malnutrition and/or co-existing diseases (especially Human Immunodeficiency Virus (HIV) disease) much more commonly predispose to chronic TB infection. Since TB is most readily transmitted by inhalation, it is much commoner where overcrowding and unhygienic living conditions are found. It is therefore predominantly a consequence of poverty and is principally a public health issue. Given the gross inequality in the distribution of wealth across the world, it is understandable that around one-third of the human population may have been infected.

Today, tuberculosis and HIV disease often go together. In stark contrast to HIV disease, TB is a disease that goes back to antiquity. Characteristic lesions have been found in Egyptian mummies over 3000 years old, and modern molecular techniques indicate that TB originated in East Africa long before then. A clinically similar disorder ("phthisis") was common in ancient Greece and the ancient Romans may have disseminated the same disease to their northernmost colony which they called Britannia. It has been suggested that the first mycobacteria originated 150 million years ago; it can be stated with more confidence that the modern strains of *M. tuberculosis* emerged from a common ancestor about 20,000 years ago.

Although many authors (including Hippocrates) had described the clinical presentation of pulmonary TB, modern pathological understanding of the disease is attributed to René Laennec, the inventor of the stethoscope, who summarised his post-mortem examination experience of TB victims in 1819 in his treatise, *D'Auscultation Médiate*. At that time, death rates from TB throughout Europe were very high.

The cause, however, was completely unknown, although as early as 1790 Benjamin Martin had guessed its infectious nature. After Louis Pasteur's demonstration of the existence of bacteria, the concept of an infectious cause became more plausible and popular. The first empirical evidence may have come from a French military surgeon, Jean-Antoine Villemin, who infected a rabbit by injecting it with an inoculum from a tuberculous cavity accessed at autopsy. The really convincing breakthrough, however, came in 1882

---

* T lymphocytes recognise and respond to the bacteria by producing interferon-γ, a defensive molecule with multiple effects including making macrophages more effective in killing microbes.

[#] Deficiency of the receptor for interferon-γ

when Robert Koch demonstrated that the TB bacilli satisfied his eponymous postulates*. A Nobel Prize for medicine soon followed. Those were the days when physicians became Nobel laureates (Ronald Ross was similarly honoured for his work on malaria at around the same time).

Robert Koch hoped a bacterial extract he called "tuberculin" could be used prophylactically in the manner of variolation/vaccination. This expectation was ill-founded, but the great immunologist Clemens von Pirquet adapted the idea for use as a diagnostic test. The size of the lump following injection of tuberculin into the skin was an indication of previous exposure to the tubercle bacillus. This work led to the discovery of a common asymptomatic carrier state von Pirquet termed latent tuberculosis. To complete this section of TB history, we should remember Charles Mantoux's technical improvement (hence Mantoux test)[#] and the development of a purified protein derivative (PPD)[Ψ] of tuberculosis by Florence Siebert.

The failure of tuberculin vaccination to elicit protective immunity led to the development of an attenuated form of *M.bovin* by Albert Calmette and Camille Guerin, which became known as Bacille-Calmette-Guerin or BCG. At the time, the most popular treatment strategy was a regime of rest, nourishing food and fresh air in sanatoria. Since sanatoria ensured the isolation of TB patients from the general public, they must have been effective at limiting the spread of the disease. Whether or not sanatoria improved the outcome for patients is less certain, but some evidence exists that for those with minimal disease, sanatorium care was indeed beneficial. Surgical treatment was also mooted during the first half of the 20th century. Perhaps surprisingly, both artificial pneumothorax and thoracoplasty[μ] were associated with some measure of success.

BCG vaccination was introduced after a dramatic and unexplained decline in mortality in Europe and North America, arrested only during the periods corresponding to the First and Second World Wars. Early controlled trials of BCG conducted between the wars and shortly after World War II had provided promising, positive results. However, the consensus view now

---

* A bacterium is proved to be the cause of an infectious disease if "Koch's Postulates" are satisfied: the organism can be isolated from the lesions; the organism can be cultured outside the body for several generations; the disease can be transferred to healthy animals; and the organism can be recovered from the animals after death.

[#] The Mantoux test for previous exposure to TB uses a cannulated needle

[Ψ] PPD is prepared from TB culture medium and is the standard extract used in the Mantoux test

[μ] Surgical procedures to allow air into the pleural cavity causing the lung to collapse and "rest".

is that while BCG seems to boost protective immunity in children, it has little or no value in adults.

Penicillin was the first of a new generation of antibiotics that had unprecedented efficacy against some gram-negative bacteria, but not mycobacteria. At much the same time, however, both para-aminosalicylic acid (PAS) and thiosemicarbazone did have some efficacy in the treatment of pulmonary tuberculosis.

Another potentially beneficial drug, streptomycin, had been discovered in 1944. A small supply had been allocated to the Medical Research Council in 1946, and an MRC committee decided to conduct a blind, randomised, controlled trial of streptomycin hydrochloride in 107 young adults with acute progressive bilateral pulmonary tuberculosis deemed unsuitable for collapse therapy[*]. At this time, controlled trials were uncommon and the only adequately controlled trial in TB (of gold treatment) had yielded negative results. The patients were either given streptomycin plus bed rest for 4 months or bed rest alone. After six months, radiological improvement was twice as common in the streptomycin group (69% versus 33%) and deterioration less common (20% versus 34%). Only 7% of patients in the streptomycin group had died, compared with 27% in the control group. Even after 12 months, the difference in the death rate (22% versus 46%) was statistically significant[#]. The trial therefore convincingly demonstrated that regular injections of streptomycin were of value in some patients with pulmonary tuberculosis. However, major improvements were most common during the first three months of treatment and strains of tubercle bacilli resistant to high streptomycin concentrations were commonly isolated from patients whose sputa[Ψ] were still positive.

The MRC streptomycin trial was planned and directed by a 15-man committee which included J. Guy Scadding. Scadding's registrar at the Brompton Hospital was John Crofton who acted as the lead clinician on the streptomycin trial at the Brompton site.

With the streptomycin experience behind him, John Crofton moved to Edinburgh to take up the Chair of Respiratory Medicine and Tuberculosis in 1952. He immediately set up a team of chest physicians (Norman Horne, Ian Ross, Ian Grant, Jimmy Williamson), bacteriologists (Archie Wallace, Sheila Stewart) and other health professionals to challenge the high incidence of TB present in the city at that time. By then, an orally-active anti-TB wonder

---

[*] See previous note. In this instance, pneumothorax is meant.

[#] The actual probability values were: 6-month radiological improvement, p=0.0002; 6-month mortality, p=0.009; 12-month mortality, p=0.01

[Ψ] Presence of TB bacteria in the sputum was an indication of active disease

drug, isoniazid, had become available. The recognised problem of drug resistance was countered by combining oral isoniazid and p-aminosalicylic acid with injections of streptomycin. Great care was taken to ensure patients' compliance with this unpleasant regimen, and over a sufficient period of time. In consequence, there was a full bacteriological and radiological cure in all patients who completed the treatment. After some scepticism, the "Edinburgh method" of triple chemotherapy was widely adopted with striking success.

First rifampicin, then other new oral mycobactericidal drugs, became available. Currently favoured treatment in the UK combines isoniazid, rifampicin, pyrazinamide and ethambutol, all of which can be taken by mouth. Combination chemotherapy virtually abolished pulmonary TB in the developed world for a time. In poorer countries, success was less marked. Even in developed countries there was a resurgence of TB incidence in the 1980s in association with the newly reported Acquired Immune Deficiency Syndrome (AIDS) later recognised as an end stage of HIV disease.

Also in the 1980s, the Conservative Government's changes to the welfare state led to a dramatic rise in homelessness amongst young people in Britain. Suddenly, it became common to see young people sleeping in shop entrances in British cities, including Edinburgh. About that time an unusual number of patients were being referred to Edinburgh's City Hospital with hepatitis B infection. Later, it became apparent that many of them were also infected with HIV. This was the cohort of young intravenous drug users .described by Irvine Welsh in *Trainspotting*. Some years later, many of them became ill with AIDS and subsequently died.

Fortunately, new cases of HIV infection in Britain are now uncommon in heroin addicts, despite the continuing popularity of opiate abuse. Nevertheless, the incidence of HIV infection (sexually transmitted, not drug-related) appears to be rising. The most serious effects of HIV infection are now effectively controlled by highly active anti-retroviral therapy (HAART), another striking example of successful combination therapy.

So while pulmonary tuberculosis remains a residual health problem in the UK, it is not the major problem it once was. The situation in developing countries is rather different. The World Health Organisation's Stop TB Strategy includes a standardised approach to diagnosis and treatment. From 1995 the DOTS programme (Directly Observed Therapy, Short Course) of rapid diagnosis by sputum examination followed by relatively cheap chemotherapy from local clinics was outstandingly effective. However, this was being conducted in the context of huge prevalence rates of HIV in some countries. Consequently, it is estimated that 1 in 3 human beings has been infected with *M. tuberculosis*; there are 9 million new cases every year and perhaps 1.8 million deaths. In the high burden countries, as many as 50% of the adult population smoke, 15% are diabetic and the same proportion have HIV infection. Other risk factors like poverty and malnutrition are common and will not be eliminated easily. The long-term target of eliminating TB as a public health concern (defined as prevalence of less than 1case per million) may not be achieved.

The most recent complication to emerge is the increasing level of drug resistance. Somewhat unhelpfully, "multidrug resistance" (MDR) is defined as resistance to just two drugs, isoniazid and rifampicin, as a minimum. The term "extensive drug resistance" (XDR) is defined by resistance to isoniazid, rifampicin, any fluoroquinone and any one of three second-line injectable drugs. Very recently, strains of *M. tuberculosis* that appear resistant to all known anti-tuberculosis drugs have emerged. It is estimated that up to 5% of all clinical isolates are MDR, posing a major threat to existing control programmes since treatment is more complex, more expensive and perhaps less effective, than for drug-susceptible disease.

Vaccination has been the most effective strategy in conquering infectious diseases, especially where a vigorous antibody response prevents primary infection. However, antibody responses are ineffective towards *M. tuberculosis*. Instead, the infection is contained by a cellular response involving lymphocytes and macrophages. BCG vaccination is helpful in young children but not so in adults and may be dangerous in the context of HIV co-infection. The original BCG has been improved by genetic engineering and numerous alternative vaccines are currently being explored. Preliminary results confer some promise but no definitive conclusions can be made at present.

The " battle with the bug", as John Crofton called it, may have been won by combination chemotherapy in the 1950s, but the war against tuberculosis continues and is of uncertain outcome. Basic research into the immunology of mycobacterial infection may ultimately lead to the design of an effective vaccine. New mycobacteriocidal drugs will continue to be discovered. A recent breakthrough has been a new diagnostic test that uses an automated molecular mechanism to accurately diagnose and simultaneously identify rifampicin resistance. However, if tuberculosis is to be eradicated at least three requirements are essential: (1) an inexpensive and accurate point-of-care diagnostic test; (2) an ultra-short therapeutic regimen that would include new drugs; and (3) an effective pre- or post-exposure vaccine. It is likely that tuberculosis will be with us for some time to come.

List of Abbreviations

ASH	Action on Smoking and Health
BCG	Bacille Calmette-Guérin
BMA	British Medical Association
BNMT	Britain Nepal Medical Trust
CCS	Casualty Clearing Station
CHSS	Chest Heart and Stroke Scotland
CO	Commanding Officer
CUMC	Cambridge University Mountaineering Club
DHSS	Department of Health and Social Security
DOTS	Directly Observed Therapy – Short course
DSO	Distinguished Service Order
GP	General Practitioner
HIV	Human Immunodeficiency Virus
IOCU	International Organisation of Consumer Unions
IUAT	International Union Against Tuberculosis
IUATLD	International Union Against Tuberculosis and Lung Disease
MBE	Member of the most excellent order of the British Empire
MC	Military Cross
MDR	Multi-Drug Resistance
MO	Medical Officer
MOH	Medical Officer of Health
MRC	Medical Research Council
MRCP	Member of the Royal College of Physicians
NCO	Non-Commissioned Officer
NGO	Non-Governmental Organisation

NHS	National Health Service
OC	Officer in Charge
PAS	para-amino-salicylic acid
POW	Prisoners Of War
RAMC	Royal Army Medical Corps
RAP	Resident Assistant Physician
RASC	Royal Army Service Corps
RCPE	Royal College of Physicians of Edinburgh
SHECC	Scottish Health Education Co-ordinating Committee
SRC	Students' Representative Council
TALC	Teaching Aids at Low Cost
TB	Tuberculosis
UICC	International Union Against Cancer (from the French: Union Internationale Contre le Cancer)
VIP	Very Important Person
VC	Victoria Cross
WGH	Western General Hospital
WHO	World Health Organisation

Chapter 1
Childhood and Boyhood

Parents

I was born on 27th March 1912 at 52 Merrion Square, Dublin. I was the son of Dr William Mervyn Crofton and his wife Molly, the second of four children. My elder sister, Patricia, preceded me by five years. My younger sister, Joan (later known as Joanna), hurried after me eighteen months later. My younger brother, Dick, arrived more tardily in 1919.

My mother's maiden name was Mary Josephine Abbott, but she was always known as "Molly". She was the youngest of the three daughters of my grandfather, Joseph Abbot, the Dean of Old Leighlin, a small cathedral town in County Carlow.

As far as I remember, my mother spent all her youth in County Carlow. Her father ran a small school in his house for a few children of local Protestant gentry, including one or more of his daughters, and was a very kind person. My mother became engaged to my father at a relatively early age, probably eighteen or nineteen, though it was five years before my father had qualified and could afford to get married. I think they met because their families were very distantly related.

By all accounts my mother was a girl of immense verve, energy and charm, which indeed she kept till very old age. She did most of the nursing in her mother's last illness, apparently a rather prolonged one, and then tended to run her father's household. I think her two sisters were less effective. All her life she had great concern for people, especially if they were in any sort of trouble. In her youth I gather she was very popular, both with her contemporaries and her elders, and of course with the people she helped. However, she was not a solemn do-gooder. She had a great sense of humour and of fun.

I imagine my own father's enormous intellectual curiosity and originality must have been a great stimulus to my mother. They started married life in general practice in rural Lincolnshire, but when, after three years, a lectureship was created for him at University College in Dublin they moved back to Ireland and soon lived in a much more stimulating professional and academic circle. As a result my mother obviously set about educating herself. Although lacking my father's very outstanding originality, I found her to be very well-read with a broad range of interests when I was old enough to appreciate such matters.

She was certainly a wonderful mother to me, caring, stimulating and encouraging. She never preached at me, but created an atmosphere which assumed that you would take responsibility for helping other people, especially if they were in difficulties. One soaks up this sort of family atmosphere unconsciously. The principles were never overtly stated. I owe her so much, probably even more than I ever consciously appreciated. Like so many mothers, she was a worrier, not about herself, but about her children or her friends. She died at the age of eighty. It was sad that for the last few years her mind had begun to go. While I was on a lecture tour in New Zealand and Australia in 1962 she went into rather rapid heart failure and died in about a week – probably a happy release.

From the time I went away to prep school I always wrote to her at least once a week when I was away from home, including all through the war years. Of course she wrote to me with equal regularity. I remember one letter, I think in the summer of 1940 when the daylight Blitz was still hitting London. She recounted that she had been driving through Piccadilly Circus when a German plane came swooping down machine-gunning. She added that she really thought the traffic police ought to alert drivers when this sort of thing was occurring! I particularly recall the wonderful reunion when I returned in 1944 after four years abroad. It was a beautiful September day. With Mother and sister Joanna (my father was working), in the afternoon we took a rug out into Park Square, opposite our house, and talked non-stop for three or four hours. All mothers, or almost all mothers, are marvellous, but I was so lucky to have had one of the most marvellous. I don't believe she ever said a nasty word about anyone or did a nasty thing.

My mother's character was loving, caring, efficient and supportive, but it was not complex. By comparison, my father's character was immensely complex. He had great intelligence, intellectual curiosity, originality and drive. He was tremendously caring to his patients and to people who depended on him, including his children, particularly when we were young. But he had a very strong personality. He knew he was always right. I often heard him say "If I say a thing is so, it *is* so!" He was a fighter, quite ruthless and critical of those who opposed his views professionally. His views had to be accepted unconditionally. He had no use for those who questioned them. Professionally therefore he tended to cooperate only with colleagues who accepted his views and who regarded him as "The Master". As I began to learn medicine, at first I argued over some of his views. But I soon found that only complete acceptance was tolerated. I had no taste for family disruption and began to avoid professional discussion. However, I have a lot to thank my father for. As a child he handled me with tact and skill. He himself had suffered when young from much small-minded discipline. He was determined that his children would be spared this. But I well remember, when I was at the difficult 11-12 age and being very uppish and critical with my mother, my father pointing out the immense time and trouble my mother took over me and how important it was for me to show how much I appreciated this and not to cause her distress. I felt very contrite and think – and hope – that I mended my ways. How much more effective than coming down on me like a load of bricks!

He was equally skilled with my sisters and brother. He was devoted to the girls, but, sadly, showed up badly, as some fathers do, when my sisters wanted to get married. He rejected their fiancés in the grimmest way. For my elder sister's wedding I had to come over surreptitiously from Cambridge to give her away, the wedding having been planned to take place while Father was away in London. My mother had already had a terrible time for supporting her daughter and there was an appalling row, which caused me also great distress, when he came back and found Patricia gone. For some years he cut her off completely – until she had her first child, when all suddenly became sweetness and light!

Exactly the same happened with my younger sister, Joanna. This was intellectually understandable as Joanna became engaged in 1939 to a German (who ran into considerable difficulties because he would have nothing to do with the Nazis). She had been due to be married, totally against her father's wishes, in September 1939. Of course it didn't happen. Joanna remained at home, with reasonably good relations throughout the war. I think she and Erich managed two letters through the Red Cross. But she stuck to her man. She did various forms of war work in London. She rejected other suitors, including a charming American billeted on my parents of whom they greatly approved. Towards the end of the war she decided the best way to get to Germany was via the American forces, joined them, got to Germany just after the peace, found her man and married him. Again she was cut off by Father until she had her first child, when sweetness and light once more descended.

Father had always wanted to do medicine (an uncle was a doctor) but he was sent to the then Royal University (later the National University of Ireland) in Dublin, less prestigious than Trinity College, Dublin, the premier University for the Irish Protestant Establishment of the time. At the Royal University he worked extremely hard, did brilliantly and ended up with a Gold Medal for his MD. This was early in the century when immunology was beginning to blossom (vide Shaw's "The Doctor's Dilemma"). People like Almroth Wright were beginning to develop vaccines for therapy[*]. Characteristically, following his own work, my father dubbed him "Sir Almost Right"!

My impression was that Father's early scientific papers, in the light of the contemporary scientific scene, were good and progressive. In order to marry my mother, there was no alternative in those days for people without private means but to go into general practice. However, after three years as a GP in Lincolnshire, the authorities in his University obviously thought he was sufficiently promising to establish for him a "Lectureship in Special Pathology" and provide him with a bacteriological laboratory. It was here that he developed his ideas and began to use vaccines of bacteria, usually grown from patients' urine, to treat a wide variety of diseases, including rheumatoid arthritis, multiple sclerosis and even cancer. I think he also used throat and sputum cultures to produce vaccines for acute infections, such as pneumonia.

Of course, as well as his University work, he was running an immensely successful private consulting practice. In that he was immensely successful. Many professional people were very impressed, though they had to accept everything my father said or he had no use for them. He began to be asked to see patients in London. In the late 1920s and early 1930s the demand grew. First he spent one day a week, then two or three, in London seeing patients. Finally demand became so overwhelming that he resigned his university post and the family moved to London in 1934.

He had a number of enthusiastic followers using his methods in the UK, later also in USA and elsewhere. It is perhaps worth quoting the view of his much younger relative, Professor William Hayes FRS (who was fathered very late in life in a second marriage, by my father's grandfather and was forty years or more younger than my father). Bill Hayes was one of the pioneers of bacterial genetics and headed a distinguished Medical Research Council (MRC) Unit in Edinburgh. Bill always said to me that my father had had many interesting insights well before his time.

My father wrote one of the earliest textbooks of endocrinology. He also wrote a book on virology. He wrote his own little book of moral philosophy. He even wrote a couple of librettos for operas by a cousin who was a composer. I suppose he was a bit of a Renaissance Man born out of his time. He died in Edinburgh in 1974 at the age of ninety-five.

---

[*] *The Doctor's Dilemma* by George Bernard Shaw (1906) ostensibly centres on a choice between treating a brilliant but dissolute artist or a worthy but dull physician, but there is much discussion derived from the immunology of the time, particularly the work of Ilya Mechnikov, and the eminent physician character in the play is believed to be based on Almroth Wright.

From my mother's point of view my father remained deeply devoted to her throughout her life. The only periods of tension I ever detected were at the times of my sisters' marriages. These caused both my parents great distress but harmony was restored surprisingly quickly. From my own point of view I owe much to my father for general intellectual stimulation. He was an admirable father in my childhood. He gave me all my educational chances. He tolerated my relative conformity. He was probably responsible for any originality in my character, admittedly vastly less than his own – though perhaps a little better controlled.

Dublin

Merrion Square is a famous Dublin landmark of classic red brick late Georgian houses looking out on a spacious square, with lawns, flower beds, tennis courts and shrubberies. At that time it was the Harley Street of Dublin where the most prominent consultants had their houses and consulting rooms. Unlike modern Harley Street[*], doctors at that time had their consulting rooms in their homes.

One end of the square was occupied by the large Georgian building and grounds of Leinster House, originally the town house of the Dukes of Leinster, later (and still) the seat of the Irish parliament. Beside Leinster House stood the National Gallery, a fine collection even then, later to become even finer when enriched by George Bernard Shaw's residual legacy, staggeringly enhanced by the profits from *My Fair Lady*[#].

These two buildings may have helped Merrion Square to maintain its social cachet into the twentieth century. Now the houses are largely converted to offices. To maintain a large house, with four storeys and a basement, needed of course a team of servants.

But even in my youth there were variants. On one side of us the house had become a convent. I have vague memories of the tinkling of holy bells through the dividing wall. I fear they made no notable impact on my tenuous religious susceptibilities.

I can time my earliest vivid memory to the probable age of less than two and a half. I have a vision of being wheeled by my nursemaid in a pram along the pavement on the north side of St Stephen's Green. My sister Joan,

---

[*] Harley Street in West Central London is famous (notorious) for its concentration of consulting rooms of private medical practitioners. Incidentally, it is very close to Regent's Park where the family lived for many years.

[#] George Bernard Shaw (1856-1950), dramatist, essayist, critic and Fabian socialist. His play *Pygmalion* (1912) was made into a successful musical *My Fair Lady* in 1956 (and filmed in 1964).

who must have been only a few months old, was in the other pram wheeled by a second nursemaid. Suddenly came the noise of a distant band. The nursemaids broke into a run. Our prams leapt forward. We arrived breathless at the triumphal Arch which led into the Green from Grafton Street, just in time to see a Guard's band, red coats, busbies and blaring brass, marching triumphantly through the Arch.

Presumably this must have been before August 1914. In that month the army, I believe, went into khaki with the onset of war. I would have been two years and five months that August. I gather I was comically stodgy as an infant. No doubt I was a trying child (perhaps most are). I have memories of what seemed to me endless sessions on an enamelled potty[*] when I was, equally endlessly and apparently often unsuccessfully, encouraged to do my duty. I have visions of one of these sessions in our empty, carpetless, dining room which doubled as a waiting room and had been dismantled while my father was away at the war.

I have two other early memories. The first was of weeping noisily as I ran round and round, and under, the nursery table, and of the nursemaid saying "Don't cry, John. You're a big boy now. You were three yesterday". The second, perhaps about the same age, was of rattling a candlestick noisily along the banisters at the top of the stairs outside the nursery. I remember looking down and seeing my father running up the stairs in a short white coat, which he presumably at that time wore when seeing patients, to still that barbaric interruption of clinical consultation. I have no memory of the final confrontation. It was presumably both effective and untraumatic. (My father had been brought up with petty Victorian severity which he was creditably determined never to repeat on us.)

I must have been a somewhat paranoid child. It was said that for a whole season I refused to eat strawberries which I thought were designed to poison me. When no-one else died from their effects, I felt safe to adventure them the following year. There was a family myth that I refused to eat fish unless it was covered with brown sugar. I find it difficult to imagine that such a vagary was tolerated. Probably my mother was a bit of a softy towards her children while Father was away at the war.

Another, I suppose very early, memory was a fear of going to sleep. As soon as I closed my eyes I began to see indefinite visions, twists and turns of vague figures, which for me were terrifying. I certainly also had some more well-defined nightmares. I remember hordes of monkeys invading my nursery and burying me under a mass of fur and claws. Of course I must

---

[*] Chamber pot or piss pot.

have grown out of the first of these though, like everyone else, I must have had nightmares from time to time.

My father's year of absence included the "Rebellion" of Easter 1916. Fortunately for my mother we had all gone down to her father's house in the country for Easter. During one stage of the fighting in Dublin the Sinn Féiners* were on the roofs on our side of the square exchanging fire with the British army on the roofs on the other.

We came back to find five bullets in our nursery, which was just below the roof. For a time my father had been a ship's surgeon in order to see something of the world. He had brought back from Burma a brass gong supported on each side by a figure of a helmeted man. This stood in the hall and was used to summon the family to meals. In the gunshot exchanges one of the figures had had his head shot off. The gong remained as a permanent and dramatic memento of that particular "trouble". I suppose my career *could* have come to a premature end!

Some time in 1916 we moved house to 32 Fitzwilliam Square. This was close to Merrion Square and was also a classical Georgian red brick square though rather smaller. It was about to succeed Merrion Square as the upmarket professional medical venue.

I was now four years old and memories become more continuous. While in Dublin we children spent much of our time out in the Square, in the early years with a nurse or governess to keep an eye on us. Later we could be left on our own there, as the gates were locked. We could be put out there to play without serious anxiety. There were many other children from the other houses. We had great fun eluding Mr Fairfield the gardener in our efforts to climb forbidden trees, construct "forts" in some secret corner or scout daringly right round the shrubberies which fringed the Square, also a forbidden activity. I can still hear Mr Fairfield's infuriated cry "*Ower* them bushes".

I made no long-term friends among the children, but I remember playing there with the children of W B Yeats[#], the poet, and James Stephens[¥], also a

---

[*] A slightly curious expression derived from the British press at the time ("Sinn Féin rebellion"), although those taking part in the Easter Rising called themselves the Irish Republican Brotherhood or the Irish Volunteers. Some members of Sinn Fein also joined the Rising. The Irish Republican Army (IRA) was formed in 1919. Today, Sinn Féin is considered the political component of the Irish independence movement, the militia ("terrorists") being the IRA (and the original or "traditional IRA" has been superseded by more modern variants).

[#] William Butler Yeats (1865-1939), poet and dramatist, winner of the Nobel Prize for literature in1923.

[¥] James Stephens (1882-1950) the poet.

famous Irish author. The Yeats lived in the Square, the Stephens just round the corner.

The war made little impact on us after my father's return but I remember the older children discussing the sinking of the Irish Holyhead-Kingstown (later Dun Laoghaire or Dun Leary) ferry, RMS Leinster, in 1918 by a German submarine with the loss of many lives. Several of the children's parents had lost friends or relatives.

News of the signing of the Armistice came to us when we were playing in the Square. We were summoned home and then taken down town to join in the celebrations. I have visions of being carried through the dense cheering crowds of Grafton Street on the shoulders of my Uncle George who was in a private's uniform (I think Canadian Royal Engineers) and was presumably on leave with my parents. We must have seen a lot on that famous day, but only this brief vignette remains.

Kiltennel

Many of my early memories are of Kiltennel in County Carlow. This was a small scattered village lying under Mount Leinster in the Wicklow Hills. It was three miles from the railway station at Borris, and had a tiny Protestant church and a large Roman Catholic "Chapel" (as Catholic churches were always called in my youth in Ireland).

My maternal grandfather was, in title, the Dean of Leighlin, and based at a small rural cathedral*. Grandfather was in effect the Rector in Kiltennel. As elsewhere in rural Ireland, the Protestant parishioners were a mere handful. I had been christened in Kiltennel church. My father often recalled having been summoned to attend the ceremony from the best rise of trout on the small local river that he had ever encountered. As a convinced agnostic (if you can be a convinced agnostic) he probably thought the fish in the hand was worth two rather doubtful spiritual preventives for his son. But, as a good father, he made the sacrifice.

My grandmother had died in middle age. With no wife, Grandpa's sister Amy, my great aunt, kept house for him. She was always known to us as "Tamer", a childish abbreviation of "Aunt Amy". I suppose when we were very small my mother or a nurse was with us, but I have memories of long periods when Tamer was in devoted charge. She had never married. For her we were very much her own children. We loved her dearly. For me she remained a loved friend till she died in her nineties in an old people's home in Dublin. Later, in our teens, and with my great friend Donough O'Brien,

---

* St Laserian's cathedral in the diocese of Old Leighlin, one of the smallest of Ireland's medieval cathedrals.

who spent so many holidays with us, we always used to call her, to her great amusement and delight, "The Duchess of Ballyhadareen".

The "Rectory" of Kiltennel was well away from the village and the church. I remember it as a cream-coloured building edged in red, with two red-bordered and red-spiked gables, and an ascending concerto of Virginia creeper. There was a small flower garden on one side; on the other a walled vegetable garden from which Grandfather would sometimes present us with strawberries elegantly served on a cabbage leaf.

A straight avenue led down to the road. My childhood memory measured it as about a quarter of a mile long. Alas when I brought my own children to see it some forty years later it had shrunk to about twenty yards. The "spacious grounds" I remembered had become Lilliputian. The neighbouring broad river which we had crossed daringly by leaping from one large stepping stone to the next, had sadly contracted to a largish brook.

To the world of the small child the grounds held excitement enough. There were extensive shrubberies where, with the aid of old pots and pans, we made our secret houses. I can still remember, when coming back for yet another visit, the thrill of uncovering the carefully concealed cache of precious, if decrepit, pots and pans. And then, with my younger sister Joanna, re-establishing domestic bliss in some hidden retreat among the laurel bushes.

Of course this continuous exposure to the charms of water carried the inevitable risks of falling in. As a very small boy I gather this was a frequent personal indulgence. I established my record one Sunday. Tamer, having had twice to change my clothes after two overclose encounters with the boundary stream, then took me up the hill to church, presumably in my best suit. But I succeeded in lagging behind and tumbled in all my finery into the little roadside stream. Poor Tamer had to forego her devotions and march me back to yet a third set of dry clothes. I have no memory of anything more than a minor atmosphere of exasperation. It says a lot for Tamer's tolerance and devotion.

Talking of "falling in", Joanna, eighteen months younger, tells me of her record. In the yard there was a pump and a water-filled stone horse trough with a narrow rim. Visiting older children dared Joanna to walk round this rim. Inevitably she tumbled in, not once but twice or three times, soaking each successive dry outfit, until she had to be consigned to bed until at least one set was dry.

I have memories of lying awake on hot, light summer evenings, with the windows wide, and the irregular grating of the corncrake in the neighbouring meadow. And of hearing a donkey braying in the distance, a queer sound, initially alarming to infant ears. But, on second thought, it proved reassuring. I had been told by someone that a donkey's bray kept the lions away.

I have a shameful memory, I trust from my very early youth. We were shown a lovely little bird's nest among the St John's Wort, with three speckled blue eggs. Everyone admired it and told me how beautiful it was. I have an incompletely suppressed memory of coming back later and surreptitiously smashing it all up. Of course the destruction was later discovered by the adults. There was much lamentation. Who could the miscreant have been? "Of course John couldn't have done anything like that". John let it be understood that of course he couldn't. I still feel guilty. Indeed I don't think I have ever confessed this crime before. Perhaps one's eighties are the time to start shriving one's sins.

In the early days trips to Borris, three miles away, were by donkey and trap drawn by "Sweet Briar", a largish brown "Spanish" donkey of a species then common in Ireland. One of the high spots of this journey was the "Fairy Wood", a romantic little grove of pine trees, carpeted green, stretching down below the road. As we passed we scoured the wood for fairies. Later, sadly, the wood suddenly was no more, no doubt yet another sacrifice to the voracious appetite for trench props in France's Armageddon mud. What a contrast between happy children spying for fairies and that bleak slaughterous hell.

Sweet Briar also served as an occasional mount, with saddle, stirrups and bridle, for my older sister Patricia, though I have no memory except of the sedatest perambulation. Some forty years later, when, as I have mentioned, I brought my family back there, I mentioned my past connection to a man I met in the road by the Rectory. A few minutes later a woman came running down the hill to greet us. She obviously had had a great regard and affection for "Miss Abbot" (Tamer) and she presented me with a faded snapshot of Patricia riding Sweet Briar I suppose nearly fifty years before!

I have two memories of how "The Troubles"[*] affected our holidays in Kiltennel. The journey was usually by train. The routine was that O'Brien's cab was booked to take us children and an accompanying adult to King's Bridge Station for the trip to Borris. For a number of years our governess was Miss Kean, always known to us as "Keanie". I remember her with a rather vague affection. I think I was a bit of a substitute for a child of her own and I gather she doted on me. I suppose she must have moved on when I was five or six, but my parents continued to visit her, sometimes with me, and I think helped her financially. They encouraged me to write to her for

---

[*] "The Troubles" in this context refer to both the Irish War of Independence (1919-1921) and the subsequent civil war (1922-23).

Christmas and at intervals. I suppose this must have gone on until I was old enough to send her a cheque for Christmas. My parents later told me that, when they visited her in her last illness, she had died with my latest cheque in her hand. I have often felt guilty that I did not do more to reciprocate, or at least reward with interest, her vicarious mother feelings for me. I am afraid the young often lack these sensitivities. Keanie has come into my mind because she was an accompanying adult on one notable occasion. We set off for King's Bridge Station with O'Brien's cab laden, as usual, with children and belongings. But when we arrived it seemed that the engine drivers were about to refuse to drive their trains – their way of striking a blow for Ireland. I think we actually got as far as sitting for some time in the carriage. Would the train depart or not? Would Ireland or the timetable win? As so often with Irish timetables, Ireland and its uncertainties came out on top. We had to return ignominiously to Fitzwilliam Square. Fortunately O'Brien's political insight ensured that he had waited to convey us back.

More exciting was one summer evening at Kiltennel. It was a lovely hot night. I woke to see my mother and Tamer crouching at the open window. Presumably my grandfather was away somewhere. Through the window came the distant sound of sawing. The Sinn Féiners were felling a magnificent Douglas Fir and an equally magnificent beech tree so that they fell across the road, thus impeding the British military traffic, and of course also the Irish civilian traffic, what there was of it. Tree felling and digging trenches across the road were common practice at the time.

The next day the military arrived. It was a Sunday. They caught young men coming out of Mass at the Catholic Chapel at Kiltennel and marched them down in their best Sunday suits to clear the trees. I remember my mother and Tamer producing tea for the troops. But I also remember being shocked to see one of the sentries walking straight through my grandfather's field of oats, instead of going round the side as we had been taught. At night we would often see fires on Mount Leinster or the neighbouring hills. We were told that these were the campfires of the Sinn Féiners.

Kindergarten

At the age of five I went to school at "Miss Wilson's". This was a private school run by two ladies for children, I imagine up to the age of twelve or thirteen. I suspect the clientele were mainly the children of Protestant professionals like my father. Most of our friends went there.

I was deposited there on the first day of my scholastic career. Immediately my mother left I made my first contribution to scholarly life by howling my head off and disrupting the whole kindergarten. I remember the kindly teacher, Miss Pollock, trying to engage my enthusiasm by showing me a colourful tiger in a picture book. I made it clear that this was no compensation for treacherous maternal desertion. My orchestration of noisy protest redoubled. My sister, five years older and in the upper school, was sent for in vain. I can't remember whether she had to take me home. I presume subsequent days were less traumatic for me, as I have little memory of them. Presumably they were also less traumatic for the school.

Indeed I think this period, I suppose from 1917 when I was five to 1922 when I went to a prep school, must have gone reasonably well. I suppose I managed the routine, but without any particular distinction. I can remember the day when I returned home and triumphantly informed my mother that I now could read. I can still visualise the page of the story, and the coloured picture, of "Princess Daffodil", which I insisted on immediately reading to my patient mother. It is also a commentary on the educational standards of the day that I started learning Latin at the age of seven.

Growing Up During "The Troubles"

Our last summer at Kiltennel was in 1921. I have brief memories of climbing the great beech tree in the grounds, and of a picnic tea in its luxurious shade during an unusually hot year. I am not sure whether our holidays there were terminated by my grandfather's retirement or by the disruptions to travel of the last year of the war against the British, followed by the civil war between the Irish who accepted "The Treaty", giving Ireland Dominion self-government, and the minority, led by De Valera[*], who wanted to hold out for a republic and total independence.

In Dublin I remember the frequent noise of firing and distant explosives. My memories are of the rattle of rifle or machine gun fire and the occasional "bomb" (as we called it). This seemed mostly as we were settling down in bed for the night, but it may be that at that time we were less distracted by our own personal occupations.

Apparently, military trucks used Harcourt Street, half a mile or so away, as a route between barracks. The opposing side shot at them from the roofs or tried to lob grenades down into the trucks. They were later covered with chicken wire as a protection to the great amusement of the locals who claimed that the Irish had put the English in chicken pens.

So frequent was the shooting during the night that, when we went on holiday to Greystones, a seaside resort near Dublin, my parents claimed that they couldn't sleep for the first few nights because of the silence!

---

[*] Eamon De Valera (1882-1975), the Sinn Féin leader who subsequently became Prime Minister and later President of free Ireland. Perhaps his greatest political achievement as Prime Minister was securing Irish neutrality during World War II.

The "Black and Tans" were a semi-irregular force recruited by the British as counter-revolutionaries. They wore black berets and trousers with khaki jackets. They were only very partially disciplined and in rural areas they were said to have committed many atrocities, presumably in revenge for ambushes and casualties. They often raided houses in Dublin, searching for arms, documents or suspects. One warm summer afternoon they raided our house in Fitwilliam Square, I suppose as a result of some misleading intelligence report. My father was out playing tennis in the Square. My mother sent me over to fetch him home to face the music. He was obviously having a very good game and was most reluctant to come ("Mother can easily deal with a little problem like this"), but, on second thoughts, he decided that perhaps he should make an appearance. However, when the searchers found his British Army captain's jacket in a cupboard they decided he must be OK. They apologied and left with no damage done.

It was just as well that they left when they did. Later my mother found a consignment of sporting cartridges in that cupboard. At the time all arms and ammunition were supposed to have been handed in to the police. My father had, of course, done this but obviously had forgotten about this particular lot of cartridges. To retain any was a capital offence – you were liable to be executed by firing squad. Later my father and mother drove out into the Dublin mountains where my mother meticulously picked the cartridges to pieces and then scattered the bits into the hedges as they passed.

Indeed Sinn Féin activists frequently raided better off houses in Dublin in a search for arms they could use. The raiders were not always very well informed. They would take anything remotely warlike. These might include ancient flintlocks or Eastern exotica brought back by one of the many Irishmen who had served the British Empire in one capacity or another. As a result I remember one or the other of us children finding on one occasion an ancient musket stuffed into a bush in the Square through the railings. Another time it was a curved scimitar, perhaps originating from some forgotten skirmish on the Northwest Frontier.

In 1921 at the age of nine, I was sent to Baymount, a small preparatory school at Dollymount, then a semi-rural suburb around the north rim of Dublin Bay toward the Hill of Howth. During term time this took me away from "The Troubles" in central Dublin, though I can remember hearing the cannonade as the newly formed Free State army shelled the Four Courts held by the Republicans, led, among others, by Erskine Childers[*]. In the end they had to surrender. Erskine, an Englishman, was later executed by firing squad. Years later, as a student and young man, I knew his two sons – Erskine and Bobby. Erskine remained in politics and journalism in Ireland, I

---

[*] Robert Erskine Childers (1870-1922), author of *The Riddle of the Sands* (1903).

think with some success. His tragic ancestry, of course, gave him much cachet with the Fianna Fáil party.

My sister Joanna, eighteen months younger, remained at Miss Wilson's. Apparently, at least at first, she still walked alone the one and a half miles to school. On one occasion an ambush occurred very close to her and she saw a man's head blown off, a pretty grim experience for a child of that age.

People must still have been trying to lead normal lives. Indeed, at the time, I never personally felt that life was particularly abnormal. On one occasion a touring opera company came to the Gaiety Theatre, probably an unusual event in those troublous times. My parents were both fond of music and decided to go to the opera, leaving Joanna and Dick (who would have been aged two or three) in the charge of the cook and the maids. Throughout my youth we always had a cook and two maids. Indeed Bridget, the cook, and Kate, one of the maids, were with us for many years and were great friends.

No doubt mother and father enjoyed the opera. But as they emerged all hell broke loose, with firing everywhere. They felt they must get back to the children. So they found their car and drove, with Father crouched over the wheel and Mother crouched on the floor beside him ready to seize the wheel if he was hit. Fortunately they got home safely. But they were then horrified to find that the maids, sheltering in the basement, had completely forgotten the children isolated at the top of the house.

I do not know how much of this Joanna remembers, but I imagine these experiences exacerbated the feelings of insecurity many children encounter. For years, after being settled down for the night, sometime later in the evening steps would be heard on the stairs and the door would open. A distressed Joanna would appear, needing maternal comfort, reassurance and resettling.

Some people in Ireland were anxious to get some sort of settlement between Sinn Féin and the British Government. The Sinn Féiners were all too conscious of the grim centuries of English mistreatment of the Irish. They felt alienated and marginalised by a different religion (or rather a different sect of the same religion, which ironically stood for love and tolerance). They had only recently had full access to education. On the other hand the British Government felt that independence for Ireland would be the beginning of the end for the British Empire. Some sort of compromise would have to be found if death, distress and impoverishment were not to go on indefinitely.

My father had as a patient a British soldier, General O'Gowan. O'Gowan had been a distinguished First World War General and knew many of the top brass in politics in London. Father had other patients in the Sinn

Féin camp. Always a man of self-confidence, with great charm and an impressive personality, he thought he could negotiate some compromise. And indeed, with O'Gowan, he journeyed to London and met Lloyd George, then Prime Minister, at 10 Downing Street. They were clearly not a formal delegation. They were there to explore what sort of settlement stood some chance of being accepted by both sides. Alas, I have no details of what went on, except that I remember Father telling me that he had strongly indicated to Lloyd George that an effective Irish government must have independent control of Customs, a proposal which at that time Lloyd George strongly resisted.

I think it was just after they returned that "Bloody Sunday" occurred. Sinn Féin Intelligence had identified a large number of British Intelligence officers in Dublin, most living among the civilian population, some with their wives. Early that Sunday morning Sinn Féin raiders broke into their houses and shot many of them, some in front of their wives. Two were shot round the corner from us. I can remember looking out of the window and seeing, through the window of their house, a slow procession of a sheet-covered stretcher.

As a result the British Government called off all negotiations. Father had no part in it when it resumed many months later. Incidentally the civil wars caused a good deal of financial anxiety to our family. Father had had many patients from rural areas referred for consultation. With the disruption of road and rail transport, few of these could now make it to Dublin. Of course it picked up when the wars ended in 1923-24. I remember my mother usually receiving six or eight turkeys at Christmas – presents from grateful rural patients.

Holidays

Just after the end of the 1914-18 war we had a holiday in Trearddur Bay in Anglesey. It was a great adventure for a seven-year old to cross by boat to Holyhead and thence to a seaside house. We had another classical Edwardian seaside holiday at Greystones, not far from Bray Head outside Dublin, partly I suspect, because professional families in those days didn't travel far for their holidays and partly perhaps because "The Troubles" made distant travel difficult.

Sometime about 1924 my mother and I were invited by my great uncle Tom for a holiday in Schull, a small fishing village in County Cork on an inlet under Mount Gabriel. The journey to Schull was entertaining. We went by rail to Cork and then on to Skibbereen. From there a steam tram took us along the side of small roads to Schull. We had a lovely holiday, bathing and boating, and with one exciting trip in a sailing boat out to an inhabited island, Cape Clare, where I remember the locals addressing Uncle Tom as "Your Honour" and pleading for tobacco.

It was just after this, I think, that, "The Troubles" now being over, my father rented Coolure as a holiday house for the family. Coolure was in Westmeath, three miles from a small town, Castle Pollard, right in the centre of Ireland and about fifty miles from Dublin. At one time Coolure had been the house of an Anglo-Irish landowner. The house itself was presumably designed to reflect its owner's social pretensions. But it was much the ugliest country house I have ever seen. It consisted of a narrow, over-tall, three storeys and a basement, more like a town house, with dull grey harling, a steep slated roof and an afterthought of a low wing on one side. It would be difficult to design a more awkward looking monstrosity. Though now very run-down, it was much better inside. One entered the house from the dull east side but most of the rooms faced west looking out across two tennis courts, the ha-ha and a tree-dotted meadow to Lough Deravaragh, a beautiful loch some eight miles by three miles in extent.

Just off the shore of the lake was a little pine-dotted island which you could reach by stepping stones. By this time our first cousins, Denis (three years older than I) and Geraldine (several years younger) spent most of their holidays with us as their father, my father's brother Dick, was in the Colonial Service, at first in Hong Kong, latterly in Zanzibar. The two children were at boarding schools, Denis at Tonbridge in England and Geraldine with my sisters at Hillcourt near Dublin.

We acquired Coolure about 1924. By this time Donough O'Brien, whose parents lived opposite us in Fitzwilliam Square and whom I had got to know at my prep school, Baymount, spent most of his holidays with us as we had become firm friends.[*]

As befits a future surgeon, Donough was much better with his hands than I was. My father gave us use of an old rowing boat. With Donough's practical skills we semi-decked its bow and rigged up a mast and sails, the latter sewn by my wonderful mother. In order to sail into the wind, we first used lee boards. These were clumsy and not very efficient, so we (I am sure mostly Donough) devised a keel. Constructing a centre-board which could be raised within the boat in shallow water was clearly beyond our technical skills. Instead we fixed planks on either side of the shallow little rowing boat keel. At one end of the planked groove we hinged the end of an iron rectangle which we had got hold of somewhere. In deep water this hung vertically, the weight counteracting wind pressure on the sails and

---

[*] They remained life-long friends, staying in touch by letter after Donough emigrated to Tasmania, Australia

preventing lateral drift when sailing into the wind. A wire was attached to the lower end of this iron keel. The wire led over a pulley in the groove and up over the stern, so that we could pull the keel into the groove in shallow water. As you can imagine all this paraphernalia made a bit of a White Knight of our boat. It was hardly an international racing yacht. But we had great fun with it. We could take two or three passengers for a sail a mile or two up the lake to a picnic in the heather-covered "bog", lovely when the heather was in bloom. On two or three occasions we took a tent and sailed some eight miles to the narrow end of the loch. There the loch forked, leaving a bushy promontory with a lovely little campsite overlooked by a steep 3-400 foot hill.

It was about this time that Donough and I started producing a holiday magazine "The Coolure Magazine". Donough's father, Dermod, was President of the Royal Irish Academy, a competent if unexciting artist. Donough had inherited some skill as a draughtsman. Thanks to an enthusiastic teacher at our prep school, I had become devoted to English, particularly poetry, and was able to splash my apprentice efforts in the magazine.

A few years later, when I was fifteen, my mother must have tired of the awkward arrangements at Coolure and felt that she wanted a house under her own (very able) control. My father leased Lough Bawn House. This was also in Westmeath about seventeen miles from Kells (the origin of the Book of Kells) and six miles the other side of Castle Pollard from Coolure. Lough Bawn was a charming two storey house set on a hill looking west down the one and a half mile lough to a distant blue hill framed by steep wooded slopes on either side of the lough, the wood on the south side being a noted heronry.

With poverty, First World War and subsequent civil wars, the house had been uninhabited for fifteen years. The encroaching trees were knocking at the back windows, the half-mile avenue down the hill was reminiscent of a post-monsoon river bed. The walled garden, said to have once contained eighty-two varieties of daffodils, was now a jungle of saplings, briars and weeds; the former tennis court a sodden and neglected sponge.

The house, grounds and 1100 acres domain were in fact entailed. But with the recent chaos in Ireland, the resultant poverty and the inanition of many of the Anglo-Irish who had lacked the belly fire to go and make careers for themselves in England or the Empire, the owner, a middle-aged bachelor with no obvious occupation, always known as "Johnny", had had to mortgage it all to the Bank. The Bank hadn't been very clever. They had not realised that it was entailed. When Johnny died a number of years later, the house and estate went to his nephew, allegedly leaving the Bank with a bad debt.

When my parents took over the house (but of course not the estate) in 1927 for, I think, a five-year lease, they had to pay all of £30 a year in rent, but also had to spend at least £100 over the five years in upgrading the house and its immediate grounds. Presumably Johnny, or the Bank, rented the rest of the estate to local farmers for grazing.

Mr and Mrs Fagan, who had been cottagers near Coolure, were installed in a flat in the basement, next to the kitchen. Mrs Fagan acted as cook and did some of the housework. Her husband looked after the grounds. Often another local woman came to help when we were all in residence.

We all helped to cut the jungle back behind the house. We rolled and cut the tennis court and erected wire round it to keep the balls out of the long grass and bushes. We had an Irish red setter called Felix. We had trained Felix to retrieve balls which went over the netting. He knew he must not collect balls from the court within the wire. He used to sit at the entrance by the tennis net with his head going from side to side like a Wimbledon fan as he watched the play. As soon as a ball went over the netting he was off like a flash. Without him we would have lost hundreds of balls.

My father was a very keen fisherman. The fishing was all on the large lochs, mainly Lough Lene and Lough Sheelin: the fishing was poor in Lough Bawn. If you caught a trout on these big lochs it was usually pretty big but often you sat in the boat all day and caught nothing. Father was always blissfully happy, fishing and gossiping away to his unvarying companion, Michael Kearney, the owner of the garage in Castle Pollard. This, for my temperament, did not make up for the boredom of spending hours in a boat catching nothing. I never became a fisherman.

Father also did much rough shooting, snipe, duck, the occasional goose. For a time I went shooting but with only very moderate success. Later I rather reacted against killing things. However I have happy memories of standing with Donough at the end of the loch, waiting in the winter dusk for the flighting duck. There would be the gentle lapping of the little waves, the gossiping of the moorhens and the comfortable asides of distant ducks exchanging confidences in the reeds. By the time the ducks started flighting in it was pretty well dark. Although we sometimes loosed off at the scarcely visible flights above us, mercifully they seldom suffered as a result. And then our own comfortable, gossiping, stroll home in the gloaming to a large tea and a wood and "turf" (peat) fire.

We spent virtually all our holidays at Lough Bawn, Father coming down at weekends. Donough O'Brien and I had a rowing boat and a canoe. We fitted a sail in the canoe but it needed a good deal of skill to prevent it blowing over. Eventually my parents persuaded us it was too dangerous.

Lough Bawn was a wonderful place for our age group, 15-22, as far as I was concerned. My mother would invite our friends to stay. The house had a large drawing room and dining room. There was an empty "library". This had one small bookcase built into the wall. It contained a series of volumes of the *Proceedings of the Irish Parliament*, for the late eighteenth century and up to the Union in the early nineteenth. The only other books were the twelve volumes of Gibbon's *Decline and Fall of the Roman Empire*. It might have been a first edition. Although in due course I read all the volumes I never looked to see the edition!

In the summer we often had tennis parties with other friendly, but impoverished, remnants of the Anglo-Irish gentry. In the moist Irish climate tennis often consisted of wet balls hurling like cannonshot across squelchy courts. In the winter we organised mixed hockey matches, fairly lethal on a field just rigged up for the day and an utter stranger to a roller. But we had great fun and only occasional trauma from stick or ball. This was lovely country for walking or bicycling on our ancient, rusting and very Irish bikes. There was also interesting archaeology quite apart from the bicycles. The village of Fore, only a mile or two away, was very ancient. Here there were the remains of an Iron Age Celtic fort, the more elaborate earthworks of a later Viking fortress, the ruins of a sixth century church – very old and simple, with a doorway consisting of two rough hewn stone pillars topped by a horizontal block – and, finally, the ruins of a fortified Norman Irish abbey, together with the remnants of two town gates. At one time it had been a prosperous place with a flourishing linen weaving trade which, as trade deteriorated, had left it a "Rotten Borough" with two members of parliament, then representing the few residual inhabitants and a couple of pubs. A mile or two away, on the Lough Crewe hills near Kells, were Bronze Age burial chambers with spirally decorated stones, which we often visited.

Later, after I went to Cambridge, a number of my undergraduate friends came to stay. Joanna would also have her friends. The household had two paraffin lamps which gave a bright light by their fitted mantles, contrasting with our usual oil lamps or candles. When we went to bed, one of these, of course, went to my parents' bedroom. The other was fought over between the boys' and girls' dormitories often with three in each, including friends. This led to light-hearted civil war. The boys made the girls apple-pie beds, with or without holly to provide additional comfort. The more skilfully endowed girls sewed up the legs and arms of the boys' pyjamas. I can still visualise Duncan Smith[*]'s face, on the first day of his stay, as he attempted to get into the blinded extremities. We later protested to the girls that such an affliction might be OK for the old campaigners, but for a new guest, fresh

---

[*] Another life-long friend.

to Ireland from the polish of English social life, it was hardly an advertisement for the charm and friendliness of Irish hospitality. The girls admitted that they had considered the point with some care. They had come to the conclusion that the rules of hospitality dictated that no guest should be left out of whatever benefits were currently on offer. The least they could do was to ensure that Duncan was fully sewn up like the rest of us. Just to make him feel at home!

What else did we do? Well, the rule was that the boys did the washing up while the girls made the beds. In the evening we played family bridge or other games. We read voraciously and widely. We continued to produce a holiday magazine, still, for old times' sake, called "The Coolure Magazine". As I got older I was writing adolescent poetry, some light, some serious – and the magazine provided an output. (Some of the serious verse was published in my school magazine at Tonbridge).

Preparatory School

In 1921, at the age of nine, I was sent to a preparatory school, Baymount. This was a boarding school. At that time many of the better off Anglo-Irish families sent their sons to such schools "preparatory" to their going on to public schools[*], either in England or to the one Protestant "public school" in Ireland, St Columba's outside Dublin, to which, incidentally, my father had been sent.

Presumably the idea was to get little boys used to being away from home and toughened up in a relatively small school, most "prep. schools" having less than a hundred boys, before being exposed to the more formidable social and disciplinary challenges of a public school.

Baymount was the private enterprise of a Mr & Mrs Scott, then I should think in their forties. They had no family and I had the impression that the school was their life. Mrs Scott was a quiet person. We saw less of her, as I think she was most concerned with running the domestic side, but I do remember her being kind to me during one of my intense bouts of homesickness. She helped me in a motherly way to settle down for the night one day after being taken out by my parents. She asked me whether being taken out helped or whether it was worse when my parents had gone off home.

---

[*] "Public school" is an absurd misnomer, as those establishments are always private and often very exclusive. The reason may be that the ancient schools were originally charitable institutions for boys from disadvantaged backgrounds. In the 19th century, this archaic expression was adopted by private schools in England offering a liberal education for the offspring of the well-off.

My memories of the headmaster, Scott, are entirely favourable. He was kind but firm. He was obviously extremely interested in his job and his boys. I remember him giving us excellent ethical talks after evening prayers. They were very much at the right level, not just formal "pi-jaws" but relevant to our own lives and very sensible. At least that is the impression they left with me, though I cannot now remember any detailed content. I have no memories of any injustice in discipline, either to me or to my contemporaries. There were no major fears. There was no corporal punishment I believe.

The chief disciplinary sanction I recall was a weekly "Card", a sort of report detailing our week's achievements in work and behaviour. I think we had to read these and then send them on to our parents. The one disastrous event I recall was in my first year or so when I was still immensely shy. Parents were allowed to take their sons out for a Saturday afternoon, perhaps once a month. I cannot remember the detailed mechanism but I think my mother must have written to me to ask if I could come out one Saturday. I was too shy to ask Scott for permission. I was spotted walking down to the gate and retrieved at the last moment. Again I was too shy to explain. Accordingly I received a damning "Card" with bottom marks for behaviour. I felt disgraced and immensely distressed.

The school consisted of about fifty boys, all Anglo-Irish Protestants aged 8 to 13. It was in a large, pseudo-castellated house presumably built in the 19th century for some successful Dublin merchant. It was on high ground near Dollymount, between Dublin and the Hill of Howth which forms the northern limit of Dublin Bay. The rooms were lit by gas mantles, though in some of the passages it was only gas "jets" giving a rather dim light. The house had a walled garden and extensive grounds which accommodated the playing fields. Some of the former stables had been adapted as additional classrooms or accommodation for staff. The teachers were both male and female[*].

I think we were well fed. Our parents were not allowed to send us sweets or chocolate, only fruit which was handed out at mid-morning break. There was a matron, Miss Smallman, who regularly examined our hair for nits, administered an occasional purgative, then an essential component of the health scene, and looked after us in a fairly objective way if we were ill.

Our normal school uniform was quite sensible: shirt, tie, grey jersey, grey shorts and, when more formal, grey jacket. However on Sundays we wore "Eton collars", broad, flat, starched collars which overlay our black jackets, black shorts and stockings, and all topped with a black bowler hat.

---

[*] The teachers were presumably *either* male or female!

We must have looked quite ridiculous. In this Victorian attire we marched the mile or two to the little Protestant church of Raheny. Later I became a member of the choir with Donough.

All of this suggests a rather favourable environment. It was certainly no "Do-the-Boys" school*. But that didn't prevent me being devastatingly homesick. For the first few weeks I wept myself to sleep. I wrote home at once "I don't like this school". I'm sure it made my poor mother quite miserable. I remember her writing that she had lain awake all night worrying over me.

I suppose it was just the sudden rupture of an all-enveloping security. Of course little boys can be pretty nasty to each other too. I didn't have the impression that others suffered so much, or indeed at all, but I imagine that many did. I was just too selfishly concerned with my own misery to pick up anyone else's, much less make any effort to help him.

There was a dreadful scene when the time came to return to school after my first holiday at home. I clung to the towel rail in the bathroom weeping and refusing to move. I cannot now remember how poor Mother, no doubt as miserable as I was, eventually persuaded me to face the music, but eventually return I did.

Of course it became better as I got older. I never liked returning after the holidays but I can remember the following morning often being in great form – I suppose I have a somewhat cyclothymic# personality. However I do think for most children separation from parents at the age of eight or nine is too traumatic. I swore I would never submit my own children to such trials. But of course it *was* educational, both academically and socially. One learnt to handle contemporaries and relate to teachers. As small boys we were able to climb on a splendid and varied holm-oak in the grounds. There, incidentally, a boy swinging above me put a boot into my eyebrow producing a deep cut which made me of temporary medical interest. I was introduced to "conkers" derived from a row of chestnut trees down a back avenue. On that avenue we played excellent games of hockey with a tennis ball, sticks made of fallen branches and rules developed by some form of consensus. I learnt to play soccer¥, hockey and cricket. The one I shone most at was hockey. I later went on to captain my school team at Tonbridge and play for my Cambridge College and St Thomas's Hospital, with a later resuscitation of activity while serving with the army in Egypt.

---

* An oblique reference to the harsh schooling (at Dotheboys Hall) described in *Nicholas Nickleby* (1839) by Charles Dickens.

Mildly bipolar.

¥ Association football.

At work I did reasonably well, but not brilliantly. As I moved up the school, there were three of us in the top form, Harry Greer, Donough O'Brien and myself. Among these I was third by an appreciable margin. French dictation was my ultimate misery. Donough's family had taken in a Belgian refugee family during the war and they all spoke French at home so he had no difficulty. Harry Greer, who was the brightest of us and a self-confident extrovert, coped quite adequately. I coped not at all (though, amusingly, I write this just after receiving a Honorary Degree from the University of Bordeaux, during which I had to use a lot of French. However I doubt if the nice, pretty, Miss McGowan who taught us, would even yet have been very proud of her efforts!).

I never knew what happened later to Harry Greer. I thought he was destined for great things with his intelligence and personality, but only a few years ago I got a hint from another Old Boy of the school that Harry's career had ended in some sort of tragedy. Donough went on to become a surgeon in Tasmania, founding a local medical society, developing services and becoming very much a leader in his community.

My greatest stimulation was from the enthusiastic young man, Mr Wood, who taught us history and who has left me with an enduring interest in it, and even more so from Miss Day who taught us English and fired us with enormous enthusiasm, especially for poetry.

At this stage the major challenge was the "Common Entrance Examination" which had to be passed if one was to be accepted in a Public School. In due course I passed this. But I suspect that I didn't do justice even to my own modest progress. For, when I got to Tonbridge, I was placed in the Lower IVth, not by any means the lowest form but not very high. At the end of the first term I came out top, was promoted to the next form, and then repeated this promotion from one form to the next for the next three terms till I found my level among the reasonably competent.

Eileen has suggested I should record my first aesthetic experience of scenery. Both my parents were passionate about the beauties of Irish scenery. I cannot remember any early childhood enthusiasm, but I do remember my first great thrill. My parents had taken me out from Baymount one summer Saturday afternoon, I suppose when I was about ten. We drove up Howth Head on the north side of Dublin Bay and picnicked on the slopes of the hill. I remember now looking south across the blue bay to the glorious lights on the Wicklow Mountains beyond. Suddenly I felt, somewhere deep in my chest, a surge of wonder and delight, the first revelation of many such wonders to come.

Public School

In September 1925, at the age of 13, I went to Tonbridge School in Kent. It was founded in 1553 by Sir Andrew Judde who was Master of the Skinners' Company, one of the ancient Livery Companies of the City of London. Judde was obviously a man of enterprise who made his pile and employed some of it to found a school for poor boys in Tonbridge, where he was born.

In 1826 the school was enlarged and rebuilt. It continued to take local boys as day-boys – there were two day-boy houses, each with about 50 boys – but most became boarders, taking the sons of country gentry and of the new and rising middle classes. My cousin Denis (three years older) had preceded me there.

Although I always regretted the end of the holidays and return to school, this was now, with prep school experience and increased maturity, no great trauma. I was no longer homesick. Although as a new boy ("novi" we were called) one started at the lowest level in the pecking order, I found this no great trial. The rules, the conventions and the discipline were clear to everybody. At least in my House there was no bullying or arbitrary or unfair discipline. However in at least one other House in the school at one stage we did hear of a set of prefects who ran an arbitrary and brutal tyranny which the masters, at least for some time, failed to detect. As complaining or telling tales was strictly against the schoolboy ethic, it may have been difficult for the authorities to find out what was going on.

My House was called "Judde House" after the school Founder. From the outside it looked like a large Victorian or Edwardian suburban house which stood on the London margin of the town, with its own grounds and tennis court. The House accommodated about 50 boys. Here we slept, ate and did our "prep"*. All lessons occurred in the main school some half mile away. A boy's primary loyalty was to his House. All one's friends tended to be from the same House. Most of the organised games were between teams from different Houses.

The most junior boys slept in dormitories of six to eight near the quarters of the Housemaster and his wife. The large windows of your dormitory had to be wide open day and night, winter and summer. In winter one's sponge often froze solid. It was a cold business getting into icy sheets at night. It took a long time to warm up your feet. I used to get into bed head first. I pushed my head and upper body down to the bottom of the bed to try to

---

* Short for preparation, the equivalent of homework

warm up the sheets a little before I was forced to come up for air. Older boys slept in individual cubicles.

A cold bath was compulsory every morning. You got a beating from a prefect if you were caught avoiding it. As there were no facilities for drying towels, in the winter you were always trying to dry yourself with a very damp towel. The residual soggy skin tended to peel off your legs.

Presumably in the interest of Victorian hygiene, the row of loos[*] opened onto a roofless passage and the doors had large gaps below and above. I suppose this reduced the smell, but it was often very cold and damp. I revisited Judde House some fifty years later, when the school started having reunions for Old Boys. New lavatories were the only change I detected. Everything else was exactly the same as when I was a boy.

The new intake, 12 to 15 "novi", were allocated to "The Big Study" with, I think, a single leader from the previous year, whose job it was to enlighten us on our duties. We each had a wooden box, officially a "tuckbox", for all our belongings (apart from clothes and night things which were kept in a small cupboard by one's bed). I think we sat on the tuckboxes. There was a large table in the middle with a few chairs round it.

The more senior boys worked in their studies, initially shared. The most senior boys each had a study of his own. Those of intermediate seniority shared studies with four or five others.

The inhabitants of the Big Study provided the junior layer of fags[#]. When a House Prefect needed some minor chore to be done he shouted "Boy!". The whole study had then to run flat out to the prefect who selected one of their number, usually the last to arrive, to do the job. In addition each prefect had a private fag from the second year, who tidied and dusted his study, cleaned his shoes, his Officers Training Corps (OTC) boots and his football boots, as well as polishing the brass buttons of his uniform before the weekly parade of the OTC. I don't remember any resentment at having to do these chores. They were accepted as part of the standard routine. Oddly enough I don't think we made our own beds. This was done by housemaids while we were at our lessons in the main school, or, on Sundays, in the school chapel.

There were about half a dozen House Prefects. They were responsible for most of the discipline. Only the most heinous breaches were referred to

---

[*] Toilet cubicles.

[#] Essentially a slave owned by a more senior pupil: fags were required to do menial tasks for their masters. There is no relationship with the American terms "fag" or "faggot" (homosexual) or with English slang for cigarette.

the Housemaster. A beating by him was a rare and significant event which made a major impact not only on the culprit but also on the House in General. Even beatings by prefects were not common. This potential sanction was normally sufficient. I myself was never beaten. Like most others I was generally conformist. A lesser punishment was to write out 50 or 100 "lines". I cannot now remember the content of the lines; I think they had to be copied from a textbook. My worst punishment, for some offence which now escapes me, was given me by a prefect who was a classical scholar. At the time of my offence I was in the early stages of learning Greek. He gave me six lines of Greek verse to learn, a very difficult task and I didn't really understand what most of the words meant

The prefects also supervised "prep", and read the roll call before all meals. You answered "sum", for "adsum" meaning "present", when your name was called. They saw that everyone took some form of exercise every afternoon. If you weren't due to participate in an organised game, and hadn't organised for yourself a game of fives, squash, rackets or tennis, you had to go for a dreary pavement run to the first milestone on the London Road and back, a chore which I almost always managed to avoid. The prefects were also responsible for putting out the light at night in the dormitories, usually with a little affable chat with the junior boys in their communal dormitories.

The Head of the House, the senior prefect, was a very important figure. He was virtually responsible for the running of the House. The Housemaster and his wife ate with us at lunch, sitting with the prefects at the High Table. He took prayers after our simple soup or cocoa and bread supper. Otherwise we seldom saw him in the boys' part of the house. My memory of him was that he was affable and conscientious and reasonably efficient, but made no major impact except as a background figure of authority.

As far as I can remember, in winter we wore dark trousers, a dark blazer, a house tie (different for each House) and a House cap. In summer we wore a stiff-brimmed straw hat with a band round it in our House colours. I think prefects wore grey trousers and straw hats winter and summer. School prefects, a select band of twelve or so, with some general school responsibilities (including reading the Lesson in chapel), wore a special band round their straw hats. One of these was appointed Head Boy, a position of special distinction. Very often it went to someone who had shone both at work and at games.

Privileges were carefully graded as one became more senior. As far as I remember no first year boy was allowed to walk with his hands in any of his pockets. In second year you put one hand in one jacket pocket, in third in one trouser pocket, in fourth in both trouser pockets. Prefects could walk arm-in-arm. It was a little like the ridiculously minor details of aristocratic privilege described by Saint-Simon at the court of Louis XIV but the nuances at Tonbridge were more firmly and inalienably defined, giving no scope for the tiffs which kept the French aristocracy harmlessly squabbling over trifles rather than expending their energies on civil war. And, unlike the French Court, one progressed by mere well-defined seniority, at least up to prefect level.

Prefects were of course senior boys. They were chosen by the Housemaster, probably after some consultation with the (usually departing) Head of the House. My impression is that the criteria mainly concerned character – whether the boy seemed capable of running things and providing leadership – though distinction at games and, perhaps to a lesser degree, work probably played some part. I suppose I must have been slightly upper middle-of-the-road in these qualities, as I was made a House Prefect in my penultimate year and a School Prefect in my final year. I don't remember fulfilling either role with any particular distinction – or any particular trauma. I know that I never beat anyone. I vaguely remember practising carefully before reading the Lesson in Chapel, one of the duties of School Prefects.

I also recall, as a School prefect, being invited, with others, to dinner with the Headmaster, Sloman, where, as a sign of our emerging adult status, we were given a glass of wine. (My parents had by this time introduced me to wine, in gentle civilised quantities, when they gave a dinner party, so it was no novelty. But of course, apart from this formal occasion for the very senior, boys never had alcohol at school). I remember, rather shyly, discussing mountaineering with Sloman, who was an enthusiastic Alpine climber, though at this stage of my career I had only scrambled and hill-walked.

At the end of my first term, one night I developed a severe tummy pain, vomited and then fainted on my way back from the loo to the dormitory. In the morning I was despatched to the school sanatorium where an acute appendix was diagnosed. This was removed under open ether, a miserable memory. Reggie Hayes, a cousin of my father's and an upper class GP in London, kindly came down, discussed my case with the doctors and attended the operation. A day or two afterwards my mother arrived. It was the end of term. Patients in those days were kept in bed for a fortnight after an operation, so Mother and I spent Christmas together in the sanatorium. The family in Ireland must have felt very neglected.

My mother was, as always, marvellous, inventing numerous diversions for a bored bedbound 13-year-old. As appendices were then taken seriously, I was kept at home to convalesce for the whole of the next term. I don't remember any particular trauma or problems when I returned to school for the summer term.

The routine at school kept the boys busy, with relatively little time for mischief. We were up at seven, woken by a large handbell rung by one of the House servants. Then cold bath, wash, roll call and breakfast. Down to the School Chapel for a brief morning service and then to our classes. A half-hour break about eleven when the School tuck-shop was stormed by hundreds of boys. Then renewed classes until returning to our Houses for lunch, the main meal of the day.

In winter this was followed by games till about 4pm when we returned for a couple of periods of classes. In summer, classes resumed immediately after lunch and games were in the late afternoon. Then back to the House for roll call and tea, followed by one and a half hours prep – for the juniors in the dining room, supervised by a prefect, for the more senior in their studies. Then a brief break for cocoa or soup and bread, after which we had evening prayers taken by our Housemaster, accompanied I think by a hymn or two. I still remember one of the standard prayers which began "O Lord, our life is one day nearer to its close....", a curious reminder to small boys. After prayers the smaller boys washed and went to bed. A prefect did a round to put out the dormitory lights. You had one weekly hot bath, according to a timetable. When your day and time came, from the list on the notice board, you asked the prefect in charge of "prep" for permission to depart for 20 minutes for your bath. As you got older, this was when you had your first weekly shave. The older boys did an hour's prep after prayers.

Once a week we had the Officers' Training Corps parade, followed by drill or military instruction in weapons and tactics. For this we wore uniform and had the chore of brasso cleaning our brass buttons and boots, for a junior perhaps also those of the prefect he served. In due course we sat an examination, both written and oral if I remember, with regular army officers as examiners. If successful, and most were, we were granted "Certificate A" which was supposed to entitle you to become an officer in wartime. I don't know how far this promise was ever fulfilled. In World War II the War Office used a much better form of examination to test for potential leadership and initiative[*].

Games ranked very high in prestige in an English Public School of the 1920s, as I suspect they do still. To be good at games carried enormous kudos. To be good at work, or brilliant at work, carried a certain rather remote regard when you were senior, someone who did rather well in an elusive world other than the one most of us inhabit. When you were more junior the danger was that you would be classified as "a little swot". It was

---

[*] Nevertheless, "educated" people were preferentially chosen to form the officer class in the Second World War. Ordinary soldiers' unfavourable perception of officers' performance may have influenced the former's determination to elect a Labour government after the war.

wise never to dream of flaunting your scholastic successes, certainly not to reveal that you worked hard for them. It was the typical English cult of the amateur. People didn't too violently object to your being brilliant, so long as you weren't seen to be actually trying!

Games were another matter. Everyone could have a go at them. This was the real world. And success in the real world really was important. In rugger[*], being small, I played scrum half, emulating my cousin Denis, who ultimately played for the school.

In due course I played for the school "Colts", the under-16 side, the house side and finally for the school first fifteen. When you had become established in the first fifteen the captain, after some interschool match, presented you with your "Colours", at a special ceremony. The "Colours" consisted of a special cap with braid and a tassel, which in future you proudly wore up to the pavilion to change for matches. In the first fifteen we played other public schools such as Uppingham, Clifton and Sherbourne. The "away" matches were quite an adventure.

My best game was undoubtedly hockey, though it carried less prestige than rugger. I rather rapidly achieved the House eleven, then the School, and ended up by captaining the School team. I was not much good at cricket. After junior experience I tended to shed cricket in the summer term and concentrated on tennis, squash and fives (a game played with the glove-covered hand and a hard ball in a small walled court) without being particularly brilliant at any of them. In games therefore I achieved enough to make me a reasonably average achiever but I certainly showed no great brilliance and never attained the semi-hero status of someone who exhibited exceptional talent.

At about the age of 15, if you were reasonably competent, you took the national "School Certificate". Up to this stage education was general: English, French, History, Maths, a little Geography, much Latin and, later, Greek. No Science. After obtaining the School Certificate you opted for Classics (then the most prestigious and often attracting the brightest boys, including Denis), Modern Languages (usually French and German) or Science. If you obtained at least four "Credits" in your School Certificate this was at that time accepted for university entrance: entrance was much easier in those days.

Unfortunately my Housemaster told me about the four Credits necessary but failed to tell me that I needed also to have five "Passes", i.e. a "Pass" in at least one further subject beyond the four Credits. As a result I didn't bother working on my fifth subject, French, and only achieved four Credits

---

[*] Rugby football

with their accompanying four Passes. So I had to retake the exam the next term. I achieved five Credits then and switched to Science. Unfortunately it meant that I had missed the introductory term in Science and had a tough time making up, particularly in the basics of Physics and Chemistry. I became passionately devoted to Biology and found no difficulty with that.

However my Biology skills gave rise to a problem for a tyro examinee. My Housemaster had recommended Sidney Sussex College, Cambridge, as a small but up-and-coming college. To do medicine they required one to have passed the University's (First M.B.) examination in Physics, Chemistry and Biology before entry. In due course I went up to Cambridge to take the exam. The Physics and Chemistry were quite straightforward. I had reasonable knowledge, allocated the appropriate time to each question and passed satisfactorily. Unfortunately I knew a vast amount about all the four Biology questions. With simplistic enthusiasm I spent most of the allotted time writing a long essay on the first question. I could have done the same on all the others, but had foolishly only left myself time to give the most staccato answers to the other questions. Consequently I failed yet another exam, fortunately the last examination failure in my career.

Luckily the exam was at the end of the Easter term and I could take a resit exam at the end of the summer term. My father, rather sensibly, suggested that I leave school at the end of the Easter term and take the exam from home. I had a delightful couple of months, mostly at Lough Bawn, working, catching frogs to dissect and drifting about the loch in a canoe enjoying the glories of May and June, which for years had been spent at school. My father said I was going to have to work desperately hard as a medical student and the break would do me good. It did!

So much for official work, but from the age of 14 or 15 I read extensively, using the excellent school library. My English teacher at my prep school had fired my imagination in English literature, in which I read widely. I read all Galsworthy's and Shaw's plays[*] and much else. I also read a good deal of popular science, especially in the biological field.

Adolescence is the age for poetry. I think I wrote my first private poem in my first year at public school and went on writing poetry. In the Middle Fifth form we were once asked, for prep, to write a poem on "A Deserted Garden". I was one of the younger members of the form and I was highly embarrassed as well as of course flattered, when the following lesson was entirely devoted to the merits of my poem. Subsequently quite a lot of my verse was published in a transient school literary magazine. I have

---

[*] John Galsworthy (1867-1933) is now remembered more as a novelist than a playwright.

continued to write poetry intermittently over the years – much of it rather personally addressed to my wife.

Religion at Tonbridge was fairly routine Church of England. At Sunday services we had frequent guest preachers for the sermon. I cannot remember being favourably impressed by any of them. Indeed it was contradictions between the views of some of these preachers that first aroused doubt in my burgeoning adolescent intellect. It seemed clear that there could be multiple and contradictory views about religion. Perhaps I should start thinking things out for myself? This was further precipitated by my being deeply shocked by a subsequent sermon. The preacher claimed that all pain and distress was sent by God as a punishment for previous sin! I hope the school authorities were as shocked as I was and that he was never invited again. But, if so, at the time I detected no such reaction among either boys or masters.

Although my father, to the horror of his Protestant Low Church family, full of clergy and missionaries, became an agnostic in early youth, he never passed this on to us as children. My mother, as the daughter of a clergyman, was a regular churchgoer and brought us up as such, with her own splendid caring morality for anyone in trouble as a wonderful example. (Sadly, my father told me late in life, my mother lost her faith after my brother Dick was killed in 1942. She felt she had prayed for his survival and had been let down.)

With all the turbulence of adolescent emotions, for several years I found my own loss of faith very traumatic, conferring a sense of loneliness and isolation. But of course this was an intellectual reaction. With my parents' fine example of caring for others, the loss of the purely theological aspect of religion if anything reinforced the "duty to one's neighbour" aspects of Christianity, which I still regard as the overwhelming moral imperative.

I made two particular friends at school, Harry Clifford and David Howarth. Harry Clifford aimed to be an architect. In those days architectural training was purely by apprenticeship, not through universities, so I lost sight of him after we left school. After many years' silence, it was sometime in the 1970s that I unexpectedly had a letter from him. He had discovered that both David Howarth and I were in "Who's Who", found our addresses and made contact. We kept in touch after that.

With David Howarth I kept in much closer touch. David didn't do much work at Cambridge and got a Third Class Degree. He then worked in London with Baird*, one of the technical pioneers of television. In 1939-40 he was in France as a war correspondent for BBC radio. After Dunkirk he

---

* John Logie Baird (1888-1946), electrical engineer and inventor.

joined the ranks of the Navy. Ultimately he became in charge of the small boat squadron which smuggled Resistance fighters into Norway. He made his name writing *The Shetland Bus*, a bestseller, about this experience and went on to a highly successful career writing popular history.

What did I personally get out of Tonbridge? Having been a very shy child it gave me increasing self-confidence, especially with the gradual introduction to responsibility through seniority and becoming a prefect. Obviously it greatly helped me in handling people and developing that unconscious social sensitivity which enables one to assess what is acceptable or possible in any particular social milieu. Apart from my, unfortunately, single term in DC Somervell's Lower Fifth form, I received little intellectual stimulus from the masters, though we were taught standard stuff with reasonable skill. The exception, Somervell[*], was a historian of some repute. He wrote a number of books, most notably the two summary volumes of Arnold Toynbee's twelve-volume *Study of History*. A tall, pale man with lots of character and humour, he was always known by the boys as "Slimy", but he was full of ideas on all sorts of subjects and a most stimulating teacher.

A public school provides an excellent basic education for the reasonably conformist, and I was in that category. However it did also prove a milieu in which I could develop and widen my own intellectual interests, though I suspect the stimulus came a good deal more from my family background than from the school. For the really original non-conformist or genius a public school may well be hell. For me it was a useful background for work in an English society whose elite is still dominated by those educated in public schools. I fear that in many ways it is a very snobbish society. I much prefer the far more egalitarian Scottish milieu. Nevertheless I suspect that my public school education was of considerable value to me in my career.

In 1977 the school had an Old Boys' reunion. Harry Clifford, David Howarth and I, and my cousin Denis who then lived in Tonbridge, attended together. I think it was the first time any of the three friends had revisited the School since leaving. It was quite nostalgic.

---

[*] D.C. Somervell (1885-1965)

Chapter 2
Cambridge 1930-33

Sidney Sussex College

I went up to Sidney Sussex College, University of Cambridge, England, in October 1930. It was the youngest of the older Colleges, founded in the late 16th century by the widow of Philip Sidney, Earl of Sussex. He had been Queen Elizabeth's Ordinancer General, responsible for state property. His family crest was the "Pheon": the Broad Arrow. He decided to use this Broad Arrow to identify government property. His initiative became perpetuated. In Victorian times convicts' uniform was covered with Broad Arrows. The Pheon in my time was also stamped on every army rifle.

The college is situated in Sidney Street. In my day there were two original front courts, Chapel Court and Hall Court. There was also a later, Victorian, Cloister Court and a large brick building dating from the 1920s, Garden Court. This undistinguished pile looked out over the large "Master's" and "Fellows'" Gardens which were beautifully kept. The Fellows' Garden had a tennis court and a squash court. The garden and courts were open to undergraduates.

In my day the interior of the Hall was the College's best feature, with a hammerbeam roof and historic portraits. At the far end the dons dined at the top table on a slightly elevated platform, sitting luxuriously on chairs. The undergraduates sat on benches at the long tables running right down the hall. We had to dine in Hall at least five nights a week. It was compulsory for everyone to wear his gown in Hall. When the dons, led by the Master, came in we all stood up. A Scholar recited the Latin grace. We then sat down and ate, waited on by College servants. We could order drinks, usually beer, from the "Buttery" just outside the entrance to the Hall proper. ("Buttery" originates from the Norman "Bouteillerie" or bottle store). Otherwise, beer drinking was mainly with friends in our rooms, after dinner, at weekends or at meetings of College Clubs. Undergraduates were not allowed to visit pubs.

The other architectural charm was the interior of the Chapel. It had been rebuilt relatively recently but in a pleasant Queen Anne style, small and attractive. There was no compulsion to attend Chapel. I don't think I ever did.

In my day there were only 180 undergraduates, all male. Normally you spent your first, sometimes second, year in College. Thereafter you had to move out into digs[*]. In digs you had your bed and breakfast but retained the obligation to dine in Hall five nights a week. This kept you in touch with your friends and the College.

Fortunately, at the end of my first year I became Secretary of the Rugger Club and then, in my final year, Captain. As these offices carried some administrative duties in arranging matches etc I was privileged to remain in College for the whole three years. Since the War the College has greatly expanded in numbers, and now includes women. There has been a great deal of additional building. All undergraduates now remain in College throughout their stay.

My rooms were on the second floor in Hall Court, one of the original 16th century courts. My sitting room was quite large, with a table, chairs, a desk, bookcase, and a couch facing the coal fire which was the only heating. It was set by one's "Bedder" every morning, but, to save cost, one only lit it in the evening. The Bedders were pleasant middle aged or elderly women, old enough and plain enough to carry little threat to undergraduate morals.

There was a very small bedroom, with just room for a bed and a washstand with basin, jug and potty. These were a relic of former times and unused. One had to walk across the court to washbasins, baths and loos – a chilly excursion on freezing East Anglian winter mornings. Your Bedder called you at seven. I think there was a communal gas ring for boiling a kettle. I breakfasted on cornflakes and bread. The Bedder made your bed and kept the room clean.

One could have breakfast or lunch in Hall, but these were expensive and I never did. Soon a group of us developed the habit of lunching in turn in each other's rooms, with the host responsible for providing the basic lunch. This became standard. It always included Cornish pasties. Mildly radical in politics, we were certainly culinary conservatives.

Jock Leslie, a Scot from a laird's family[#], was opposite me in my first and second years and we became great friends. He was reading science. We both played rugger and later we climbed together in Scotland. A second member of the group was Dafydd Jenkins, a native Welsh speaker, who read law. A third, Basil Engholm, I had vaguely known at Tonbridge, though he was in another House. I got to know him very well at Sidney; he achieved a

---

[*] Lodgings in a private home. Traditionally, landladies were informally regarded as acting *in loco parentis*. This form of accommodation was common as late as the 1970s.

Local landlord and member of the aristocracy in Scotland.

Double First in Law. The fourth friend was Duncan Smith who also read Law. The fifth was David Howarth, my close friend from school.

Duncan Smith was the most politically interested and most radical of our group. As we now know, from subsequent scandals, there was a strong communist group among staff and students in Cambridge at that time. I was quite unaware of it, probably because it did not affect my own College. At first I was uninterested in politics. But the great Economic Depression hit Britain in 1931, following the disastrous stock market collapse in the USA in 1929. In the UK the economic crisis resulted in a split in the contemporary Labour party government. The Prime Minister, Ramsay Macdonald, and the Chancellor of the Exchequer, Philip Snowden, broke away to form, with the Tories, a "National Government". This resulted in cuts in unemployment pay, gross increases in poverty and the "Hunger Marches".

The National Government had much public support, at least among the middle classes. Increasing awareness of social costs began to give my emergent political consciousness a radical bent. My views were never the slightest bit communist. To me communism was vaguely foreign, extreme and dangerous. Perhaps through my ignorance and lack of incentive to study it, it had none of the attractions of Marxism's claim to be a science of history and politics. It was this claim, together with social caring, which probably captured the imagination and adherence of some of the highest intelligences at Cambridge. Of course the Soviet government took good care to conceal the cruel and extensive breaches of human rights associated with the alleged "dictatorship of the proletariat", in fact a dictatorship of either one man or a few at the top.

The first year of university is a marvellous time in your life. You are beginning to feel yourself an adult. New stimuli come at you from all directions, most notably from new friends with different backgrounds. You sit up till two in the morning discussing what, for you, are new ideas on all sorts of subjects.You are probably blissfully unaware that for hundreds of years successive generations of young people have also sat up till two in the morning arguing over the nature of beauty, the basics of civilisation, and many of the other exciting problems which you and your friends think they have just discovered.

That sounds like the typical patronising comment of an old man. And of course it is. But equally that process provides a vital element of university education. It is at least as important in developing your mind as reading literary criticism of Shakespeare's sonnets or studying the muscle reflexes of the frog. It is also many orders of magnitude more enjoyable.

There were other social outlets. I played rugger two or three times a week as a scrum half. We were a small College, highly unlikely to provide a team which would shoot us up the intercollege league. I suppose it was the College's modest pretensions which enabled my very modest games talents to take me to Secretary and Captain. We played for fun rather than ambition, against other Colleges and various East Anglian clubs. I was a better hockey than rugger player and was persuaded to play for the College, at least intermittently, during the Easter term.

The College had a number of social clubs. I belonged to two of these. In one we read plays, drank beer and had an annual dinner. The other was slightly more intellectually pretentious. We met in the rooms of the "Senior Tutor", a bachelor with overall responsibility for undergraduate welfare. I suppose there were about twenty of us. We took it in turn to present something. I can only recall presenting one on Leonardo da Vinci, which I imagine was pretty inadequate. We also had a few outside speakers.

In spite of these social occupations, I worked pretty hard. We started with a 9am lecture in the medical school. We were then at lectures, laboratories or dissecting rooms until 5pm or after. Back to work in my rooms till "Hall". This was "First Hall" at 6.30pm for the first year, "Second Hall" at 7.30pm with the dons, subsequently. Back to work after Hall till my tea-break with Jock Leslie at 9pm. Then work again, normally till 1am, though stopping at midnight if I had to play rugger the next day.

We had no advice as to the most effective ways of working. I really didn't learn to work effectively till I started clinical work after leaving Cambridge. At school we learnt partly by taking rough notes on the science teacher's address and then making fair copies of our notes for his comment. Looking back, this was a gross waste of time, certainly at university. It is perhaps a measure of my intellectual immaturity that it took me so long to recognise this. It was also perhaps a sign of immaturity, and of the then lack of any education on learning methods, that, though I put in long hours in term time, I did very little work in the vacations.

We had official tutorials from Fellows, usually in groups of three or four. We wrote some essays for these tutors. Compared to what I have heard of Oxford tutorials, with their in-depth one-to-one help and accompanying intellectual challenge, these were very inferior. I got little out of them. Apart from the club with the Senior Tutor, and an occasional tea with the Master and his wife, we had little contact with the dons.

My Father knew the Professor of Pathology, Professor Dean, who was also "Master" (Head) of Trinity Hall College. He kindly invited me to lunch and advised me. He suggested that I should try to achieve my "Second MB" exam (Anatomy, Physiology and Biochemistry) in four terms (instead of the usual two years) and go on to complete the first part of the Natural Science Tripos (Comparative Anatomy, Embryology, Physiology and Zoology) in a further two terms, leaving my final year free to do an in-depth Natural Science Tripos Part II in Pathology. For Part I the Physiology was similar to the Second MB but the other subjects had to be mastered in two terms instead of the normal two years.

This programme also involved an extra term in the Long Vacation in the summer. In order to complete my dissection of the human body for Second MB I also had to organise six weeks at the London Hospital in August and September. I hit a sweltering heatwave. I can still recall that curious cocktail of heat, dissecting room flesh, the acrid fumes of formalin and the odours of Whitechapel.

With Long Vac Term plus my dissection at "The London" my first year's long vacation consisted of two weeks at our Irish home in Lough Bawn, before returning to Cambridge for my second year. This involved taking my "Second MB" at the end of the autumn term followed by two terms of pure "Natural Science". I was rather fascinated by Comparative Anatomy and actually did some additional reading on the origin of man in the vacation. I gathered that, in consequence, I did quite well in that subject, adequately in Physiology but poorly in Zoology. With only two terms and little academic guidance it was difficult to know what to swot. I only achieved a 2-2 overall.

I enjoyed my final year in Pathology Part II. This involved morbid anatomy, immunology, bacteriology and a first introduction to statistics and the history of public health. Although I learnt a lot and discussed a lot I obviously didn't do a good examination and only achieved, again, a 2-2 degree. I think retrospectively that one of my examination errors was to fail to stain a meningitis specimen for tubercle bacilli and so to miss the diagnosis – somewhat ironical in view of my future career!

One of the delights of university is, of course, one's new friends. In those days these tended to be entirely male. There were two women's colleges, Girton and Newnham. There were a number of women medical students. They were expected to sit separately in the two front rows at lectures. Although my youthful pathological shyness was by now greatly diminished, it remained pretty powerful as far as girls were concerned. Indeed our close group of friends rather light-heartedly founded "The Five Mile Club". Its basic rule was that members were forbidden to have anything to do with a girl within five miles of Cambridge! Dafydd Jenkins was the Secretary. I kept what we thought at the time were amusing Minutes.

Holidays and Hills

There was a three week gap between the end of the summer term and the beginning of the Long Vac Term in July, In my first year (1931) four of us – Jock Leslie, Dafydd Jenkins, David Howarth and I – took a boat for a week on the Broads. We had a splendid week of relaxed endeavour with no distinguished exhibition of seamanship. Thereafter Jock invited David and me to come for a couple of weeks to Scotland, based on his ancestral home, Kininvie, near Dufftown in Banffshire.

We returned from the Broads to Cambridge and set off north. David had an ancient motorbike with curving uplifted handlebars which we christened "The Monarch of the Glen". Jock had a sidecar in which I was ensconced, surrounded by tents and blankets.

Basil Engholm was already involved with Nancy, his future wife. He had invited her up for the May Week Ball in Sidney Sussex, just after the end of the summer term. I have a memory of myself lying more or less supine in the sidecar, cocooned by impedimenta, when Basil and his terrifying beauty appeared above me on the pavement to bid us bon voyage. I was covered with confusion. Fortunately I was promptly whisked off towards the Great North Road, the then straggly and primitive ancestor of the present A1.

The Great North Road ran through all the towns and villages. These were the black days of the great economic Depression. I have visions, in the Northern towns, of rows of unemployed men leaning against walls, hands in pockets, watching us go by – we were so much more fortunate than these poor men. I remember once, having gone astray one evening, asking our way through some small town in the Sherwood Forest area. When we stopped to enquire a very drunken man gazed down at me in the sidecar. It obviously stirred a fuzzy memory of wartime (1914-18) experienced long since. Out came "Fifteen days in an open boat and only a bean a day"! We laughed at the time. We wouldn't have laughed if we'd been through it ourselves. We had all the insensitivity of youth.

I remember stopping at "The Last Pub in England" for a beer. We topped Carter Bar about nine o'clock on a June evening. I can still recall the intensity and excitement as I gazed for the first time at the beauty of the Scottish hills fading northward in the evening light, hills which were to mean so much to me in later years. Crossing Carter Bar really felt like entering a new and unknown country.

We had had, on the way up, intermittent mechanical problems with the Monarch of the Glen. Being then, as now, a mechanical moron, I left these to the other two. As we approached Edinburgh the current problem was a crack in the Monarch's aged exhaust pipe. This was ingeniously, if temporarily, remedied by wrapping it round with a sheet of canvas. This served suavely enough when the Monarch was in motion and the canvas was adequately cooled by the air draught. But when stopped by the traffic in Lothian Road the canvas began to smoulder, threatening perilous inflammation to the Monarch's carburettor just above.

Like the Monarch's exhaust, David was suffering hiati in his aged coverings. Wear and tear on the Broads had provided the final challenge to the seat of his only trousers. In consequence he was embarrassed to descend from the Monarch to douse the incipient conflagration lest it expose his all too obviously deficient rear.

A further stop at a garage achieved less potentially lethal therapy and we proceeded into Edinburgh. It was lunchtime. Jock's family had a flat in Edinburgh, but it was shut up; everyone was at Kininvie. The only place Jock knew where one could find lunch was the Caledonian Hotel, then as now in the top rank. So to the "Cally" we proceeded in all our disreputability. David had delicately donned his mackintosh to spare the blushes of the upper classes. He only removed it after his shameful posterior was safely installed in a chair at the lunch table, reversing the procedure before rising.

After lunch we proceeded north. It's a long way from Edinburgh to Dufftown in Banffshire. We arrived at Kininvie at about 3am in gathering daylight. Next day I awoke to another world. Kininvie had been built by one of Jock's ancestors in 1490. The original building was a Peel Tower with a spiral staircase. David and I shared a room on the second storey. Just outside our room was a rounded central depression on the staircase. The legend was that the wife of one of the ancient lairds had misbehaved and was imprisoned for years in a room at the top of the tower. Her ghost would descend and turn on its heel at this depression outside our door.

Jock's grandfather had commanded the Cameron Highlanders (as did later Jock's elder brother, David). His father had been a solicitor in Edinburgh, but had been severely wounded in the 1914-18 war and died prematurely in the 1920s. Consequently the house and estate were run by Jock's mother. She came from a landed family, her father a General with an estate near Wick in Caithness which he had been awarded by a grateful country after the First World War. Her parents had disapproved of the match and she and Jock's father had had to elope. Mrs Leslie was a woman of great character to whom I became much attached.

Mrs Leslie had managed to keep things going after her husband's death. She achieved this by letting the house, with its shooting and fishing, for three months in the summer to a succession of rich Americans. Sadly, this source later dried up as a result of the Great Depression of 1929. In the later 1930s they had to sell out to a Leslie cousin who had had the foresight to marry a margarine heiress. Thereafter it went through a succession of owners.

I was now in a somewhat feudal household. One of Jock's uncles, General Leslie, was staying there with his wife. The General was a very pleasant and affable chap. I think at the time he was Quartermaster General, or the equivalent, of India. He had a large car and a chauffeur (who later turned out to have impregnated one of the maids during his stay). The General's wife, accustomed to the duty of keeping innumerable more junior officers' wives in their place, was a formidable memsahib, viewed by the family with quiet amusement tinged by a touch of apprehension. Fortunately she did not greatly intimidate us. It was clear that she possessed little power to affect our promotions as none were in prospect.

As I have said, David and I slept in the original tower. The "modern" wing of the house was 18th century. There was a beautiful dining room with three floor-to-ceiling windows. The walls were lined with mass-produced portraits of somewhat wooden-faced ancestors. As an introduction to our enormous breakfasts, everyone ate his porridge strolling about the room. We had been warned to bring our dinner jackets. In the evening we found a housemaid had laid out all our clothes on our beds, the socks carefully folded to ease foot insertion. Jock and the General wore Highland dress.

The prime object of our visit was a trip to the Cairngorms. We were joined by Jock's elder brother, David, and by Stephen Cumming, who was at another Cambridge College. We had been given permission to spend the week in the stable loft of a stalkers' lodge where we slept among the hay. We carried our clothes and a week's food. We had a very wet July week. On the one fine day we climbed Beinn Macdhui, crossing an extensive snowfield below the summit. We had another brief excursion to the West, to a brief rain-soaked camp in Glen Brittle in Skye, marred by the three tyros having forgotten one of the tent poles! Three very damp adventurers decamped and fled to the feudal delights of Kinivie before I returned to the (medical) Long Vac term in Cambridge.

At the same period the following year (1932), Jock again invited me and David north. Jock and Stephen had joined the Cambridge University Mountaineering Club (CUMC) and learnt the basic techniques of rock climbing and rope work. They invited us to join them in Glencoe to learn the elements. We had a lovely camp by the river at the top of Glen Etive. We walked across the moor in a heat wave and set about climbing the famous Crowberry Ridge. We were first given elementary instruction in ropemanship and belays. This was my first real rock climb. The conditions were ideal for a beginner. No shivering on shelves in icy blasts waiting for the next man to come up or the leader to overcome some technical difficulty.

When not climbing or bringing the next man up I sat and gazed across the loch-strewn wastes of Rannoch Moor to the dramatic distant peak of Schiehallion. I remember the thrill of arriving at, and surmounting, the final Crowberry Tower and the little traverse from the Tower to the summit. I found no difficulty with the climbing which I greatly enjoyed. I immediately became a convert.

We went on to do the Aonach Eagach Ridge in Glencoe and then on to Skye. We had a glorious week's climbing on the wonderful Cuillin gabbro rock, so rough that you can almost, like a fly, hang on to it upside down. These were the days of nailed boots. To Scottish mountaineers "rubber-lubbers" were a deeply inferior species. Their methods were considered analogous to cheating at cards. Our ropes were real old-fashioned hemp ropes, kinking into unexpected and awkward angles when wet. There were no carabiners, no nuts to be wedged into cracks to ensure security above a drop. Above all, inserting a piton into Scottish rock was held to be equivalent to making a pact with the Devil. It would ensure permanent allocation to a particularly lurid Calvinistic hellfire. Climbing was a sport for committed amateurs, not one to be besmirched by pseudo-professional aids. *Chacun pour soi* or perhaps *"en ensemble"* against space and gravity. It was great fun and luckily we got away with it.

We climbed to the glamorous rock nipple of the Cioch, protruding from its precipice, and on above to the ridge and so to Sgurr Alistair. We climbed the long unconquered "Inaccessible Pinnacle". The weather did us proud. For a week you could have held up a lit match on any of the summits. But, just as joyful childrens' parties are liable to end in tears, so a Skye week, however shot through with sunshine, is liable to finish by some Celtic Jupiter Pluvius pulling the loo chain. In the corrective deluge we left a day early.

Cumming-Crofton Route

The following year, 1933, Jock and I decided again on a climbing holiday in Scotland. By this time I was also a member of the CUMC and there was to be a CUMC Meet in the Cuillins of Skye. But before that Jock Leslie, Pat Baird (a fellow geology student of Jock's) and I felt we would celebrate the completion of our examinations by taking our BA degrees by proxy and so have a week or two exploring the possibility of climbs in North West Scotland before going on to Skye..

None of us had climbed in the North West before. Indeed very few people had. With the warm wet west wind the rock was reputed to deny handholds by the profusion of its vegetation; we were advised to carry an effective gardening tool. We managed to buy a curious mini-handaxe equipped with a spike on the reverse. Fitted with a sling of lamp wick, it seemed – and proved – just the thing for scraping out holes. (How attitudes changed in the next 50 years. We had then felt that Nature's overprovision spoiled useful handholds. Now it would be felt that we were the spoilers of nature's bounty!) Belays were also said to be rare. So we brought an ordinary domestic poker to be thrust into soft slopes as a somewhat tenuous longstop.

I led a pleasant, if not particularly exciting, new climb on Stac Pollaidh, that lovely little mountain topped by pinnacles and tumbling towers of Torridonian sandstone like a mediaeval cathedral. We gazed across the glen and spotted a promising looking buttress, Sgurr an Fhidhleir on Ben More Coigach, which we knew was quite famous but so far unclimbed. This proved one of our most exciting climbs. But we didn't see much of it, as it was a day of mist and pouring rain, which started just as we began to climb. If we had done it in good visibility and better conditions perhaps it would have seemed less challenging. But viewed from afar in my old age it still looks a good buttress and the climb has got into the textbooks. This, like our other new climbs, was thanks to Pat. We all recorded the climbs afterwards but it was Pat who wrote them up for the SMC Journal[*] so that some have become standard.

We also did a pleasant new climb on An Teallach. From An Teallach we went south across country, bivouacking, and did a couple of new climbs on A'Mhaighdean, one of the remoter Munros. The first proved to consist mainly of just a couple of tricky pitches, on one of which I disgraced myself by having to use a knee, another minor heresy. The second, up the Pillar Buttress, was much more charming with lovely views, especially from a little overhung niche near the top where we all assembled and which we nicknamed the "cabine à trois".

Then on to the CUMC Meet in Skye. We had a week or so of delightful climbing on standard routes. We led some beginners up the more straightforward stuff. The only difficult route I remember was the Cioch Direct, which was then classified as "Severe". We had obtained permission to take a party to the island of Rhum, then privately owned. The Club hired a boat and about ten of us climbed Askeval and Halleval, the highest peaks, without detecting any exciting rock climbing routes .

That was not the end of our month-long mountaineering holiday, to be savoured before all my closest friends and I left Cambridge for the next steps in our careers. My Scottish friends had long talked of the famous unclimbed Mitre Ridge in the Cairngorms. Five of us decided to attempt it: Pat Baird,

---

[*] Baird P.D. Exploration in the North West. *Scottish Mountaineering Club Journal*. Nov. 1933. Vol. XX. No. 116. pp 83-91

Jock Leslie and I plus Stephen Cumming and Sandy Wedderburn, then the President of the CUMC and a redoubtable climber.

The Mitre Ridge on Beinn a' Bhuird was somewhat remote. This must have partly accounted for its continued virginity, though a number of previous parties were said to have attempted it. To give ourselves maximum time we decided to camp in the corrie at its foot. Next day dawned gloriously again. It soon grew very hot. We had done a reconnaissance the evening before. Pat, Jock and Sandy had decided to try a direct route from the lowest point of the almost vertical ridge up to the final tower. Stephen and I noted a vast vertical crack in a corner on the right side of the ridge. This ran almost from the base up to the final tower. It looked airy and exciting. It might prove possible. The rock is granite, with vertical and horizontal cracks. But the edges of the granite cracks tended to be rounded which gave less easy foot- and finger-holds.

We found a reasonable couple of initial pitches up a wall from which we could traverse into the crack. We took it in turn to lead. My memory is the belays were sparse and some of the pitches were long. It proved an exhilarating, difficult and exposed climb. Indeed it is now listed in all the climbing guides. It is regarded as the best climb in the Cairngorms. I have little claim to immortality but I suppose the "Cumming-Crofton Route" will remain in the books for at least some years to come[*].

Being only two and "leading through" we reached the final tower well before the other party. The tower was separated from the main mountain by a few easy steps leading to a small final wall of 20 feet or so. I decided to make the final pitch as direct as possible. I went straight up. A few feet up, for the first, and I trust last, time in my life I came off. I only dropped a foot or two before managing to find holds to stop me. I then wisely compromised with an easier crack slightly to the right. I brought up Stephen and we relaxed in the heather in the blazing sunshine and an equal sense of blazing satisfaction.

We waited for the others. They soon appeared below the tower. They reported that the first two pitches had been very difficult but the rest fairly straightforward. Sandy was then leading. He was obviously anxious to make the final pitch up the tower as direct and exciting as possible. He edged gradually and painfully upwards. Stephen and I became apprehensive. Above Sandy the angle first steepened and then gradually merged into what

---

[*]First written up by Jock Leslie (Leslie E.J.A. "The Mitre Ridge" *Scottish Mountaineering Club Journal* April 1934, Vol. XX. No. 117. pp 183-188), a more recent description by Robin Campbell, " Mitre Ridge (Cumming/Crofton Route)" can be found in *Classic Rock* (2007) published by Baton Wicks. Both John's son, Ian, and a grandson, David (Ian's nephew), subsequently climbed the Cumming-Crofton route.

appeared to be an impossible overhang. But Sandy persisted. With twenty or so feet of rope out suddenly he dropped vertically. With astonishing skill Pat held him and the belay held Pat. Luckily Sandy was uninjured and managed to climb back to Pat's stance. That evening we picked up his hat in the corrie 600 feet below! He finished the climb more circumspectly if marginally less heroically.

A very happy party assembled at the top. It was very, very hot. We later heard that it had been 90F[*] in Dufftown that afternoon – a rarity in those parts. We found a little burn on the plateau, stripped and rolled in. I don't think we bothered to go on to the summit of the mountain a little further away.

---

[*] 32^0Celsius

Chapter 3
Medical Student & Junior
Doctor in London 1933-39

Clinical Student

In my student days Cambridge University had no clinical school. We did our pre-clinical studies in Cambridge itself. Then almost all students went on to one of the London Teaching Hospitals for their clinical medicine. However, we took our Final Examinations in Cambridge.

I had sought advice from medical friends as to which hospital I should apply. St Thomas's was the one I chose. The reasons now escape me. It was one of the larger and older hospitals, one of the few mediaeval monastic hospitals that had survived the depredations of King Henry VIII. It was pleasantly situated on the Thames just opposite the Houses of Parliament. Here Florence Nightingale had initiated modern nursing; its nursing standards were said to be superb. Presumably I had also learnt that the medical and teaching standards were high.

I had made a formal application while still at Cambridge and travelled down to be interviewed by the Dean. As far as I remember, the only subjects he discussed with me were sport and athletics. My sporting record in rugger and hockey were presumably regarded as adequate and I was accepted without difficulty. I began my clinical studies in September 1933.

At that time my family were still living in Dublin, but my father was travelling to London each week to spend several days dealing with his steadily expanding consultant practice. One of his pupils, Michael Brady, was a devotee of my father's vaccine treatments. I think he came from a successful Dublin business family and presumably had inherited money. At any rate, he owned 149 Harley Street where he lived and practised himself and where he also provided a consulting room for my father. He and his wife kindly gave me a room in the top storey where I bed-and-breakfasted and studied. Regent's Park Tube station was less than five minutes' walk away. I could catch a train from there direct to Waterloo, only ten minutes walk from St Thomas's. With the development of my father's London practice, the whole family would be moving to London in February 1934 when, of course, I would join them.

The Bradys were very good to me. Their most memorable kindness was to ask me to join a social-cum-debating club to which they belonged. This was a rather upstage affair. I had the impression that it consisted mostly of people on the rise, now on the fringe of the London non-aristocratic elite but with ambitions to join it. For our meetings we wore full evening dress, white tie and tails. We had an elegant buffet supper in some nice place (I don't think they were private houses) and then debated. What we debated I fear I can now no longer remember.

I had participated once or twice in debates in Cambridge, learning by heart beforehand my minor and rather stilted contributions. But now I suppose I was maturing. I found myself more articulate and my brief interventions seemed to go down well. I began to become more confident in public communication, later a major component of my life. It was the Bradys who gave me that chance.

In those days the study of clinical medicine at a London teaching hospital was very much an apprenticeship. We had a few lectures. We had some initial teaching on how to elicit clinical signs in sick patients. But the bulk of the time was spent in the wards. The Ward Sister allocated each new patient to a student. The student then took a history of the patient's illness and examined him or her. He then wrote it all up in the patient's notes. It was the student's notes which were kept above the patient's bed. When the consultant did his round it was the student, not the house physician or house surgeon, who presented the case.

When in due course I myself became a house physician we were the first generation who were expected to write up the patient's notes ourselves. From then on it was the house physician's notes that were kept beside the patient.

We worked in pairs. Each member of the pair was expected to know all about his colleague's patients as well as his own. If his colleague was absent the other member of the pair presented his patients to the consultant. We followed our patients through to discharge, writing appropriate progress notes. We were expected to be present if the patient was having any special investigation and, of course, if he or she was undergoing a surgical operation. It was very good clinical training.

The consultant's rounds, normally twice a week, were mainly for teaching. After presentation by the student, there was discussion of the possible diagnosis and treatment with the students on that "Firm", usually eight to twelve. There was much question and answer. The registrar on the Firm, a young doctor in training, would also do one or two teaching sessions in the ward, though he spent most of his time seeing outpatients.

There were normally two consultants, a registrar and a house physician, or house surgeon, to a Firm. The junior consultant mainly saw outpatients but did one teaching round a week in the wards. He usually had a personal responsibility for only five or six beds out of the thirty or so (fifteen of each sex) run by the Firm. The senior consultant had the rest. The students sat in with the junior consultant while he saw outpatients. Teaching was conducted *pari passu*.

At some stage we put in brief sessions at specialised units such as Eyes, Ear Nose and Throat, Tuberculosis, Venereal Disease, Public Health etc. In view of my later involvement with tuberculosis, it is curious that there are only two things I can remember from my brief visit or two to the Tuberculosis Department, which was stuck away in decent isolation in the basement. One was that you should carefully distinguish "Tb", indicating "tuberculosis", from "T.B." indicating "tubercle bacilli". The other was a peculiar squiggle to be sketched on a diagram of the chest to indicate the presence of "rhonchi" – particularly squeaky noises heard through the stethoscope.

We had a short series of initial sessions to introduce us to clinical medicine. These were conducted by Dr "Ikey" Jones, the chief doctor to the Metropolitan Police – Thomas's was their official hospital. I remember his recounting, for our admiration, the skills of some of the great clinicians of the past. I recall him describing "Sir Somebody Something" doing a ward round when Ikey Jones had been his house physician. "Sir Somebody would stand at the foot of the bed. "Put out your tongue, my man, he would say". The patient would put out his tongue. Sir Somebody would turn to me and say "I don't like it, Jones, I don't like it". And sure enough his patient would be dead by next morning. What a wonderful doctor that man was!" Apart from these brief sessions with Ikey Jones, for the first three months we were allotted to "Casualty" (equivalent to the modern Accident and Emergency Department). There we acted as assistants to the junior doctors on duty. We learnt to stitch up cuts. We opened boils and minor abscesses: no antibiotics in those days and lots of boils and abscesses. We assisted with minor surgery, including giving "gas" as anaesthetic. This was before the days of intravenous anaesthetics.

We were on duty for only four or five hours a day; morning, afternoon or evening sessions in turn. At this stage there was little bookwork one could do. We had not yet started on studying real disease. So I had plenty of time on my hands. With no family yet I used it to have regular sessions in London's art galleries and museums; very educational, if not in medicine.

As already indicated, games were an important part of student life. Initially I played rugger. But I found that, with only one game a week, I could not keep in good enough training for the physically exacting position of scrum half. I switched to hockey and played regularly for the hospital. It was the game I was best at.

There was a students' club opposite the hospital where we took our lunch and tea. It also had a couple of squash courts. This was an excellent way of getting intensive exercise quickly and could be played after dark. I played at Thomas's and thereafter fairly regularly, except in war years, until into my forties.

After my three months in Casualty I moved into the wards and started reading the textbooks on clinical medicine. Clinical medicine was so much easier to learn than preclinical. I was seeing clinical medicine every day. Every evening I read up the conditions I had been seeing, besides working gradually through the textbooks. I was continually building a scaffold of experience on which to hang theoretical knowledge. In consequence theoretical knowledge was much more likely to stick. I also learnt to write rough notes as I read. These could later be used for swift revision. I read *The Lancet* and *British Medical Journal*. I ventured into a series of books on "Recent Advances" on subjects that interested me. Accordingly I was usually able to take a fairly full part in discussions at teaching sessions. This was an excellent way of acquiring knowledge and of getting it to stick.

At one stage, while doing surgery, with your partner, you did a "Major Week". This involved living in for a week, sleeping in a room in Casualty. You saw all the emergency admissions with the doctors, day and night, and so were frequently called out of bed. You were summoned to the wards to pass catheters or help with various procedures. You assisted at emergency operations at night. Very educational!

These were still the years of the Great Depression. This had started in Britain in 1931, two years after the disastrous Wall Street Crash. In paediatric outpatients there was plenty of malnutrition. I remember feeling ashamed to be going home to a good dinner, when many children, and their parents, had not enough to eat. We saw plenty of rickets in the children and telltale signs of previous rickets in the bodies of many adult patients.

In obstetrics we had to deliver 20 "normal infants", this is to say normal, uncomplicated births. This was partly done "on the District", when my partner and I went out with the midwife to do deliveries in the home. Here again we saw real poverty – bugs climbing up the walls in some houses. Our job was to ensure cleanliness and safe birth. Of course we were guided by the experienced and skilled midwife who was used to the inevitable improvisation in very poor homes – and indeed to teaching apprenticeship obstetrical skills to tyro students. Excellent education, medically and socially.

Presumably because there were insufficient inpatient births in St Thomas's, we were seconded for several weeks to one of the London County Council hospitals, St James. This was said to be one of the best of the local authority hospitals, but I found it a rude shock.

The organisation was extraordinary. I suppose there were several hundred beds, including medicine, surgery, obstetrics etc. Yet the Medical Superintendent had personal clinical responsibility for all the beds, besides his heavy administrative load. He was assisted by a number of younger doctors, poorly paid and working in sessions. They seemed to be of variable quality and varying conscientiousness.

We were encouraged to see as much as we could of all disciplines in the hospital. We lived in and only had to give limited time to our obstetrics, so that we saw a lot and learnt quite a lot. But the patients were treated like cows, a sort of mass-produced medicine. For instance, all emergency admissions to Casualty were stripped naked before they saw the doctor. When he came, the sheet was tossed back. I have visions of a poor old lady, so treated. When the sheet was tossed back, it was obvious that she had a fractured neck of femur. Her feelings, her embarrassment, were totally disregarded.

We attended an antenatal clinic run by the overworked Medical Superintendent. He rushed from one patient to the next, carrying out vaginal examinations, with the nurses desperately trying to get screens around in time but often too late to give the poor woman genuine privacy.

We happened to be there in late April and early May. The local authority bureaucratic rules apparently laid down that the central heating should be turned off on 1 May when summer was read off on the calendar. I found one of my patients shivering with cold in her bed. So I asked one of the nurses to give her an extra blanket. This resulted in a torrent of abuse from the Ward Sister, scandalised that "one of her students" should dare to do such a thing. However the patient kept her blanket.

This experience, and what I heard of other local authority hospitals through most of the country, have always made me determined to resist any suggestion of putting the National Health Service (NHS) under local authority control. I believe one or two local authorities were better – Middlesex, some Surrey hospitals and perhaps Lancashire. Scotland does not seem to have been much better. Before the NHS began, the City Hospital in Edinburgh, the main infectious diseases hospital and with a large tuberculosis section, had no X-ray apparatus and a minimum of equipment. It was the City Treasurer's boast that rates had not been raised for years. The services, and the sufferings of the patients, were commensurate.

I kept up with my Cambridge friends, particularly Basil Engholm and Duncan Smith. Basil was at the Ministry of Agriculture in Whitehall, Duncan at the London County Council headquarters. Both were very close to St Thomas's. We usually lunched together once a week, either in a simple café or buying a box of sandwiches and eating them in St James's Park nearby.

My student partner throughout these years was Denis Keall. Denis had done a Part II Tripos in Pathology with me at Cambridge and I had got to know him there. It was natural that we teamed up when we both moved to St Thomas's. He was the son of a solicitor in Perth, Western Australia. We shared a keen interest in medicine and became firm friends. Later, when the war came, he joined the British RAMC[*]. Soon after the war he returned to Perth, having not seen his parents for fifteen years. He became a consultant in the main teaching hospital in Perth and ended up as the senior physician and President of the Australasian Thoracic Society.

In February 1934 my family moved to London from Dublin. My father had acquired a 30-year lease of 22 Park Square East. This was Crown property. It was part of an array of excellent houses round Regent's Park built for the Prince Regent in the 1820s. (The original Regent Street was part of the same project but was rebuilt in the 1920s.) Park Square was just off the Marylebone Road. We looked out on to the pleasant square to which we had, for a consideration, a private key. It was only a few doors away from the present site of the Royal College of Physicians. Park Square was only a few minutes walk from Harley Street and so endowed with the appropriate socio-medical aura for my father's rising consultant practice.

The family's introduction to London life was unfortunate. There had been a good deal of nostalgic distress in leaving the beauties of Ireland, the charming surroundings of Georgian Dublin, the holiday house at Lough Bawn and the many friends for London's impersonal metropolis – even though we were to live in a particularly attractive part of that metropolis. Alas, the family was greeted with one of the densest and greenest of London's notorious pea soup fogs, a fog which lasted for their first fortnight. Their major furniture was to come by sea. The fog also blanketed the sea and grossly delayed transport. We must have had some sort of beds but I remember we at first ate our meals off the top of a trunk.

My elder sister Patricia was already married to a doctor in Dublin. My younger brother, Dick, had succeeded me at Tonbridge School. So there were only my sister Joanna, eighteen months younger, and myself, with my

---

[*] Royal Army Medical Corps

parents, to experience the gloomy initiation into the glories of domestic life in the Capital.

But in due course, with all my mother's energy and domestic skills, we settled in happily. Having not lived at home since the age of nine, I thoroughly enjoyed it. It was a large Regency terraced house. The beautiful Nash houses surrounding Regent's Park were covered with cream coloured plaster. In terms of the Crown leases they had to be simultaneously repainted every few years. We looked out on to Park Square. The park itself was a two minute walk away. In the summer evenings I often walked up there and did my studying in the Rose Garden. We were close to Regent's Park Tube station and I could be in Thomas's in half an hour. The house was capacious, a basement and four stories. We always had a cook and two maids. Two of the maids had bedrooms in the basement; the cook had hers on the top floor. On the ground floor was a large dining room which also served as a waiting room for my father's patients. His consulting room was next door. Behind this was a one-storey wing, presumably built in what had previously been the garden. Now it contained a "morning room" where we normally had our meals and where my father's secretary was accommodated during working hours. A serving lift, operated by rope, was used for bringing food and other materials up from the kitchen. There was a little area in front of the basement, below the street level, which led to a coal cellar under the pavement.

On the first floor were the front and back drawing rooms, separated by folding doors so that they could be elided for major social occasions. The drawing room had two floor-length windows looking out on to the Square and over the busy road leading up to the Zoo and North London. There was a narrow balcony but, with the noisy traffic, we never used it. Instead we had a minor garden, with tubs and pots and seats in summer, on the flat roof of the morning room, with access at mezzanine level.

On the second floor was my parent's bedroom facing the Square, with an adjoining bathroom, and Joanna's bedroom. On the top floor was my own bedroom at the back of the house, a small spare room, and the cook's bedroom. My parents found the traffic noise irritating, as cars changed gear just outside when they accelerated up from the traffic lights in Marylebone Road. For me, my window looking out at the back of the house, the traffic was a more distant roar to which I rapidly accommodated. Indeed when I woke in the morning I could often make a pretty good guess at the time by the extent of the traffic noise, which steadily increased from the early hours.

Gradually I got to know London. At first I learnt about the local areas around different Underground stations. Later I learnt bit by bit to join these areas up. With the family, at weekends we often went into the country. The Chiltern Hills were reasonably accessible from North London were we lived.

Father also belonged to a golf club in that area. In the summer we often visited Oxford or Cambridge to see the College gardens. Later my father bought me a second hand car for £10! It was an old, round nosed, two-seater Morris Oxford with a "dicky". This was a sort of boot with a lid which could be lifted up to give two additional seats.

Holidays

During these clinical years we were given two weeks holiday every three months. These I spent mostly climbing with friends in Scotland or Wales. Sometimes I got a lift with a friend, sometimes my old car managed to carry me there. In the winter it was best to park it on a steep slope at night so that it could be pushed off to get started in the morning.

My memories are particularly of winter campings in Scotland. One January I went with Pat Baird and John Kendall to Glen Coe. We had a splendid, very cold but largely dry, week and did a number of climbs, including several on Buachaille Etive and the Church Door Buttress on Stob Coire nan Lochan. We had two sleeping bags apiece and took it in turns to be the first to emerge from our ice-cocooned bags to light the primus and cook breakfast. We had to remember to take our boots into our sleeping bags at night. Otherwise the boots would be frozen hard in the morning and impossible to enter.

We went on to Ardgour, across Loch Linnhe, to climb a recently discovered buttress. We established camp on the elbow of a burn and had a fine climb. During the night the heavens opened. The sky torrented down on us. We decided to hog it out in our sleeping bags for the day. The burn had been a good 6-8 feet below us, but in the early afternoon I glanced out of the tent from my book and saw the water shooting past, just about to overflow and sweep us away. We hurriedly dressed, gathered our soaking tent, and retired ignominiously to a hotel in Fort William.

On another occasion there was to be a March "Meet" of the Cambridge University Mountaineering Club in Glen Coe. As senior members some of my friends and I were to help to train the new recruits. Some of us decided that it would be fun to have a couple of days beforehand climbing on the great 1,000 feet cliff of Ben Nevis. We had arranged to stay in the Scottish Mountaineering Club hut. Seven or eight of us were to meet at the bottom of the path at 7pm, coming from various parts of England and Scotland. Of course it was dark at that time of the year. We set off with our equipment and torches. As we got further up a blizzard began. Soon the path was buried in snow. We couldn't find the hut. Every now and then we thought we had spotted its dark shape against the snow, but it always turned out to be a small boulder a short distance away.

By 11pm we gave up and retreated. Some of the party had problems in the blizzard with cramp and exhaustion. But we got them all down. At the bottom of the path is a distillery. The night staff allowed us to sleep on the top of the moist warm vats until the day staff came on at 6am. We then retired to the Youth Hostel in Glen Nevis which the warden kindly opened for us. We were pretty tired, so we spent the afternoon in the local cinema in Fort William. Next day we climbed the Ben by the standard path. The weather was fine but cloudy, but we had to battle through soft knee-deep snow. We took it in turns to lead. The ascent took us five hours, but we made it and got down before dark.

Then on to a lovely campsite beside Kinghouse Hotel in Glen Coe. The less penurious were staying in the Hotel, but the paupers were allowed to camp outside. The views were superb, especially of the snow-covered Sron na Creise gleaming in recurrent sunshine. At that time, in winter, I don't remember seeing any other parties in the glen. Certainly, in our previous January camp, we only saw one man and his dog on the hills during a whole week's climbing.

My main memory of this particular Meet was my leading a party of three up a previously unclimbed gully. It was a snow and ice climb and proved very difficult. I was very relieved eventually to get them all to the top just in time to descend on the other side before dark.

We also had several very enjoyable climbing holidays in North Wales. I belonged to the Climbers' Club which has a pleasant, bunkered, hut near Lake Ogwen. This was pretty comfortable. It had a stream nearby. Sometimes, in the winter, when we came hot off the hills, we stripped off and plunged into an icy pool, bouncing out again like a shell from a howitzer with a quick sprint to a dry towel and hot cocoa.

Back in London, I also developed my cultural education. The Old Vic theatre was ten minutes walk from St Thomas's. It twinned with Sadlers Wells theatre in North London. They alternated ballet, opera and plays (such as Shaw's *St Joan*, Shakespeare, etc.). Their ballet was the beginning of what became the Royal Ballet. It was amateurish at first but quickly developed. I remember my first sight of Margot Fonteyn, then only fifteen, floating across the stage like a wisp of genius from a better world. And then there were all the galleries and museums.

Qualification

Nevertheless, I worked very hard. I often studied in bed for an hour or more before breakfast. I was usually home soon after six. I did an hour or so's work before dinner and at least two hours afterwards.

With all this effort I was quite a successful student. I entered for one of the major prizes and won it, possibly for an essay on pneumonia. In those days one worked at the hospital on Saturday mornings. I then went on to play hockey or rugger in the afternoon.

It was very much up to you how hard you worked. There were no exams after leaving Cambridge until your Finals two and a half years later. Ignorance could be shown up on ward rounds where there was much question and answer. The less enthusiastic and more idle tended to linger at the back of the group and tried to avoid the teacher's eye, but the better teachers ensured that everyone was tested and stimulated. Naturally, however, enthusiastic students received a larger share of the give and take. This I personally found very stimulating and great fun, especially as I think I usually showed up pretty well. Clinical medicine was clearly proving my forte.

There was a habit in those days for students to take the "Conjoint" Final Examinations as a lead up to those in the University (Oxford, Cambridge or London). The Conjoint was a joint examination set by the Royal College of Physicians of London and the Royal College of Surgeons of England. When you passed you qualified for medical registration. It was regarded as a somewhat easier option than the University examinations and could be taken and passed six months earlier. You could take it in individual sections at intervals, e.g. pathology, medicine, surgery, obstetrics, which made revision easier.

I thoroughly enjoyed pathology. Of course I had been well grounded in academic pathology in Cambridge. St Thomas's also had excellent teaching in the subject. Every day at 1.30pm there was a demonstration of current post-mortems. A notice was put up each day in the Students' Club listing the post-mortems to be demonstrated. Many staff and the keener students would walk over after lunch for the demonstration. The patient's doctors, often including the consultant, would attend and give the clinical details. The pathologist would then show what he had found and there would be much teaching and discussion. Everyone learnt a lot.

Later, postwar, when I worked at the (Royal) Postgraduate School of London at Hammersmith Hospital, the same system was followed. Whenever a post-mortem gave the promise of interest many staff attended. I was surprised and disappointed, when I later came to Edinburgh, to find how poorly post-mortems were attended by staff and, indeed, students. I had previously thought that Scotland was the home of good pathology, but found the clinical/pathological liaison very poor. We managed to build it up to some extent in my own Department and so, later, did some others. But it has never developed as a general culture in the medical school.

I started my Conjoint Finals with what was for me the easiest option, pathology. I raced through it pretty easily, as indeed I did for the subsequent parts. Most people took the Cambridge University examinations in two parts, medicine and then obstetrics and surgery, but one of my teachers, Hector Goadby, strongly urged me to take the whole exam in one go. Fortunately his confidence proved justified and I had little difficulty in getting through.

First Jobs

In those days there was no compulsion to do junior hospital jobs after qualification. You were registered right away. Many went straight into General Practice. Others went to peripheral hospitals to do jobs in internal medicine, surgery or obstetrics. Specialist training was a long and penurious affair. Junior "House Jobs" were unpaid – in St Thomas's we even had to pay for our laundry. Then, if you were both competent and fortunate, you might land a Registrar job. This was usually in your own teaching hospital. London teaching hospitals in those days were very inbred. Registrars and consultants were seldom appointed from another hospital.

After a number of years as a very poorly paid registrar you might be lucky to hit a vacancy for a consultant job at your own hospital and succeed in the very hot competition for the job. You would likely be in your thirties by then. After that you began your consultant practice, with rooms in Harley Street or its surroundings. That's when you gradually began to earn your money. As a consultant you were not paid for your hospital work. You relied largely on the students you had taught, subsequently working as GPs, to refer private patients to you. You would have private beds in a nursing home or use the private wing of St Thomas's. You might land a useful steady income, in addition, as a consultant to some insurance company.

All this had to be worked up gradually. It was unlikely you would be able to afford to marry until you were well into your thirties. If you wanted to marry earlier, you either had to have a private income or go into General Practice.

In St Thomas's there were only four House Physicians jobs and four House Surgeons jobs available for the fifty or so students qualifying each year. So you usually had to wait about a bit even if you were ultimately successful in landing a job. I can't remember how long I had to wait, probably six to eight months. I filled in the time, as did others, by working as a "Clinical Assistant" in several departments, Diabetes, Electrocardiography and some others. The job was mainly concerned with seeing outpatients.

The House Physician and House Surgeon jobs were for a year. You spent the first six months in Casualty doing minor surgery and seeing the many patients with medical conditions who came to Casualty because they could not afford a GP, or who were sent up as emergencies by GPs.

All patients were seen by a "Lady Almoner", the title being a mediaeval monastic relic. She was the predecessor of the modern Medical Social Worker. Officially her primary duty was to assess what the patient could pay. If he was too poor, he didn't have to pay at all. However the Almoners were excellent, caring women much concerned with the patients' social problems and adept at knowing of charities or charitable funds that could help. I think it was my experience of their help, and my admiration for their qualities, which stimulated my own life-long interest in the social aspects of medicine and my close life-long cooperation with social workers in meeting these challenges.

St Thomas's was the first school to train social workers. I believe it was the devoted and caring nursing, and equally devoted and caring social workers, more than the doctors, which created the very different atmosphere from the routine, impersonal and often not very competent clinical drill I had experienced in the London County Council hospital while doing my obstetrics.

We who were going on to become House Physicians in our second six months, did rather more medicine and less surgery during our Casualty period. We also had to give anaesthetics in the operating theatre, usually for the less formidable operations carried out by the more junior surgical staff. I did not find anaesthetics to my taste. It was still the days of open ether or gas, though we had some machines. It was before the introduction of the merciful initial intravenous anaesthesia which now merges the patient peacefully into slumber. That came a little later. The induction of anaesthesia was still very unpleasant for the patient. Mostly I found anaesthetics boring, if things were going well, but anxious when facing the occasional difficulty in which I was having to cope after relatively little preliminary training or experience.

Of course in Casualty you took your turn of evening and night sessions. This was when you really saw life. Every now and then you had an invasion of uproarious drunks, pouring with blood after some violent altercation. However in those days national alcohol consumption was lower than now. We did not have the tidal waves of weekend drunks which break in a bloodstained foam of ignoble trauma on the hapless staff of modern Accident and Emergency Departments.

As a Casualty Officer you were the first doctor to see each emergency, medical or surgical. We called in a more experienced senior if we found it was something major and needed admission, or a problem beyond our competence. We learnt a lot from this. Then there were the patients with "Munchausen Syndrome". These were curious people, apparently passionately addicted to medical attention. It seems it gave them a feeling of importance and fulfilled some deep need for in-depth personal concern. They had learnt to simulate various medical conditions, perhaps after some genuine original experience. This might have led to recurrent abdominal operations if, as was frequent, they had effectively simulated some abdominal emergency. The scars might accentuate the impression, for the doctors, of a genuine physical problem. To reinforce the picture a patient might bite his cheek and spit blood into his urine so as to arouse appropriate medical concern. Of course, some were primarily after drugs. A number would go from hospital to hospital, sometimes deliberately attending in a period when they knew that there would be a new influx of young doctors on duty, who would be unlikely to have seen them before. They might, however, be spotted by one of our experienced porters who would alert us to a possible problem.

Sometimes one's heart would go out to some poor person coming up in the evening with desperate toothache. We had been taught how to take out teeth. So one might agree to give him or her a whiff of gas and manage to yank out the grim torturer. But softening of the heart was always a bit risky. The news might spread very quickly. A row of miserable faces might soon be planted on the waiting benches. Poor people could not afford dentists. In any case in those days there was little emergency dentistry available.

In the Wards

After six months I moved into the wards for what was one of the happiest six months of my career. At last one had responsibility. At last one was actually caring for patients oneself.

My main chief was Dr Forrest-Smith, a Harley Street consultant, I suppose then in his fifties. He was a sound, not very imaginative, physician with a pleasant rather formal personality. I probably learnt a certain amount from him. He did two regular ward rounds a week. These were largely taken up with teaching students. One of my jobs was to help him to choose the most appropriate patients on whom to teach. I might incidentally get help from him on a problem. More useful and instructive was a non-teaching round which he did on Sunday mornings. Then we had a more one-to-one contact.

Our "Firm" had half a male and half a female ward, some 30 beds in all. Curiously the male and female wards were at opposite ends of the long corridor of the hospital and on different floors. So I had plenty of exercise going from one to the other. Forrest-Smith had most of the beds. His junior consultant, perhaps in his late thirties or early forties had only four or five. His main job was to conduct outpatient sessions in which I was not involved. Besides teaching in outpatients he usually did one ward teaching round a week. He was a curious eccentric man. I was not impressed with either his knowledge of medicine or with his judgement. He had a slightly manic "shop window" which presumably had sufficiently impressed an interviewing board to appoint him as a consultant, though, very unusually he had been trained at another London teaching hospital, St Bartholomew's. In briefing him about patients on whom he was to teach I sometimes had to be careful to ensure that he didn't confuse different patients and so get shown up before the students.

The registrar of the Firm spent almost all his time in outpatients, apart from one or two teaching sessions a week in the ward. He was not usually available to advise me with problems. The one really valuable source of advice was the Resident Assistant Physician (always known as the RAP). There was only one RAP for the whole hospital (I think about 600 beds). He lived in and appeared to be on duty 24 hours a day and seven days a week. In practice he had overall day-to-day responsibility for all the "medical" (as opposed to surgical or obstetric) beds. It was he who decided when each patient should be allowed home. But he also saw all the "medical" emergencies, day or night, and made the final decision about their admission. (If he thought the patient needed admission but was not appropriate for a teaching hospital he would send him or her on to one of the London County Council hospitals).

The RAP was usually selected as the best of the contemporary registrars. His standard was accordingly high. He often later went on to become a consultant in the hospital. In my day the RAP was John Bishop Harman. He was very bright indeed and a very nice man. He had acquired the Membership of the Royal College of Physicians and the Fellowship of the Royal College of Surgeons within three months of qualifying. Both were the most difficult of higher qualifications and seldom both obtained by one individual. Shortly after his achievement, the laws of both Colleges were changed. One was only permitted to sit the examinations much later and after appropriate postgraduate experience. Harman was a wonderful support. With his day and night experience he was probably the best opinion on a medical emergency in London, but also very good right across the field. In spite of being out of his bed often several times a night, he was always helpful and patient. I learnt a vast amount from him. He died a few months before I wrote this (in March 1996). I learnt from his obituary that his daughter Harriet is now a member of the Labour Shadow Cabinet. I wrote to her to say how much I had owed her father so many years ago.

But the person from whom I learnt most was Sister George, the Sister in charge of my male ward. She was relatively young – I would think in her thirties – very intelligent, very caring and very experienced. She knew a great deal of medicine. For her I was always "the doctor" yet, with consummate tact, she would gently guide me into appropriate action. And of course I soon learnt to ask her advice. I developed an enormous respect for her, especially when I considered that every six months she had to start educating yet another raw recruit like myself, and do it with the same calm patience and diplomacy.

My other ward Sister was older and an excellent nurse. She had less of an intellectual grasp of medicine than Sister George but we also got on very well.

The standard of nursing care at St Thomas's was superb. This had been Florence Nightingale's hospital. It had been built to her design, a series of ward blocks facing across the Thames to the Houses of Parliament, joined on each of the floors and the basement by long corridors. (The Royal Infirmary of Edinburgh was built to the same Nightingale design. This was subsequently copied, from the RIE, in the teaching hospital of Magill University in Montreal, which was partly founded by Edinburgh graduates.)

It was very competitive to be accepted for nurse training at St Thomas's. You had to be "a nice girl" both intellectually and socially. There was a snob element. It was said that you had to have a Bishop behind you to be readily accepted. You also had to evince a passion for nursing. Once admitted the student nurse was treated like a slave and ruled with iron discipline. They only wanted girls who were so passionate about nursing that they'd put up with anything.

In my day the Matron was indeed a formidable woman, who ruled her staff with a rod of iron. Everyone was terrified of her. When The Presence moved down a corridor you could feel the Cold Front moving ahead of her, stilling all but the most respectful and deferential activity, not only in nurses but in all staff. Even medical students were momentarily awed.

The Ward Sisters were the standard bearers of this devotion. They too ruled their nurses with a rod of iron. All their nurses were expected to know all about all the patients in the ward all the time. The "Report" at each changeover of staff (night staff to day staff etc) was extremely detailed and was attended by all nurses coming on duty. From a House Physician's point of view this was marvellous. Each nurse always knew what had been happening to every patient. They were a delight to work with and of course were very nice girls. In those days certainly no one came into nursing for the money. The Ward Sisters were paid £90 a year. I think some of them, if not all of them, still slept on the ward in their own bedrooms.

Theoretically the nurses were not supposed to mix socially with either doctors or students. If someone did take a nurse out for the evening – and of course they very frequently did – the escort was not allowed to see her back to the Nurses' Home. They had to part at the other side of Westminster Bridge. The girl then proceeded, alone and unprotected, back to the Nurses' Home!

One of my fellow house surgeons became engaged to a nurse. She felt she must confess to the Matron. She sought an interview and deferentially reported "I thought I should inform you Matron that I've become engaged to a member of staff". Matron's only reply was "Doctor or porter?"

The aunt of my old Irish friend Donough O'Brien had been a nurse at St Thomas's early in the 20th century. On the river side of the hospital, facing the Houses of Parliament, was an attractive broad walk along the half-mile or so of the hospital blocks. In the summer many staff and students would stroll along it at lunchtime. But at that period nurses were instructed that, if a group of them were walking there and saw an approaching group of students or doctors (who were, of course, all male) the nurses had to about turn and walk the other way. I suppose all this was a relic of Florence Nightingale's efforts to establish nursing as a profession for "ladies" and live down the early nineteenth century image of nursing as a job for Sarah Gamps[*] and prostitutes.

The outlook of the hospital over the Thames was delightful. I have memories of being hauled up to emergencies in the middle of the night and the peaceful atmosphere after the problem had been dealt with. The city lay silent about me save for the lights and faint engines of tugs and barges still moving romantically up and down the river. Somehow the feeling of that peace, against the background of at last doing such a wonderfully worthwhile job, mingled to give me much inner satisfaction and support.

We worked extremely hard. In those days we were expected to do most of our routine biochemical and haematological laboratory investigations ourselves. We had a laboratory in the basement where we repaired after our evening meal for a couple of hours' work. Thereafter we did a detailed night round checking on our patients. This did not usually finish until after midnight. It was often lightened, especially if there had been some emergency to cope with, by cocoa, sandwiches and gossip with the night nurses in the ward kitchen.

We were supposed to have every second weekend off. In practice I usually found there was so much to do that my weekend started at 6pm on Saturday. I was back on the job on Sunday evening.

---

[*] Disreputable character in *Martin Chuzzlewit* (1843) by Charles Dickens.

Every four weeks your Firm was on a "Major Week". During that week your Firm took all the medical emergencies. You were called down to Casualty to see any potential admission. If you agreed that the patient should come in, you called in the RAP. It was he who made the final decision. This meant that you were out of your bed usually several times a night for a week. If you had such an admission as a patient with diabetic coma, you might be up all night doing repeated blood sugars and adjusting the treatment accordingly.

I had the excitement that the first effective treatment for a bacterial infection, sulphanilamide, became available just as I started in the wards as a House Physician. This was highly effective against the streptococcus. Although the streptococcus commonly caused nasty, but not fatal, sore throats, if it infected wounds or entered a surgeon's pricked finger or that of a doctor doing a post-mortem, the bacteria could enter the bloodstream and be rapidly fatal. The drug was less effective against the common cause of pneumonia, the pneumococcus, but at least one was able to give the patient a drug that might help. Previously one had had to depend merely on oxygen and good nursing.

My most impressive success was a young woman with meningitis. My chief had seen her in private practice. He diagnosed that it was probably tuberculous meningitis, at that time 100% fatal. I did a lumbar puncture, from which we grew the pneumococcus. My chief said that this was equally likely to be fatal. But we filled the patient up with large doses of sulphanilamide and she recovered, probably one of the earliest patients to do so with the new drug[*].

Another novelty with which I experienced early use was the "iron lung" for poliomyelitis (known to the laity as "infantile paralysis"). This was an acute infection with a virus which settled in the nervous system and caused paralysis. Sometimes the paralysis extended to the breathing system. Formerly this had been fatal, but now the patient could be put in the iron lung. This enclosed the body in a sort of rounded coffin with his head sticking out. A machine rhythmically sucked the air out of the iron casing. This caused the patient's chest to expand and suck air through his mouth into his lungs. When the pressure relaxed, the elastic recoil in his lungs expelled the air. With the machine he was breathing mechanically.

As you can imagine, this required frequent adjustment and attention both to the patient and to his machine. With luck, after days, weeks or months, the paralysis would recover. Some patients died. In some others there was

---

[*] Pneumococcal meningitis was commoner in children than in young women. However, I believe that only a minority of such patients at any age died from the disease.

little recovery and the patient might spend years in the machine. Fortunately my young man's breathing recovered in a few weeks, though he was left with some limb weaknesses.

All this was, of course, a monastic existence but one had a wonderful sense of total devotion to a wonderful job. One did, of course, often get very tired. Although our bedrooms were somewhat Spartan, and dominated by our ruthless master, the telephone, we were very well fed. The food was excellent and the staff very fatherly and caring. They would always keep food if we were delayed and try to provide it at the odd hours which so often resulted from the job. There was always a large jug of milk and, surprisingly today, a large jug of beer, on the table.

The Next Stage

That immensely happy and rewarding six months came to an end. What next? If I was going to become a consultant somewhere, there were two major hurdles ahead. First of all I had to pass the very difficult examination for the Membership of the Royal College of Physicians. As an indication of the difficulties, I was conscious that the brightest student of a previous year, who collected all the prizes all the way through his career (including his preclinical years which he had also spent at St Thomas's) had failed the Membership examination five times. That hurdle hopefully surmounted, I had then to land a registrar job at a teaching hospital. Registrar jobs I think lasted three years. So vacancies came up only intermittently. There would be none at St Thomas's until later 1939 or 1940.

A number of St Thomas's graduates frequently had similar problems in awaiting opportunities for longer term posts in London or elsewhere. There was a tradition of filling the time, and at last earning some money, by becoming a Civilian Medical Practitioner at one of the army hospitals in London. These posts seemed to be a St Thomas's sinecure. They were used by the RAMC when they were short of General Duty Officers at their London hospitals. You were paid so much a day (it was 28 shillings), but you could be sacked at a day's notice if a suitable RAMC officer became available.

My professional earnings so far had amounted to a pound or two for signing the odd cremation certificate on a deceased patient. My father had generously continued his allowance. I think this was still £2 a week, but I had found this quite adequate for my monastic needs as a House Physician. It was splendid at last, at the age of 25, to release him from supporting me. The army job was said not to be all that exacting and would give adequate time to study for the membership examination.

I first spent a month or two at the Royal Herbert Hospital at Woolwich. This served some local Base Depots. Many of the patients were very young recruits, often admitted with short-term minor illnesses or reactions from smallpox vaccinations. Not very exciting challenges from the medical point of view. Then I had the opportunity of moving to the Army's most important hospital, the Queen Alexandra's Military Hospital at Millbank. It was just beside the Tate Gallery (and indeed is now converted to an extension of the Gallery, having been released by the Army). The main RAMC School of Medicine was nearby.

Clinical problems from other military hospitals in the UK, or from anywhere in the then worldwide Empire, were referred to Millbank. The head of the medical side was the current Consultant Physician to the Army, a General. When I first arrived it was General Priest. He soon retired to be replaced by General Biggam, fresh from being professor of Medicine at Cairo University. When, in 1952, I came to my Chair in Edinburgh, I found him, now Sir Alexander, as the very effective and charming Postgraduate Dean, busy with organising postgraduate education for the vast post-war pilgrimage to Edinburgh from all over the Commonwealth.

Both of the Generals were excellent physicians. In addition a number of distinguished London consultants in specific specialties (cardiologists, neurologist etc) could be called in to advise on difficult problems.

I was given charge of the main medical ward. There I had day-to-day responsibility and personally carried out most of the minor procedures. My immediate superior was a competent army medical specialist, a Major, with the General as a more remote consultant.

In practice I did most of the work of the ward. I learnt a lot and greatly extended my experience, including a first contact with some tropical diseases. I got on very well with my superiors.

Occasionally I had to sleep in as Orderly Officer and deal with night emergencies in any of the wards. But when I had any patient who was acutely ill I always drove down late in the evening to do a night round. The shortest route from home to the hospital was through the West End via Bond Street. I was often amused by the hopeful salutations of the rather upmarket Daughters of Joy of that area – but rather surprised that they should think that my aged car might be carrying a sufficiently affluent potential client.

Besides the complicated, and inevitably more long term, patients brought in from abroad, we admitted many young soldiers with pneumonia, probably a product of the greater chances of infection in crowded barracks. By now we had a new sulphonamide, sulphapyridine, which was much more effective than its predecessor against the pneumococcus, the commonest cause of pneumonia. It was very rewarding to see its effect on these young men, often admitted extremely ill. I think my very first medical publication was a letter to *The Lancet* concerning some side-effects of the new drug.

From this post, a very happy and rewarding one, though carrying little prestige to boost my future career, I took the examination for the Membership of the Royal College of Physicians in London in January 1939. At that time you first sat the written papers. Only if you passed these did you go on, three weeks later, to take the very stiff clinical and oral examinations. The ultimate hurdle was the "Final Viva Voce examination" by the President of the College, supported by two Fellows; I think the Senior and Junior "Censor".

The written papers included a voluntary section involving translation of two medical passages from French and from German. These, if done correctly, gave extra marks. In preparation I had been learning medical German, and reading French medical publications.

After the written examination of course I discussed the papers with fellow examinees. I came away from this discussion very depressed, sure that I must have failed. I nearly neglected to skim through my planned revision in preparation for the pathology and oral examinations, but finally decided that I should persist.

In due course I was informed that I'd passed the papers and should present myself for the clinicals and orals. In the clinical my "long case" was a poor man with classical tabes[*] (a late neurological complication of syphilis now, mercifully, since penicillin, virtually unknown in Britain). The symptoms and signs were so classical that I was sure that there must be some cryptic complication to provide a further challenge to my clinical skills. I couldn't find anything other than tabes. Fortunately this proved correct. The challenge proved to be in one of the short cases. The longer of these was a nice little girl, accompanied by her mother, who appeared to have a congenital abnormality of her heart. She turned out to have an additional hidden complication. To begin with I took a little time to make friends before taking a history and examining her. This paid off. Her mother dropped me a hint that there was something more. I found she had Horner's syndrome[#], an eye change due to interference with a long nerve which runs down from the neck to curve round the aorta and return to the right eye. It had presumably been compressed by the cardiovascular abnormality.

---

[*]Tabes dorsalis (locomotor ataxia): neurological manifestations of tertiary syphilis. These include severe leg pain, abdominal pain, double vision and eventually blindness, and most characteristically, unco-ordinated walking.

[#] neurological condition defined by signs and symptoms resulting from paralysis of the sympathetic nerves in the neck.

When it came to the orals my examiner proved to be a well known postgraduate teacher from the Middlesex Hospital. After I had examined the pathology slides, he first made encouraging noises about my progress so far. He added "I see you did your languages well too".

After a series of questions on pathology and clinical medicine he finally put up on a viewing box an X-ray of the chest. This showed what seemed to be cavitated tuberculosis in both lungs, and a pneumothorax, with a fluid level on one side. But there was also an obvious abnormality, with thickening, of one clavicle (collarbone). I took the examiner through the lung and pleural changes. He then asked if there was anything else. I replied that there was an obvious abnormality of the left clavicle. He asked me what I thought it was. I said I had been taught not to make more than one diagnosis, but it didn't look to me like tuberculosis. He asked what I thought it did look like. I said it looked like Paget's Disease (a disease sometimes affecting the elderly giving a loofah-like appearance on the X-ray). This proved correct.

My examiner apparently used this tricky X-ray from time to time for both postgraduate teaching and examinations. Many years later a Middlesex graduate I knew went to my examiner's last postgraduate teaching round at the Middlesex Hospital before he retired. There was a large farewell attendance. He showed the same X-ray. He added that in his many years of experience only one postgraduate had ever got it right and he was now Professor of Respiratory Diseases in Edinburgh. I felt very flattered – or perhaps very lucky!

After this exchange, I moved on, somewhat encouraged, to wait with one other colleague for a summons to the "Final Viva" by the President and his two formidable inquisitors. Soon the summonsing official entered but fortunately announced "You will be glad to hear, gentlemen, that the President does not wish to ask you any further questions". We entered the presidential room. The President shook our hands and congratulated us. We passed out through the other door. A secretary greeted us with her congratulations, but quickly added the final question, "Do you have your cheque books with you, gentlemen?" With perhaps unjustified optimism we had. We had been appropriately warned beforehand. You paid a fee for taking the examination. If successful you paid a further substantial fee for being enrolled as a member of the College.

This final part of the examination had been held in the College itself, then housed in what is now the Canadian High Commission building in Trafalgar Square. I emerged, treading on air, into the Square and reeled down Whitehall to look for a telephone box. I rang my thrilled father with the happy news. I then walked on down Whitehall, past the Houses of

Parliament and along the Embankment to the hospital, rejoicing that this was positively my last examination. I happily completed my day's clinical work.

A few days later I was delighted to receive a personal letter from the Registrar of the College, Sir Letherby Tidy, one of St Thomas's consultants. He congratulated me and told me that I had done extremely well in all parts of the examination. This was a great boost. I also had a kind letter of congratulation from Lord Lugard, a famous African administrator and a patient of my father's.

It happened that very shortly afterwards my services would not be required by the Army for a couple of weeks. A regular RAMC officer was expected on temporary attachment. I could therefore have an unpaid holiday.

It was January. None of my climbing friends could, or would, come away. So I drove north alone to the Western Highlands. My original plan was to establish food dumps, via the east-west roads, leave my car at Kyle of Lochalsh and then walk cross country south, camping and picking up my food en route. I would return by the Mallaig railway, roundabout back to Kyle to pick up my car. But, for my ten days in the Highlands, I only had two hours when it was not snowing or raining. It was much too grim for my original scheme, but I did a lot of hill-walking. I climbed all the Munros of the Five Sisters of Kintail and also those on the other side of the glen. I found that if I hurried my ascent I got out of the rain into hail, which was much less wetting. There had to be much compass work. I mostly camped, trying to find the least wet spot, which often proved to be the bank on the side of the road above the drain. I did, however, spend a couple of nights, by myself in the ancient Inn in Glen Shiel. At least one day was so awful that I read in my sleeping bag all day. The only time I got wet at night was when camping beside the road after climbing Craig Meggie[*]. During the night very wet snow fell and with its damp weight bent my flysheet and roof down so that the melted snow leaked though over my sewn-in groundsheet. I woke in a pool of water and retired to the car for the rest of the night. My challenging holiday was a brisk contrast to hospital medicine and the stress of the examination.

In January 1939 a vacancy for a registrarship at St Thomas's Hospital looked as if it would not occur before 1940. A few months later a registrar post was advertised at another London teaching hospital, the Westminster. I knew that most London teaching hospitals only appointed their own graduates, but I decided to have a go.

---

[*] Perhaps Creag Meagaidh is meant, a Munro north of Loch Laggan.

The Westminster administrator informed me that I would be expected to call on all the physicians at their consulting rooms. I telephoned their secretaries to make appointments. I trailed around from consulting room to consulting room in the medically sanctified Harley Street milieu. I cannot remember how many there were or the details. My one memory is of calling on Sir Adolf Abraham*, in his Queen Anne Street rooms. The waiting room and consulting room carried carpets in which I practically sank up to my knees. The elegant Sir Adolf greeted me in his cutaway tail coat. His career had undoubtedly been facilitated, apart from his medical achievements, by having been an Olympic sprinter.

The consultants were pleasant and affable, but of course the job went to one of their own graduates, Clarence Gavey. He was obviously a good man. He later became a consultant cardiologist at the hospital. Ironically, when during the war I was promoted to Lieutenant Colonel and Officer in Charge of the Medical Division in the Military Hospital in Malta in 1944, Clarence was one of the two medical specialists under my command!

---

* Presumably Sir Adolphe Abrahams (1883-1967), elder brother of Harold Maurice Abrahams (1899-1978), 100m sprint champion in the 1924 Olympic Games held in Paris, France.

Chapter 4
Me and Hitler 1939-45

Curtain-raiser

In May 1939 Hitler's downfall became assured! Crofton J. joined the British Army's Supplementary Reserve Category C, an exotic subsection confined to specialists in medicine or railways. The reason seems to have been that these officers were thought to require no peacetime training in military matters. I was aged twenty-seven and could hardly have been regarded as a very high powered specialist.

I had started at the Royal Herbert Hospital in Woolwich. However, after a few months I moved to the Queen Alexandra Military Hospital at Millbank, as previously described. For me it was splendid experience in medicine at a time when soldiers often acquired rheumatic fever, tuberculosis, infectious diseases and various tropical exotica, as well, of course, as various rarities which might turn up in any part of the world. I found clinical work absolutely fascinating; and seemed to have a certain facility for it. The intellectual challenge, the contact with patients and their infinite ranges of personality, the satisfactions of achieving diagnosis and successful treatment were all enormous fun. The recently discovered sulphonamides were beginning to treat successfully some previously grim diseases such as pneumococcal pneumonia, which has indeed remained a lifetime interest.

So here I was, on the strength of the MRCP, acknowledged, perhaps rather shamefully, as an RAMC specialist, though admittedly still highly supplementary. In August 1939 an RAMC officer was going to take my place for two weeks, so I was to be temporarily sacked – no 28 bob a day. Accordingly I thought I might get in one more holiday before the war started and fixed with one of my friends, Ashley Greenwood, to climb in the French Alps. In those days France was remarkably cheap, though we travelled third class, with additional tourist reduction, and mostly bivouacked or slept in climbing huts.

We went to the Dauphiné and had a few days splendid climbing. I have a memory of a lovely bivouac in the last alp below a glacier on the Écrins and the stars wheeling over the opposite ridge. I have a memory of coming down to a hut after that climb. There was a party of French Scouts there, singing happily in the evening. Would they look back to this evening as their last taste of happiness? I don't remember having any particular personal apprehension. I suppose, since the Germans had marched ruthlessly into Czechoslovakia in March, we all knew war would come and nature had helped us to suppress or ignore the horrors on which my generation had been brought up in the aftermath of the First World War.

After five days the weather broke. After a dim wet day or two, forced into a little hotel in La Bérarde, we decided it might be a better bet to cross into Italy, south of the Alps, and attempt Monte Viso, one of the larger of the Southern Alps. It went on raining. After a day or so we started early one morning for Monte Viso, but the rain poured down and the rain soaked rocks came after it, so we decided to reserve our bodies for a more worthwhile cannonade. We had managed to get an Italian paper and deciphered the news of the Soviet-Axis pact. This obviously cleared the decks for Hitler and I persuaded Ashley that we had better get back across the frontier as soon as possible. In fact it was closed the day after we crossed.

Nothing except rain for the first ten miles of the French side; not a soldier or a gun, not a person. Then a man ran out of the first house and cried to us "Mobilization". So we knew it was on.

We were soaked through and would have to stay at a hotel. In the first and second little towns we came to, all the hotels had been taken over by the military. At the third town, only the Hotel Majestic was open – a long, long way above our normal social aspirations. It was almost empty. One or two elderly couples, with women in long frocks, were at dinner. Ashley had no dry shirt or dry shoes and I was only marginally better. So we must have been unique diners for that hotel. But, fortunately, "C'est la guerre" and all was forgiven.

After dinner, miraculously, the sun appeared. We took a little walk and met an elderly English couple who said all transport home would now be horribly crowded with the mobilization and the English hurrying back. It would be better to wait a few days till things settled down. But of course I knew that Hitler needed his answer and where would the war effort be without Crofton?

So next day off to Besançon to collect our luggage and to stock up with food for what might have been a long and difficult journey. We shared our wooden seated third class railway carriage with First World War veterans in their forties or fifties, now recalled to the colours, who seemed very gloomy and depressed. It was a tribute to the French railways that we arrived in Dover only two hours late. A day or two later the radio announced that reservists should not wait for call-up papers but report at once to their mobilization centres. I was off.

Mobilization

I was to report to Shorncliffe Military Camp, near Folkestone. But first I had to get a uniform. So I went off to Moss Bros., who specialised not only in hiring out evening dress, or grey toppers for royal garden parties, to temporary or impecunious gentlemen, but were also military tailors, reputedly expert at instant matching of a uniform to even the most unexpected physique. In half an hour I was improbably metamorphosed into an officer and a gentleman, topped off by the two pips of the lieutenant.

I packed my bags and set out for Folkestone on 28th August, five days before war was declared. I didn't really know what to expect. My reading about the First World War had indicated that one slept on the floor of a barn, but I had forgotten that I was now an officer and gentleman. In the event, the men did sleep on the floor of barns (or the equivalent, the floor of the huts of the Army Educational Corps at Shorncliffe), but the officers were accommodated in the Majestic Hotel in Folkestone, duly commandeered for this major contribution to the war effort.

On the way down in the train I had shared a carriage with a regular officer – in the first class now, no longer the wooden seats of French third class mobilization. He gently pointed out that the sword-frog on my Sam Browne, thoughtfully provided by Moss Bros., was now archaic. I blushingly removed it.

In the next few months it was just as well there was a period of phoney war. Whatever the rest of the British army was like – and my impression was that it was patchy, with both very good and very poor units – the RAMC in 1939 was incredibly inefficient. The deficiency seemed to reside mainly in the officers. The regular NCOs[*] and men had been well trained and I always found them reliable and efficient. But in war you have to look to the officers for initiative. The peacetime RAMC, with its strict routine, its regulations and its narrow well-defined responsibilities, was a poor training ground for those who might have to make quick decisions in the face of disaster. Indeed the senior officers I met in these early months didn't seem capable of making any decisions at all. They were like fish in small aquarium tanks, gently weaving their fins and gills, sucking in the odd morsel descending to them, and oblivious of life hurrying by outside. If someone upset the water tank they would be left gasping, as many of them indeed soon were.

However, in a couple of years, by 1941, the Corps had become first class. By that time those at the top had got rid of the less competent senior regular and territorial officers and the amateurs from civilian life had learnt

---

[*] Non-commissioned Officers

the job. Six years later, when I was travelling back from Germany in a demobilization train, I remember overhearing through the thin partition, some officers in the next carriage reminiscing over their war experiences. I was proud to hear them agree that the one lot that had never let them down was the RAMC.

The first administrative triumph was to mobilise the reserves three days before the regulars to whom they were due to report. The result was that one overworked, but remarkably efficient, staff-sergeant at Shorncliffe appeared to be in sole charge of mobilization of several hospitals, a couple of Casualty Clearing stations and a Field Ambulance or two. I was attached, as a medical specialist, to No. 5 General Hospital, which was to form part of the British Expeditionary Force to France. But meantime most of us were set to carry out medical inspections on the vast numbers of reservists who were pouring in from numerous units. We had no instructions about the criteria for fitness, the numbers were overwhelming, and most of the reservists were keen and did not emphasize any disability. So unless there was something obviously wrong they were passed. The result was that for the first few months in France we spent a great deal of our time invaliding out men who should have never been accepted in the first place.

Meantime, in my own unit, one or two senior territorial officers had turned up. A vague identity began to emerge. A good many of the men had been celebrating on the way, which added a minor spice to any attempt at organization. Fortunately the weather was glorious.

As September 3rd, and the declaration of war, approached we began to make our preparations. It seems ridiculous in retrospect, but the expectation was that the Luftwaffe would immediately start attacking us. All the tuberculosis sanatoria had been emptied to make room for casualties evacuated from the cities (this later contributing to the sharp spread of the disease). Children had been sent into the country. Obviously Goering's planes would make straight for the vital targets at Shorncliffe!

So we spent the last day or two before the war mobilizing our men, drunk or sober, to dig slit trenches. On the day war was declared I was made Orderly Officer and so was to stay up at the camp with the men while the remaining officers fell back in their usual good order to the bar at the Majestic Hotel. I had the men hard at it digging their trenches. There was only about one gas mask available for every three men. I met this challenge by dividing them into groups so that they could go sniff, sniff, sniff, in rotation! I had a patrol going round listening for the air raid warning siren from Folkestone and two men by the telephone to take messages about the approaching raiders. About midnight, satisfied that the British genius for improvisation had done its inadequate best, I retired to my camp bed in one of the huts and slept like a log.

After a peaceful night I went down by truck for my breakfast at the Majestic Hotel, only to be greeted with "How did you get on in the air raid last night?" Apparently about 3am some unidentified plane had been spotted over the Channel and the alarm given. All the other officers had spent several hours in the cellars. But my patrol had heard nothing, my telephonist had heard nothing and certainly I had heard nothing. Providence had clearly thwarted my well-laid plans and spared the men (and me) an uncomfortable night in the slit trenches sniffing at our shared gas masks.

The war had started. But no one could find our Commanding Officer. We knew who he was. General Headquarters knew who he was. The only person who didn't know that he was our Commanding Officer was the man himself. He was a recently retired regular and had been happily engaged as an Air Raid Warden somewhere in Shropshire. No one had informed him that he had been recalled to the colours, made a full Colonel and assigned to our rather blunt-edged spearhead of the British Expeditionary Force. But at last our CO turned up at Folkestone to command us. He proved to be an affable, pleasant, dapper little man who was very good at organizing social events. He arranged one or two dances for the officers and the nursing staff. We were all more or less ordered on to the dance floor. As I was very shy with girls and no dancer, some of the earliest casualties of the war must have been the trampled toes of the Queen Alexandra's Imperial Nursing Service, as it was then rather grandly called.

The next game, after "Find the CO" was "Find the Equipment". It was supposed to have been carefully stored so as to be instantly available. Over and over again every military store in Southern England denied having it. Finally, in despair, someone sent a wire to the General Headquarters of the British Expeditionary Force. Magically, one of the persistent deniers immediately coughed it up.

France: The Phoney War

After 48 hours' embarkation leave with our families, we sailed in convoy from Southampton to Cherbourg on the night of 11th October 1939. We zig-zagged in a stormy sea. Once more I was Orderly Officer and dossed down on the floor of the large lounge, crammed with smoking, and often vomiting, troops. I am normally a good sailor but in the morning, for the first and, I hope, last time, I was briefly seasick. We then travelled by train to a small third-rate seaside resort, Le Tréport, near Dieppe. Here we were to erect our base hospital on the golf-course atop the 300 foot chalk cliffs. The officers were billeted in a local hotel or in the golf club. We younger ones awaited orders or instructions. But for what seems in retrospect like weeks absolutely nothing happened. That's not quite true: one evening the CO dined the local mayor in our mess and on another he organised a dance with the nurses.

We knew our hospital was to be a tented one. The wards were to be in what the army called "Marquees, Hospital, Extending". These were never used in peacetime and no-one in the unit knew how to put them up. After a week or two of idleness, and after discussing it with some of my friends, I asked the CO whether I could have a sergeant and a squad and try to find out how to put up one of the marquees. With some difficulty, we succeeded. So we thought we'd put up another. That started it. I finally found that, without at any time receiving any orders or instructions, I'd become Master of Works and eventually put up the whole hospital. It really was quite extraordinary. What did go on, if anything at all, in those senior officers' minds? The CO and everyone else seemed pleased, but in a totally passive way. If I'd been instructed to put it up, I'd have thought it out much more carefully in advance. As it was, it was a matter of one thing leading to another and a pretty amateur performance of course. When I realised what was happening to me, I began to take advice where I could get it. There was a nice young Royal Engineers officer who was a great help. I remember our triumph when we had jointly designed, and he had constructed, a bedpan washer. No other hospital seemed to have one of those. In our excitement you might have thought we had evolved the British Secret Weapon that would win the war.

Soon the autumn gales started. All of us on the construction site got soaked. My father sent me out his fishing waders. These plus a ground sheet and a tin hat proved a good combination. The northwest storms roared up the cliffs, creating a vacuum which sucked our massive marquees up into the empyrean. Over and over again we had to turn out in the middle of the night to batten them down. We almost had to set the tent-pegs in concrete.

Disappointingly perhaps, in early December, just as our hospital was completed and ready to open, I was posted to No.1 British General Hospital in Dieppe. This was already well-established, open and very busy. The Surgical Division was in the Casino, the Medical in the Metropole Hotel, both on the seafront. I presume they were both destroyed in the Dieppe raid of 1943.

I looked after the officers' ward and a ward for the more difficult medical problems, besides seeing a number of patients in consultation with colleagues and doing my share of Orderly Officer when, besides inspecting the kitchens and the men's meals, one was first on call for emergencies. My memory of the latter was mainly of bleeding tooth sockets (as the army dentists tried to cope with the horrors of prewar British teeth), bleeding noses and the occasional routine medical or surgical emergency. Among the troops there was an epidemic of meningococcal meningitis, which fortunately responded to the then available sulphonamides, and later of, appropriately enough, German measles (rubella). I caught the latter quite badly myself and had to be off work for a few days.

It was rewarding and interesting work. I had some keen young colleagues and a good regular army medical specialist, a major, with whom I got on very well. But the senior officers were once more out of the aquarium. The Lieutenant-Colonel in charge of the Medical Division in which I worked was a rather silent Irishman. I don't remember him ever doing anything except drink, equally silently, at a table in a neighbouring café or in the bar of the mess. The franc was very low in comparison with the pound and drink was dangerously cheap.

Our Commanding Officer had the reputation of being the best dressed man in the RAMC. He certainly looked it, but his Savile Row uniform and red tabs seemed to be backed largely by sawdust inside his skull. One day the Adjutant-General from General Headquarters arrived to inspect the hospital. Presumably the CO knew he was coming but he seemed to have told no-one else, certainly not anyone as junior as I or my colleagues. Suddenly a nurse told me that a battalion of Top Brass, gleaming with red, had come up the stairs and was in the ward below. I warned all my staff. The orderlies hurriedly made the beds even more tidy and Sister and I awaited the Coming. In fact the Coming never reached us. It was too taken up with the shambles below, where all the nurses had fled at the sight of the Apocalypse and no-one could find the Medical Officer among the innumerable hotel bedrooms of which the ward consisted. When someone eventually did find him and informed him, he rushed hurriedly out of one of the little rooms and trampled painfully on the Adjutant-General's toe.

The next day our CO solemnly called a meeting of all his officers. He informed us that, for the first time in his career, had had "received a raspberry" from his superiors. In future all officers must be in their wards from 9am to 1pm. As I, at least, was then starting work at 8am or before and usually working to at least 11pm, these instructions were received with a certain amount of silent irony.

Sometime about February or March 1940 I received notification of my promotion to Major. I hasten to add that this was not a recognition of any gallant or distinguished service but just because the authorities had now decided that all medical specialists should be so graded. Of course at that stage my officers' ward was full of regulars or territorials of some service. They were deeply shocked at the thought of a major aged a mere twenty-seven.

In the later winter I was posted once more, this time to No.3 General Hospital a few miles inland among the Normandy apple orchards. It was far more cohesive than either of my previous units, with friendly pleasant junior staff who got on very well with each other.

Here for the first time was a CO who seemed quite effective. He was a silent man, but appeared to know very well what was going on. One of the minor problems was that every medical alcoholic in the UK seemed to have heard that drink was cheap in France. By chance or intention they kept on being posted to this unit. One might trip over their horizontal forms on the way into breakfast. Somehow the CO knew. Within a few days they had been posted up the line. Within a few weeks one often heard they had come back down again under close arrest. Not perhaps the ideal way of dealing with the tragedies of alcohol, but at least an improvement on the aquarium syndrome.

Fortunately when I arrived at the unit I was blissfully unaware that the junior officers had greatly resented the prospect of having to receive some bloody young prig of an upstart major as a senior officer whom they would be expected to salute. However after one or two had resentfully fulfilled this military obligation and I had laughed at them and told them to stop being silly, the atmosphere soon thawed and we became firm friends.

Professionally, unfortunately, the CO insisted that medical specialists should not have direct charge of patients but only act as consultants. Of course I, with my fellow medical specialist, a charming middle-aged Harley Street psychiatrist, saw all the interesting or difficult problems, but it is not the same thing as having at least some patients under one's direct charge.

Among our medical problems turned out to be a number of patients with meningococcal septicaemia. These are patients in whom the bacteria (meningococci) circulate in the blood instead of causing meningitis (inflammation of the membranes of the brain). These patients ran a chronic variable fever, with joint pains and occasionally red spots on the skin. We were very puzzled at first but as there was an epidemic of meningitis we suspected that this might be an unusual manifestation. But, in spite of many blood cultures, we were at first unable to prove it. Eventually the bacteriologist and I speculated that, as it was a very cold winter and the blood had to be carried from the tents to the laboratory a mile or so away to a house in the village, the bacteria might have died of cold on the way. Accordingly we tried first heating the blood in the incubator and then insulating it on its way up and back from the tents. After that we began to get positives, knew where we were and could cure the patients with sulphonamides.

The spring came, with blossom, birdsong and glorious weather. We remained very busy. The poor Poles had been crushed. In April Norway was invaded. Then, suddenly and at last, Hitler's western blitzkrieg began. The Phoney War was over. The real thing had begun.

France: The Real War

As so often in the war, at first nothing much happened as far as we were concerned. The radio reported that the British Army had advanced into Belgium to meet the oncoming Germans. One evening there was an air raid in Dieppe. I had a very sick patient and had just had him given a sedative and got him off to sleep when the warning "gas" came over the telephone. So we had to wake the poor dopey man and put on his gas mask, as well as, of course, our own. (By this time we had one each). Presumably someone in Dieppe had smelt high explosives and misinterpreted it as gas. We didn't keep our masks on for long.

To clear the beds for casualties we evacuated home what patients we could. In the event we did not receive many wounded, but I remember my first experience of seeing severe psychiatric casualties. These were men who had been subjected to intensive dive bombing. The German dive bombers, one after another, would hurtle down almost vertically, making a hideous screaming noise, drop their bombs and sweep up again. To the attacked this was a very unnerving experience. Later it was found that if you were in a slit trench the chances of being hit were quite small. Moreover as the bombers rose from their dive they slowed down and were easy and very vulnerable targets. For this reason the Germans later discarded them.

At that time all the horrors were new and our patients' experiences had been very terrifying. Some of the men were quite unable to speak. They behaved like tiny infants. I remember one who, if he heard a plane in the distance, lay whimpering under his bed. I understand that with rest and sedation, most such patients made a good recovery. Later, improvements in training, especially battle training, reduced the terrifying novelty and such casualties became much rarer.

Eventually we were told that two major convoys of wounded were coming to us. They never arrived. In retrospect this was obviously because the German armoured divisions had swept across the lines of communication and cut off the convoys. But we didn't know that at the time. We waited in expectation and with frustratingly little to do except wait. Then I came down to supper in the mess one evening and was informed that, immediately after supper, all specialists were to parade with minimal baggage ready to move elsewhere, destination not specified. We presumed we were going to be sent forward to reinforce units in more direct contact with the enemy. In fact we were piled into ambulances and, to our chagrin, found ourselves going off in the opposite direction. In the darkness we saw Rouen burning in the distances as we passed. There were streams of refugee cars, many with mattresses on their roofs as some sort of pathetic protection against bombs or machine guns.

I was sitting beside the driver of my ambulance. Sometime in the night he fell asleep and we swerved towards the ditch. Fortunately I was awake and seized the wheel. Next day we arrived at Le Mans, far to the southeast.

One of my friends whom I met later in the war, a regular, was at that time a surgical specialist in a small military hospital at Arques, a few miles to the north of our own. The day we left they suddenly saw the German armour on the main road half a mile to their north. But the armour turned west and streamed past them all through the day and night. This was the dash to the coast to cut off the British and French forces at Dunkirk. It was not a comfortable position for a Base Hospital to find itself in the front line. The CO panicked. Eventually my friend (very bravely for a regular) had to say to his CO "I'm sorry, Sir, but I'm afraid you'll either have to go sick or I must put you under arrest!" He went sick. They then managed to get their patients away, the CO included.

Presumably, with the enemy on our doorstep, the high-ups had decided that specialists were in short supply and that they were the most important personnel to save from capture. We felt very ashamed when we found what had happened to us, especially as the nurses had not been evacuated. However, thanks to Dunkirk, later they all got away too.

Back at Le Mans, after an hour or two, we were put on a train crowded with troops and refugees. Having had no sleep overnight I managed to doss down on the floor of a crowded corridor with people trampling over me at intervals.

Eventually we found ourselves at La Baule, on the south coast of Brittany, where all the bits and pieces of the RAMC, variously dispersed by the retreat, were being concentrated. There was one hospital in a large hotel. With some difficulty, as there were so many doctors available, I managed to get some work in it. There I met some splendid young wounded or sick from the Highland Division. Unfortunately most of that Division were captured or killed. Our patients were the lucky ones who were evacuated before the Division was completely cut off. This Division was later reconstituted and became famous in the Army's advance from Egypt to Tripoli.

The weather was glorious; the war news far from glorious. In a week or so I was once more posted, this time north to a hospital in Rennes, the capital of Brittany, then a moderate-size provincial town.

I went up by train and found myself sitting opposite a girl who was British and had had some interesting adventures. She had volunteered for the war effort and was told that the most useful thing she could do was to go to Spain and learn Spanish which was needed by British Intelligence. So off she went. She rented a room with a Spanish family and attended lessons. Her hostess was horrified when one day she went out for a walk with some Spanish citizens who were also studying in the house. However, she was a Catholic and had taken careful note of local customs. Thereafter she went to Mass every morning. With this morally unassailable background she found her social life much less inhibited. Anything she did was now respectable.

When the balloon went up she was advised by the British authorities to beat it to Bordeaux and find a boat for Britain. But at the frontier the Spanish authorities would not allow her to cross. She told me they were checking with her Spanish contacts "to see if she loved Franco". Of course Franco was quids in with Hitler and would certainly come in on Hitler's side once he was sure the Allies would lose the war. So she was stuck at St Jean de Luz for three weeks while everything collapsed in France. The result was that when she was eventually allowed out of Spain and reached Bordeaux there was no chance of transport to England. She was now aiming further north.

Things looked grim, but turned out quite satisfactorily. When we arrived in Rennes I took her along to the Railway Transport Officer and asked him to help. He said he would do his best. After I returned to the UK I had a letter from her thanking me and telling me that he had tagged her on to the staff of the British Embassy who were in the course of evacuation from Paris through Rennes. That ended the brief "Incident of the Beautiful Refugee". She was indeed a nice, pretty girl. I hope she married and lived happily ever after.

The Rennes military hospital was in some 19th century university buildings. The Allies' disintegration continued. The patients were evacuated, together with the nurses and half the male personnel.

The rest of us were divided into a Casualty Clearing Station and a Field Ambulance (to which I was allocated), but, beyond the listing of our names in one or the other, no obvious steps were taken to equip or organise us. We waited, with little real news but plenty of rumours of the approaching enemy.

I had only just joined the unit and was only beginning to know people. The younger officers kept their nerve but we were worried about our seniors who seemed to be calming theirs by drinking too much, and that too early in the day. I was shocked one afternoon to meet a senior major reeling down one of the corridors on a bicycle, a very bad example to the men. Of course these older men were expected, and were expecting, to see out the war at a relatively safe and routine base hospital. At their age (I thought they were old but I suppose they were mid-forties to early fifties), it is obviously more difficult to stand up to your world falling to pieces around your ears.

Fortunately disaster struck at ten o'clock in the morning when everyone was sober. An air raid warning went and we heard the approaching planes. Everyone scurried to the shelters in the basement. As I passed the telephone exchange I saw that it was unmanned. This hardly seemed appropriate for a hospital, especially during an air raid. I'd only just arrived. I hardly knew anyone. So I thought I'd better man it myself.

I had a book with me. It happened to be *The Worst Journey in the World*, by Apsley Cherry-Garrard, recounting a grim winter expedition in the Antarctic. I remember sitting there, trying to concentrate on the book, feeling all alone in an apparently empty hospital, with the planes going over and over and the bombs beginning to crash. At first they were not too near, but then there came a series of terrific explosions though obviously some little way away. They continued. Then a young soldier came running into the hospital and found me in the exchange. He said the planes had caught an ammunition train parked beside two troop trains, a British and a French. It was still exploding and there were large numbers of casualties. Could we send help at once?

I went down to the shelters, found my then CO, a territorial major, told him what had happened and asked if I could take a colleague, some orderlies and a couple of ambulances and see what I could do to help. Again the aquarium reaction: "Oh, if you want to, yes, go ahead" But absolutely no initiative on his part. Another young officer offered to come. I found the sergeant-major, who gave me a sergeant, a corporal and about six orderlies. We collected bags of shell dressings, some Thomas splints (for broken legs) and morphia, found a couple of ambulance drivers and set off with the young soldier as guide. The remainder stayed solidly in their air raid shelters.

On our way we were stopped by a French civilian. His wife had been hit, could we come? My colleague hurried in. Flying glass had severed her carotid artery. She was dead. We hurried on down a little lane towards the railway sidings, the explosions, continuously small (presumably small arms) and intermittently enormous (shells or bombs?) getting louder and louder. We found a corrugated iron shack, open down one side, partly screened by a bank from the railway and the worst of the explosions. Here the heroic French rescuers were carrying the wounded. Later there was a French medical team there also. The place was already crammed with injured men. Naturally the French and British handled their own. It was flat out and non-stop for the next six hours. Little time for niceties. Sometimes the morphia had to go straight in through the clothing. The explosions continued, sometimes with metal rattling down on our roof. Fortunately none came through. We had many horrible injuries, including lots of fractured femurs; I remember one poor officer with both his femurs broken. We ran out of Thomas splints and morphia. I sent a man back for more of both. Not surprisingly, he failed to return. For a time we had to use rifles as splints. So I sent the corporal. He did come back, good fellow. We couldn't pause for even a few minutes, though I think at one stage someone gave me a cup of coffee.

The French behaved splendidly. So did my men, who worked like Trojans, so did the wounded. In spite of our hurry I think we didn't forget that it was important to make the patients feel you cared about each one as a person.

Finally, about four or five in the afternoon, they said they thought they'd got everyone out who was still alive. We went wearily back to the hospital. But we didn't get inside. There was a long convoy of ambulances drawn up. I was told my bedroll was already aboard and I was to get in.

The air raid shelters had apparently rallied round. They had been admitting, dressing and operating on our casualties all day. Now half the staff were being evacuated with them to Nantes, en route for England. I was with the other half which was to go to St Malo and, with luck, would be evacuated from there.

Rumour had it that the roads were bombed to hell and St Malo destroyed. Rumour was always a jade. We had an easy run in the sunshine. When we reached St Malo the harbour was empty. Ships could only get in at certain stages of the tide. We lined up, with another unit, on the quay. I think we were handed out some rations. I chatted to a Belgian refugee. He told me he had heard on the radio that the French had offered an armistice but that Hitler had said he would only accept it if the British gave in too. It is interesting, retrospectively, that I laughed and pointed out that this was a completely absurd suggestion.

We expected a long wait, and perhaps not to get off at all, but in about an hour a small Danish ship came in, with a single British naval officer on board. The ship came up to the quay. With no ceremony he whipped us all on board and we were off. I doubt the ship was there more than a quarter of an hour.

Of course we were expecting air, and possibly sea attack. I was too tired to be frightened. With the rest I dossed down on the deck and slept well into the next day. We arrived in Southampton in the late afternoon. Only then could I wash the blood from my hands.

We were put into a long and crowded troop train. The men, of course, were in third class carriages, the officers far away in firsts. As we set off, the senior officer in charge (I still hardly knew him, my arrival in the unit was so recent) remarked that it was going to be difficult to find the men among the many other troops. He was impressed, and I felt a little priggishly proud, when I said I'd made a note of their carriage numbers.

We moved slowly through the night to Leeds, with many stops where splendid ladies, who must have stayed up late in the night, gave us sandwiches or cakes. Of course this was the peak of the post-Dunkirk patriotic spirit, a great surge after the relative routine of the phoney war – indeed a surge which carried right on till 1945. Just then anyone back from France was a hero, however little he'd done to deserve it.

Looking back on this incident, the most bloody of my personal war, I was young at the time and impatient with my seniors. But they must have rallied round and done a good job in the hospital while we were doing the first aid. It obviously was a fine effort to have handled all those casualties and got them away and back to England. The major, who was acting CO and who had seemed so inactive in the cellars, was awarded a DSO[*]. My impatience was perhaps exacerbated when I met him later in England (he had been with the Nantes evacuation) and he asked me accusingly what I'd been doing all day when they had been working so hard dealing with the casualties!

Egypt: The first phase.

The RAMC returning from France were concentrated in Leeds. The headquarters of the two units to which I was successively attached were based in the pavilion at Headingley Cricket Ground where, from time to time, test marches are played. For me there followed an idle six weeks. As far as I remember, I had virtually no military duties. With some friends I took a bus out to Ilkley and walked on the moors. I read some medicine. I started on the 18th century novelists. I attended the quarter sessions of the local courts and was intrigued to note the parallel with medicine in the law's efforts to get truth out of witnesses, the difference being that patients are usually at least trying to tell you the truth and witnesses may often be trying not to.

Then I received a posting to yet another hospital, No. 8, though its persona happened to be enshrined within the same cricket pavilion. One day we were told to draw tropical uniforms. We were sent on a week's embarkation leave. We had no idea of our destination except that it was presumably hot.

One evening we were entrained and sent off north, arriving in Glasgow late at night. I remember being silently cross with officers who telephoned

---

[*] Distinguished Service Order

their wives and told them where they were. Security was still very bad. Next day we embarked on the *Andes*. She was a brand new passenger liner, designed for the South American run, which had not yet made her maiden voyage. There were 1500 troops aboard, including our own and a New Zealand hospital. The officers were pretty crowded – I think there were 8 of us in a largish cabin – the men very much more so. Officers were theoretically first class passengers and we ate like lords. We also had an excellent cellar.

The long sea voyage could have been boring but it was not. There was the excitement of getting into the tropics. We often saw flying fish, once or twice a whale spouting in the distance. We put into Sierra Leone for refuelling but, wisely, no-one was allowed ashore. Our ship was moored well out, beyond the range of enemy mosquitoes. Other ships were less fortunate. Later we saw them celebrating several burials at sea. Afterwards we heard that these had been from malignant malaria* missed by doctors inexperienced in tropical medicine.

We arrived in Cape Town. We were only the second Middle East convoy and were wonderfully looked after, local volunteer families taking care of groups of officers or men. We were moved round to Simons Town and I was able to go ashore for two successive days, being looked after charmingly by a young accountant and his wife. We actually went to the top of Table Mountain, but time only allowed us to do it by cable car. (I climbed it, alone on my own two feet, some eleven years later in 1951).

We arrived in Suez on 20th September 1940. While we had been peacefully voyaging, the Battle of Britain had been at its height. Bulletins used to be posted on the ship's notice board every day recounting the news as heard over the radio. It was very hot when we arrived in Suez. In those days we all had to wear topees. Later troops only had to wear them for the first two weeks in the Middle East. We went up along the canal by train for an hour or two and were then trucked to a transit camp in the desert. Another disembarking unit had left the UK without being issued with tropical kit. Their transport failed to arrive at the station. Their CO marched them up to the camp. They had two deaths from heat stroke. The lesson was not quickly learned by all commanders. A year or two later troops were being poured into Iraq to meet a possible German threat as the enemy advanced through Russia and might later turn south through Iran or Turkey. It was some time before recurrent heat stroke deaths persuaded the authorities that men must not be disembarked in the Gulf in the midday heat.

---

* *Plasmodium falciparum* malaria, the other three malaria-causing plasmodia being considered benign.

It was found that in a few weeks men acclimatised and thereafter trouble only occurred with exceptional exercise in exceptional heat.

We only had a few days in the Transit Camp. Then we were entrained to Alexandria where we soon opened our hospital in a beautiful modern Italian school, its white walls glorious with bougainvillea.

It was a busy, but not an overwhelmingly busy, time. The officers were comfortably billeted in a hotel. I worked hard all the morning, often played games in the early afternoon (I had my last game of rugger there), returned to the hospital about four and worked till a late dinner about nine o'clock, returning afterwards if I had anyone seriously ill. Although there were plenty of trivia, I began to see tropical medicine: malaria, dysentery (plenty of that) and sometimes exotica such as leishmaniasis. There were a large number of "short term fevers", usually diagnosed, without much evidence, as "sandfly fever", a recognised entity. There were wardfuls of infectious hepatitis (jaundice). Our hospital seemed efficiently launched and administered, though of course we were not exposed to any sudden disaster as we had been in France.

Again, for me, it lasted about six weeks. In early November I was posted to a Casualty Clearing Station in the Western Desert at Dabha[*]. The Italians, after entry into the war a few months previously, had advanced from Benghazi over the Egyptian frontier to Mersa Matruh and stuck there. They were now opposed by Wavell's tiny force. We had assumed that Egypt was already stuffed with troops. In fact when we arrived there was not even a complete Division. But Wavell's men included the "Desert Rats", later the 7th Armoured Division whose morale, initiative and desert fighting skills soon made them famous. Later I met many of their officers. They were mostly from cavalry regiments turned into armoured units, tanks or armoured cars. They were from aristocratic or county families. They had a certain mediaeval dash and charm since, for them and their ancestors, a gentleman's only acceptable occupation, apart from managing his estates, was war. Simple chaps but brave, splendid in battle. At first their officers insisted on leading their men into battle without helmets and with their heads out of the tops of the tank turrets. So many had their heads blown off that strict orders had to be issued that turret covers must be firmly closed in battle.

The road ran west from Alexandria a few miles in from the coast. I got a lift out on one of the unit's trucks which had run into Alexandria for supplies. Our Casualty Clearing Station (CCS) was the only one in the Desert at that time. It had been established some time at Dabha which, if I

---

[*] Anglicised spelling of the place variously spelt as Ad Dab'Ah, El Dab'a etc.

remember, was about half way between El Alamein (not yet famous) and Mersa Matruh. The railway also ran towards Mersa Matruh. At Dabha there were a few mud huts and a rail stop. The CCS was about a mile away. It had one or two army huts used as wards for more serious cases, for the operating theatre, for administration and for the officers' and sergeants' messes. The other wards were in tents sunk three or four feet in the ground for protection against air attack. We slept in tents, similarly dug in.

Inland from the CCS was a low ridge, perhaps 100-150 feet high, beyond which rolling sandy ridges stretched inland. The sea was a couple of miles away, separated from us by a salt marsh and then sand dunes. The salt marsh held a low scrub. In the autumn many birds were migrating south and we would see quails and others in the marsh. Unfortunately at that time I had less knowledge and interest in ornithology. Later we had one or two rainstorms and flowers appeared temporarily in the salt marsh.

Scorpions were common. They looked aggressive in a cheerful, busy sort of way, but I saw no casualties. Poisonous centipedes were an occasional diversion. I had one amusing near miss. The officers' mess loo lay about 100 yards from the mess. It was a wooden box-seat with a lid, over a deep trench latrine, delicately surrounded by a sacking screen. One damp cold morning I lifted the lid and was about to sit down. Fortunately I looked behind me and saw that a poisonous centipede had got there first.

Life was very happy in the CCS. The staff were young, keen and friendly. The CO, a territorial, was also relatively young and competent. I had only had very short postings in each of my previous units and little time to get to know people well. Here I was able to be in close contact with the men and soon knew everyone in the unit by name. For a month or two we had a splendid routine. There was little fighting up front. About five o'clock every evening a train came down and offloaded a convoy of sick. We worked hard all the evening dealing with them. We had a mobile laboratory attached with a keen pathologist. He and I cooperated closely in investigating the fevers. We wanted to try to see what all the short-term fevers really were. We didn't, as it proved, have enough time together to get very far, but we did make early diagnoses, for instance by diagnosing typhoid on the second day through the blood cultures we were carrying out as a routine.

Next morning we sorted the patients out into those who would only have to stay with us a few days and could then return to their units, those who were too ill to move further, and those who should be sent to base hospitals in Alexandria. We usually finished by lunchtime and went off by truck for a bathe in the sea, returning later in the afternoon to meet the new convoy.

We had many visitors from other units. The New Zealand Division had recently arrived but their commander, Freyburg, would not allow them to be used until they were fully trained. Later experience in Greece showed how wise this was: in contrast to the first Australian Division which, only semi-trained at that time, were exposed to action well before they were fit for it. The New Zealand "Div Cav" (Armoured Cars) were not far away and we saw quite a lot of them, an early experience that began my lifetime admiration and affection for New Zealanders in peace and war. Their army medical units were superb.

It had still been very hot in Alexandria in early November, when I left. It was hot during the day in the desert, but very cold at night. From mid-December it became pretty cold unless you were out in the sun. Sea bathing was now more heroic, though you could thaw out in the sand dunes if sheltered from the wind.

Every now and then a sandstorm blew up from the south. It was like a thick yellow pre-war London fog – but it stung. Sometimes it was difficult to find one's way from the mess to one's tent fifty yards away. The sand got into everything. At meals one had to have one plate under and one plate over the food. It was impossible to operate. Sometimes everyone just had to hibernate. We could do little work: I read a lot lying in my tent.

We had an area of rolled sand where we played hockey against other units. There were now some Indian units about. Hockey is an Indian national game. Although I had captained my school and played for my college at Cambridge and St Thomas's, I was inferior to most Indian players. Nevertheless we had great fun and it was a good way of getting officers and men together.

We also rigged up a deck tennis court outside the mess. The ground was rough and one day I tripped, fell and fractured a small wrist bone, the scaphoid, which put me in plaster for three months. Christmas came and I found the plaster useful for cracking nuts. I claimed that my injury was incurred while capturing two enemy tanks single handed, but no-one found this convincing. Six nurses were posted up to us in December and lived in dugouts on the ridge. Being the only women in the Western Desert Force, as it was then called, they had a busy social life, but they also humanised our Christmas and were excellent in the wards.

Early in 1941, Wavell's famous advance started, astonishing everyone by its dramatic success, with rapid defeat of the Italians, vast numbers of prisoners and the unexpected opportunity for the army to advance hundreds of miles. Soon our surgeons were sent forward as a mobile team, taking most of our transport. Then our CO was posted elsewhere and I found myself, to my astonishment, appointed acting CO for a few weeks. With efficient NCOs and no major challenges it did not prove very exacting.

Before all this there had been one amusing incident. This, of course, was the year before Pearl Harbour and American entry into the war. The Americans, though still theoretically neutral, had a military liaison officer with General Wavell. This officer developed severe tonsillitis and was evacuated to us. Of course it was policy to be as nice as possible to the Americans in the hope that we would soon be allies. We were warned that the patient must be treated with particular attention. Of course he had to be admitted to the officers' ward, one of the large tents sunk in the ground. During the night we had one of those sudden rainstorms which occasionally occurred in the desert in winter. In the morning there were a couple of feet of water in the officers' ward, fortunately not quite reaching the mattress of the bed. Wavell and his staff took that moment to arrive to visit the VIP. However the patient was much better. He and the top brass took it all very cheerfully. Everyone concerned was greatly amused.

The American had recently been a military attaché in Berlin and had been there during the first British air raid on the city. This, of course, had been greatly played up by our press and radio. I enquired hopefully whether it had been a grim experience. He replied, to my chagrin, that he'd been very busy at the time and hadn't noticed anything very much!

Sometime in late February our unit was recalled to Alexandria for refitting. We were sent to a camp just outside the town. It was easy to visit my old friends at the hospital. We soon learnt that we were to go with an expeditionary force to Greece. The Greeks had been heroically resisting an Italian assault and had largely halted them at the Albanian border. Greece was not yet at war with Germany, but Hitler was rapidly forcing successive Balkan countries into subservient agreements. Yugoslavia and Greece seemed clearly to be the next two on the list. I started to learn modern Greek.

Greece 1941

On 11th March 1941 we sailed from Alexandria in a large convoy for Greece. The British medical officers were allocated to different ships. I was the only Britisher on a small ship, built in Denmark but manned by Greeks, that was carrying the New Zealand 19th Infantry battalion. The ship was grossly overloaded. Trucks were lashed down all over the decks. To accommodate the large numbers of men, extra bucket latrines were also lashed to the rails.

We ran into one of those formidable Mediterranean storms. With our top heavy overloading our captain had to risk the submarines, leave the convoy and go and shelter behind the south coast of Crete. We ran low in food. As Medical Officer I was in charge of hygiene. After such a storm you can imagine the state of the lashed latrines, with loosened lashings and seasickness adding to their normal hazards. I said to the cheerful New Zealand corporal of the Hygiene Squad "I'm afraid, Corporal, you'll have to clear up all this mess". An hour or two later I came back and asked him how things were going. "Sweet as a disey (daisy), Sir, Sweet as a disey!" A splendid lot, the New Zealanders.

When the storm abated we sailed round to one of the ports on the north coast of Crete to collect food and so that I could land my few sick patients. I went ashore and had a brief view of that lovely island in its early spring green, striking after six months of sand. I arranged for my sick patients to go to a British hospital and, with a New Zealand and a Greek officer, we went to some farms looking for food. The Greek saw and fancied a turkey. With wonderful Cretan generosity this was immediately presented to him. That night we had a special dinner to celebrate our survival. Present were the Greek ship's officers, the New Zealand officers, myself - and, of course, the turkey. I had managed to compose and stutter out a brief speech in Greek thanking the captain for bringing us through. It was a gay international occasion.

A day later we sailed up to Piraeus, the port of Athens, past the Isle of Salamis, site of the great Athenian naval victory over the Persians. Here, later, sadly several British ships were sunk and I lost some of my friends from the unit. That day the sea was blue, the land green, the sun shining on the snows of the surrounding mountains. It was very beautiful – a lovely curtain so soon to rise on tragedy.

We had a few days attached to the British Military Hospital just outside Athens. At the time the Parthenon was closed to all except military personnel. I was able to get up to it at nine o'clock one morning and had an hour there all to myself. After so much literary build-up I had expected an anticlimax but of course it completely captivated me as it has captivated so many generations.

In a bookshop I met a professor from the British School at Athens and we had a long talk. He said the modern Greeks were very like the classical Greeks, highly intelligent, highly political and almost totally unable to cooperate with one another. This war, admittedly under the leadership of their then dictator, Metaxas, had made them more united than ever before – or perhaps since facing Darius and the Persians some two thousand five hundred years previously.

Soon we moved up to just outside Larissa in northern Greece, where we were to set up our CCS in tents. It was a beautiful site, on rolling, grassy downland with wild tortoises wandering about. Not unnaturally many of these soon carried soubriquets in their shells inscribed by the men. In the evenings a rosy-cheeked, white bearded, classical shepherd with a crook would take his flock past the camp. We looked north down over a flat wooded valley, with a broad river twisting across it and beyond it the sheer snowy peak of Mount Olympus. Towards our northwest were other snowy ranges where the Greeks were face to face with the Italians.

We busied ourselves erecting our CCS. As there were no patients, I took on the hygiene, planning and supervising cesspits and deep trench latrines, a discipline I found curiously intriguing, perhaps evidence of some sinister Freudian twist in my subconscious. One or two interesting new officers had joined the unit in Alexandria. There was a very nice Israeli doctor, fair-haired, calm, pipe-smoking, in many ways typically British. Sadly he was later drowned when his ship was sunk during the evacuation. Also Martin Herford, who later proved to be one of the most able and most highly decorated soldiers in the RAMC. In due course he rose to the rank of full colonel and collected an MBE[*], an MC[#] and a DSO and bar. He had only joined the RAMC in Egypt, having had considerable adventures getting there. When the Russians attacked Finland in the autumn of 1939 a body of British volunteers was raised to help the Finns. Martin went as their medical officer. They arrived a day after the Finns signed their armistice and then had considerable difficulty in getting out again. Some of the volunteers were Irish and were therefore technically neutral. They got out, on their Irish passports, through Germany and then joined the British Army! Martin, after a number of months, managed to reach Stockholm, obtained an interview with the Russian ambassador there, a formidable lady with an aristocratic background, and persuaded her to grant him a visa to travel through Russia to Turkey. From there he reached Alexandria and joined the army. He was therefore a very new and junior lieutenant but he soon showed his quality when the real war started.

At first we were on basic rations, bully beef and biscuits, but soon bread became available. The RAF established its advanced base at the airfield at Larissa. There films were to be shown once a week. I only saw one. It was *Dawn Patrol*, a tragic film about the Royal Flying Corps in the First World War, with many of the heroes being shot down. What astonishing lack of imagination to show such a film. Many of those watching it were themselves shot down in the next few weeks.

---

[*] Member of the most excellent order of the British Empire

[#] Military Cross

The Yugoslav government was bullied into making yet another subservient agreement with Hitler, but they were immediately overthrown by their countrymen. Germany promptly bombed Belgrade and its army stormed in before the Yugoslavs could mobilise. We saw some of their tattered remnants and met a few of their officers. Germany simultaneously declared war on Greece. The German army was soon over the border. We began to hear the steady continuous rumble of artillery to our northwest. The Larissa airfield was massively attacked by the Luftwaffe. Most, if not all, of our planes were shot down or destroyed on the ground. We had no more air cover.

Casualties began to pour in. Our junior officers were taken away to man hospital trains improvised from cattle trucks. Our two surgeons worked day and night in the operating theatre. There was only one specialist anaesthetist; our CO acted as a second. That left the radiologist and myself as the only doctors available for everything else. We took it in turns to admit the unending stream which continued day and night while the other one did what he could in the wards. We snatched sleep when we could, but got very little.

Disposing of the dead was a major problem. It was very difficult to spare orderlies to dig graves. We had been expecting nursing sisters, who fortunately got no further than Athens. I am afraid, in our desperation, we had to use their already prepared deep trench latrine for interment. But at least the padre read the burial service over them.

The main road to the Front looped round our camp and was frequently machine gunned by enemy fighters. We had a large red cross laid out and hoped that that would stop them attacking us. To give them credit, it did. But my tent was on the top of a little hill in the loop. When I was trying to sleep there, I would hear the plane, and then the bullets plugging up the hill straight for me. In fact the pilot usually took his finger off the button. But of course one could never be sure and had to nip into the slit trench. It didn't help one's sleep.

The orderlies were marvellous. They had to take far more responsibility than was proper, as the radiologist and I, having sorted the patients on admission, had only time to deal with the most severe cases and to determine who needed surgery. We had a number of wounded German prisoners and helped them as much as we could. I remember one poor fellow whose wedding ring was causing intense agony to his wounded swollen finger and how grateful he was when I gave him a shot of anaesthetic and got the ring off with a metal cutter.

I suppose this went on for a couple of weeks. At night I tried to snatch some sleep on the stretcher in the admission tent but one seldom got as much as an hour before another convoy of casualties arrived. The noise of the guns came steadily nearer. Streams of men from broken Greek units poured back along the road and our own forces were clearly in retreat.

Our CO was excellent but the higher Command of the RAMC was not. I believe we did not receive a single order in writing. One evening an Australian Division passed back along the road and when they had gone the CO discovered that we were more or less in the front line. He was told that, if he could get his patients away, we were to fall back on an abandoned New Zealand hospital twenty miles or so to our rear. There was a Friends' Ambulance Unit available. These young men, conscientious objectors to fighting, were absolutely splendid – calm, courageous, efficient, marvellous with patients. One of the other ambulance units said that they would not take the German wounded. I explained that in that case I would have to stay and look after them and be captured. So they took them. All the patients and all members of the unit got away, but we had to abandon our equipment – including our enormous protective Red Cross.

We moved back to the site of the New Zealand hospital where we managed to get the patients on to one of the improvised ambulance trains. Afterwards I heard that Martin Herford was attached to one of these. Every time the Luftwaffe came over, which was very often, the driver stopped the train and lay in a ditch. Finally Martin borrowed a revolver and rode in the cabin with the gun in the driver's back. The train kept going.

At first we thought we would be staying at the site of the NZ hospital, which had been abandoned with all its equipment. Having got the patients away we were just issuing some food when a German bomber appeared overhead, dived and released a few bombs, its rear gunner opening up as it came out of its dive. Fortunately no-one was hit.

Then we were told we were to move away south. We tried to salvage some of the equipment by piling it into the empty ambulances and started away – ironically over the Pass of Thermopylae. I had had very little sleep for the past ten days. I lay down in the back of an ambulance and went dead to the world.

At this point I will stand aside and try to analyse my feelings at that time. Over the previous stressful couple of weeks, with little sleep, gross overwork and recurrent danger, I was certainly apprehensive during the few moments when I had time to think. When in contact with patients or the men I tried to exude cheerful confidence. I was a bachelor and the youngest of the remaining officers. If anyone had to stay and be captured with the wounded it would be me. At any time I might be killed. I was interested to find that I had a certain looseness of the bowels. I had read in First War literature that this was a common experience in one's first battle. To a somewhat lesser extent the apprehension, but fortunately not the bowel trouble, continued for the rest of the retreat.

Later I contrasted this with my experiences during the bombing of Ismailia. There I was, as you shall hear, much closer to death. But somehow I found it much more exhilarating. I experienced brief periods of fear rather than continuous apprehension. I think there were several elements in this contrast. An important one was that if one was wounded one would be evacuated to a hospital among friends and not captured. A second, that I had already experienced danger in France and Greece. A third, and I believe an important one, was that that experience provided a challenge to leadership, at first among patients, until the hospital was evacuated; later, among the men, as officer in charge of the air-raid squad.

Returning to Greece, we travelled all night and next day set up a receiving station for casualties and sick. We only had our trucks. The ambulances had moved on. Fortunately the weather was fine. We had almost no equipment. Some of what we had had was lost when one of the trucks was bombed and set on fire. The patients had to lie on the ground. We tried to make them comfortable along a bank, which gave some sort of backrest, and either in or under lorries. Their only source of water was a mug which I carried in my belt. But I found a certain professional satisfaction in trying to make sure I was doing the best that could be done under the difficult circumstances. Moreover I had managed to get some sleep during the previous night's travel.

After 36 hours there we transferred to the control of the Australian medical administration. This proved vastly better than the British. We actually received orders in writing. The Australian Deputy Director of Medical Services (DDMS) visited us briefly – we'd never seen his British equivalent. He ordered us back to join the other CCS in Greece, an Australian one, which still had its equipment and was grossly overworked. It was established on a hillside near Delphi.

We moved back, the air almost continuously packed with German planes, the roads with refugees. For a few days we worked flat out with the Australians. Both men and officers were splendid (as indeed I found with all Australian medical units). We must have created a good impression. I was flattered to find one evening a bottle of beer tucked into my jacket pocket, goodness knows by whom, presumably a gesture of appreciation.

The air was still continually filled with Nazi planes, bombing and strafing the road. But they respected the Australian unit's Red Cross and we were not attacked. I remember on Hitler's birthday they appeared particularly active and seemed to leave streams of celebratory smoke which we speculated might be part of the celebrations. In fact, of course, they were only vapour trails, then new to us.

One soldier told me that, during the retreat, he was out in the middle of a field with his trousers down relieving himself when an enemy aircraft swooped down on him machine gunning. But the pilot then circled away, returned and chucked him down a tin of preserved meat!

At midday one day we were very busy loading a lot of casualties to clear beds for more. To encourage our tired men I was busy helping to shift stretchers into the ambulances and trucks. One of the Australian privates said admiringly "You're the first fuckin' officer I ever seen doing a stroke of fuckin' work". Our CO called me urgently and said that we were off back to Athens and put me straight into a truck. No time to say more than an instantaneous farewell to our Australian friends.

In Athens we slept on the floor of the school. With my exhaustion I slept very well. The next day we were told we would entrain in the evening for the Peloponnese. Come the evening I was asked if I would march an Australian company down to the station; they had lost all their officers. They told me that when things had become really grim their officers had piled into the available transport and made off. These were the early inadequately trained Australian Divisions. It was the first and last time during the war that I ever marched a column of troops. I am proud to say that we made it to the station. For Crofton a great military achievement.

Then started a tedious journey in a long troop train. We were all piled in cattle trucks, officers and men together. I remember I lay on the floor reading a novel about family life in classical China. There was a large contingent of Cypriot Pioneer Corps on the train. With daylight came the German aircraft seeming to swoop on us about every half hour, firing as they came. Each time they did so the train stopped. When it stopped the Cypriots leapt out and streamed away across the countryside. Panic is infectious but, with a little firm handling, our men creditably stayed put. I don't know how many Cypriots missed the train each time it started moving again.

The train stopped at the station at Corinth and we descended to fetch water. As we did so the dive bombers came down. I remember lying in a gutter about six inches high and hoping, without much confidence, that it would protect me as the bombs fell. Surprisingly none of us was hit.We moved on slowly into the Peloponnese, scene of so many wars, including the one between Sparta and Athens, so marvellously recorded by Thucidides[*],

---

[*] Greek historian and naval commander (c460-c400BC). His *History of the Peloponnesian War* consciously aimed to be an impartial account.

which Toynbee[*] claims was the beginning of the end of Hellenic civilisation. Soon we were stopped by a staff officer who said the line was being bombed to hell further on. We must detrain and proceed by road to Argos.

We had some food, boarded trucks and went on to near Argos. There we were distributed over the hillside under the trees and bushes for the night. Fortunately the weather remained splendid.

All next day German fighters came over at intervals machine gunning the woods, presumably suspecting troops were there. During the day we were told that when darkness came, which was relatively late in mid-May, there would be an evacuation from a nearby beach to destroyers standing off. The sick were collected and put under my charge. I think I ended up with about eight of them. Only a couple were really ill, one with rheumatic fever; this is dangerous to the heart and the patient must not make any exertion himself; he must be carried. I had six or eight orderlies to help me. At dark we moved down to the beach, carrying the most sick.

We had been told that each man could only take one side pack and his water bottle. Food would be provided on board. I remember my luggage included Sir Henry Tidy's splendid fat little *Textbook of Medicine* in note form, my small case of medical instruments, my stethoscope and Hugo's *Italian* which I thought might occupy me when incarcerated as a prisoner.

There followed a few hours of utter shambles. Most of the troops at that beach were from an untrained Australian division which had quite lost its discipline. There was only a single landing craft. Every time it beached the troops, quite out of control, would rush on to it. The overloaded craft would then ground. It could not be got away until some of the men were forced or persuaded to come off again. The unfortunate Australian officer in command was in despair.

Finally we were told that the destroyers had gone. They had to be out of aircraft range before daylight. The rest would get away the next night. The landing craft came in once more. I consulted the exhausted beach commander and suggested that it would be best for me to take the sick on to the landing craft where they could lie down and be transported in some comfort. He agreed and we hurriedly brought them on. Sadly, after we had pulled off, I found that two of our excellent orderlies had gone missing in the darkness.

Two thirds of our own unit had managed to embark earlier in the night. In due course they were landed in Crete where later half of them were captured. The other third, with some other miscellaneous men, were on the

---

[*] The English historian, Arnold Joseph Toynbee (1889-1975).

craft with my group. Its crew seemed to consist of an officer, a midshipman and a couple of sailors. They were splendid, as indeed the navy always was when I encountered it. They had been at this for nights. The officer had had down his back, the streaks of a near miss of machine gun bullets from a German fighter. He told us that he was going to move up the coast and find a sheltered hidden cove. We would lie up there till the following night.

At daybreak we landed in a little cove surrounded by wooded hills. There was a stone boathouse with a corrugated iron roof. I decided that this was the best place for my medical squad and the patients. The rest of the troops hid up in the woods or under the bushes. The naval crew beached their craft and did the same.

Once more at regular intervals over came the enemy fighters machine gunning around. Twice they swooped on our boathouse. Fortunately the bullets hit the stone walls and none came through the roof. No-one was hurt.

At some time during the day a local Greek fisherman turned up. He came storming in with best American English, talking about "those damned bastards", the Germans, and asking if he could help. This was typical of the Greeks. Everyone from the British army I met, then and subsequently, said that the Greeks behaved magnificently throughout this grim retreat. I gave him as much money as I had and asked him if he could get us some food. He came back an hour or two later with what he had been able to find, which wasn't very much. One of the efficient orderlies had saved a little stove. We were all very hungry.

The orderly offered me the food first but I had some sort of concept that in a crisis the proper attitude was that it should be officers last. I said it should be patients first, then men, and I would take anything left. None of us had very much.

As dusk fell the troops and the sailors reassembled on the little beach and re-embarked. The naval officer said that we would travel hard all night and land at dawn near Monemvasia, not far from the southern tip of Greece. The final evacuation would take place from there the following night.

We grounded in a little bay as daylight came. The first men were wading ashore and we were still on board. Some of those ashore had taken off their wet trousers and were wringing them out when over came a dive bomber. I have a vision of a group of white bottoms disappearing hurriedly and headlong into the bushes. A string of bombs were dropped but missed. The midshipman, who looked about sixteen, fought back with his Bofors gun.

When the plane had gone, we carried the sick ashore and found, not far away, a bushy little hollow which seemed the best we could do for them.

The landing craft had backed out into the bay. As it did so, three more dive bombers appeared and attached the craft, one after the other. The brave little mishipman continued to fight back with his gun. The boat was holed by a bomb and had to be grounded, but fortunately none of the crew was hit.

Later in the morning the surgical specialist of our unit, a regular RAMC major who was now our senior officer, found me and suggested that he and I should seek out the authority in charge of the evacuation. During our search we saw some of the New Zealand Division coming in. The German planes were raiding, bombing and machine gunning. We were struck by the calm, disciplined, orderly movements of the New Zealanders when under fire. So different from our experience two nights previously.

Eventually we found the British Headquarters in another little wooded hollow. They were having lunch and offered us some. Having had little to eat for 38 hours we accepted. I was desperately hungry but was embarrassed to ask for more. We ensured that we collected food to take back for the patients and for the men of our own unit.

Later in the day we received our official orders for evacuation. We were to go up on to the road, line up in order of units as directed, and then move out along the causeway to the ancient Venetian castle at Monemvasia where we would embark. On the road I was to hand over my sick patients to a New Zealand field ambulance.

There were many units awaiting evacuation and this was to be the very last night when it was possible. We were disappointed to find that we were near the bottom of the list and felt sure that we would be left behind. I suppose priority understandably went to the fighting men. We reached the road, found the New Zealand field ambulance and parted, with mutual regret, from our patients. I had given my man with rheumatic fever my sleeping bag and told him, and the New Zealanders, that he was on no account to walk. He was to be carried on board. Later I found him in a ward in a hospital in Egypt. He had been told to walk aboard. I hope he suffered none of the potential medical complications. He seemed all right when I saw him.

In spite of our apprehensions, the evacuation was superbly accomplished. There must have been several thousand men, British, New Zealand and Australian. Organisation and discipline were excellent. Fortunately here the destroyers were able to come right in to the quay. I believe they got everyone away. We ourselves were on board by 2.30 am, 800 of us crammed into a destroyer. Yet within half-an-hour there was a rating coming round the decks handing us hot cocoa. These men were subject to air attack all day and working flat out on the evacuation at night.

They had been doing this for days or weeks. Yet they always remained efficient, disciplined and courageous. Once more I saluted the navy.

In a few hours we were uneventfully in the harbour of Souda Bay in Crete. There we were told Crete could not take any more troops. We were transferred to a ship and set sail for Egypt. I stretched out on the deck and slept the sleep of the exhausted. During the night the convoy was attacked by something. There were gunfire and explosions. I opened one eye and sank back to sleep. I was too tired to be frightened.

Next day we arrived at Port Said. There I remember seeing for the first time jeeps being unloaded and driven down the quay. I was astonished at the dinky-toy-like vehicles, soon to become so familiar.

Egypt – 1941- 42

The one third of our CCS, which had been evacuated on the last night, was assembled in a camp in the desert where, after the Crete debacle, the other survivors of the unit joined us. Half of the Crete contingent had been lost on the march south across the island, some because their feet gave out. Our Israeli officer and our nice cheerful dental officer had both been drowned when their ship was sunk as it left Piraeus. Another junior officer, posted to a hospital train, had been captured. Martin Herford, after many vicissitudes, had also got away from the western side of the Peloponnese.

I was sad to learn that our unit was to be converted into a mobile surgical hospital and that this would not carry a medical specialist. So I must go. I was temporarily attached to No. 2 General Hospital sited in the desert halfway between Suez and Cairo.

The hospital was extremely busy and I was soon up to my eyes in work. We were entirely tented. The amateurs were coming up. The OC[*] Medical Division was a consultant from University College Hospital in London and first class. I shared a tent with three others and soon made a number of very pleasant new friends.

It was May which in Egypt is the hottest month owing to the fierce "Khamsin" wind blowing up from the baking deserts to the south. In fact this proved to be the hottest month in Egypt for 50 years. On one occasion it was 117°F[#] in our tent and it remained about that level. I appreciated the dauntlessness of the British one day when I came in to lunch in the mess tent and was served with roast beef and Yorkshire pudding, followed by a hot steamed pudding – luxuries by UK wartime standards but here perhaps

---

[*] Officer in Charge.

[#] 47^0 Celsius

symbolic of the heroic British Lion's determination not to compromise even with the elements.

I began to feel more and more tired. I thought it was the heat, and the hard work, until one evening I vomited before supper. I then took my temperature and found it was 104°F*. I spent a day or two in my tent but my temperature remained up. I was admitted to the officers' ward where my colleagues competed to see if they could feel my spleen – I later gathered that everyone could do so except the medical specialist in charge of me. In a few days my blood culture showed that I had typhoid. It must have been an unusually long incubation period, but it seems most probable that I had collected the infection in Greece. During the retreat our water sterilising tablets had been lost in the bombed and burnt truck and we had to use uncertain water. However we heard of no other cases among the CCS staff. Of course my inoculations were well up-to-date, but these were by no means an absolute protection; I later saw a great deal of paratyphoid.

At that time there was no treatment for typhoid except nursing. In fact once I knew I was ill and did not have to go on working I felt much better; I could just rest and wait to recover. They did not isolate me. I was in one of the large "Marquees, Hospital, Extending" with which we had struggled in France and shared it with about 30 other officers. It was so hot that they removed the walls to let a little air in. We lay on our beds in the sand and sweated it out. Soon I was well enough to get out my *Hugo's Italian* and started to learn the language, certainly in much more pleasant surroundings, at least psychologically, than the prisoner of war camp where I had expected to study.

As I began to recover it still took a little time to become negative for the typhoid bacillus. After a month, when I was free from infection, I was given a month's sick leave. The father of one of my Cambridge climbing friends worked in business in Cairo. He and his wife kindly asked me to spend three weeks with them in the delightful suburb of Maadi. I remember the beauty of the jacaranda trees which lined the streets and were then in full bloom. I had a pretty quiet three weeks recovering and then went on for a final week in Alexandria where I stayed with a surgeon, John Watt, who had been a contemporary at St Thomas's, before returning to work. It was another couple of months before I felt really fit. In those days typhoid was a nasty disease from which people often died; it caused major mortality in the Boer War. My attack was severe enough, but I was never desperate, perhaps because I had some immunity from my inoculation.

---

* 40° Celsius

After my sick leave, I suppose in early July 1941, I was posted to the military hospital in Ismailia, halfway down the Suez Canal. This was a peacetime British military hospital in wooden huts, as Ismailia was a peacetime military station. It was a small hospital and carried only one medical specialist.

I did not have many weeks clinical work. Air raids started soon after my arrival. The Germans were now in Rhodes and the Canal had come within range. We had slit trenches dug beside each of the wards. There was a double air raid warning system. The first siren indicated that the planes were approaching the Canal, the second that they were coming for us. To begin with most of the raids seemed to be elsewhere in the Canal.

If I remember, we took it in turn to command the air raid squad. At any rate I was on one night when the planes really did come for us. This was not surprising, as the peacetime hospital had been built just beside the peacetime airfield, now in active operation. In consequence we were not allowed to show the Red Cross.

As the raid started I whipped round and ensured that all the patients had been got into the slit trenches. The planes came in to attack one by one. A number of bombs fell on the hospital, severely damaging wards. I was surprised to find it quite exhilarating to nip from slit trench to slit trench making sure that everyone was all right, no-one hit, and generally trying to keep up morale. Remarkably no-one was hit and morale was excellent, but in the morning it was clear that much of the hospital was severely damaged. It was decided that the patients should all be evacuated to hospitals in safer areas.

Then started a rather curious period in my military career, a period which lasted several months. Having lost my hospital patients I took charge of the local "M.I. (Medical Inspection) Room". This consisted of a sort of general practice health centre for the troops. One dealt with the minor problems and sent the men with more serious problems to hospital. I held a sick parade at 7am, which usually lasted several hours, and a shorter one at 6pm. The afternoons were usually free, though the nights were often devoted to air raids, necessitating an hour or two in the slit trenches or behind the sandbags of the air raid centre in the battered, but evacuated, hospital. It was summer and we were near the water of the so-called "sweet water" canals (fresh water) so that mosquitoes were prevalent, thirsty and enterprising. Although it was hot I wore long sleeves and trousers, and even socks over my hands! No effective insect repellents were available at that time.

Ismailia was a delightful centre. Here the Canal ran into the Great Bitter Lake. There were green lawns, and even woods. For a time I had to take a sick parade for a Cypriot labour unit on the other side of the Canal. This involved a pleasant drive in the early morning sunshine along the edge of the lake, past a little pine wood and then by ferry across the Canal.

A Cypriot sick parade was a comic experience. I was told that at home the men expected their womenfolk to do most of the hard physical work. They had joined the army for the money and were surprised and distressed by the work expected in return and by the discipline. One's sick parade was therefore enormous. It mainly consisted of skrimshankers, often feigning the most improbable, bizarre and indeed laughable symptoms and signs. At first I took it lightly, merely writing the miscreant up for "Medicine and Duty". The numbers became very large. The excellent (Turkish) Cypriot medical sergeant told me I would be inundated unless I took firm measures. So at the next parade I signed up one particularly obvious deceiver as "Malingering". He was firmly disciplined by his CO. Next morning my sick parade had shrunk by 80%.

Another interesting experience was when the CO of a searchlight unit, busy with the air raids, asked me to check the mental state of a new draft which had come out from the UK. He said they were very decent chaps and excellent at digging trenches or concreting, but directing searchlights was quite a skilled business and they were hopeless at it. Would I check their IQs. I was no psychiatrist and none was available locally. I managed to get hold of a few tests for basic mental skills and put the 100-150 men through them. They were very decent chaps, many were fine-looking men physically, but most of them had no idea how many minutes were in an hour, how many hours in a day or the difference between north, south, east and west. At the end of a couple of exhausting days I found myself asking, like jesting Pilate, "What is truth?" and finding myself a little uncertain of the answer. I am sure that what had happened in the UK was that the various searchlight units, heavily engaged in countering the intense air raids on Britain, had been asked to draft men for units abroad and had naturally chosen their least useful members.

One incident was my only experience of a murder case. I was called early one morning to see the body of a young British officer who had been shot dead as he slept in his tent. Knowing that this would probably turn out to involve a legal trial, and vaguely remembering the famous forensic medical textbook of Sydney Smith (at that time, though I did not know it, one of my predecessors as Dean of the Faculty of Medicine in Edinburgh), I made a very careful examination of the body. I also remembered as advised by Sydney Smith, to write equally careful notes right away while my memory was fresh. This was just as well, as the court martial took place several months later. It proved very useful to be able to brush up my memory beforehand.

Later that day our young pathologist and I carried out a post-mortem in the hospital post-mortem room. This had been bombed. It had no roof and one wall had been blown out. The pathologist fortunately had a copy of Sydney Smith's book. We were able to switch steadily from body to book and back again, so as to make sure we did the job properly. We were both young and neither of us had previously faced a murder case.

The story behind the murder proved to be a sad one. A Sikh corporal had committed some major misdemeanour for which he had been reduced to ranks. For him this was appalling loss of face and a dreadful disgrace. The authorities knew that this would be the attitude of a proud Sikh and so posted him to another unit, which happened to be in Ismailia. To exorcise his disgrace, that night he had shot the first white officer he found. He then stole a truck and disappeared. Eventually he was stopped somewhere near the front line and arrested. On his way back in the truck, handcuffed and escorted by military police, he managed to edge up to one of the policemen, snatch his pistol and shoot him too, though fortunately not fatally.

Some weeks later, when I had to attend a preliminary "Summary of Evidence", I saw the murderer, a tall, young, dignified, handsome, turbaned Sikh. This time they were taking no risks. His hands were handcuffed behind him; a rope was attached to the handcuffs and held by a helmeted soldier; two others, also helmeted, crouched behind the prisoner with fixed bayonets pointed at his back. However he marched along bolt upright and with considerable dignity.

Some months later I gave my evidence at the court martial in Cairo. I was intensively cross-examined by the defending lawyer, who wanted to prove that the murder had occurred after the departure of the accused, but my evidence was fairly straightforward. The pathologist had a tougher time but had also prepared his evidence with care. The cumulative evidence against the murderer was, of course, overwhelming. He was found guilty and, in due course, shot. I was told he faced death bravely, smoking a last cigarette.

At Ismailia I had another legal experience when I was asked by a man in the unit to act as the "Prisoner's Friend" and defend him in a court martial. He was one of the hospital orderlies, a tough Geordie from Tyneside. He was alleged to have sloshed a sergeant in the dark one night.

Courts martial are remarkably fair. They are weighted heavily in favour of the defence. The defence is provided in advance with a detailed summary of the evidence against the prisoner and no additional evidence can be called at the court martial itself. On the other hand the defence does not have to show its hand in advance. I therefore knew beforehand exactly what the prosecution witnesses would say. In cross examination I managed to tie the witnesses down to a precise time for the crime, which may well have been incorrect, and then to produce witnesses to prove that my client was elsewhere at that time. I suggested that in the darkness and blackout it must have been a case of mistaken identity. To the chagrin of the unit administration he was found not guilty. As you will hear, I later had the opportunity of once more exercising my kindergarten legal skills on his behalf.

Apart from these episodes and the air raids, my job was largely routine and, for a limited period, quite enjoyable. I worked all the morning and an hour or two in the evening, but the afternoon was nearly always free. There was an excellent peacetime Officers' Club down by the Great Bitter Lake, with green lawns and shady trees. I spent most afternoons there, bathing and reading – sometimes medicine, sometimes other books. My mother had sent me out a complete Shakespeare. Over a number of months I read it from cover to cover, marking, and sometimes learning, the most exciting poetry. I interspersed my reading with long swims in the warm, but rather sticky and very salty, water, hence the name, Great Bitter Lake.

Then one night we had a major air raid. I was in charge of the air raid squad. Our action station was on the balcony at one end of the one-storey administrative block. It was situated by the telephone and behind a wall of sandbags. That particular night the planes roared in low over the hospital to attack the air field. They came in a series of waves. They dropped both large and antipersonnel bombs. During one of the raids a ward went on fire, though of course at this time it was empty as all its patients had been evacuated. I thought we had better put the fire out, shouted "Follow me, Air Raid Squad" and dashed off. When I arrived at the fire and looked behind me, I found that only the sergeant was there. Fortunately the fire was a minor one and soon out. I tore strips off the squad and they behaved well thereafter. After that attack I rang the air raid headquarters and asked whether if there was a further attack we should try to deal with fires while the bombs were actually falling or, as seemed sensible as the wards were empty, wait until there was a gap in the bombing. The major at the other end of the phone at first said we should go out and deal with any fire whatever the conditions. I said I was, of course, quite prepared to obey an order but, as it would be putting my men's lives at risk, I would like the order in writing. He promptly amended his instructions to what I had suggested.

A few more waves came over. Some strings of anti-personnel bombs fell across the hospital. Then suddenly there was a wall of white flame in front of me, a deafening explosion, the roof came down and the place was filled with acrid smoke. One man was whimpering and terrified but unhurt. To my surprise no-one was dead. No-one was even wounded. But instead of the administrative block there was a twenty foot deep crater. I measured it later; the edge of the crater was fifteen feet from us. It had been a 1000 lb bomb. The main strength of the explosion seemed to have gone upwards; our wall of sandbags had saved us, both from the blast and from the falling roof. This was my nearest escape from death during the war. Having survived, I was surprised to find myself quite exhilarated. I had not had time to be really frightened as the bomb fell and the pleasure and surprise of having survived seemed to inhibit retrospective apprehension, or indeed apprehension during the further waves which followed.

After the raid I went carefully over the hospital site and prepared a detailed report on the bombs that had fallen, where they had landed and the subsequent damage. It was thought that there might be time bombs, so the whole site was officially put out of bounds for a day or two. I had to creep in, really against orders, to retrieve some essential medical equipment which I needed for my patients.

Another night, when I was not on duty, I was woken by the air raid siren as I lay in my quarters, a peacetime stone building. I had been up a lot in the raids and was very sleepy. I said to myself "I'll just snooze till the second siren" and turned over. But apparently it *was* the second siren; I must have slept through the first. A few minutes later I opened an eye and thought "The moonlight is very bright outside" – and then there was the most resounding explosion, seemingly about 20 feet away. The "moonlight" was from the flares dropped by the raiders and this was the first bomb, almost on top of me. With the explosion I shot out of bed. My previously dozing suprarenals must have also shot out about a pint of adrenaline. My pulse seemed to be about 400 per minute. I am sure I did a record dash to the slit trench. Bombs fell all round, but again no-one was hit. When the raid was over and I returned to my room, I found a large hole in the wall and a large hole through my sleeping bag. So it was just as well that I had not *completely* slept through the alarm!

About this time I was surprised to receive an official letter telling me that I had been "Mentioned in Despatches" for my work in Greece – presumably for my record rearward dash in the face of the enemy. I was quite surprised to be told that I had also been recommended for a "Mention" for my work during the air raids in Ismailia but it had been decided in Cairo, quite rightly, that in view of the dangers civilians were undergoing at home, no awards would be given for work in air raids in the Middle East.

In mid-January 1942 I was again temporarily posted, this time to No.19 General Hospital at Geneifa, which I later came to know so well. Geneifa is in the desert between Ismailia and Suez about a mile south of the Great Bitter Lake and overlooked by a couple of rocky, sandy 400 to 500 foot peaks, affectionately known as the Big and the Little Flea.

The hospital was close to the main Infantry Base Depot. There were vast numbers of troops in the area and we were very busy all the time I was there. At that period there were 1200 British beds and 200 prisoner-of-war beds in a wired-off area attached. The POW hospital was staffed by Italian doctors and orderlies, the British hospital being administratively responsible and providing specialist advice. The hospital was in widely spaced long huts on a sloping sandy site. There were nursing sisters in charge of wards, with male orderlies. We had captured many Italian medical personnel and some of their orderlies served as batmen, others in wards, medicals being "neutral" under the Geneva Convention. The Italians were excellent medical orderlies, if well supervised, many of them better than their British opposite numbers. They responded well to friendliness and personal interest.

As patients the Italians tended to be very apprehensive. However worried one was about an ill patient one had to remain extremely cheerful and confident, and keep a fixed smile on one's face. They were far more sensitive than British patients to the slightest sign of anxiety in the doctor; immediately it would be "Ah, Mama mia, Mama mia!" and the patient would relapse into general despair.

The Italian doctors were nice chaps but not well trained, and they were very unconscientious about their patients. If an Italian or German prisoner patient was seriously ill, one of the British doctors would go up to see him last thing at night; we knew the Italian doctors would never bother.

By the time of my second spell at the 19th General Hospital, a year later, the Italian doctors had been replaced by Germans. These were a great contrast. Having had only a brief wartime medical training, and Hitler having got rid of many of the most distinguished teachers, they were often ignorant, but they were very keen to learn and were, if anything, hyperconscientious. In contrast to the Italians, they would be likely to stay up all night with a patient even though this was not really necessary.

With Italian patients, doctors, orderlies and batmen, there was a stimulus to resuscitate the Italian language which I had started to learn when I had typhoid. It is a beautifully easy language to acquire, at least in basic form, and I had plenty of opportunity to use it.

Indeed there was plenty of opportunity to practise languages in the hospital, then and later. We had Italian and German prisoner-of-war patients, Greek-speaking Cypriots, Free French, Belgians and Arabs. At first we were provided with interpreters. These were at about the level of waiters from Cairo and were hopeless in dealing with medical problems, however skilled they may have been at interpreting *bombe glacée* or enquiries about the less reputable nightclubs. One would ask "where is the pain?" There would then follow a long and spirited exchange between the patient and interpreter which I might endeavour in vain to interrupt. Then the interpreter would turn to me and say "No!" I found it much better to try to learn a little of each language myself. I made out tables in an exercise book listing standard medical questions, and answers, in the five commonest languages. This worked quite well if the patient answered briefly and to the point. It was much more difficult if he raced off into a long vernacular description of his woes.

Later on, when I returned to No.19, another 200 beds had been added in an African Section. There we often had very serious linguistic difficulties, sometimes having to use two interpreters, one of whom knew the patient's tribal language and Swahili, and the second Swahili and English. You can imagine the false trails to which this often gave rise. Sometimes it had to be largely veterinary medicine, though one tried to look kind!

At any rate, when I did manage to acquire a little of the more straightforward languages, I could spot when the interpreter was going wrong, as of course was his usual habit. I soon discarded the interpreters as a waste of time except for the more obscure languages.

No 19 was an excellent hospital, with a keen professional staff. The OC Medical Division was Eric Boland (later Sir Eric Boland). He was a Guy's consultant and after the war the Dean of Medicine there. As a combatant in the First World War he had been seriously wounded and had lost an eye. A glass eye was thought to be dangerous in wartime so he wore a black eyeglass through which he appeared to observe you with steely ferocity. For the first three weeks I endured this distant, silent and formidable inspection. Eventually he apparently decided I was all right, thawed completely and we became great friends.

One of the other medical specialists was George Komrower, later a distinguished paediatrician at Manchester. The OC Surgical Division was Ian Aird, later to write a famous surgical textbook and to become Professor of Surgery at the Royal Postgraduate Medical School in London. One of the surgical specialists was John Swinney, whom I had met earlier in the war and who was later to become a Professor of Urology in Newcastle; at some time during my stay I acted as his best man when he married one of the sisters.

For a bachelor, life in an officers' mess, with a fascinating job, was really ideal. I had a room of my own, if I wanted to be on my own, company when I felt like it, and lots of interesting work. I nearly always slept out under the stars, a little cold for six weeks in mid-winter but otherwise ideal. The sky was almost always clear; I got hold of a star map and began to learn the constellations. In the mornings I usually woke about six and studied languages or medicine for an hour before getting up.

This period gave me four months or so of intensive introduction to tropical and other relevant diseases. Although we were very busy, we were better staffed than when I returned a year later. So we had time for clinical meetings. I played a certain amount of hockey. We sometimes went down to the Great Bitter Lake and bathed, or walked up the Big or Little Flea.

While I was there Headquarters in Cairo set up the first medical meeting for Middle East medical specialists. Boland arranged for us to stay at a hotel beside the Pyramids. I got up early one morning, arrived before the hordes of guides, climbed the Great Pyramid and had half-an-hour all by myself on the top. This was a most moving experience, taking one back 4000 years to that fantastic early achievement of a remarkable, if not very *sympathique*, civilisation.

In these pre-DDT days, bed bugs were a problem. Later they began to infect some of the medical wards at No.19, emerging at night from cracks in the lath-and-plaster walls to torment the patients. I had a canvas folding camp table. Somehow they invaded that. The little brutes would bite my bare arms through the canvas while I was writing. Finally I put the table through the heat steriliser. This destroyed the bugs but also, unfortunately, destroyed the leather so that I had to discard it.

During this Cairo visit we went one evening to a Cairo cinema. In the row in front of me was an officer with his girlfriend in a low-backed tropical dress. In an interval I spied a bed bug on her neck and back running around and obviously tickling her. What does a gentleman do? Deftly pick it off and dispose of it, thus risking being called out by her escort? Say "Madam, excuse me but you have a bug on your back. May I beg the privilege of removing it?" The cowardly Crofton was clearly no gentleman. He was much too shy to do anything. He just left the poor girl to suffer. No mention in Despatches for bug-removal.

This pleasant period of work among good doctors and good friends was terminated after four months by my being recalled to rejoin the Ismailia hospital unit, now reconstituted as No. 54 General Hospital of 200 beds. We were to proceed to Eritrea.

Eritrea: June 1941 – February 1942

We embarked at Suez and sailed down the Red Sea to Massawa. This must be one of the hottest and most humid places in the world, certainly the worst I have experienced. The few local British went about with towels round their necks to mop up the streams of sweat.

Our hospital equipment was unloaded and packed into cattle trucks for carriage to Asmara. Asmara, the capital of Eritrea, was only 70 miles away but 8000 feet up. Eritrea had been occupied by the Italians since the nineteenth century; they had only conquered Abyssinia[*] in the 1930s. With one junior officer and some men I was put in charge of the baggage in the goods train, while the rest of the unit proceeded in a more comfortable passenger train. We had to sleep in the cattle trucks at the quay in Massawa awaiting an engine. In that heat it was far too hot to be able to turn on your side. You had to sleep spread-eagled on your back with streams of sweat trickling into each ear.

The next evening we set off overnight for Asmara. We stopped briefly at intervals. If I had been more experienced I should have put a man in every truck. As I did not, when we arrived at Asmara we found a certain amount of equipment had been stolen *en route*. I should have thought of that possibility, though, equally, someone local should have warned me.

The climate in Asmara, at 8000 feet, is delightful, warm and sunny during the day and with air like the proverbial wine. It was a little cold at night; one could have done with some heating but, with wartime restrictions, we could only have a fire in the mess on a guest night, which was only an occasional event. The three months of the rains were quite tolerable, as the rainy periods were totally predictable. Each day it was warm and sunny until about 11am. Then the clouds would come piling up from the Red Sea. About 1pm it would start pelting with rain. This would continue until dusk, about 6pm, and then stop. Meantime the country was turning green, there were masses of flowers and great drifts of butterflies floating over the long grasses or the crops.

Much of Asmara had been constructed by the Italians. The buildings were quite good. It is situated on a plateau with dramatic hills in the distance towards Abyssinia. We were to open our hospital in the huts of an ex-Italian military hospital three miles outside the town. By that time the Abyssinian campaign had been successfully concluded. Most of the British troops had been withdrawn, leaving only an occupation force and the British military administration. Consequently we had very few patients. Most of the time there was only one medical, one surgical and an officers' ward in use. I ran the medical and officers' wards but this was by no means a fulltime job. So I also took on the hospital hygiene. I had a hygiene squad of Eritreans who had been conscripted into the Italian medical corps. The *serjente* was a delightful man who spoke excellent Italian. This further increased my language practice, as did most contacts with the locals.

After his experience with the Italians, the *serjente* was at first very puzzled by the pernickety hygienic ideas of the British: latrines, drains and all that. But ultimately he began to appreciate their appeal and became

---

[*] Now called Ethiopia

enthusiastic. One day I was charmed to receive a letter from him, of course in Italian, asking for a latrine to be provided for his village nearby. I passed this on with a strong recommendation, emphasising how valuable would be this contribution to civilisation and also the potential boost to British prestige! Of course I received the standard administrative answer that, desirable as it might be, "funds would not allow …..".

Another incident in the local hygiene saga is worth recording. There was an excellent British missionary doctor from the Sudan who had been brought in to run the civilian public health. He told me that when he arrived, Asmara had open drains and virtually no hygiene. He decided that a public lavatory would be a great leap forward. In due course the project was approved, the institution erected and the guardian appointed. One day my friend was showing some visiting dignitary round his public health achievements. He proudly brought him to their crowning glory, the new and magnificent public lavatory. They arrived just in time to observe the official guardian performing his own functions against its outside wall!

The hospital, like so many military hospitals, at least in wartime, was a series of large huts with tin roofs and linen ceilings, presumably largely to improve the appearance. The officers' quarters and bedrooms were in partially divided sections of one of the huts. During the rainy season the rats came in from the rain and retreated above the linen ceilings, scampering noisily above our heads and occasionally producing a damp stain on the ceiling.

My most interesting job was to act as medical consultant to a vast hospital complex for the large numbers of Italian prisoners-of-war. I did a medical round there twice a week and saw the difficult problems. The POW hospital complex was about 30 miles away from Asmara 2000 feet lower down. I was taken down there each time by an Eritrean driver. It was a beautiful drive, by zigzag roads down very steep mountains covered with prickly pear and red-hot pokers. In the distance were dramatic hills with great smooth, almost vertical, granite slopes leading up to shapely rounded tops. The Eritreans were terrifying drivers, taking the steep hair-raising corners downhill at breakneck speed. I would frequently feel I had to shout, fiercely or imploringly accordingly to my degree of terror, "Piano! Piano!" ("Slowly! Slowly!") but never with more than the briefest of effect.

Getting into the Italian POW hospital was quite a business. It was guarded by Indian troops who were far greater sticklers for the precise letter of their orders than any British troops. Although of course I had a special pass, quite often I had to call out the Officer of the Guard before I was allowed in. In contrast, in Geneifa, the POW hospital attached to No. 19 was guarded mostly by British troops who were often very casual. Of course there was much coming and going between the POW and the main hospital as the prisoners had to be sent into the British section for X-rays etc. One day three German officers escaped by just holding out a bit of paper to the sentry and walking through. Of course they didn't get very far. They were picked up on the train for Palestine.

There was much fascinating medicine in the Italian hospital. Mussolini had claimed his Abyssinian campaign as a triumph of preventive tropical hygiene. This of course was pure Fascist fantasy. The troops had every tropical disease in the book, including exotica like relapsing fever.

The Italian doctors were pleasant men. Most of them were not very knowledgeable but there was one good physician. With my steadily improving Italian and frequent visits I came to know them well and we became very friendly.

Nearby there was an American civilian hospital. The Americans, of course, did not come into the war until Pearl Harbour in December 1941, but had already given, and continued to give, very considerable aid under the "Lease-Lend" policy.

With the Mediterranean closed to our sea and air traffic by the Luftwaffe bases in Italy and North Africa, planes were flown to the Middle East across tropical Africa to Eritrea and thence up to Egypt. In Eritrea the Americans had established a civil organisation for repairing and servicing planes and had brought their own civilian hospital to support them. Incidentally, in the trip across Africa the pilots usually spent the night at Takoradi in Ghana. This was a malarial hot spot and they often developed severe malignant tertiary malaria after they arrived; I had a great battle saving one of them who had developed the life threatening cerebral malaria.

I saw something of the American doctors. They were, perhaps surprisingly, short of some things and we helped them out. Like ourselves they had no pathologist. None of their doctors was used to doing post-mortem examinations, whereas I had done quite a few in my time. So I occasionally lent them my ghoulish assistance. This included a post-mortem on a very odd case. He was a young man of about thirty. Very unusually for his age, he was said to have had several "coronary attacks" in the USA. He was clever but extremely highly strung. He had made up his mind that he was soon going to die and had decided that he would do so abroad. So he joined the American firm doing the plane repair work in Eritrea. One day he had one of his attacks of cardiac pain and was admitted to their hospital. The electrocardiogram showed nothing. A day or two later, as the doctors did their ward round, he announced that he was going to die that afternoon. They repeated the electrocardiogram, which was normal, and strongly reassured him. Later in the morning he said "I'm going to die after lunch".

He was again reassured, but after lunch he sat up suddenly in bed and then fell back dead. This, of course, was before the days of cardiac resuscitation.

I was asked to do the post-mortem but found nothing except some slight scarring of the heart which could have been the remnant of old trouble. His coronary arteries appeared normal. At that time no-one had yet appreciated the connection, in the relatively young, between coronary heart trouble, especially sudden death, and tobacco smoking. I remember nothing about his smoking habits or even whether they had been recorded. However, in view of the period and his temperament, I expect that he was a heavy smoker; we know now that this notoriously predisposes to sudden cardiac death. A major discharge of adrenaline-like substances, due to his anxiety, may well have pre-disposed to cardiac irregularities and death, when existing on top of his heavy smoking. Nevertheless his accurate prediction was remarkable.

One of the first jobs given me on my arrival in Asmara was to report on the mental state of six officers of the military administration who were under close arrest on various charges of corruption. Having spent most of the earlier part of the war retreating, Eritrea was the first place the British had conquered. There was a considerable civilian Italian population, no doubt accustomed to the routine Mafia techniques of corruption. The whole set-up must have presented considerable temptation to the less reliable of the conquerors. The peccadilloes apparently became somewhat of a scandal. Gold bricks were said to have been thrown around in the local nightclubs. One requisitioning officer was reported to have built an elegant house, at government expense, for himself and his Italian mistress. Eventually a senior intelligence officer, dressed up as a lieutenant, was sent down from Cairo. By frequenting bars and nightclubs he soon collected plenty of evidence. Hence my tricky assignment. It had fallen to me because the nearest psychiatrist was fifteen hundred miles away in Egypt.

Needless to say my six miscreants were perfectly normal mentally, if not morally, but they produced some interesting stories. One of them was an excellent young man who I was sure was innocent and indeed should never have been put under arrest. He had come from a relatively poor family, had gone out to India and was doing well on the staff of *The Times of India* when the war came. In the Abyssinian campaign his RASC* unit was in charge of military supplies to the front line troops along a 400 mile route through the wildest country. Ridiculously, his was made an accounting unit. Operational units were supposed not to have to keep detailed accounts because, while fighting with the enemy you cannot be expected to keep tabs

---

* Royal Army Service Corps

on every little item. Because some of his material was missing or unaccounted for, he was arrested. I am glad to say that in due course he was found "not guilty".

The other one who sticks in my memory was a handsome man of about thirty-five, rather upper class and self-confident. But he certainly gave me the impression of being an unscrupulous twister. I believe he was up on some twenty charges. Perhaps because of his basic skills, the only one ultimately held proved was that of stealing two tyres. The court martial obviously thought that was good enough and cashiered him.

Later I had an analogous and more curious problem. I came back to the hospital one evening to find that an officer had been admitted to my ward under close arrest. A long and fascinating story emerged.

This young man, from a distinguished school and university, had been in the civil service in the Sudan. The Sudan service was regarded as the elite of the colonial administration. It was alleged that you needed a double blue and a double first to get into it.

When Eritrea was conquered they needed some experienced administrators to assist the untutored officers seconded from the army. A few from the Sudan service, including my patient, were accordingly seconded. He was put in charge of a newly conquered District. Meantime in Asmara he had met a Hungarian girl, said to be an experienced demi-mondaine, and had fallen head-over-heels in love with her. She came to live with him on the job. This caused a considerable scandal. There were rumours that people bribed her to obtain what they wanted, either administratively or in the magistrate's court. He was told to get rid of her. In fact she just went underground (or under the bedclothes) and they continued to cohabit. Finally it became too much. He was posted elsewhere in the Middle East to some other job. He was forbidden to return to Eritrea.

Prior to this I was told there had been one other remarkable incident. He had gone back temporarily on leave to the Sudan. In his baggage he had a large very heavy trunk and seemed to be very anxious about it. This aroused the suspicions of the Sudanese customs officials. They opened it. Inside, of course, was the lady!

After some months in his other job, elsewhere in the Middle East, my patient heard that there were plans, through the Red Cross, to repatriate enemy women and children from Eritrea and Abyssinia. His girl, as a Hungarian, was an enemy alien. He thought he would never see her again. He obtained leave and then applied to the Governor of Eritrea for permission to visit Eritrea. This was refused. Nevertheless he managed to fiddle a place on a plane and arrive in Asmara.

The British head of the military police, a senior and well-decorated officer, was sent to the airport to arrest him. The police chief had known the young man well and was fond of him. He decided the best thing was to shove him into my ward as sick. Of course he knew all about the story; much of it I learnt from him, the rest from the patient.

As one would expect, the young man was a very pleasant, intelligent chap, though, totally, madly, unreasonably infatuated with the girl. (I say "unreasonably", but that may not be fair; I never met her). I had to produce a report saying just that. He was only sick with love. However I added that I was not a psychiatrist; I thought it would be quite wrong to condemn an individual on a psychiatric report by a physician untrained in that discipline. I recommended that he should be sent the 1500 miles to Cairo for a proper psychiatrist's report.

Accordingly, he was sent off to Cairo, via the Sudan and thence down the Nile. Being under close arrest he was put in the charge of an Indian medical officer who was being posted to Egypt. I heard later that *en route* the patient gave his escort the slip, managed to make contact with some of his friends in high places in Cairo, and the charge was dropped. Indeed I was told he eventually managed to marry the girl. Let us hope they both lived happily ever after. He seemed a very nice young man.

In Eritrea I was also involved with further legal problems, this time once more as the "prisoner's friend" rather than as an amateur psychiatrist. The miscreant was the same tough Geordie whom I had defended in Ismailia when he had been charged with slugging a sergeant. On this occasion he was alleged to have slugged a military policeman during a disturbance at a dancehall and had then escaped. He had jumped on an ambulance going back to the hospital, had been pursued by a military police (MP) car and finally arrested. It all looked pretty bleak for him. But when I took a detailed history I learnt that, when the police car got near, he had jumped out of the ambulance and fled across country, pursued by the MPs. One of these was an American who had eventually taken out his revolver and shot at my client, who then stopped and gave himself up. I realised that this gave us a chance. I knew that MPs were strictly forbidden to shoot. It seemed highly likely that they would all deny that there had been any shooting. On the other hand I found that there had been several witnesses on the ambulance who had seen and heard the shooting. If I could prove that the MPs were lying this would obviously make the rest of their evidence unreliable. And so it turned out. My client was found "Not Guilty".

I had one other interesting moment in the court. When the prosecuting officer was bringing out evidence from one of the other witnesses, things didn't look very promising and I asked to cross-examine the witness on certain points. This the presiding officer refused. He said I had already had my opportunity. I replied that, of course, I must accept the ruling of the court, but I asked that it be recorded that I had made the request and been refused. I knew that the rules of courts martial were extremely strict and that the defence must in no way be impeded. The presiding officer knew it too and climbed down. I got my re-examination.

Once more every miscreant up for court martial for miles around requested my services. But my interest was in medicine, not law – fascinating though it is – and I said I would only defend the men from my own unit.

Among my few patients was for a time a man with a classical presentation which I had read about in the textbooks but not encountered in practice – the "delusions of grandeur" associated with the early stages of General Paralysis of the Insane, due to syphilis of the brain. He was a seaman who, when at the wheel of his ship coming up the Red Sea, began to see things that no-one else saw. Accordingly his captain thought it best to put him ashore as sick. And so he fell under my care pending transfer, always a slow and delayed business in this remote area of the Middle East, to the more skilled attentions of the distant psychiatrist.

One day I was showing a medical Squadron Leader from the RAF round the hospital and we came to this patient. "Oh yes", said the patient when I introduced them. "I used to have a uniform like that – but of course with a lot more stripes on my sleeve, *and* my seven VCs!"

Later on, before my patient was borne away to better things, we were informed that the Duke of Gloucester was coming to Eritrea and would pay a Royal Visit to the hospital. I suggested to the Commanding Officer that my patient would certainly claim royal status and that it might be appropriate to arrange a formal meeting. I was firmly instructed that the patient must be securely battened down under double hatches for the entire duration of the Royal Visit. (My CO was a splendid, informal and quite efficient man. He was impatient with the more ridiculous traits of military bureaucracy, and of official protests when he disregarded them. He said he kept a special basket for letters which started "Please explain....."!).

While I was in Eritrea, I had one week's leave and went with a friend down to Keren. This is at 6000 feet, 2000 feet lower than Asmara. It had a lovely climate, not too hot during the day but still not cold at night. West of the little town of Keren is a very steep jagged ridge, perhaps 1500 feet high, which had been the major obstacle to the British advance. All movement in the valley below was obvious from the ridge and the Italians only had to lob grenades down if the troops came to close quarters. For weeks our men had to cower in what cover they could find below the ridge. It was eventually turned by a night tank attack through the only gap.

For us at this stage the ridge and its surroundings made delightful holiday walking and scrambling. We also went off for a couple of days cross country walking. We ran pretty short of water. The river we aimed for proved to be dry. Indeed we slept in its dried out bed. But we obtained some water from the locals. On our way back we lost the path in dense bush and ended up with a long, arduous and hot scramble down an almost vertical river bed and then across a parched plain. Again we were out of water and quite desperately thirsty when we reached the other side of the plain where, to our joy, we found a positively biblical well behind a large boulder and below a cliff. It was complete with shade from great spreading trees, a flock of sheep and a little shepherd boy. It took all our discipline to fill our water bottles, insert our water sterilising tablets and wait for an agonising half hour before we drank.

Soon I became very restless, partly because we were so far from active operations. I felt guilty to have so little work in so safe a place when Tobruk was under siege. I felt I was doing little to help win the war. In addition I was the only medical specialist for 1500 miles. In that area and that medical field I knew much more than anyone there, but I realised that I could easily get too cocky and think I knew more than I did. I needed to mix with people who could put me right. So I applied for a transfer to a more active area. But almost at once, after eight months in Asmara, the whole unit was transferred back to Egypt where I was posted yet again to the 19th General Hospital on the Canal at Geneifa.

We returned to Egypt, via Masawa and the Red Sea, in the *Aquitania*. This large transatlantic liner was empty except for our small unit but was still fitted for the intensive troop-carrying involved in shipping reinforcements to Egypt before the battle of El Alamein some months before. The decks had three tiered bunks, three deep, and we learnt that the men had slept in three batches – each bunk used by three men over the twenty-four hours. All this, of course, was in addition to the vast numbers between decks. And it must have taken at least six weeks to sail from the UK round Africa.

Egypt again: February 1943 - February 1944

The 19th General Hospital in Geneifa had grown even bigger with the vast pre-Alamein influx of troops to the nearby main Infantry Base Depot for Egypt and the Middle East. We had, I think, some 2400 beds at this time, including 200 beds for prisoners of war, now mainly German, and a 200-bed West African hospital attached, to which we acted as medical specialists.

The clinical staff had almost completely changed. The Officer Commanding the Medical Division was now Guy Scadding, a distinguished young academic physician from the Postgraduate (now Royal Postgraduate)

School in London and the Brompton Hospital, the main postgraduate chest hospital in the UK. He was some five years older than I. He taught me a vast amount. We had very similar interests and became great friends. After the war he gave me all my chances.

Junior doctors came, often for a few days or a week or two, then were posted up the line. There were a number of other specialists, opthalmologists etc, who were a little more long-stay and had similar non-medical interests. We used to refer to ourselves as "the Booksie Boys".

But for much of the time we didn't have many minutes to be booksie. The hospital was immensely busy and we were often very short of junior, non-specialist, doctors. Medically it was one of the most intensive years of my life. With many beds and a rapid turnover, there were inevitably very difficult medical problems, so that I had a heavy burden of medical consultations in all parts of the hospital, besides the detailed direct responsibility and paperwork, sometimes for as many as 180 beds.

Compared to a year previously, there was an even greater variety of countries and races among the patients: British, Australians, New Zealanders, white South Africans, Free French, Belgians, Cypriots, Arabs, tropical Africans of many kinds, South Sea Islanders; and Italians and Germans as POWs. There was a nearby Indian Army hospital to which I was also occasionally called for consultation.

If it was a remarkable experience of men, it was also a remarkable experience of diseases. We had wards full of diphtheria, scarlet fever, measles, chicken pox, and sometimes typhoid and paratyphoid. We had a nasty epidemic of poliomyelitis. Later we had both louse-borne and flea-borne typhus. I had charge of the typhus ward. At that time it was a grim disease with no specific treatment and the mortality was high. Nursing was all. Fortunately the nursing was superb: I had a splendid sister in charge. Laboratory methods were just being developed which could differentiate the louse-borne from the flea-borne types. I kept careful notes and, after the war, wrote my MD thesis on the subject.

When we admitted our first patients with typhus, and knowing that it was spread by fleas or lice, we decided that the clothes of all patients being admitted should be carefully examined and then sterilised. As this obviously was a potentially dangerous operation I thought I should do the first batch myself. I was in the middle of going through one man's clothes when a flea about the size of a small elephant leapt into the air, landed briskly on my arm and bit on it, raising in due course a large bump. Fortunately no typhus eventuated. Indeed that was the last creature of any kind which we found in any of the patients' clothes.

In addition to all the above, we saw malaria, leishmaniasis and many other tropical diseases. One hot evening, when the blazing Khamsin wind was blowing from the southern deserts, a Cypriot was admitted with a high fever, up to 107°F[*]. I found nothing specific on examination but initiated the usual investigations. To keep his temperature under control (higher fever might have been fatal) I put him in the middle of the ward under a fan and asked the nurses and orderlies to bathe him with ice at regular intervals throughout the night. Next morning I again examined him carefully. Something about his forehead struck me. I laid my hand on it and it felt a little lumpy. This I had read was the first clinical sign of smallpox. No smallpox had then been reported in the Middle East but Guy Scadding and I decided at once that he should be isolated with full precautions. Within a day or two the diagnosis was all too obvious. This in fact was the beginning of a major epidemic, with appreciable mortality, and I saw many more cases (including our radiologist who had a mild attack). It is a fantastically infectious disease and, in spite of all precautions and isolation, many hospitals had secondary cases – no-one quite knows to this day, but probably dust from the dried scabs of the terrible eruption gets carried long distances by air currents and wind. Future generations of mankind will owe an immense debt to the World Health Organisation which has now virtually certainly rid the world of one of its most terrible and terrifying afflictions. Of course each time we saw a new case, we revaccinated all staff and patients within miles, including ourselves.

Later I had another unexpected "first". One Saturday evening I was asked to go and see a patient who was very ill and had a temperature of 105°F[#]. I examined him carefully. The only thing I could find was a slight erosion of his scrotum and slightly enlarged glands[¥] in one groin. Although plague had not been reported at that time in the Middle East I initiated full isolation and precautions so as to be on the safe side. Guy Scadding was away in Cairo for some conference so I was unable to consult him. I also did the usual investigations, including blood culture. The only chemotherapy we had in those days was a drug belonging to the second generation of sulphonamides and which was very effective in pneumococcal pneumonia so I put him on this. The next day, Sunday, he was much better and his temperature was down. When Guy returned on the Monday I said lightly "we've had a case of plague while you've been away, ha, ha, ha!" – now thinking this much less probable. But later that afternoon the laboratory

---

[*] Almost 42°C. A higher temperature could indeed have been fatal.

[#] Above 40°Celsius.

[¥] Inguinal lymph nodes.

reported the culture as positive for plague*. Great excitement! Again this was the beginning of an epidemic, but another hospital was nominated to have a special plague unit and I saw no more. Since then I have always recommended plague patients to come to Crofton – 100% cure in his series of one!

The work was fascinating but exhausting, great masses of routine mixed with major and often very anxious problems, all too easily missed if you weren't continually on the alert.

For much of that year I worked from 8am till midnight, with only the briefest break for meals; and of course often up at night for various clinical crises. I used to try to stop work between lunch and tea on Sundays and this was often the only break in the week. On one occasion our Commanding Officer, with kindly intent to give me a break, sent me off to Cairo for a day to a course, I think on nutrition, not realising the vast amount of work I would have to catch up on when I returned. However it did give me the opportunity of meeting Fay, my brother Dick's widow, who was now in the Army Cypher Department at GHQ. I'm afraid she was rather shocked to see how tired I looked; I hope she did not repeat her impressions too truthfully in letters to my mother.

However it was a satisfying year professionally. I certainly felt I was doing something useful for the war effort. And, of course, the war was now beginning to go our way. The 8th Army was advancing steadily towards Tripoli; the 1st Army and the Americans had landed in Tunisia and were gradually overcoming the opposition. Later in the year Sicily was invaded. On the Eastern Front the Russians had won the epic victory of Stalingrad.

Suddenly, in February 1944, I received an official notification that I had been promoted to Lieutenant-Colonel and was posted to be Officer Commanding the Medical Division of a hospital in Malta. It was just before my 32nd birthday – but of course promotions come early in wartime.

Malta: February – September 1944

I had a pleasant trip from Alexandria to Malta on the *Oranje*, a Dutch hospital ship, with a Dutch crew and British medical personnel. As far as I remember, it carried no patients on this voyage which took 2-3 days. The climate in Egypt in February is lovely, pleasantly warm in the daytime without being too cold at night, and of course always sunny. We had this climate on the voyage, but my first month in Malta was far from the British

---

* Presumably *Yersinia pestis*.

conception of Mediterranean weather. We had rain, stormy winds or gales and, to me, spoilt by several years in Egypt and Eritrea, bitterly cold.

There had been several military hospitals in Malta when it was a base for the invasion of Sicily but the war was now moving on to Italy and the last of the more mobile hospitals had left the day I arrived, leaving only the military hospital in Imtarfa, the peacetime military barracks more or less in the centre and highest spot on the island. This was perhaps cooler in summer but well exposed to storms at this time of year. The hospital was in the standard dull architectural style of pre-war barracks, quite unlovely.

Malta, of course, had had a terrible and heroic time and a frightful battering from many months of intensive bombing. Fleet after fleet, trying to bring food and relief had been sunk. The worst problem, perhaps, had been the shortage of food. Those RAMC officers in our mess who had been through the siege had on average lost two stone in weight.

In the officers' mess I found some familiar faces. My opposite number, the OC Surgical Division, was Bob Nevin, who had been Resident Assistant Surgeon at St Thomas's Hospital when I was a House Physician. Somewhat embarrassingly, one of the medical specialists, now my junior, was a Michael Hudson who had been senior to me at St Thomas's; the other was a St George's man, Clarence Gavey, who was also older than I and more established; immediately after the war he became a consultant cardiologist at St George's. But they were very kind to their tyro OC Division and we got on very well. Indeed Michael was later my best man when I was married just after the war ended.

The last, largely ineffective, air-raid occurred soon after my arrival and seemed to cause little damage. There were still a lot of troops on the island and we were pretty busy, though much less hectic than I had been in Egypt. Of course I had to learn the administrative work of my new job, but I still spent most of my time clinically. The Commanding Officer, though a nice man, was a bit of a stickler for formalities. All my previous COs had usually given their orders verbally somewhat informally, which made for a friendly atmosphere. This CO gave his in nasty little formal notes, however trivial the subject, and without any previous discussion. Moreover he absolutely forbade any discussion of "shop" in the mess. With busy doctors who had a daily need to exchange information and ask advice about their patients, it was far easier to do this in the mess where we all met for meals than to march perhaps from one end of the hospital to the other to find the man in his ward. It was a ridiculous rule and of course we had to break it all the time, but always having to look over our shoulders to make sure the CO wasn't around.

I thought I had done enough in acquiring the rudiments of my patients' languages, but here were two more. Many of the patients were Maltese and spoke only Maltese, a Semitic language which had probably come to the island through Phoenician and Carthaginian, with plenty of subsequent additions from Arabic and Italian. I added this to my notebook and picked up the elements, much more difficult than German, Italian or French, as it had no bases in common with any Indo-European language.

The second language was Serbo-Croat. Soon after I arrived, the hospital was told to open a section for Yugoslav partisan patients, which was put under my administrative charge. These were mostly patients with long-term illnesses, such as chronic nephritis or tuberculosis, both of which were common among the partisans.

They were splendid people, both men and women. There was quite a problem when the British, very naturally, arranged separate wards for the men and the women. The women said they had fought and lived with the men and should go on doing so. In fact the partisans had a disciplinary code which absolutely forbade even mild relations between the sexes and this had been, and continued to be, strictly enforced. However, they yielded to our old-fashioned ideas.

They had their own ways of enforcing discipline. Each ward was a sort of soviet of its own. If anyone did something wrong, the first step was for every other patient in turn to tell him off. If this was unsuccessful, he was sent to Coventry – nobody spoke to him for so many days, or till he confessed and rectified his fault. It seemed to work pretty well and was fine for the majority who were happy to conform. But it was miserable for the occasional individualist or a man with an original mind.

There was much illiteracy in Yugoslavia in those days and big efforts were being made by the more educated to teach the long-term patients to read and write. I received complaints from the NCO in charge that lavatory paper was being consumed at a rate which would have done credit to the most Augean of stables. When I tackled the very nice Yugoslav doctor who acted as both interpreter and liaison officer he was delighted to acclaim this as evidence of the Yugoslav Renaissance – it was, of course, being sacrificed to literary rather than intestinal ardour. We arranged for a more appropriate substitute and the coefficient of loo-paper consumption fell back to a more appropriate level.

Of course I got to know the Yugoslav doctor well. However, I'm afraid I handed over clinical responsibility for the Yugoslavs to one of the medical specialists and chickened out of learning the medical patois of yet another language.

One curious incident with the partisans reflected the sad history of Yugoslavia. Before the war that country[*], a confederation of some of the smaller Balkan states – Serbia, Croatia, Montenegro etc – established after the 1914-18 war, was a kingdom with a young king, Peter, on the throne. As the Nazi threat moved nearer, through fascist governments in Bulgaria and Hungary, the Yugoslav government shifted accommodatingly to the right and was induced to make an agreement with Hitler, giving him among other things, if I remember correctly, the right of passage for the German army to help the Italians in their ineffectual attack on Greece, which had heroically resisted them for so long. There was an immediate mass protest in Yugoslavia. Its government was thrown out and the agreement with the Nazis abrogated. As I have mentioned earlier, the Germans immediately made a mass air attack on Belgrade and invaded before the Yugoslav mobilisation had got going. The Yugoslavs were overwhelmed. King Peter fled abroad, taking with him his small navy. In due course Tito[#] started his very effective, communist-led, resistance in which King Peter, for obvious reasons, had no part. Another more right-wing character, Mihailovich[¥], also led an official resistance, which I think professed loyalty to Peter. But in due course it became clear that Mihailovich had come to some agreement with the Nazis that he would not bother them if they didn't bother him. Churchill and the allies therefore put their backs behind Tito, who was successfully holding down many German divisions. They withdrew help from Mihailovich but continued in a minor way to support Peter and his navy, though I do not know whether that navy ever made any real contribution to the war effort.

All this is the background to a request which reached me through the (British) Royal Navy for a rating in King Peter's navy, which was stationed in Malta, to visit his wife, who was a partisan in one of our wards. He shortly arrived, accompanied by a Yugoslav naval officer and a British naval liaison officer.

---

[*] In fact, Yugoslavia was a federal state comprising seven countries or nations - Slovenia, Croatia, Serbia, Montenegro, Macedonia, Bosnia and Herzegovina. The last two were combined as a single member of the federation. Although fairly homogeneous ethnically (mostly Slavs), religious divisions led to the violent break-up of the federation in the 1990s, and a realignment into predominantly Orthodox Christian, Roman Catholic Christian and Muslim independent states.

[#] Marshall Tito was the military nickname adopted by Josip Bros (1892-1980) who became the post-war President of Yugoslavia.

[¥] Dragoljub (Drazha) Mihailovich (1893-1946), Yugoslav army colonel who led the Chetniks, an anti-communist resistance group that allied itself with the Germans and the Italians. He was executed by the post-war Yugoslav Government.

The partisans were very anti-Peter. They said that his navy was well paid, privileged and did nothing. The partisans received no pay at all. Anyone who joined it, including the husband, they regarded as a deserter who had "sold the sum of things for pay". As the little party arrived at the hospital, the partisans gathered round like a pack of threatening wolves. You could almost literally hear the growls.

I interviewed the visitors. I said the husband could see his wife, but only if she were prepared to see him. I then interviewed her. She had said her husband was a deserter. She absolutely refused to see him. The disconsolate party departed, shepherded by a couple of protective British NCOs and accompanied by the growls and threatening murmurs of the pack.

One of my official functions was to be doctor to the Governor General, then Lord Gort. Gort had commanded the British Expeditionary Force in France at the beginning of the war and had been sent to Malta at the grimmest period of the siege. All British planes had been destroyed by the Luftwaffe and Malta was virtually defenceless against the remorseless bombing. In several of the relieving convoys, most of which were destroyed or dispersed by the Luftwaffe from convenient bases in Sicily or Italy, an attempt had been made to fly off fighters to the island from one of the British aircraft carriers in the convoy. But of course this was observed by the enemy who promptly destroyed them as soon as they landed and before they had time to refuel. Gort realised that this was the crux and concentrated the whole organisation to ensure that immediately the planes landed they were refuelled and took to the air at once. The Luftwaffe bombed empty airfields which were promptly repaired and the fighters then managed to land again. Next day, for the first time, they downed many of the enemy. This enhanced defence helped the surviving ships of the next convoy to get through, including a heavily damaged merchantman with enough food to save the island from starvation. This crucial ship, however, had to be nursed with difficulty and literally supported to allow its heavily damaged hulk to limp into the harbour. This was the turning point of the siege.

My impression of Gort was of a very nice, friendly but not highly sophisticated or intellectual man. Although I only met him medically, or socially at friendly lunches at Government House, and had no opportunity of watching him develop grand strategy, my impression would have been that he could be good at tactics – as indeed he had so decisively shown – but that I would have put him in charge of a brigade rather than an army. What scandalous presumption by a militarily moronic medico!

At one of Gort's lunches I met his nephew, an officer in the Guards, who was recovering from wounds received in a gallant action for which he was later awarded a VC. A very pleasant modest young man.

One of my other duties was, in the company of two Maltese doctors, to pay official visits of inspection to the island's only tuberculosis sanatorium. You must remember the horrors of tuberculosis in those days, with a mortality of at least 50% and everyone terrified of it. The sanatorium was run by devoted nuns who were obviously doing their best, but the poor patients were obviously very frightened and morale seemed pretty low. The place was black with flies. I think the only useful contribution I made was to suggest methods, learnt from my experience of army hygiene, for the control of the flies.

I was notified that, as I had now completed more than four years abroad, I was due for home leave.

Northern Ireland and the Great Romance September 1944 – September 1945

I went home on a cargo ship returning empty after delivering supplies. Fortunately, by this stage of the war the once bloody and fatal route via Gibraltar had become reasonably safe. Nevertheless, we went well out into the Atlantic to avoid aircraft attacks from Europe where the terrible post-D-Day battles were still raging. It took us a fortnight to get to Liverpool.

It was a thrill to get on to a train in Liverpool and to travel through green fields after so many years of sand. I remember being struck by the great pink swathes of rosebay willowherb which had spread explosively in the bombed and burnt areas of England. (In Canada they call it "fireweed" as it moves in after forest fires).

I had first to report to the RAMC Base Depot at Crookham near Aldershot. I was immediately given a month's disembarkation leave and took the train to London. With military security etc, my parents did not know I was coming and in fact were on a brief and well-earned holiday in Wales. They immediately set off back: my father later told me that it was the only occasion in their married life on which my mother had actually urged him to drive faster! (He was a fast and rather terrifying driver). It was a marvellous reunion, all the more moving for our having lost my brother two years before. I remember the next day sitting out on the grass in Park Square where my parents lived and my mother and me talking non-stop for four hours.

They in fact had had a much more dangerous war than I had, having been in London throughout all the bombing and, in recent months, through the waves of V1 buzz-bombs. I experienced a few during that leave. You heard the engine coming and knew, when it cut out, it would either dive directly or slope down and then explode. You never knew whether it was coming at you. During my leave the first V2s landed on London. These were the rocket borne bombs. They were far more destructive than the V1s but you were spared the anxieties of anticipation as you did not hear them coming: if you heard the explosion, you knew you were all right.

Earlier in the war my parents had spent all their nights in the coal cellar, converted to an air-raid shelter, or under the reinforced table in the basement kitchen. Almost all the houses in the neighbourhood were destroyed. In that large area round Regent's Park, mostly fashionable Nash Regency houses looking out over the park, I believe that only five houses were still inhabited at the end of the war. Most had been destroyed internally by firebombs but still had their outer shells.

Later, I felt ashamed to have consumed so much of their meagre rations on my leave. Army rations were much more generous than civilian rations and I was used to feeding rather well.

I was equally touched when I went to dinner with my old friends the Engholms. Basil had been my contemporary at Cambridge and was now high up in the Civil Service. He was private secretary to the Minister of Agriculture (very important in besieged Britain), working desperately hard and seeing all the Cabinet papers. For my dinner with them they provided their last bottle of by then unobtainable wine.

Basil got me a ticket to attend Parliament during one of Churchill's reports on the war. I found both his presentation and the whole debate fascinating and stayed on all day. Of course it was one of the great occasions and the galleries were packed. I sat beside an American general who was deeply impressed.

My sister Joanna, I think, was also away when I arrived home but came back a few days later. She was working as a secretary for the American Army. She had been due to marry a German in September 1939. But she remained faithful. I think they managed to exchange one or two letters through the Red Cross during the war. Through working for the Americans she was later able to go with their army to Germany, found her man and married him. He was ten years older than she. He had been too old to have done military service between the wars. The result was that he had been a civilian interpreter in Italian throughout the war and had survived.

During my leave I applied to be allowed to visit my other sister, Patricia, in Dublin. But the War Office replied that one was only allowed to travel to (Southern) Ireland to visit parents or children. But, whether by kindness or by chance, at the end of my leave I was posted as OC Medical Division in a hospital in Bangor, Co Down, in Northern Ireland. There I departed in October 1944. From the British province of Northern Ireland one was permitted to travel to the Republic of Ireland and in due course, in spring 1945, I had a delightful weekend with Patricia and her family in Dublin. Of course by far the most important thing that happened to me in Ulster was that I met my future wife and laid the foundations for many years of blissful marriage.

Anyway, in October 1944, I went to Northern Ireland and took over my job from John Richardson, who had been a year senior to me at St Thomas's. The hospital was in a school in Bangor and the officers' mess in a small adjoining castle. Northern Ireland had been packed with troops before D-Day, including large numbers of Americans, but now they were much fewer, mostly training units. My medical colleagues seemed to be mainly elderly, by army standards, or unfit, or ex-prisoners-of-war or, for the first time in my career, women. We were, however, quite busy. Some of the recruits were from the Republic of Ireland. I found it nostalgic to hear so many accents and modes of expression which had been so familiar to me in my youth.

The war in Europe was still grimly at work. After rapid advances following the lethal post- D-Day battles, the attempted British advance at Arnhem in September 1944, with its heroic but unsuccessful airdrops, had sadly failed. Temporarily things had ground to a halt. Then followed, the last great, and unexpected, German offensive in February 1945, contained with difficulty and succeeded by the later advance of the Allies into Germany in March and April, the suicide of Hitler at the end of April and the final German surrender in early May.

The medical specialist in my division, Wilson Johnson ("Johnny"), was a Belfast man, in civil life a GP and also in charge of the Queen's University health service. One of his duties was to do outpatient sessions at another military hospital which was established in Campbell College, a boarding school in peacetime. He told me that there was a "grand wee lass" in charge of one of the wards there. In May 1945 I first met "the grand wee lass".

In pre-war Britain, before the NHS, if you wanted to become a specialist in medicine it was very unlikely that you could afford to marry until you were over the age of thirty. The most junior training posts were unpaid, the more senior very poorly paid. If you wanted to marry in your twenties you had either to have a private income or go into General Practice.

Up to this time I had never contemplated marriage. I was too junior before the war and, although I had become a Lieutenant-Colonel in early 1944, there was war, uncertain future, and few opportunities to meet girls. However in early May 1945 the European war was over. I became aware that the years were creeping up on me. I was already thirty-three, an age at which, in peacetime, most men had married. Pre-war, with my single-sex public school and entirely male university friends, together with my shyness with girls, I had got to know very few girls. There had been no women doctors in the RAMC in France or in the Middle East. My chances of meeting any woman with similar interests in five and a half years of war had therefore been minimal.

In May 1945, one of my colleagues suggested that our Officers' Mess should hold a "Guest Night" and invite some of the staff of Campbell College to dinner. Accordingly, a week or two later, the dinner was arranged. Among others I was introduced to Lt Eileen Mercer RAMC, "the grand wee lass".

Before dinner we all had a little walk in the grounds. I "happened" to walk with Eileen. She noted and named some of the wildflowers, a subject of which I was pretty ignorant. She was obviously very knowledgeable. I immediately decided my botanical ignorance should be remedied.

It was a chilly evening. With this, the euphoria of the end of the European war and the need to be good hosts, the Mess Secretary had arranged for a welcoming fire in the Mess. After dinner several of us, including Eileen, were standing chatting in front of a very warm blaze. Whether it was the heat, or the wine or the dinner, Eileen suddenly fainted. What could any responsible physician do but catch her in his arms?

A few days later I felt it my duty to pursue my botanical studies, to pursue the medical follow-up and (purely incidentally) to pursue my botany teacher and my patient. But I was still very shy with girls. I had greatly to screw up my courage to telephone her and invite her out to dinner. I carefully plotted not to use the telephone in the Mess, where I might be overheard. In the evening quiet I stealthily crept down to the public callbox in the hospital and rang the Campbell College Mess. Yes, Lt Mercer was there. I tentatively put my invitation to dinner. I received a rather surprised acceptance. I had got a toe in the door!

There followed several dinners – in places carefully arranged to try to avoid the prying eyes of colleagues. We found we had more and more in common, both in interests and in background. Eileen was clearly very able. She had successfully competed for a place in Somerville College, Oxford, and later achieved (as she was told unofficially) the second place in her finals at Oxford. Besides her medical and botanical skills she obviously had wide interests outside medicine, fostered by her parents and by her many non-medical bright friends at Somerville. In every way she was obviously a marvellous girl.

Soon we were going for walks up Cave Hill, a lovely wild area on the north shore of Belfast Lough, with fine views down over the Lough. Many romantic memories there. Sometime about July 1945 we were both given a routine week's leave which overlapped. Both our families were in London. But it turned out that Eileen's mother was highly suspicious of what she visualised as a stuffy old Colonel, behaving either as a Nasty Old Man (I was indeed seven years older) or as a Baby Snatcher. Eileen found that her leave programme had been almost completely filled. All I could "snatch" was one afternoon at the cinema.

It was easier when we returned to Ulster. None of our colleagues had spotted what was going on. On one occasion, which afterwards caused us secret amusement, Eileen was ticked off by one of her female colleagues for failing to salute me when we met.

We had so enjoyed our walks together, and we were both so keen on mountains, that we planned, one weekend at the end of August, to go down for the day by train to Newcastle, Co Down, not far away, and climb Slieve Donagh, the highest of the Mourne Mountains. Alas, just after we had made the plan, came an order from the War Office posting me to a hospital in Germany. I can still envisage, and still feel flattered by, Eileen's sad face when I met her at the Officers' Club in Belfast after phoning her with the news. We were not yet formally committed, though I was hoping we were in the final straight.

The imminent posting seemed particularly distressing. The Japanese war was still on. Big offensives were clearly planned in the Far East. All the more recent intake into the Forces were expecting soon to be posted there. Eileen would certainly go. I, having already spent years overseas, would probably stay in Europe. It might be years before we met again.

It was a gloomy parting when I prepared for my week's embarkation leave. But almost at that point, what sadly proved death, misery and disaster for so many Japanese proved salvation for us. The two atom bombs were dropped. The Japanese surrendered. The war was over. Eileen would now not have to go.

It was with a particularly gladsome heart that I celebrated VJ Day during my leave in London. With my old friends the Engholms I walked down to the Mall to see the Queen, in Procession, proceeding to open the new Parliament* after the Labour Party had swept the board at the recent election. It was a lovely summer day.

During this leave I had to go alone to meet Eileen's parents for the first time. Eileen's mother was at that time in a nursing home recovering from a hip fracture resulting from a fall. Of course later her mother and I became very dear friends. The stuffiness of elderly colonels was forgotten.

---

* The UK Head of State at the time (David Windsor) was a king, "George VI". His queen was in the procession but would not have opened Parliament.

It was in the middle of our courtship that I was told I would shortly be posted to Germany. Sometime in early September 1945 I embarked at Tilbury for Antwerp and from there by train to an officers' transit camp in Bruges. This was comfortably sited in a hotel where I had a couple of nights and was able to wander through that lovely town seemingly untouched by the destructions of war. Then a long, long, slow, slow train journey to Hamburg.

The hospital to which I was posted was a former German barracks in Luneberg, a small town near Hamburg and on the edge of Luneberg Heath where the last battle and the final surrender had occurred. I was only two months in Luneberg. The hospital was busy, but not overwhelmingly so.

I hadn't yet formally proposed. Indeed I never did. But somehow a more-or-less daily correspondence through the army postal service soon moved into a clear assumption. A rash admission at one stage by Eileen that she'd "burnt her boats" made it clear that we were finally on the beach together and it was too late for her to sail away.

We agreed to put an engagement notice in the Times. I would have been very embarrassed by the duty of taking her to a jeweller's to choose an engagement ring. I was secretly relieved that "the exigencies of the service" made this impossible. I appointed my mother as proxy and sent her £25 (worth a bit more then, but no fortune). She and Eileen went together and made the choice.

By now I knew I would be demobilised about the end of November 1945. By now we also knew that, the war being over, women in the Forces could be demobilised immediately if they were getting married. We fixed the wedding for 14th December 1945.

En route from my hospital at Luneburg to be demobilised in Britain, I was being driven to the station in a town some miles away. On one of those long straight narrow tree-lined roads my driver tried to slow down behind a line of slowing traffic ahead. He put his foot on the brake. Nothing happened. To avoid colliding with the traffic ahead he naturally swung out. Unfortunately just at that moment another line of traffic emerged in the opposite direction. We hit the leading car head on. I went through the windscreen and found myself by the roadside picking teeth and blood from my face. At my best I could never have been classed as a handsome bridegroom. I certainly couldn't now. My wedding was three weeks away.

And so back to the hospital where I had just said my farewells. A broken nose was more or less straightened. A great vertical gash across forehead and nose was meticulously stitched. The dentist provided a couple of substitute teeth. After five days I pursued once more my chastened way to home and beauty.

Eileen gallantly agreed to put up with a shop-soiled article. I climbed into my demob suit. I put on my new hat. I visited briefly my parents. I went over to see my bride for a few delightful days before she herself was demobilised. She had just served for long enough to be promoted to Captain and was thus to earn a minor increase in demobilisation gratuity.

We were married in a Presbyterian church in Kensington as Eileen's parents were Presbyterians. There were still wartime fuel shortages. There was no heat in the church. Fortunately I was entitled to wear uniform, which was warm enough. I did not have to hire a formal wedding suit. Eileen was a beautiful bride in traditional white. The church was full of friends and relations, loyal and enthusiastic, if chilly. Our joint photograph later appeared in the London Evening Standard. As a marriage between a Colonel and a Captain "They Should Be Well Suited" said the caption.

We moved on to a much warmer wedding reception laid on by Eileen's parents in a neighbouring hotel. I then carried her off in an elegant chauffeur-driven car to the Savoy Hotel in the Strand, an up-market start. We had dinner in a small good (and surprisingly German) restaurant, also in the Strand. Next day I had again grandly fixed a chauffeur-driven car to take us to Euston *en route* to our honeymoon in a less grand hotel (now a youth hostel) on Derwentwater in the Lake District.

After a splendid ten days' walking and climbing, with mixed weather, we returned for Christmas with Eileen's parents. Again we had one final elegant car from the station to Putney. I assured Eileen that she'd better make the best of it. She'd never have it again. (In fact she didn't till we both went to Buckingham Palace for my knighthood ceremony in 1977).

Reflections on the Second World War

Luneberg and Hamburg were full of the most extraordinary mixture of Allied troops, civilians of many nationalities released from slave labour and concentration camps, as well as undemobilised Germans. To me, in a short stay, the spectrum of uniforms was indecipherable. I met, I think as patients, two women who had been in concentration camps. One was a young German who had helped some prisoners to escape and was sent to Auschwitz. She was a cellist and was put in the camp orchestra which, with the ghoulish psychopathology of the Nazis, often had to play during executions or punishments. The other woman was a Hungarian who had been in a female concentration camp somewhere working as a sort of orderly. On one occasion a female guard ordered her to light a fire in one of the rooms. She objected as this was not one of her duties. The guard threatened her and ordered her to do it. She found the guard's whip lying about and put this on the fire. The guard saw this and took out her revolver to shoot her. Just at that moment the (male) Nazi commandant came in and stopped her shooting!

This woman had subsequently worked for the British military administration. The officer for whom she worked treated her very kindly at first, but then started making sexual advances. Victory, as I had seen in Eritrea, can be very corrupting. I was shocked that, when I was being demobilised, my CO said that there were lots of German sheets in the store and I should take as many as I liked. This, of course, would have been looting, which was strictly forbidden but was in fact rampant. I would have felt thoroughly guilty, and of course I declined.

During my stay, the trial of the guards of the Belsen concentration camp was going on in Luneberg and I attended one day of it. My impression of the guards was that many of them were of low intelligence. Mentally backward people are often very cruel if they are not carefully controlled. Belsen was one of the terrible camps which was over-run by the British Army. When they found it, it was filled with thousands of dead, dying or barely living skeletons. It was this that first brought home to our army, and then to the British public, the full horrors of the Nazis. A friend in a Field Ambulance, who was early into the camp, said he had never seen British troops so trigger-happy. If a German guard looked crooked he was shot. I believe that when the Americans over-ran Dachau they were so horrified that they shot all the guards out of hand. There was no Dachau trial.

A contrast to this terrible aspect to Germany was Hamburg. This also had been horribly bombed, with ruins and piles of rubble. There is a lovely lake in the city with the rich merchants' houses in their gardens around it. Like my parents' surroundings in Regent's Park in London, they were virtually all burnt out.

A surviving hotel had been turned into an Officers' Club and on two occasions I was able to go to concerts. The first was a moving concert performance of *Fidelio* by the resuscitated Hamburg choir and orchestra. The emergence of the prisoners from the dungeon into light symbolised the beginning of the German emergence from the savage darkness of the Nazis and was sung with touching emotion. The other was, in marked contrast, a charming concert performance of *The Marriage of Figaro*. What a counterpoint these two performances were to the bestial history of Belsen being unfolded in the trial a few miles away.

By looking back more widely on the world scene, I am convinced how very essential it was to fight this war. Of course we knew that at the time, but the full horrors of the Nazis' arrogant, bestial and perverted cult of cruelty, their anti-civilisation, was only revealed to most of us when the concentration camps were liberated and we had contact with those who had been so viciously racked and torn by the Gestapo and its minions. In ancient times Attila and Tamburlaine had butchered and tortured with the ruthless wildness of a savage barbarism. In our day Hitler had tragically debauched all the resources of a modern state to turn it from one of the most civilised nations of Europe into the very embodiment of evil.

Of course his cruelties rebounded. His brutality turned all the occupied nations against him. This must have been one of the few wars in history which had to be fought – at least after the pusillanimous failure of politicians, notably the British, to give effective backing to the League of Nations in stopping Japan in China or Mussolini in Ethiopia. These failures gave Hitler a clear run.

One of the benefits of such a crisis is, of course, to produce cohesion and mutual support in a society. It was this spirit that fostered, during the war, the sense of social responsibility which resulted in the great postwar reforms of the welfare state and the foundation of the National Health Service. During the great depression in the early 1930s, malnutrition was rampant. We still have problems of poverty in the UK, but it is a relative poverty, not the absolute poverty of severe malnutrition or starvation, previously common in Britain.

If society on the whole benefited in cohesion and social advance, at least for 20 to 30 years after the war, I personally benefited from the war in several respects. As a young man I was very shy, especially with my seniors. The war gave me the opportunity of command and initiative. It greatly increased my self-confidence. I vastly increased my experiences of people, people of many different social backgrounds and indeed of many different nations. I served in thirteen different army units, often with considerable turnover of staff, so that I made many friends. After the war there was almost nowhere in the UK where I did not have a friend.

I visited, at government expense, a number of different countries, serving in France, Germany, Egypt, Greece, Eritrea, Malta, and Northern Ireland, calling in at Cape Town and Durban on my way to the Middle East, and spending some leave in Palestine, Syria and Lebanon.

Although I was fortunate mostly to be busy in my professional work, I had considerable periods between jobs, in transit camps or travelling. During these periods I read very widely outside medicine – and a fair amount of medicine as well. The *Lancet* and *British Medical Journal* reached me most of the time, though of course often after long delays; I found the *Lancet*, which arrived rolled up, was very useful in darning socks, which I usually did myself as most batmen were hopeless at it – (this was when socks were wool only and quickly developed holes in the heels).

Professionally I had wide experience, especially in infectious and tropical diseases, though lacking in the diseases of older people. I collected enough data from my work with typhus to write my Cambridge MD on it just after the war.

I cannot claim that the military history of my personal war was very notable. The times I was in active units were the times when we were suffering defeat after defeat. When we began winning the war I was mostly in base hospitals. I calculate that, combining France and Greece, I retreated about a thousand miles during the war and never advanced at all!

I was lucky to be a bachelor throughout the war. For some of my married friends the separation was very grim. How lucky I was to meet the right person just when the war was ending. We have never since had to be separated except for a few weeks on professional foreign tours in which, when our children grew up, Eileen was able to share.

*John (aged 10), with brother Dick (4) and sisters Patricia (15)
and Joanna (9); 1922.*

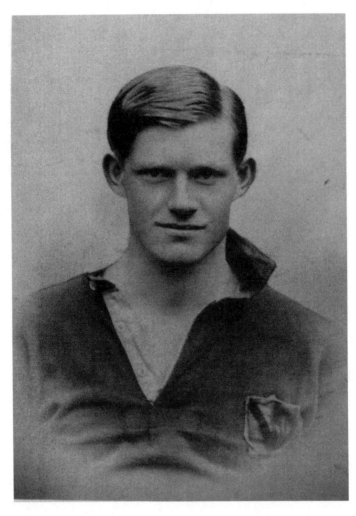

John playing rugby for Sydney Sussex College, University of Cambridge.

John climbing Dent Blanche, Swiss Alps; 1938.

John, in RAMC, Egypt.

Wedding of John and Eileen, December 14ᵗʰ, 1945; with William & Mary ("Molly") Crofton (left) and Edith & Richard Mercer.

John's children and parents, 1955; (from left to right) Richard (7), Pamela (4), Patricia(4), Alison (3) and Ian (in mother's arms) taken at Park Square East, London.

John with colleagues in Southfield Hospital, Edinburgh, 1950s.

John, City Hospital, Edinburgh, 1972.

John and some extended family in editor's garden, 2000. From left to right, back row: Sally Mumford-Crofton (daughter-in-law), John, David Kilpatrick (son-in-law; editor), Ian Crofton (son), Jeanne Féaux (granddaughter), Laura Kilpatrick (granddaughter), Alan Kilpatrick (grandson); front row: Archie Crofton (grandson), Claire Crofton (granddaughter) and Eileen (wife).

John, aged 97, taken on Eileen's 90th birthday.

Chapter 5
The Battle With The Bug

Background

The tubercle bacillus, *Mycobacterium tuberculosis*, has a long ancestry. Its forebears were probably hived off from a group of similar bacteria that lived wild in nature, picking up a living where they could. At some time in evolution certain of these species must have adapted to a parasitic life in animals. Notable among these was the bovine tubercle bacillus, *Mycobacterium bovis*, which afflicts cows, badgers, camels and other animals and formerly caused much human disease through infected milk.

We do not know exactly when the human bacillus first infected man. Tuberculosis produces characteristic disease in bones which has certainly been found in Nubian mummies back to about 2,000 BC. So tuberculosis has probably been established in the Middle East for at least 4,000 years. It is thought also to have had a long history in China and India. Silk from China came to Rome in early imperial days. We know, from Hippocrates's descriptions of "phthisis" (wasting) that the Greeks, and presumably the Romans, were afflicted. We also know that there was Roman trade to India across the Indian Ocean by the first century AD and that Roman products reached China. The tubercle bacillus may well have gone with them.

On the other hand in some parts of the world we know the disease is a relatively recent arrival. A skin test[*] usually produces local swelling and redness if the person has ever been infected. Most infected people overcome the infection without developing the disease, but they remain skin test positive for many years, often for the rest of their lives. Forty or fifty years ago skin-test surveys in remoter areas of Africa showed few positives among the population. For instance in Rhodesia (now Zimbabwe and Zambia) a Colonial Service doctor told me in the 1950s that the high positivity rates were all along the railways. The rate in the communities decreased to very low levels as he tested in districts far removed from it. In the 1950s rates were also very low in hill areas of Nepal away from the established trade routes. In East Africa the Arab slave traders probably brought the disease to

---

[*] The Mantoux test in which an injection of tuberculin into the skin provokes a cell-mediated response in those previously exposed.

the coast. It must have spread up the inland slave routes at an early stage. No doubt the European slave traders had the same effect on the West Coast.

Tuberculosis had almost certainly not existed in the Americas before contact with Europeans. It may well have been one of the diseases which, after Columbus's visits, exterminated the Indians of the Caribbean. In America, in contrast to Europe, there had been no natural selection favouring those genetically resistant to what was for them a new disease. In a limited area of Canada in the nineteenth century, where statistics were actually collected, one tenth of a local Indian tribe died of the disease each year for the first few years after contact with Europeans. There was a similar explosive epidemic in Eskimos* in the north of Canada after contacts with the rest of Canada greatly increased following the Second World War.

Tuberculosis may well have come north into Europe with the Romans. Scrofula, tuberculous lymph nodes in the neck which often break down the skin and produce discharging sinuses, seems to have been widespread in mediaeval times. But the great European explosion came with the overcrowding, malnutrition and general poverty accompanying the massive expansion of city slums during the Industrial Revolution. In England in the early nineteenth century one in seven deaths was attributed to tuberculosis. By mid nineteenth century tuberculosis was the commonest single cause of death in adult life. Keats, the Brontë family, Chopin, Paganini all died of it. The list is endless. As I used to tell my students, no self-respecting poet, artist or musician dreamt of dying of anything else! But many, many more ordinary, less articulate people found it just as grim to be tossed to and fro, toyed with and finally finished off, by this savage cat-and-mouse disease. Over and over again it would offer temporary improvement. There would be a transient burgeoning of hope. Then, with a cynical smile, the Mephistophelean bug would slip the trump card of relapse out of his sleeve. And later, all too often, the final fatal black Ace.

Curiously it was not only in Africa, America and the South Seas that tuberculosis was a late arrival. Before the later nineteenth century it seems that there was little in rural Ireland or the remoter parts of the Scottish Highlands. As a result, people from these areas had little inherited resistance. When they came to work in the industrialized areas they often developed the dreaded "galloping consumption" which might carry them off in two or three months.

In England tuberculosis mortality seems to have peaked in the mid nineteenth century, in Scotland a little later. Thereafter it fell fairly steadily, apart from increases in the two World Wars, 1914-18 and 1939-45. The

---

* Inuit is now the preferred term.

slow but steady fall in mortality was probably mainly due to gradual improvement in social conditions. Of these better housing – with reduction of overcrowding reducing the chances of infection – and improving nutrition were probably particularly important. An additional factor may have been the weeding out by death of the more genetically susceptible members of the population before they had fully reproduced.

By the mid nineteenth century, and up to the late 1940s, there were so many people coughing tubercle bacilli, and so much milk was infected with the bovine bacillus (to which man is fully susceptible), that most people became infected by the time they reached adult life. The spread of tuberculosis among cows may well have been due to their being kept in crowded conditions in towns in the early stages of the Industrial Revolution.

Whether you developed the disease depended partly on the size of the dose of bacilli you received and partly on your body's defences. How strong your defences were in turn depended on many factors, including perhaps your genes. But good food and good living conditions were the most important. The poor suffered most but the rich were far from immune.

As the Industrial Revolution spread to other countries in Europe and America the pattern of increase of tuberculosis roughly followed that in England. When, in turn, social conditions subsequently improved, there were similar falls.

The fall in disease, due to improving conditions, was only gradual. There was a formidable reversal, an increase in the disease and in death, in Britain and Europe during the 1914-18 War, followed by a fall to a lower, but still high, level. During the 1939-45 War there was another great increase, especially in the devastated countries of Europe, but also in Britain. Within Britain the increase both in the prevalence of the disease and in the mortality was particularly high in Scotland. In most countries involved in the war, mortality and incidence of tuberculosis began to fall after the war ended. Apart from Portugal, Scotland was the only country in Europe in which both continued to rise.

Much of the increase was in young women. Perhaps during and after the war they were working more outside the home and receiving more infection. Many of these young adults had lived through grim conditions in a childhood which coincided with the severe economic depression of the early 1930s. In addition housing conditions in Scotland were far worse than in England. Gross overcrowding was much more prevalent and had improved much less between the wars.

By the time I went to Edinburgh in 1952 there had been some fall in Scottish tuberculosis mortality, following the introduction of the early streptomycin, and later para-aminosalicylic acid (PAS) treatment in 1948-49, but the numbers of new cases both in Scotland generally and in Edinburgh, were still increasing year by year. There was great public concern and deep anxiety among the population.

The first controlled trials

In the USA, soil biologists had been stimulated by the world-shaking discovery and success of penicillin. They had been looking at soil fungi in the hope of finding something that might affect organisms not susceptible to penicillin, including the tubercle bacillus. Eventually Selman Waksman and Albert Schatz had discovered another antibiotic, streptomycin[*]. Streptomycin had knocked off the bacillus very effectively in the test tube. But many such substances proved much less effective, or much too toxic, when used in experimental tuberculosis in animals. The guinea pig was the classical animal for such tests. It was very susceptible indeed. One felt that the poor little brute had only to catch a glimpse of one tubercle bacillus on the horizon to turn up his toes and expire. But the work by Feldman and Hinshaw, of the Mayo Clinic in the USA, had shown that streptomycin prevented and even reversed this grim process. The drug did not seem to be toxic to animals, or in preliminary trials to humans. A formal trial in human tuberculosis seemed to be both justified and hopeful.

But streptomycin was in very short supply. Fortunately the generous Americans were prepared to make a limited amount available to the British Medical Research Council for trial in human tuberculosis. The MRC already had a Tuberculosis Research unit, headed by Philip D'Arcy Hart. Philip was a British pioneer both in tuberculosis and in coal miner's pneumoconiosis. Accordingly the MRC set up a committee to plan such a trial. This committee included Guy Scadding. It also included Professor Bradford Hill, a statistician.

It was Bradford Hill who persuaded the committee to carry out what came to be called a "controlled trial" of the new substance. It is difficult now, when controlled trials have become the standard way of testing new treatments, to remember how revolutionary this was. Previously, perhaps because most treatments were pretty ineffective, a new treatment came into use because of the clinical impression of its value, and because of powerful advocacy by one or more dominant members of the medical profession. Its introduction could have some of the confrontational characteristics of the English legal system. For instance, in my studies of the nineteenth century German medical literature for my MD thesis in typhus I had found that one week in a medical journal there would be a paper from some big professorial

---

[*] It is now generally believed that Albert Schatz (1922-2005) did indeed discover streptomycin, but Selman Waksman (1888-1973) stole most of the credit.

knob advocating a particular treatment. The next week there would be a "Reply from Professor So-and-So". This would be extremely offensive. I remember one which said that "Nur ein Dummkopf" ("Only a thickhead") could have advocated his colleague's treatment, as proposed in the previous week's journal. His contribution had revealed abysmal ignorance of the whole subject. The difficulty is that in many diseases Nature cures at least some patients. But, understandably, both the patient and the doctor naturally prefer to attribute the cure to the doctor's treatment. Of course an occasional treatment, such as penicillin for certain lethal infections or liver extract for pernicious anaemia, or insulin for diabetes, had been so dramatically effective that the results were incontestable.

In pulmonary tuberculosis, assessment might be much more difficult. At that time roughly half the patients died within five years of diagnosis. Others might relapse later. But some, especially those with milder disease, recovered. Trial by just giving the drug to a group of patients might therefore give a confused and uncertain answer. Bradford Hill pointed out that there was only enough drug to treat a limited number of patients. He therefore suggested that it was entirely ethical that patients should be admitted to the trial and, to avoid bias, be allocated at random to the treatment or control group. The control group would have the best available previous treatment. To avoid bias the doctor must not make this decision: he could write the patient's name on the next envelope, open the envelope and the card inside would say "Streptomycin" or "Control". Each group would have its progress carefully recorded. Such measurements as improvement of the X-ray, where bias might enter, would be unbiased: the films would be read by a team who did not know whether the patient had or had not received streptomycin. The disappearance of tubercle bacilli from the sputum was also a very important criterion and less subject to bias.

The trial was ethical because there was only a limited supply anyway; because no one knew whether streptomycin would work and whether it might damage the patient; and because the controls might be able to receive treatment later if the drug proved effective. It might well prove safer to be a control who did not receive the new drug.

In the first place, therefore, it was decided to carry out the controlled trial on patients with advanced pulmonary tuberculosis of bronchopneumonic type, whose outlook normally would have been very poor. Trials were also conducted on the most dangerous forms of tuberculosis, miliary tuberculosis (widespread disease due to spread through the bloodstream) and tuberculous meningitis. As these two forms of tuberculosis were virtually 100% fatal, no controls were necessary. Any survivors would be a major advance.

These initial MRC trials of streptomycin had at first shown dramatic improvement in the streptomycin patients compared with those who had received only the best previous treatment of care and bed rest, but after a few weeks or a month or two the patient's bacilli often became resistant to the drug. We were back to the cruel cat-and-mouse act: improvement, this time often dramatic, followed by tragic, and often fatal, relapse. It was concluded that streptomycin treatment could only be an adjunct, perhaps to make patients fit for collapse therapy[*] or surgery.

Fortunately during 1948 para-aminosalicylic acid had been discovered by Lehmann in Sweden. This was one of the few effective drugs to have been designed on rational grounds, rather than found by the "philosopher's stone" trial and error approach which had given us streptomycin. It had been noted that salicylates stimulated the growth of tubercle bacilli in the laboratory. The research workers speculated that chemically modified salicylates could be inhibitory. If the metabolic pathway promoting bacterial growth is regarded as a lock, and salicylate as a sort of key, then a neo-salicylate acting as a warped key, could jam up the lock and prevent growth of the bacilli. Eventually, it was found that para-aminosalicylic acid, later always known as "PAS" was effective. In the laboratory it stopped the growth of the bacilli. It appeared to cause no damage when fed to laboratory animals and seemed to suppress the disease in them. Unlike streptomycin, which had to be given by injection, it was absorbed from the intestine and so it could be swallowed as medicine. Preliminary trials in patients suggested that it had some effect.

The MRC Committee therefore thought it was justifiable to try this new drug in patients. This trial showed that PAS did suppress the disease, though less dramatically than streptomycin. Unfortunately here again, when the drug was given alone the tubercle bacilli often became resistant to it after a few weeks. But the most important finding was that if both streptomycin and PAS were given together far fewer patients developed resistant organisms. The tragic relapses under treatment, which we had seen with streptomycin after development of drug resistance, did not occur, or at least were much rarer.

A disadvantage of PAS was that it had to be given in a rather high dose. This caused nausea and vomiting in many patients so a further trial was carried out comparing different doses given in different ways. This trial showed that a larger dose given twice a day was importantly better than the same total daily dose given in four equal, but smaller, amounts[#].

---

[*] Artificial pneumothorax to collapse the lung and allow it to rest

[#] Presumably the nausea was no worse at the higher dose (which might have been feared) and so it was better to feel sick twice a day rather than four times a day.

I have always thought that Austin Bradford Hill failed to receive adequate recognition for the introduction of controlled trials. These had at last given a scientific basis for advances in treatment, and across the whole range of medicine. They greatly speeded up both the introduction of genuine advances in treatment and the discarding of the ineffective or spurious. I think the only previous trial which had approached this technique was a study by a naval surgeon, Lind*, in the eighteenth century, of the use of lime juice in treating scurvy. This had largely been forgotten until the controlled trial was rediscovered and systematised by Bradford Hill.

Some time in the mid 1960s, when I was Dean of the Faculty of Medicine in Edinburgh, our Medical School, as I suppose happens at intervals, was asked (no doubt among many others) to make a nomination for the Nobel Prize in Medicine. We nominated Bradford Hill, but, alas, he didn't get it. However at least we were later able to get him a very well deserved honorary degree.

Apprenticeship

I had had only incidental contact with tuberculosis in the army. Though armies consist of fit young men, tuberculosis was not infrequent. In the Middle East, once the diagnosis was made the patients were transferred to tuberculosis hospitals in South Africa.

During these years I had become interested in chest diseases, particularly in chest X-rays and their interpretation. My interest was further stimulated by serving for eighteen months as a Medical Specialist under Lieutenant Colonel Guy Scadding. Before the war Guy was already a rising star in the academic chest world, one of the few who combined skills in both tuberculosis and other chest diseases. He was already a consultant at the Brompton Hospital, the leading chest hospital in Britain, and also one of the founding members of staff at the new Postgraduate Medical School of London (now the Royal Postgraduate Medical School) at Hammersmith Hospital, which was to become a spearhead of academic medicine in Britain. I learned an enormous amount from Guy. We became lifelong friends. He gave me all my chances.

The government had arranged that young doctors coming out of the services should be eligible for supernumerary jobs in teaching hospitals to prepare them for civilian practice. Accordingly, at the beginning of 1946, I obtained one of these (worth £650 a year) at St Thomas's Hospital. I had no choice but to do neurology and diabetes. At that time St Thomas's had no chest department, only a somewhat despised tuberculosis section tucked

---

* James Lind (1716-94), author of *A Treatise of the Scurvy* (1753).

- 145 -

away in a basement. In fact most of St Thomas's had been bombed and destroyed during the war. Almost all the actual beds were now in a temporary unit in Surrey. The old hospital mainly housed outpatients and casualty departments.

Fortunately Guy Scadding suggested that I should do a couple of sessions a week with him at the Brompton Hospital as a Clinical Assistant. These were unpaid but would clearly be very useful experience. Later I applied for a new and more academic physician's job at the Central Middlesex Hospital, one of the few good municipal hospitals in the UK. This was one of the first such jobs advertised. We cancelled our holiday which we had already booked in Ireland so as to be available for interview. But there were over a hundred applicants and I wasn't even short listed for interview. No job. No holiday.

Fortunately at this moment the Brompton Hospital decided, with government assistance, to start some new Registrar (junior training) posts. I applied for one of these and in due course got it. Great relief. The anxiety of even such transient unemployment gives me some faint whiff of the devastation of long-term job deprivation.

I had indeed six weeks' unemployment pending the job starting. So I got down to finishing a thesis for my Cambridge M.D. I had kept all my notes on the typhus cases I had seen in the Middle East, where I had run a typhus ward, and had already started to write my thesis on this subject. I had great fun dipping into, and summarising, the highly controversial and abusive nineteenth century German literature on the subject, and the slightly less spiteful British. My aim was to lend a spurious air of scholarship to a somewhat pot boiling concoction. However I had the advantage that there were not many people in Cambridge who knew much about typhus. So perhaps my thesis was passed "nem.con" as there was no-one knowledgeable enough to be "con".

For the M.D. one had not only to write a thesis but, if it were accepted, then attend at Cambridge to write a set essay on a related subject, followed by a viva voce examination. I sat in solitary glory to write my essay. The Regius Professor, Lionel Whitby, said that the point of the essay writing was mainly to ensure that I'd actually written the thesis myself! Anyway the essay and viva voce also achieved a "Nem. Con". Next day, in a hired MA gown and hood, I knelt in scholarly submission before the Vice-Chancellor and rose to my feet a real Doctor. Until that moment I had been firmly addressed by all concerned as *Mr* Crofton with the emphasis on *Mister*.

To return to the main theme, I had three happy months at the end of 1946 as a Registrar to Guy Scadding. I learnt an enormous amount both from him and from the endless discussions with other junior staff. My fellow

Registrars, Neville Oswald, Ken Robson and Howard Nicholson all went on to become distinguished consultants at London teaching hospitals. Guy Scadding was the most academic member of the Brompton senior staff. He was accordingly made Dean and afterwards developed the academic side of the hospital. As he was also on the staff of the Postgraduate Medical School at Hammersmith he had his hands full.

As Guy's Clinical Assistant I had already been working with him. That part of the job involved working the whole of Saturday, as I had done previously. In the morning we did a medical outpatient clinic. In the afternoon I ran an artificial pneumothorax refill clinic. This was for patients who were working. The patients had to attend regularly to have more air put into their pneumothoraces. I think I ran this clinic for two to three years before there was a merciful change. Our outpatient clinic was moved to Thursday afternoon. We saw our outpatients till 5pm and then I went straight on with the pneumothorax clinic till 8 or 8.30pm.

It had been decided that the first controlled trial of streptomycin in the treatment of tuberculosis would be carried out at a number of centres throughout the UK. The trial would be coordinated by the MRC's Tuberculosis Research Unit with Marc Daniels mainly responsible.

Guy Scadding then, as Dean, asked me if I would be prepared to act as coordinator of the trials at the Brompton Hospital, funded by the MRC. He thought this would take up about half of my time. He also said that Professor John MacMichael (later Sir John), the professor of medicine at the Postgraduate School, had suggested that Guy, with his commitment at the Brompton, needed a half-time lecturer to assist him with his responsibility for thirty beds there and his teaching commitments. Guy asked if I would be prepared to take on the two jobs. Of course I was thrilled: research, clinical medicine, teaching and working with someone for whom I had such admiration and affection.

In those hectic post-war days everything seemed to be fixed on an "Old Boy" basis, which might now be regarded as unethical, even if the eventual results were no different. The post wasn't advertised. I had lunch at Hammersmith Hospital with Guy and John MacMichael and started in January 1947.

The job at the Brompton required a good deal of tact and persistence. All the physicians had agreed to participate in the trial, I had diplomatically to ensure that they did indeed enter patients and then that, once entered, the treatment and observations were carried out meticulously according to the protocols. I had also to see that the results were fully recorded. It was a lot of work but it was also enormous fun. In addition it had the advantage that I saw a wide range of disease throughout the medical wards. It was a very good way of getting to know all the staff, senior and junior. The Brompton was a small, very friendly hospital. And of course there was the excitement of participating in new developments, not only in tuberculosis but in the whole range of chest disease. The surgeons were pioneering many new techniques. Several of them, notably Clement (later Sir Clement) Price-Thomas, were stimulating teachers and enjoyed discussions and arguments with younger colleagues, even juniors like myself.

I continued in the same status for two to three years. I then left the MRC's service and became the equivalent of a Senior Lecturer in the Brompton. Later Guy Scadding was made Professor of Medicine at the Brompton. He could then give less time to Hammersmith, so I took over two thirds of the beds there and only spent one day a week at the Brompton. In 1951 I was made a Senior Lecturer at the Postgraduate School.

At Hammersmith much of my research was in non-tuberculosis fields, but in tuberculosis I worked closely with Denny Mitchison, at first when he was a bacteriologist at the Brompton and later when he transferred to the Postgraduate School where he eventually became a Professor of Bacteriology. Before that he had spent several years in Madras setting up the laboratory for the Indian Tuberculosis Research Unit there, which was supported by the British MRC. Denny came from a famous intellectual family. His mother, the novelist Naomi Mitchison, was a Haldane, daughter of the famous Oxford physiologist JB Haldane and sister of JBS Haldane the geneticist. Denny's father was a Labour MP, later Lord Mitchison. Two of Denny's brothers also became professors. Denny was as you might expect, a most stimulating colleague. Later he had a MRC Tuberculosis Bacteriology Unit of his own. He, Georges Cannetti and Noel Rist of the Pasteur Institute in Paris proved in that generation the world leaders in the bacteriology of tuberculosis.

I was also immensely stimulated by Marc Daniels of the MRC's Tuberculosis Research Unit, who was the central coordinator of the trials and from whom I learnt an enormous amount about the epidemiology of tuberculosis. We were all devastated by his death from a rare liver cancer at the early age of forty five, shortly after I moved to Edinburgh. We had become close friends with him and his wife, Kay. Kay came to stay with us after all the trauma of his death. Marc, in this short post-war period, had made, through the meticulous conduct of successive trials, outstanding contributions to the control of tuberculosis. After his death his father endowed a Marc Daniels Memorial Lecture at the Royal College of Physicians of London. In 1960 I was proud to be invited to deliver this lecture. In it I was able to summarise the work we had done during the first few exciting years in Edinburgh. This could be regarded as both a legacy from Marc and a tribute to his memory.

I have omitted one bit of personal research in connection with the early streptomycin trials. In these early trials a number of patients, after a few weeks on treatment, developed nausea and vomiting. It was clearly due to the streptomycin, as it ceased if the drug was stopped. I thought this might be due to an allergic effect and that it might be mitigated by the newly evolved antihistamine drugs. We did a "double blind" trial of adding antihistamines or placebo (neither doctor or patient knowing which patient was receiving which) and clearly showed that the antihistamine switched off the vomiting. As it turned out, the vomiting must have been due to an impurity in the early streptomycin samples; later it proved no problem. We published our results. Others read our paper and wondered whether the antihistamines might have a specific anti-vomiting, as well as an anti-allergic, effect. This proved correct and antihistamines became the basis of many standard anti-seasickness pills. A nice example of "serendipity", a term used to indicate that when one is trying to do research with some particular object one in fact achieves quite a different one by fortunate chance.

Edinburgh: Philip's "Edinburgh System"

In late 1951 I was appointed Professor of Tuberculosis and Respiratory Diseases at Edinburgh University. I started work there at the beginning of 1952.

The Edinburgh Chair of Tuberculosis had been created in 1919 for Sir Robert Philip. As a young man Philip had studied in Vienna, then probably the most outstanding medical centre in Europe, soon after Koch's discovery of the tubercle bacillus in 1882. Philip was clearly greatly excited by the possibility that this opened up for the prevention and treatment of this terrible disease. When the young physician, panting with intellectual ardour, stimulated by both Koch and Vienna, returned to Edinburgh and expressed his enthusiasm to his stodgy seniors, he was patronisingly assured that "phthisis was played out" and advised to turn to some other endeavour. But, as his subsequent career showed, Philip was a strong character and took little notice. He proved to have a genius for influencing the influential and for extracting money from the rich. He knew what he wanted to do and he did it. He pioneered organisational methods for the control of tuberculosis which were later followed, first nationally and then internationally.

Philip realised that, if tuberculosis was an infectious disease, its spread could be limited by isolation of its victims. Patients with less advanced disease, who had some chance of recovering, could be put into hospital and their resistance to the disease enhanced by good food and bed rest. Patients with advanced disease, and little hope of recovery could be put into long stay hospitals, looked after and isolated until they died. Families of patients could be carefully examined so as to pick up at an early stage any who had been infected. At this early stage they were more likely to benefit from the limited treatment available at that time.

Gradually Philip put this scheme into operation. He first opened a "Dispensary" for patients and their families in two rooms above a shop on The Mound*, now marked with a commemorative plaque. Later the Royal Victoria Hospital was built and opened for the more hopeful cases. Advanced and hopeless cases were isolated in the special wards in the City Hospital for infectious diseases run by the local authority. It is difficult to know now whether all this contributed to the decline of tuberculosis. With rising standards of living, the national mortality had been slowly declining since the middle of the nineteenth century. There was no notable acceleration in the decline after Philip began his work, but of course his methods were only gradually introduced. A statutory responsibility to do so was placed on local authorities in an Act of Parliament implemented from 1911. Philip was closely consulted in the drafting of this Act.

In the late nineteenth and early twentieth centuries, and parallel with Philip's work, sanatorium treatment was introduced, first in Germany and America and then widely in richer countries. This relied on country and mountain air, good food, initial bed rest and, in many sanatoria, later gradually increasing exercise to build up patients' resistance against the disease. Vast numbers of sanatoria were built all over the world. It is difficult to know whether they did any good. But at least, like Philip's scheme, they isolated potential infectors at least temporarily. That this was indeed useful is shown by the sharp increase in attack rate and mortality in the UK when the sanatoria were emptied at the end of 1939 so as to provide accommodation for the expected influx of air raid casualties (though of course the influx did not start until a year later by which time many of the sanatoria had been re-occupied by patients). Of course other wartime factors played a part here but it would be surprising if the sudden release of large numbers of infectious patients was not an important contributor.

Philip's system was in place throughout the UK at the time when streptomycin was introduced in 1947-48 and before the launch of the NHS. In 1948, with the introduction of the National Health Service, and after the pioneering work on non-tuberculosis chest disease at the Brompton Hospital, the tuberculosis dispensaries were converted into Chest Clinics, though tuberculosis still remained the dominant part of their work. This system made it relatively easy to organise cooperative controlled trials throughout the UK. Moreover the excitement of streptomycin, and the broadening of

---

* A steep street in central Edinburgh linking the Old and New Towns.

the specialty to include chest disease in general, attracted many able young doctors, fresh from war service, who were delighted to participate in such exciting work.

The challenge in Edinburgh

When I was being considered for the Chair, the Professor of Medicine, Stanley Davidson, and the Professor of Therapeutics, Derrick Dunlop, invited me up to have a look at the situation. These two had done an enormous amount for Edinburgh medicine by recruiting a number of outstanding young physicians from England to academic posts in the medical school. This had caused great fury in some of their more nationalistic and conservative Scottish colleagues. Stanley asked Ian Grant, then still a doctor in training but later to earn a major national and international reputation, to show me around. This he did with his usual intelligence, and the acerbic comments, which I was later to know so well[*], on the more shaky aspects of Edinburgh medicine and its purveyors. I subsequently wrote, for Davidson and Dunlop, a memorandum on what I believed needed doing. It is possible that this influenced the selection committee to offer me the Chair.

In Edinburgh, as in Scotland generally, the mortality for tuberculosis, which had risen sharply and remained up during and after the war, had begun to decline since, following the first streptomycin trial, the drug had become generally available for use. But the number of new cases was still rising steeply. Although there were some 400 beds for tuberculosis in the city, there were long waiting lists. Patients often waited months, even a year or more, for admission. They might well die before their turns came. There was great public concern. Shortly after I came to Edinburgh the Edinburgh Presbytery of the Church of Scotland held a Tuberculosis Week to draw the attention of the authorities, especially the National Health Service authorities, to the tragic situation for so many patients.

The services for tuberculosis were organised in a way that seemed to me highly unsatisfactory, though this was the pattern throughout most of the British Isles. One group of doctors saw patients at the Chest Clinic, made the diagnosis and were responsible for their care until they were admitted to hospital and then again after they were discharged. These doctors were also responsible for checking the patients' families and other contacts.

Another group of doctors looked after the patients in hospital but had no further responsibility once they were discharged. It seemed to me that,

---

[*] After his retirement, Ian Grant was a regular contributor to *The Scotsman* newspaper correspondence columns on a variety of topics.

especially with the complexities of the newly unfolding treatment ("chemotherapy" as it came to be called) and the major psychological, family and social stress of the disease, continuity of care was essential to give the greatest chance of success and to sustain the morale of the patient and his family. Moreover it would be a great stimulus to the doctor to avoid failure. Previously, in many places, when things seemed to be going wrong with a patient, the outpatient doctor would put him down for hospital admission, often achieved only after long delay. Later the patient might be discharged, often still with a positive sputum, with a note that "maximum hospital benefit" had been achieved. Both sets of doctors could therefore get rid of their failures, at least temporarily.

When I arrived in Edinburgh I was theoretically in clinical charge of 400 beds in three different hospitals in the city. In the hospitals I was the only physician of consultant status, though there were a number of junior doctors. (Only consultants were supposed to have ultimate clinical responsibility for patients). Another consultant, let us call him Dr Z[*] as I shall have to be unkind to his memory, was in charge of the main Chest Clinic and had junior doctors under him. Dr Z had no beds but he kept the waiting list for hospitals and it was he who decided who should be admitted. I was allowed to do one outpatient session a week at the Royal Infirmary, the major teaching hospital, but I could only admit any patient I saw there with the agreement of Dr Z. To do him justice I had little difficulty about this.

I had agreed to accept the Chair only if I were also provided with beds for non-tuberculosis chest disease. In due course 30 beds were allocated for this at a fourth hospital, the Northern General Hospital[#].

Dr Z was very senior, indeed he was due to retire in three years. I was relatively young (39) and had had no extensive responsibility for patients with tuberculosis – just 5 beds of my own at Hammersmith Hospital and some experience under Guy Scadding at the Brompton Hospital. Indeed my predecessor in Edinburgh, Professor Charles Cameron, had announced to the junior staff that he was going to be succeeded by "a young registrar from a municipal hospital in London". (Up to the introduction of the National Health Service in 1948 Hammersmith Hospital had been run by the London County Council, though the clinical staff had been provided by London University through the Postgraduate Medical School of London).

It was clear that it would not be easy to work with Dr Z. I had previously outlined how I thought things should ultimately be run. The Chest Clinic

---

[*] Referred to as "Dr E" in Isabel Gillard's account of tuberculosis treatment at that time in *Circe's Island* (2010).

[#] This hospital was demolished in 1996 to make way for a supermarket.

should come into the same organisation once Dr Z retired. Fortunately in due course Dr Z retired a year early. When we later discovered the haphazard way in which Dr Z used chemotherapy, which sometimes seemed to border on the psychopathic, I uncharitably wondered how many patients' lives were saved by his early retirement. This judgement may indeed have been uncharitable, a product of my relative youth and enthusiasm. It was early days in this form of chemotherapy. Our group was thinking and working continuously on the problem. Many other people, indeed probably most other people besides Dr Z, were using the drugs badly. As our knowledge and research accumulated, I tried as tactfully as I could to pass some of it on to Dr Z and his colleagues, but it had little effect. As we shall see, for a number of years we had similar problems with many other consultants throughout the UK and indeed abroad, so perhaps one should not be too beastly about Dr Z.

I am afraid I am probably prejudiced by some of the horrifying stories which patients told me or my colleagues. At that time the highest rate of tuberculosis was in young women. They often seemed to be particularly beautiful young women. Whether tuberculosis boosted their coefficient of pulchritude, or whether a high coefficient of pulchritude made them more susceptible to the disease, or whether having a high C of P made them more likely to be kissed by sputum positive young men, is a problem science has failed to resolve. Shortly before I moved to Edinburgh, a young woman from the city was referred for continuation of her treatment to the artificial pneumothorax clinic which I ran at the Brompton on behalf of Guy Scadding. She told me that when she had been in a young women's ward in Edinburgh, at that time run by Dr Z, he would come into the ward and tell them "You are all rosy apples, rotten at the core!" What a horrifying thing to say to girls in the grip of the disease that would probably kill at least half of them. And what an appalling canker to plant in their youthful self image.

There was worse. Another woman told a colleague that she had been in one of the Edinburgh hospitals, the Royal Victoria Hospital used for milder disease. Without any warning an ambulance arrived one day and took her off to the City Hospital where the advanced cases were cared for. The next time Dr Z came round to the City Hospital she asked him why she had been moved. He looked at her and said "You see, my dear, there is no post mortem room in the Royal Victoria Hospital". Do you think I am uncharitable when I label him as a psychopath? In the Chest Clinic the patients were treated like cattle, handled with unthinking discipline, mitigated only by the devoted efforts of the nurse in charge, the splendid health visitors and the social worker. These did their best to make things less awful.

When our group took over the Clinic two years later, we completely reorganised it. We made major efforts to change the atmosphere, to make every patient feel that we thought he or she was important to us, and was a person not a "case". To set an example, when a patient came into my consulting room I always stood up, welcomed him by name and shook his hand, as indeed I always had done with all my patients.

Early reorganisation, new consultants.

To return to early 1952. Before arriving in Edinburgh I had gathered that there was serious concern about tuberculosis among both the general public and the health service authorities. It therefore proved not too difficult to persuade the Regional Hospital Board to provide for two more consultants. Accordingly, within six months Norman Horne and Ian Grant were appointed.

Norman had been a lecturer with my predecessor Charles Cameron. Cameron was a difficult character, but he had an encyclopaedic knowledge of tuberculosis of all types. He had believed in doing everything personally, including putting plasters on tuberculous joints, taking X-rays and developing them himself. He had taught Norman all his skills – the hard way I gathered. Norman's skills were immensely useful to me, both practically and for my education. I was still new to orthopaedic tuberculosis, and not particularly adept with my hands. He proved an immensely able colleague, combining outstanding skills both as a clinician and as an administrator, contributing much to our joint research and pursuing projects of his own. Motivated by a strong religious faith, with his obvious sympathy and integrity he was excellent at handling colleagues, staff and patients. Forty years later we were still working happily together (on our book *Clinical Tuberculosis* for Third World* doctors). His own book on the chemotherapy of tuberculosis, written first with Ian Ross a few years after we started, reached at least seven editions. Norman soon established a national and then an international reputation.

Stanley Davidson had ensured that Ian Grant, as an outstandingly able young physician, had been thoroughly trained. This had included several junior posts at the Brompton Hospital. He proved to be a superb clinician, with the originality and drive to develop new services. He kept up a steady stream of important clinical research throughout his career. He had a strong and vigorous personality. The world for him was black and white, mostly more black than white – and if you were black you were pretty firmly black! He was not an easy colleague but he worked vigorously with us all in the

---

* Here and later, John uses this now outdated expression. The currently preferred or "politically correct" term is "developing countries".

initial difficult and exciting years and made many contributions to our joint efforts. In the early stages I had asked him to concentrate on non-tuberculosis chest disease, though he also dealt with tuberculosis, while the rest of us concentrated on the enormous tuberculosis problems.

The third consultant was Ian Ross. In 1952 he was already a consultant working partly at East Fortune Hospital in East Lothian and at Bangour Hospital in West Lothian. It was suggested by the Regional Health Board that he was more needed in Edinburgh. Like the other two doctors he had already the Membership of the Royal College of Physicians, at that time fairly rare in people who were dealing with tuberculosis, who tended to have the Diploma of Public Health. He proved quiet, intelligent and hardworking, and made many contributions, including running a very successful clinic for patients suffering from both diabetes and tuberculosis, then an important problem, until, in his early forties, he suffered a sudden coronary infarction. He was admitted to the Royal Infirmary but had a further severe attack while the house physician was actually taking his history. He fell back unconscious. One of the registrars was scrubbed up for a coronary catheterisation next door. Hurriedly summoned, he carried out open cardiac massage (it was before the days of external cardiac massage and "the kiss of life"). Ian very slowly recovered. He was unconscious for some days and then gradually regained his speech. But unfortunately the period of oxygen deprivation had deprived him of, perhaps, the top 1% of his IQ and he never recovered his previous brilliance, that subtle intellectual grasp and drive which had made him outstanding. He had to be content with relatively routine duties, and the back-up of his colleagues, until his retirement nearly twenty five years later. Two or three years after his retirement he had his final coronary returning from a rugby football match. But in his early years he made notable contributions to our work.

We four consultants worked very well together. We devised a federal scheme. Clearly I had to give primary attention to the overwhelming problems of tuberculosis. Accordingly we agreed that Ian Grant should take two thirds of the 30 beds for non-tuberculous chest disease at the Northern General Hospital and I would take a third. Ian would concentrate on the non-tuberculous side but would have some tuberculosis beds at the City Hospital, where Norman Horne would take over the rest of the 200 beds there for tuberculosis. Ian Ross would take the 100 or so tuberculosis beds at the Royal Victoria Hospital and I the 60 beds at Southfield Hospital, which included 20 children's beds. Later, to try to meet the desperate situation, we found some discarded old huts and rehabilitated them in the grounds of Southfield Hospital to produce another 20 beds. Norman looked after a further 20 beds in a small hospital unit for children's tuberculosis at Lasswade. We agreed to share the teaching and cooperate in research, of which more hereafter.

Within eighteen months of these consultants being appointed we were able to devise our overall organisation to meet the tuberculosis problem in Edinburgh. The NHS authorities were very happy that we should take the total responsibility for tuberculosis in Edinburgh from January 1954.

The tuberculosis outpatients services were almost all based at the Royal Victoria Dispensary, so for the first three months I took over responsibility for its reorganisation. Thereafter Jimmy Williamson joined us as Dr Z's replacement and I handed over the administration of the clinic to him. This included the responsibilities for contact tracing and cooperation in prevention with the Department of the Medical Officer of Health. I had, with my colleagues' approval, already made the principal changes, but Jimmy proved to be a superb administrator and organiser. He also did some excellent epidemiological research. A few years later, when we had got the tuberculosis situation under control, Jimmy felt he must find a fresh social and medical challenge and became one of the pioneers of geriatric medicine. He started in Edinburgh and then moved to Liverpool as one of the first Professors of Geriatrics in the UK. From there, in due course, he was invited back to Edinburgh to fill the newly founded Chair. A man of immense charm, wit, intelligence and ethical drive, I have boundless admiration for what he has achieved. My admiration is echoed in many countries.

Good organisation under good leaders is the basis of tuberculosis control. When we took over in 1954 there were some 400 patients on the waiting list. Many had been waiting many months. We had a basic 400 beds for tuberculosis within Edinburgh but we managed to increase these by a further 100 and were provided with a further 100 beds for Edinburgh patients at East Fortune Hospital in East Lothian. We divided the city roughly into five sections. Each of our teams took over the waiting list patients from one of the sections. We devised a priority formula which summarised the medical and social priorities for each patient according to the degree of illness, the risk to other members of the household, such as young children, and the social circumstances. Once a week each team sat down to review its list. Each patient was known personally to some member of the team. For priority patients we looked around the wards to see whom it was least risky to send home in order to create a bed. To our astonishment the waiting list of 400 was reduced to nil within a year and thereafter we were able steadily to reduce the number of beds needed for tuberculosis.

Cooperation with the Medical Office of Health

In the past there had been little love lost, and many personality clashes, between my predecessors and successive Edinburgh Medical Officers of Health. The Medical Officer of Health, in the pre-NHS period, had the major responsibility for tuberculosis, not only from the public health point of view but also from the clinical point of view. After the initiation of the NHS he ceased to have responsibility on the clinical side but maintained his responsibility for the preventive aspects. I went to see the then MOH, Dr Henry Seiler. I found him very charming and cooperative. We were easily able to agree that our primary objective must be the control of tuberculosis in the city. We must not fight about threats to each other's patches or about our mutual assignments of responsibility. We would manage things mutually without fighting. In practice this worked out very well.

To facilitate cooperation we held an informal lunch once a month. This was attended by the MOH and his assistant with primary responsibility for tuberculosis, by all the consultants of our group, by the doctor in charge of the Mass Radiography Unit and by a representative of the Edinburgh General Practitioners, as most of our patients came to us via GPs. No minutes were kept but the system worked very well. I tried to make sure that the MOH and his staff received every possible credit, if anything more than was due. In many fields I have found that this is the best possible way of getting maximum cooperation, and further cooperation in the next round. One should get no particular credit oneself for any presumed unselfishness in doing so. In due course the credit seems to have a habit of returning to base, having benefited others on the way. It's an ultimately selfish, but highly successful, technique.

With the MOH's staff, Jimmy Williamson and junior staff in training, every three months we reviewed all tuberculosis deaths. This was to ensure that none were due to deficiencies in the service. Some proved to be phoney. A GP might sign up a death as due to tuberculosis when the only evidence was that the patient had had tuberculosis many years before, with no evidence of recent activity and death clearly due to something else. Sometimes the resultant correspondence required considerable tact but hopefully might prove educational. We continued these reviews, of course with steadily diminishing lists of deaths, until my retirement in 1977.

In the early stages we had a large map in a special room in the clinic, with red pins for new notifications. This was so that we could pick out areas with many cases and, when necessary, have a drive to get as many local people as possible to attend a mobile miniature X-ray van. In this way we could pick up some cases early and hopefully identify local infectors.

In addition, in the same special room, we listed under each consultant all his patients out of hospital still with a positive sputum. These were known potential infectors. The list was a useful stimulus to each consultant to get his patients removed by cure. Later we just circulated the list every three months, instead of posting it up. If a patient appeared twice on the list, at an interval of three months, the consultant would be asked why the patient had not been made negative: at least two negative cultures were required before he was removed. All of us were therefore submitted to ongoing audit.

Southfield Hospital

My own wards were at Southfield Hospital. This had been a Victorian country house built by the then owner of the *Scotsman*. It stood in impressive grounds just south of Liberton, a former village* that had been incorporated into the southern margin of Edinburgh. The adult beds were in the main house. A light and airy 20 bed children's ward had been built in the grounds, as well as an X-ray department, physiotherapy department and bacteriology laboratory. The hospital had originally been provided for Sir Robert Philip by the Royal Victoria Hospital Tuberculosis Trust. At the same time the Trust had bought a farm across the road where Philip established the first tuberculosis-free herd of milk cows in Scotland, probably also the first in the UK.

When the NHS was established in 1948 the Trust handed the "Southfield Sanatorium and Colony" over to the NHS and the farm to the Chair of Tuberculosis. There I and my family spent eight happy years. We had a beautiful view over the farm to the Pentlands, a pleasant garden, and my main hospital was just across the road. But my non-tuberculous beds were on the other side of the city; and I had to go in to the University for lectures and meetings and to the Royal Infirmary for outpatients. Moreover I was almost daily called to one hospital or another in consultation. I sometimes had to visit five hospitals in the same day and hardly ever spent all day at Southfield. This load somewhat decreased as other consultants were appointed and established their reputations.

Personal responsibilities

These early days were enormously stimulating. There was a highly challenging job to be done. The tuberculosis problem was frightful, but the new drugs, if they proved as powerful as we hoped and if we could learn to use them properly, seemed to give exciting hopes for the future. My splendid new colleagues were enthusiastic and were not fixed in the previous treatment tramlines of bed rest, sanatorium treatment and artificial pneumothorax.

Perhaps arrogantly, I did not think much of the previous organisation. I tried to be tactful, especially as a non-Scot. While Dr Z was still there we could only reorganise the hospital service, but once he went we were virtually given *carte blanche*.

---

* It is believed the name derives from Leper's Toon, having been the site of a colony for lepers excluded from Edinburgh.

Tuberculosis is very much a social disease. In London I had worked closely with medical social workers and held a weekly "social round" in which every patient was considered from the social point of view. It was not difficult therefore to make our approach far more personal, friendly and constructive.

The research proved equally stimulating and paid off far more rapidly than any of us expected. We were able immediately to utilise our results in our routine practice. By using the insights gained from our research, our treatment results soon proved better than anyone had so far achieved anywhere in the world, indeed far better than we ourselves expected, though for a number of years our figures were not generally believed. Indeed we were accused of rigging them.

Equally, our meticulous attention to treatment detail and the endless trouble we took to see that all patients, including alcoholics, down-and-outs or psychopaths completed all treatment, resulted in an astonishingly rapid decrease in new cases – far more rapidly than we had expected and far more rapidly than has ever been recorded elsewhere in the world. This was partly because we inherited a very bad situation which was being poorly handled and was getting worse. We replaced it with good organisation in which we were able to apply our research results immediately to practice and apply them to all known tuberculosis patients in the city.

I had already done a good deal of postgraduate teaching in London. I now had much more of this. It further increased as our group became known, with many visitors and postgraduates from abroad. I also had to teach in the Diplomas of Public Health and of Tropical Medicine. For this I had to learn about the epidemiology of tuberculosis. Marc Daniels had taught me a good deal. Fortunately, in 1952 an excellent book was published on the epidemiology written by a Dr Clarke of Northern Ireland[*]. I had to give twenty lectures on tuberculosis to undergraduates, as well as a number on non-tuberculous chest disease. Edinburgh students were highly lectured at that time, often five lectures a day. I was later partly instrumental in greatly reducing their lecture burden. I also had to lecture in the biennial postgraduate course on internal medicine set up by the Edinburgh Postgraduate Board for Medicine.

For me personally it was a marvellously euphoric period. I was creating and running, with my colleagues, our own show. Although the problems we faced always seemed formidable at any one time, and I often felt impatient at delays in getting things done, every now and then one was able to look back and be pleased and surprised at what we had achieved. Also, as a bunch of

---

[*] Probably *Causes and prevention of tuberculosis* (1952) by Brice R. Clarke.

enthusiasts, we attracted very good junior staff, later from all over the UK. Teaching them was enormous fun. Of course it was very hard work, I was in my office soon after eight and never home before 7.15pm. We had dinner at 7.30. I usually read the paper till 8.30 or 8.45 and then worked till 10.45 – writing, preparing lectures or dictating letters on to a machine (at that time a sort of flimsy gramophone record). I read the medical journals over breakfast. When particularly pushed I started at 6am, occasionally 5.30am. In due course I found I could not reduce my sleep to six hours for any prolonged period without, after a week or two, getting very exhausted. I remember that, after a few desperate weeks of short sleep, I nearly fainted after giving a lecture at York. Later I cut sleep only intermittently or just before a holiday when I knew I could make it up.

It was a long week also. In those days an NHS "session" was supposed to be three and a half hours. A full-time consultant was expected to do eleven sessions a week (5½ days). In the first few years I reckoned that I did at least twelve clinical sessions a week for the NHS. Research, teaching, administration, reading and writing had to come on top of that. In later years my NHS load eased, as the tuberculosis load eased, my consultant colleagues took an increasing proportion of the work and we somewhat increased our staff. In the early years my main weekly round on adult tuberculosis patients was on Saturday mornings, indeed I worked on Saturday mornings until retirement. I tried always to take Saturday and Sunday afternoons off to be with the family, but I usually worked in these evenings unless we had a social engagement. I mostly managed Sunday morning free but quite often had to go and advise on one or more clinical problems either in my own wards or in consultation at another hospital. It was a hectic life but enormously stimulating. Fortunately Eileen was marvellously understanding and supportive and I spent every moment of my limited spare time, and all my holidays, with her and our marvellous children.

Tributes to colleagues

I should make it clear that my colleagues contributed at least as much as I did in pioneering the methods of tuberculosis control which proved so outstandingly successful. We five consultants all ran our own clinical units, but, as far as tuberculosis was concerned, we made joint decisions by consensus. I remember us sitting together one day and saying it would probably take twenty years. To our astonishment the job was largely done in eight from the start of 1952 or in six if it is dated from our taking on the complete responsibility in 1954 when Dr Z retired.

Nor must I leave this early clinical period without paying a tribute to three outstanding women who made so much difference to the lives of our patients. You must remember that at that time tuberculosis was a grim disease. Patients were terrified of it and so were their families. Diagnosis was a disastrous blow. Up to then half the patients with pulmonary tuberculosis would die of it. There was enormous need for psychological and social support. In Edinburgh in the past this support had too often been lacking. I had the impression that patients had been treated as diseased bodies – to be disciplined, to obey orders and to be processed firmly through the system, such as it was. A good matron can make an enormous difference to both staff and patients. She can create among her nursing staff a caring atmosphere with real concern and support for the patients. She can inspire them with her own sense of the rewarding value of their work. She must be a good organiser, but a considerate boss. She has to handle doctors, senior and junior, with tact and subtle firmness. She has to make sure that they take nursing realities into serious consideration.

In my experience the above combination of talents is rare. But Miss Archibald, the Matron at Southfield through most of my time there, possessed them to the full. She was a quiet, middle-aged, unruffled woman who did a wonderful job with the minimum of fuss. I usually asked the most senior of my juniors to handle the medical administration, but in practice most of the administration, including the management of the large gardens and grounds, was by Miss Archibald.

An example of her concern and her skills, was Mr X. He was in his fifties and deaf and dumb. He was picked up in one of the Edinburgh lodging houses (always with a high tuberculosis rate: we tried to survey the lodgers every six months) with advanced tuberculosis. He had only done a total of nine months work in his fifty odd years. He was admitted filthy and, literally, lousy. But as he improved with treatment it was realised that he was basically intelligent. He rapidly picked up card and other games the men played, and he usually won. He seemed to have an excellent personality. Matron and the occupational therapist tried him at different sorts of work (I can't remember whether he was literate, but probably he was not). Eventually they found that he loved helping the gardeners; like most tuberculosis hospitals and sanatoria we had extensive vegetable gardens. He turned out to have green fingers and he obviously adored the work.

But, with his handicaps and background, it was quite another thing to find him a job. For months the social workers and others tried. It was Matron who finally found him a gardening job in a Church of Scotland home in the west. Away he went, cured and able to lead a real life at last. From time to time he came back to visit us. He appeared, dressed in a smart blue suit, self-confident, a man with a purpose in life at last – salvaged by developing tuberculosis!

A second fine woman was the Senior Social Worker, at that time still known as "Lady Almoner". Miss Peggy Wood must then have been in her fifties. Like many of the early Almoners she was obviously from the upper middle classes. With gray hair and fine features she looked an aristocrat. She was confident, practical and down-to-earth. Superficially she had little of the sentimental, but underneath she had all the ethical drive. For years she had done her splendid best to mitigate the social horrors of the disease, often at least as grim as the physical. In this, I suspect, she had had relatively little positive encouragement or help from an unimaginative medical staff. Many of our patients came from the still desperately grim slums of Edinburgh, with all the problems of poverty, alcoholism, family disruption and the social stigma of the disease. Later, when our group took over the whole problem, I did many home visits and saw how dreadful things were. Of course Miss Wood greatly welcomed our intense interest in the social side. Her own vast experience of the shattering social effects of the disease and of the problems of the local scene, together with her knowledge of the best local sources of help, enabled us often to improve the lives of patients and their families greatly, quite apart from curing their disease. Indeed for some people the disease proved a bit of good fortune, as they were helped to cope with social problems which they would never have solved on their own.

In praising Miss Wood I should at the same time pay a tribute to the large number of other medical social workers with whom I collaborated over more than thirty years. They have all been wonderful. It has been a joy to work with them. And without exception they have been such nice people. I have often wondered whether it is because medical social work attracts only exceptionally nice people, or whether it is that medical social work makes them exceptionally nice.

My third tribute is to the wonderful Miss Euphemia Liston, the Chief Nurse at the Royal Victoria Dispensary. Dispensaries were, I believe, a nineteenth century invention, or even an eighteenth. They were originally places supported by charity, where public spirited physicians provided free diagnosis and treatment for the sick poor. Outdated by the coming of the NHS one of these in Edinburgh, long used for undergraduate teaching, ultimately became one of the elements of the new University Department of General Practice – the first in the UK.

The Royal Victoria Dispensary was founded by Sir Robert Philip, only six years after Koch's discovery of the tubercle bacillus in 1882, as a centre not only for dealing with the tuberculous patient himself but also a centre for screening the family of patients with early or more treatable disease and for trying to minimise further spread of the infection. As we have seen the original Dispensary was in two rooms over a shop on the Mound. Sometime in the 1920s or before, Philip needed more space and acquired a disused church in, appropriately enough, Spittal Street (though of course "Spittal" is

"Hospital"). This was metamorphosed quite appropriately. In our day the interior was excellently redecorated by the administration. Over the years many young doctors working with us remarked that it was far the most pleasant and well run outpatient clinic in which they had ever worked, a tribute to our 1952 reorganisation.

Philip was obviously a great man. I am sure that, in terms of the time, he was a humane man. But I suspect that, also in terms of the time, for highly educated professional men, making their living out of private practice and generously giving time, unpaid, to hospital or dispensary practice, the sick poor were a slightly different species. "They don't feel pain like we do" etc.

When Miss Liston first came to the Royal Victorian Dispensary, I suspect in the 1930s, one of the small rooms contained pathological specimens in glass jars. These were used by Philip in his teaching. The *pièce de résistance* was a large glass jar containing a vertical section through a dead boy used to demonstrate the tuberculous lesions distributed throughout his body. It was in this room that stretcher patients were left to await their turn to see the doctor! One of the first of Miss Liston's innumerable humane initiatives was to make a curtain to hide the horrific jar from the sad, apprehensive eyes of the sick.

During the tuberculosis epidemic of the war and post-war years, Miss Liston carried much of the burden. It was she who took the histories from the patients, she who listed the contacts, she who comforted and explained, she who did much of the organisation. And all this in a medical atmosphere still dominated, I suspect, by the attitude of doctors giving routine and objective services to the sick poor, still a slightly different species.

When I first knew her Miss Liston must have been well into her fifties. She was a big, red-faced, buxom, upright woman, arms literally and/or metaphorically akimbo. Clearly directional, she gave her orders in a firm loud voice: very much the Queen Bee in her own particular hive. With this character, having run the place for so long, having been the linchpin of all the better things that happened there, it would not have been surprising if she had greatly resented my arrival in 1954 to reorganise the clinic. This included a decision that the doctors should take the histories themselves; an appointment system for the patients instead of endless waiting; evening clinics for working patients; the whole system turned upside down.

But I think Miss Liston quickly saw that we really cared what happened to patients, that we were prepared to take trouble to get things right and that we enormously appreciated her own contribution. She threw herself into the reorganisation with astonishing and creditable enthusiasm. She continued equally enthusiastically until her retirement a number of years later. When she did retire, we tried hard but unsuccessfully to get her a national award. She at least deserved an MBE, much more so than many a slick entertainer.

I must also pay a tribute to another fine group of women, the Health Visitors attached to the clinic. When, in the early stages, for lack of beds we had to start treating many patients at home, the Health Visitor would visit regularly to make sure all went well; for new patients the consultant usually went with her on the first occasion. She also checked on treatment and problems arising after the patient was discharged from hospital. It was she who discovered and listed the home contacts and made sure they came up for examination. She tended to know most about the home background. In our "social sessions" on the problems of our hospital patients we always had a Health Visitor present; she liaised with her relevant colleague about social problems and decisions. The Health Visitors also supervised home treatment. We would never have been so successful in completing treatment on almost every patient, including alcoholics, tramps, psychopaths etc, without the devoted work of these wonderful women.

Administrators are the classical whipping boys of doctors – sometimes because doctors have to blame someone for their own deficiencies. Bear with me while I add one more member to my pantheon. Just as I came to Edinburgh, Alec Welstead was appointed Secretary to the Group which included all the tuberculosis hospitals and the Royal Victorian Dispensary. He had had tuberculosis himself and so was sympathetic to what we were trying to do. Alec was a tall, quietly effective man. He was no bureaucrat sitting on his bottom in an office. He was always out seeing people, hearing about their problems and trying to help, a competent, effective catalyst to action. When we went to him with a difficulty, instead of (like some administrators) listing all the impossibilities, it was always "Let's see how we can best manage it" and, however difficult, he usually succeeded.

I was on two hospital Boards of Management, Alec's Group and the Northern Hospitals Board (where we had our non-tuberculosis beds at first). The contrast was extraordinary. I am sure it was how the respective Secretaries put the business to their Boards. In Alec's Board we only considered important matters and decided by consensus, usually on Alec's tactful lead. The other Board's Secretary was a former local authority bureaucrat. As every smallest detail was put to the Board, and with no lead at all, the Board argued lengthily over every little item and often only made a decision by a formal vote. Endless discussion on nonsense and little on really important issues. It was the only administrative committee in which from time to time, I could not conceal my frustration and even fury. In 1960 I was glad to move my non-tuberculosis beds to the City Hospital, under Alec, and resign from the Northern Board. Alec was by far the most outstanding hospital administrator I met during my career.

When, in 1954, we inherited large numbers of patients whose bacilli, through previous mistaken treatment, had become resistant to the standard drugs, we had to ask the Board for very large sums of money for the few and very expensive reserve drugs as they became available. With Alec's support they accepted my hope that this would prove money well spent, not only in giving the patients a chance of cure but in preventing the spread of particularly dangerous types of bacilli. We were able in due course to demonstrate that it had paid off. Moreover, partly as a result, large numbers of beds could be released for other purposes, mainly geriatrics, a major long-term financial saving.

Alec had all the administrative problems of our tuberculosis reorganisation, including (later) the 1958 mass radiography campaign in which over 80% of the adult population of Edinburgh were X-rayed within three months. Also, as tuberculosis decreased, he arranged the move of my Unit to a new University Department in the City Hospital, which he conjured and adapted out of existing buildings on a minimal budget. As tuberculosis decreased, he arranged the tricky metamorphosis of many of the tuberculosis beds to geriatrics. All this he achieved in the most friendly, painless, modest and economical way. I never felt he received enough credit for his quiet but effective efforts. He later became Secretary of the Borders Health Board.

Tuberculosis Research

At the beginning of 1952, a new anti-tuberculosis drug, isoniazid, appeared on the scene. This had been evolved more or less simultaneously in Germany and the USA. It seemed very promising. The dose was small; it did not have to be injected; it could be swallowed as a pill. It seemed to have few toxic effects on the patient. Moreover it was cheap.

In 1952 we participated in a further cooperative MRC controlled trial which demonstrated that isoniazid was highly effective and fulfilled all its early promise, though, as with other drugs, the tubercle bacilli soon became resistant to it unless effectively combined with streptomycin and/or PAS. One of the trials showed that if streptomycin injections were given twice a week, with daily isoniazid, some 15% of patients would develop first isoniazid and later streptomycin resistance – it took a long time for this danger to be recognised outside the UK.

Early reports from the USA had shown that patients gained weight so rapidly, and felt so euphoric, that it was suspected that these effects might be directly due to the drug and not merely secondary to its effect on the tubercle bacillus. We decided to do a double blind controlled switch-over trial on ourselves. We took either isoniazid or a placebo, ignorant of which we were receiving. We recorded our moods and how we slept. We were weighed weekly with our backs to the scales so that knowledge of our weight would not influence our food intake. After a number of weeks, without knowing it, the isoniazid group were switched to placebo, and vice versa.

We showed that there was no direct effect. Weight variation was similar on isoniazid or placebo. I remember one of my colleagues who thought isoniazid was "super"; he felt absolutely marvellous. It turned out that he was on placebo at the time! This shows how important it is to design such trials with great care.

In order to coordinate and record all this work, and the detailed case studies which I shall describe later, we needed more pairs of hands (and brains). For me one of the attractions of Edinburgh for potential research in tuberculosis, as well as being a relatively self-contained epidemiological entity of some half million population, was the potential of the Royal Victoria Hospital Tuberculosis Trust. This Trust controlled, for that time, quite a large sum of money. It had originally been raised, through Robert Philip's initiative, to finance Southfield as a professorial unit in tuberculosis and also Philip's salary as professor. When the NHS started in 1948 the Trust handed over Southfield and no longer had to pay its running costs. The university had long since taken over the professorial salary. The Trust money was now allocated for welfare payments to patients with tuberculosis and for research. But no-one had used anything much of the research money. The Trust proved eager to do so. We soon had a Clinical Research Fellow, Derrick Turnbull (later to become a consultant in Manchester) and a Bacteriological Research Fellow, Sheila Stewart, together with adequate sums for running costs and technical help. Sheila's laboratory was initially established at Southfield later moving to the City Hospital when my unit was transferred there in 1960.

These facilities, together with the meticulous and devoted work of Archie Wallace, in charge of the main tuberculosis laboratory at the City Hospital, enabled us not only to conduct our share of the MRC trials but also later to initiate, through the Tuberculosis Society of Scotland (now the Scottish Thoracic Society), a series of Scottish collaborative controlled trials. The facilities also enabled us to make our most important contributions, the detailed study of the causes of failure of treatment. As we shall see, these causes turned out to be avoidable. We were soon able in our own practice to avoid these errors, but unfortunately, it took a good many years to persuade others. Indeed the errors still persist in many parts of the world, particularly in Asia.

I will deal with the Scottish controlled trials first as they are quite straightforward. I cannot remember whether the Scottish Society already had a Research Committee or whether we helped to initiate it. If it had existed I don't think it had done very much. As we gained confidence in the effectiveness of chemotherapy it seemed to us, certainly to me, that the classical bed rest, even for patients with minor X-ray lesions, with a negative sputum and few symptoms, might not really be necessary. What a difference for such patients if they could continue their normal working lives, apart from taking chemotherapy, instead of having to lie on their backs, in or out of hospital, for months and months.

With some difficulty, as the concept was at that time so revolutionary, we persuaded our colleagues throughout Scotland that the trial was ethical, but of course it needed even more effort to ensure that they actually entered patients to the trial. Patients were then allocated at random either to having at least three months' bed rest plus chemotherapy, the normal practice at the time, or to continue with their normal lives apart from taking chemotherapy, which most specialists at that time would have regarded as very risky. A panel of us read the X-rays "blind" (without knowing to which group the patient belonged) at weekly sessions, and other relevant data were recorded. Of course, as everyone now knows, the patients leading normal lives were as successfully cured as the bed rest group, a dramatically revolutionary conclusion at that time.

The British MRC, about the same time, were conducting, with the Indian MRC, their trial in Madras, comparing hospital or sanatorium treatment with treatment at home – usually in slum conditions. But they were trying to give their patients as much bed rest as possible at home. Our trial was the first in the world where patients were deliberately continuing their normal lives.

With the extensive X-raying of the population by Mass Miniature Radiography carried out at that time, many patients were found at X-ray to have doubtfully active lesions. These were usually watched carefully with regular repeated X-rays to pick up clear signs of activity needing treatment and regular sputum examinations. We initiated a controlled trial comparing different periods of preventive chemotherapy with the normal watching procedure. We found that, with the longer periods of treatment, we could prevent all development of overt disease. The lesser periods were more effective than no treatment but some patients did develop active disease. However these then recovered with the new standard treatment.

In 1958 some Americans discovered that patients varied in the rate at which their bodies broke down and disposed of isoniazid. They suggested that the "rapid metabolisers", getting rid of their drug more quickly, would need a higher dose. All patients should therefore have their drug blood levels checked and the dose adjusted appropriately. Of course this appealed to "high-tech" Americans – lots of expensive laboratory work. As the British already gave doses a third lower than the Americans, and as I was pretty sure that I had had no failures in patients with initially sensitive organisms, I analysed my Edinburgh patients to date. The rate at which their sputa had become negative fell on an almost embarrassingly even downward curve. All (100%) had become negative by ten months of treatment. I wrote a letter to the widely read *American Review of Tuberculosis* (now the *American Review of Respiratory Diseases*), including the curve and giving details of the patients and their treatment. Many of them of course had far advanced disease. I think this killed the new American concept internationally, but more slowly in the USA. It was also the first publication in the world to claim 100% success in the treatment of pulmonary tuberculosis.

To prove the point about the importance of drug levels we later did a collaborative controlled trial in Scotland, through the Tuberculosis Society of Scotland. We randomised patients into receiving either high or low doses of isoniazid and measured their blood levels. We showed that there was nothing to be gained by higher doses.

In the 1950s some doctors had used corticosteroid drugs (cortisone etc) to help control allergic reactions to anti-tuberculosis chemotherapy. They had been surprised to see, in some of these patients, rapid clearing of the X-rays. They suggested that these drugs might be of value in routine treatment. This seemed somewhat paradoxical, as corticosteroid drugs were known to decrease the effectiveness of the body's defences. Indeed the development of tuberculosis was a well known risk in patients on long term treatment with these drugs. Results from many countries, none of them controlled trials, were confusing. Some reported much improvement, some the reverse.

On the basis of our own detailed studies of failures, we suspected that the deterioration had occurred in patients whose bacilli, owing to mistaken treatment, had become resistant to the drugs being used and that deterioration would not occur if the corticosteroids were covered by effective chemotherapy. It seemed worthwhile conducting a proper controlled trial through the Tuberculosis Society of Scotland. This trial was duly launched, coordinated and reported by Norman Horne. It was the world's first such trial. It showed that the X-rays did clear more rapidly in the corticosteroid patients, who received three months of the drug. Of course they, and the control group, received full chemotherapy and had initially sensitive bacilli. The patients felt very much better more quickly than the controls and gained weight more rapidly. But, in the point crucial to ultimate cure, the rate at which the sputum became negative, there was no difference between the two groups. Nevertheless we had hoped that the corticosteroids might prevent longterm damage and scarring of the lungs. But at twelve months there was no difference between the X-rays of the two groups; the corticosteroids had speeded up initial clearance but had had no longterm benefit. Nor had the corticosteroids done any damage, confirming our suspicion that deterioration reported by others was probably due to unappreciated drug resistance.

All these were useful trials, and all of them were world "firsts". They required initial push and meticulous control, but no great intellectual effort. Our studies on failure were much more intellectually challenging, and ultimately more important in preventing the failures which were still widespread and regarded by most specialists as inevitable in handling a ruthless and fatal disease.

At that time, understandably, specialists tended to think of tuberculosis of the lung in terms of its classical pathology, especially as much of the pathology could be revealed by X-rays. It was known, for instance, that if a patient was left after treatment, with an open cavity (hole) showing in the X-ray, he only had a 20% chance of still being alive in five years. But it seemed to us that X-rays and pathology were like the shadows on the wall in Plato's cave. What was really important was what the enemy, the tubercle bacillus, was doing in the patient's body. It was he that had to be dealt with, not the shadows, though the shadows might follow, and to some extent reflect, his activities.

As an aside, I may say that at one stage we did a study (unpublished) to see whether, from the X-rays, we could guess in detail what the pathology of the lung would be. We did this on patients who were about to have their lesions removed by surgery. (Much surgery was at that time done in order to prevent relapse. We later, as others did, showed it to be unnecessary). Interestingly, if we only saw a single X-ray of the patient, with no history of his treatment or progress, our guesses were often mistaken. But if we had all the details of treatment and bacteriology, and a row of successive X-rays, our guesses of the detailed pathology usually proved remarkably accurate.

For our studies of failure we had a sadly rich field. We had already learnt a lot, and were still learning, but most specialists still regarded failures as inevitable and had little insight into what they were doing wrong. We therefore inherited many patients who, even by our standards at that early stage, had received bad chemotherapy, one drug at a time, drugs in combinations we had found unreliable, or adding a new drug to a combination when the patient started deteriorating. We thought it likely that he would only deteriorate if his bacilli had become resistant to *all* the drugs being used; adding a new drug was equivalent to giving the drug alone, with the inevitable development of resistance to that drug also. This is, even now, sadly a common error in some countries.

At weekly sessions we considered these patients in great detail with our group of physicians, Research Fellows and bacteriologists. We kept detailed records. Initially we considered other possible causes of failure. For instance failure of the patient to absorb the drug or failure of the drug to penetrate the actual lairs where the bacillus lurked, but evidence of various kinds made these explanations improbable.

At an early stage we learnt that failure of outpatients to *take* the drug was a potential cause of failure. Patients were so terrified of the disease that we initially thought that every patient would be obsessional in swallowing his lifeline. But of course as one begins to feel better the disease may begin to lose its terrors. The patient may have higher priorities than taking his medicine. This is now recognised as a major problem worldwide. One of my colleagues, Jimmy Simpson, who sadly died from a coronary attack in his forties, developed a test for PAS in the urine of patients. He then went on to check the urine samples of a hundred patients supposed to be continuing their drugs after discharge from hospital. Twenty five of the first hundred tested were negative. Thereafter all outpatients on treatment had their urine tested as a routine when they attended. We never told them what we were doing and I only knew two patients out of many hundreds who guessed. If we had a negative test we specially emphasised to the patient the importance of drug taking and got him back early for checking. If his urine was repeatedly negative we readmitted him to complete assured treatment. We owed it to him. We also owed it to others whom he might infect if he lapsed.

Even in the MRC trials there had been a small percentage of failure with the best drug combinations. But the MRC had allowed up to two weeks' other chemotherapy before admission to their trials and we found, by detailed studies that, with bad chemotherapy, resistance could be well on the way by then.

Our studies showed that minor errors in treatment, a drug omitted for a week or two, a single drug for a week or two, one drug given daily and a second intermittently, a weaker combination (eg PAS + isoniazid without streptomycin), all could give rise to failure. The bacilli became resistant first to one drug and then, losing that drug's cover, to the second drug etc.

Research in the laboratory had shown that in any population of bacilli a very small proportion were naturally resistant to any one drug ("resistant mutants"). If a drug was given alone, the sensitive majority was inhibited but, if the patient's defences were not strong, the few naturally resistant bacilli would be at an advantage and could grow up and replace the sensitive populations. The chances of mutants being simultaneously resistant to two or three drugs were infinitesimal. If two drugs were given each would suppress the few mutants resistant to the other.

Unfortunately we soon learnt, as did others, that patients with drug resistance resulting from poor treatment could infect others with their resistant bacilli – which we came to call "primary" as opposed to "acquired" resistance. In practice we found that "primary" resistance was usually to only one drug, but in the early days, when it was routine practice to start treatment with two drugs, Norman Horne and Ian Grant each encountered one patient, who later proved to have been infected with a bacillus resistant to one of the drugs, who then developed resistance to the second drug. As resistance tests took some weeks one had to start treatment without knowing whether the bacilli were fully sensitive. We therefore began, in the early 1950s, to start all patients on at least three drugs until we knew they had been infected with fully sensitive bacilli. If the bacilli proved resistant to one of the drugs, there was still a pair which would be effective in preventing any further resistance developing. To our astonishment we then found we were achieving cure in virtually 100% of new patients. We could salvage even patients admitted almost moribund by adjusting their plasma electrolytes (often hypokalaemia[*] in such patients) or by adding high doses of corticosteroids to control toxicity until the chemotherapy could take effect.

Some people thought that low degrees of drug resistance might not be of great importance. It might be coped with by increasing the dose of the drug. To examine this point we had to do a very careful and complex exercise in surveying the detailed records of patients who had failed treatment. It was very difficult for me to clear time for it. I could only spare time after dinner in the evening, not the best time of day for intellectual effort. Our bacteriological Research Fellow Sheila Stewart, kept all the vast details about the patients. She knew what each analysis session was going to be like and usually had a couple of hours' sleep in the afternoon beforehand! I had to substitute wifely pints of black coffee. Somehow we managed ultimately to crystallise ten years' work into a definitive paper[#].

Our studies on these patients also showed that a number who had had unsatisfactory chemotherapy behaved as if their bacilli were resistant to streptomycin, but the standard MRC test reported them as sensitive. We felt sure that it was the tests that were inadequate. Sheila Stewart and Archie Wallace devised a test which confirmed this and conformed with clinical data. The MRC revised their method appropriately. All this taught us that, with meticulous bacteriology and meticulous adherence to good drug combinations established by careful controlled trials, with no fiddling about because of minor side effects or panic about slowness of progress, all new patients with pulmonary tuberculosis, however ill, could be cured.

In 1958, as mentioned above when discussing isoniazid and dose, I had published in a letter to the *American Review of Tuberculosis*[¥], my own early

---

[*] Low potassium in the blood.

[#] Stewart SM, Crofton JW. The clinical significance of low degrees of drug resistance in pulmonary tuberculosis. *American Review of Respiratory Diseases* 1964; <u>89</u>: 811-829

[¥] Crofton J. "Sputum conversion" and the metabolism of isoniazid. *American Review of Tuberculosis* 1958; <u>77</u>: 869-871 series with 100% success in patients with initially sensitive bacilli. In the same year we published our combined results[*] These were similar. But in addition we had analysed relapse rates in pulmonary tuberculosis after differing periods of chemotherapy. In the early stages we had expected many relapses in this notoriously relapsing disease. Naturally we had given longer treatment to patients with more advanced disease. We found 22% relapses after 0-6 months' treatment, 7% after 6-12 months', 1% after 12-18 months' and none in those receiving more than 18 months' treatment, though these were far the worst cases. These findings were largely confirmed by further study by the MRC and it came to be generally accepted that a minimum of 18 months' chemotherapy, with the drugs then available, should be the standard, at least for severe cases. A number of years later, after the introduction of rifampicin, it was found that, with this powerful drug added to the others, effective treatment could be reduced to 6 months. The effectiveness of the standard treatment that we had introduced in Edinburgh for the standard period which emerged from our research in preventing relapse was later shown by a large scale analysis of the Edinburgh cases by Norman Horne.[#]

To prevent the expected relapses, we, as many others, at first asked the surgeons, after the patient's sputum had become negative, to remove remaining diseased parts. Our research group, Sheila Stewart and Derrick Turnbull, did multiple cultures from these diseased lungs. As there was so much demand for surgery, patients often had to spend many months, first to get their disease under initial control with chemotherapy, then to wait, still under chemotherapy, for their turn for surgery. In my 1960 Marc Daniels Memorial Lecture at the Royal College of Physicians of London I put the clinical and research results together: the relapse rates closely corresponded to the proportion of patients with positive lung cultures after varying periods of chemotherapy.[¥]

Convincing Others

Most people were not getting as good results – mainly because they were still committing the errors that our research had taught us to avoid – and they could not believe our results.

---

[*] Ross JD, Horne NW, Grant IWB, Crofton JW. Hospital treatment of pulmonary tuberculosis. *British Medical Journal* 1958; 1: 237-242

[#] Pearce SJ, Horne NW. Follow-up of patients with pulmonary tuberculosis adequately treated by chemotherapy. Is this really necessary? *Lancet* 1974; 2: 641-3

[¥] Crofton J. Tuberculosis Undefeated. *British Medical Journal* 1960; 2: 679

Sri Lanka

My first opportunity to affect treatment abroad was in Sri Lanka (then Ceylon). In 1954 there was an enthusiastic and influential Minister of Health who had decided that tuberculosis was a major problem in his country. I was asked to accompany a London thoracic surgeon, Donald Barlow, to advise. The government had also asked for the assistance of WHO[*] who sent Professor Robert Neubauer of Ljubljana in Yugoslavia. We were asked to write a White Paper on tuberculosis for the Ceylon Government. We worked desperately hard for six weeks with the help of an excellent local physician, John Wilson. (In spite of his name he was a Tamil from Jaffna in the north of Ceylon and was also a Christian Methodist. I had already taught him in the UK while in London.).

Although at that time our research in Edinburgh was in the fairly early stages, as a result of the White Paper six chest physicians from Ceylon were subsequently sent to spend a year in our Department, when our research was more advanced. With John Wilson, backed by an enthusiastic Minister, and with appropriate local adaptations, a national programme was developed which successfully utilised the relevant Edinburgh techniques.

Canada and USA 1955

In 1955 I was asked to speak on tuberculosis at a joint meeting of the British and Canadian Medical Associations in Toronto. I was able to report my personal results so far, with 100% cure in new cases of pulmonary tuberculosis and no relapses. Unfortunately I was so busy at the time I did not publish this paper; it only appeared in abstract. However it made quite an impact in the local press and was mentioned in the Edinburgh newspapers. I remember being a little overwhelmed at the size of the audience which I addressed in a hall which took fifteen hundred. I was preceded by speakers on other antibiotic subjects of more interest to GPs. A number left when I started speaking on tuberculosis, but I still had a formidable audience.

I then crossed into the USA and lectured in Minnesota, Los Angeles, San Francisco, Denver and New York. At that time there was great interest in tuberculosis in USA. I had many discussions and arguments and made many friends but I am not sure that I had any very major influence on methods of treatment which remained extremely patchy in the USA for a number of years.

---

[*] World Health Organisation

Turkey and Yugoslavia 1956

In 1956 I visited Turkey and Yugoslavia on a British Council lecture tour. Of course my lectures and discussions outlined the results we were already achieving and described how to avoid failures. Although the trip to Turkey, which included Istanbul, Ankara and Izmir was a very interesting one, I am not quite sure how big an impact I made on their future practice. Several further visits to Turkey to attend conferences did not suggest dramatic progress, though in the 1970s Mustafa Artvinli, a lecturer from Ankara, spent a year with us. He later went back to be a professor and must have spread good practice.

In Yugoslavia I was hosted by Robert Neubauer with whom I had worked so happily in Sri Lanka in 1954. Robert, who by that time knew me well, readily accepted our work. I lectured in Belgrade, Zagreb and Sarajevo, as well as Ljubljana. I later gathered that, with the tragic Balkan capacity for schism, Yugoslavia chest physicians split into "Croftonites" and "Anti-Croftonites" and continued an intellectual civil war for a number of years. Of course at that time Yugoslavia was firmly and ruthlessly united politically under Tito's eccentric form of communism. I had insufficient knowledge, or insight, to know whether the professional split was along ethnic lines. Perhaps, because Robert Neubauer, a Slovene, backed my claims, Serbs may have rejected them.

India

In 1957 I had a brief visit to India, primarily to attend the International Union against Tuberculosis's World Conference in New Delhi where I chaired a session. However I only had a minor part in the programme and I think made little impact. I went on to give lectures in Delhi, Madras and Bombay. I doubt whether I affected practice to any extent.

Norway and Sweden

Also in 1957 I visited Scandinavia. I think Norway had already picked up our ideas through a visit to our Unit by Hans Jacob Ustvedt, one of the professors of medicine in Oslo, who had achieved high prestige in tuberculosis by writing an influential book, as well as by his outstanding personality and intelligence. In fact Hans Jacob had primarily invited me to lecture to the Norwegian Medical Society on the techniques of controlled trials. So my visit, and discussions about tuberculosis, may only have re-emphasised what they were already doing. That year I was also asked to lecture to the Swedish Medical Society at their meeting in Gothenburg and visited Stockholm. I think the Swedes were fairly rapidly influenced by what we were doing.

USSR

Finally in 1957 I was also, with three or four other British, invited to attend an all-union tuberculosis conference in Moscow. Stalin had only recently died and this was the first time they had been allowed to invite foreigners. Though they listened to us politely I doubt I made much impact.

Finland

The following year another visit, to Finland, had a much more successful outcome. I had been invited by their national Medical Association, after a visit by a senior Finnish specialist, Dr Salmonkalio, to our Department. In 1958 tuberculosis was still an enormous problem in Finland, after the deprivations of the War.

At that time few Finns spoke English. I had prepared my slides in Finnish, through the courtesy of my Finnish hosts, and they laid on a sentence by sentence interpretation. I think the content of the lecture, together with my comments on individual problem patients, convinced my hosts and revolutionized their treatment. The lecture was translated into Finnish and published in their principal medical journal. Many years later, in the 1980s, I was invited back to participate in the Jubilee of the Finnish Tuberculosis Association and was formally presented with a medal. I was even more flattered, at the preceding scientific meeting, to be passed a note by an elderly specialist who had been at my original lecture thirty years before. The note said "You came to us like Lutherus!"

Germany

In 1959 I was asked to lecture at the main tuberculosis research institute at Borstel near Hamburg in West Germany. The Director, and most of the large audience, clearly did not really believe our results or my arguments. In subsequent years I noticed that the Director often seemed to get hold of the wrong end of the stick about a number of relevant matters. He was very influential in Germany and this is probably why things took so long to come right there. There seemed to be only one member of the audience, later a professor in Berlin, who was really impressed by what I said, and it took him a long time to persuade his colleagues to change their unsatisfactory practices.

Retrospectively I have a certain sense of guilt over this. After my visit to Borstel I was asked to become a member of the Scientific Council of the Research Institute. I was subsequently asked to attend several meetings of the Council but failed to do so. This was partly due to the difficulty of getting away for several days from my very hectic responsibilities in Edinburgh, and partly because it was not clear whether they would pay my expenses – and European flights were indeed expensive. I now feel ashamed about this. If I had attended regularly, could I have altered their thinking and so saved a lot of unnecessary suffering and death in Germany? Many years later my attention was drawn to an article in a German journal advocating the treatment of tuberculous patients with mares' milk! These were poor people whose tubercle bacilli had been made drug resistant by bad treatment. Some doctors obviously had no idea how to prevent this happening or how to cope with it when it did.

Poland and Czechoslovakia

In 1960 a lecture tour in Poland and Czechoslovakia under the auspices of the British Council was much more satisfactory. Both countries then had enormous postwar tuberculosis problems. In Poland I remember being horrified by an entire hospital given up to children with tuberculous meningitis, which, before the introduction of chemotherapy, was always fatal. However my principal host, Professor Marion Zierski of Lodz, was also the chief postgraduate teacher of chemotherapy. Under the communists all chest physicians had to come back for training every five years, so he had plenty of opportunity of spreading the good practice he had acquired. Indeed he subsequently organised excellent controlled trials in Poland and established a high reputation internationally. He had previously visited our Department in Edinburgh and this is probably why I was invited. We have remained close personal and professional friends ever since my visit.

I remember that one lecture to a large audience in the beautiful mediaeval town of Cracow was followed by no less than three hours of discussion! What I said may have been controversial – claiming 100% cure as a reasonable objective – but it obviously aroused not only argument but interest.

I went on to Prague where, with Noel Rist of the Pasteur Institute in Paris, I lectured to their relevant national society and visited a number of centres elsewhere. Noel Rist, with another bacteriologist, Georges Canetti, also of the Pasteur Institute in Paris (both of whom had visited us in Edinburgh), were our only influential international supporters at that time. Our combined impact certainly revolutionized treatment in Czechoslovakia. Everyone seemed to become rapidly convinced.

The IUAT International Trial

It was in 1960 that Noel Rist suggested to me, at the World Conference of the International Union against Tuberculosis in Istanbul, that we might convince the world of the correctness of the Edinburgh claims, and so induce them to adopt the meticulous methods that would prevent failure, by conducting an international trial of chemotherapy with standard protocols. In view of the scepticism and individualism of many of our international colleagues, Noel and I thought it would be unwise to suggest a trial of "Edinburgh chemotherapy", however named.

Our colleagues thought that failures occurred because some pulmonary disease was too severe to respond to chemotherapy. So we ingeniously dressed the trial up as "A Study of the Causes of Failure of Treatment in Pulmonary Tuberculosis". Of course we believed that there should be very few failures if proper treatment was meticulously given.

We proposed that only far advanced pulmonary tuberculosis, however severe, would be admitted to the trial, and the possible causes of failure of treatment would be carefully studied. But we laid down in the protocols specific standards of chemotherapy along the Edinburgh lines (but carefully not designated as such).

No one at that time had carried out an international trial of the kind we envisaged in any disease as far as I know. It would clearly be a novel and difficult operation needing high organisational skills as well as outstanding diplomatic talent. Before moving to Edinburgh I had worked with Reg Bignall of the Institute of Thoracic Medicine at the Brompton Hospital. I thought that Reg had the obsessional qualities and tactful personality to make a success of it. Moreover he too was sceptical of the Edinburgh results. He certainly would not be accused of fiddling the figures in our favour. Noel and I were delighted when he accepted our invitation. He carried out the trial brilliantly and, quite rightly, was accorded great credit for its success. And indeed he was later made the coordinator of the Scientific Committees of IUAT.

In order to convince people we hoped that, by sticking to good meticulous treatment and not mucking about with it because of minor clinical upsets or slow improvement, they would see with their own eyes on their own patients the success of such a policy. This we believed would lead them in future to use the good methods consistently and meticulously. We chose for each country an outstanding unit with a local national reputation. If the trial went as we hoped we thought that the national prestige and influence of such a centre would spread the message to others in that country. We selected such units in each of twenty-three countries.

Somewhat to our surprise, most centres, most of the time, carried out the trial very well. But perhaps it was an advantage to the trial that some clinicians, for the same sort of reasons as had mistakenly influenced them in the past, sometimes broke the protocols and messed about with the treatment. There were admittedly a few very early deaths in those on good treatment who had been admitted nearly moribund. Apart from these, all the failures were in patients in whom the clinician had broken the protocols and given other treatment. In those who stuck to the laid down treatment the results were virtually uniformly successful. Perhaps I should add that all patients were, of course, from those newly diagnosed. Although there were few with organisms primarily resistant to one drug I don't think there were any with multiple primary drug resistance.

Reg Bignall reported the results at a further international conference of the IUAT, as far as I remember in Rome. By then he himself had become convinced by the results and made clear that the major cause of failure was failing to keep to the laid down chemotherapy and/or messing about with treatment. In the formal programme of the meeting I was also asked to comment on the results. I took great care *not* to say "I told you so", *not* to emphasise the Edinburgh precedents and to try to give the participating clinicians – and, of course and very justifiably, above all Reg Bignall who had done such a marvellous job – the major credit. I was determined not to risk resentment or confrontation which might have damaged the chances of general adoption of good treatment. This was not really as unselfish or as creditable as it may sound. Those who really knew about the subject also knew that the principles of the successful treatment derived from the work in Edinburgh. We got plenty of credit in the long run. But of course the change in professional opinion was enormously rewarding. Instead of people making snide remarks, or talking behind our backs about our unreliability, or accusing us of fiddling our figures, at last they knew, as we had learnt long since, that in pulmonary tuberculosis patients with initially sensitive bacilli, 100% cure was a reasonable and achievable aim. But of course most of them almost immediately felt that they too had known it all the time! We are all human.

The Marc Daniels Memorial Lecture

In my Marc Daniels Memorial Lecture in 1960 I reviewed my own personal results and our research over the previous seven years. As a confirmation of our claims I had shown that the decline of mortality from tuberculosis in Edinburgh had been more rapid than in any other centre, both in the UK and abroad. I had also demonstrated the preventive effect of ensuring that all known patients received meticulous chemotherapy. A previously steeply rising rate of new cases in Edinburgh had been reduced by 53% within three years. (A rate of decline never remotely matched anywhere else in the world as far as I know). I had shown how our clinical results, and low (later negligible) relapse rates, fitted well with detailed studies in the elimination of bacilli from lungs removed after various periods of chemotherapy. (You will remember that these operations were done when we still, as others, thought this might be necessary to prevent relapse). Further experience, and the experimental work, had later confirmed that, if treatment was sufficiently prolonged, surgery was unnecessary.

The slow diffusion

Although the International Union trial, and perhaps the Marc Daniels Lecture and other papers by my Edinburgh colleagues, had convinced a number of leading academics in the UK and abroad, it was many years before good, meticulous treatment was given by all clinicians even in the UK, much less abroad. For instance forty miles from Edinburgh in Glasgow bad treatment was not uncommon up to twenty years after we had ensured that all patients in Edinburgh received good treatment. Things were fairly slow in the USA where doctors tend not to be influenced by non-American research. They were particularly slow in Germany and, of course, in USSR.

Later, with the introduction of powerful new drugs, rifampicin and pyrazinamide, it became possible to give much shorter treatment. We had originally shown that no relapses occurred if patients were given at least eighteen months of treatment involving streptomycin, isoniazid and PAS. With the new drugs, controlled trials – largely by the British Medical Research Council in cooperation with local services in East Africa, Singapore and Hong Kong, and later confirmed by cooperative trials by the British Thoracic Society in Britain – showed that it was possible to reduce the time of treatment, first to nine months and then, by giving four drugs for the first two months, to a total of six months. Such "Short Course Chemotherapy" is now generally advocated. Although the new drugs are more expensive, Third World patients treated with them are much more likely to complete treatment and be cured. The cost per cured patient is much less than the cost of wasteful, uncompleted and unsuccessful longer term treatment with the old drugs. The general principles remain the same as we had laid down: give meticulous drug combinations of proved efficacy, keep your nerve if the patient does not improve as quickly as you expect or if he experiences minor side effects. Do not change or vary treatment except for clear indications, such as a serious reaction to an individual drug. When patients have had previous bad or risky treatment with unreliable drug combinations, the problems can be difficult and require much intellectual effort. We showed that most such patients could be cured if treatment was tailored to their specific problem. But in relatively few centres in the world were these problems adequately addressed; and the same is probably still true. If good, standard treatment is properly given the problem should not arise. The principles of attacking these difficult but entirely avoidable problems were outlined in several publications from our Department or from those trained by us. As I have mentioned, many years after I "retired" I summarised them in a lecture given in Barcelona to the Academy of

Medicine of Catalonia and in a subsequent publication in the journal of the International Union[*].

Over these years, and indeed until my retiral, we had very large numbers of visitors from all over the world. We had a succession of junior and senior postgraduates from many countries who worked with us for weeks, months or, sometimes several years.These brought back our methods to their own countries. I myself made many visits abroad. In the 1960s I visited New Zealand, Australia, Brazil, Germany, India, Sudan, Algeria, Tunisia, Malaysia, USA and Canada; in the 1970s Israel, Egypt, The Argentine, Uruguay, Peru, Canada, Hong Kong, India, Bangladesh, Sri Lanka, Pakistan, Sweden, Norway (twice), Iraq (twice), Brazil, USA (several times), Nepal; in the 1980s Thailand, Nepal (twice), Bangladesh, Kuwait, Spain, Sudan, Yugoslavia, Zimbabwe. In addition I made many contacts through the International Union Against Tuberculosis and Lung Disease (as the IUAT became) and a large international correspondence.

The Third World (Developing Countries)

Once it was clear that patients with tubercle bacilli sensitive to the standard drugs could virtually all be cured, granted that they were given the right drug combinations for the right time, it followed that the disease in the community could be controlled. The basis of that was, of course, good organisation.

In Britain there was the basis for this organisation, originated by Sir Robert Philip. In the Third World organisation was usually poor. Tuberculosis was often the Cinderella of medicine and was unlikely to attract outstanding doctors. There was a shortage of trained manpower and of resources of all kinds. There was little money available even for antituberculosis drugs.

I had been associated with the International Union against Tuberculosis since 1953 when I gave my first paper at its World Conference in Madrid. Thereafter I met many of the world leaders at its meetings and through its scientific committees. We had many discussions. An early controversy relevant to Third World problems was with the Americans. Experimental work had found that tubercle bacilli that had become resistant to isoniazid proved less damaging to guinea pigs, which are normally rapidly killed by the bacillus. Humans have better resistance. Walsh MacDermott of Columbia University in New York was deservedly a world leader. He had been involved with early chemotherapy trials, including some of the first

---

[*] Crofton J. The prevention and management of drug-resistant tuberculosis. *Bulletin of the International Union against Tuberculosis and Lung Disease* 1987; 62: 6-11

trials of isoniazid in patients. He extrapolated the guinea pig results to assume that isoniazid resistance was unimportant clinically. If a patient's bacilli became resistant under treatment they would cease to be dangerous to him or to others. So treatment with this very potent and cheap drug, alone, was the obvious solution for Third World tuberculosis.

But in Edinburgh we had had a number of patients who had been primarily infected with isoniazid-resistant bacilli from other patients who had had previous bad treatment. Our research had shown that these bacilli were clinically important: treatment failure occurred and the patients deteriorated. So I had many arguments, public and private, with Walsh. Sadly with very little effect. He was a man of great charm, with whom I personally got on very well. Our arguments were always very friendly. When I got him really cornered with the evidence, he would quickly change the subject by some wisecrack which made everyone laugh.

Unfortunately he was senior and highly influential internationally. WHO at first accepted his assurances and advocated using isoniazid alone in the Third World. Later experience of subsequent clinical disasters proved that Walsh was wrong. Everyone quietly forgot his advice. Meantime there had been a spread of consequent drug resistance in a number of countries.

The British Medical Research Council (BMRC) did a splendid job in addressing Third World problems by scientific work in the countries themselves. Its first effective controlled trial was the demonstration in Madras, in association with the Indian Medical Research Council (IMRC), that patients could be as effectively treated at home in the slums of Madras, as they could by receiving the same treatment in a sanatorium. Sanatorium treatment was, of course, very much more expensive. This, and subsequent trials, owed their success above all to the drive, organising ability, enthusiasm and tact of Wallace Fox who went on to become the acknowledged world leader in the field, together with his bacteriological colleague, Denny Mitchison.

The BMRC/IMRC, led by Wallace, then went on to carry out a series of trials working out the cheapest methods that could be effective. They organised these trials, in cooperation with the local medical services, in India, Singapore, Hong Kong and East Africa. In rapidly developing countries with good organisations, such as Hong Kong and Singapore, the methods were quickly implemented in routine practice, with highly successful results. But in most of Asia, Africa and Latin America, organisational and other inadequacies prevented any really effective national control programme. It might exist on paper, but in practice, in most countries, achieved little.

Meanwhile WHO had decided that in most poor countries it would be impossible to ensure nationwide, effective treatment and control through a specialised tuberculosis service. The resources were simply not available. So a standard plan was developed to "integrate" the tuberculosis service into the general routine services: Health Posts or Health Centres providing primary care, District Hospitals etc. Many such plans were made on paper, few succeeded in practice. The demands – on motivation, training and supervision – were just too great. One of the exceptions was Algeria where they were fortunate to have outstanding leaders and through their oil, reasonable resources.

Our own contribution to these problems, at this time, was not very great. Tuberculosis had become only a minor disease in Edinburgh and was running that way in the UK. I personally was heavily engaged as Dean of the Faculty of Medicine from 1963 to 1966. Immediately after that I started, with Andrew Douglas, to write our postgraduate textbook *Respiratory Diseases* which was published in 1969. As soon as that was finished I was asked to be a Vice-Principal of the University during the interesting period of student militancy. This took me to 1971. Shortly afterwards I was elected Vice-President of the Royal College of Physicians of Edinburgh and thereafter President (1973-76).

Meantime the Edinburgh group continued to have some influence. In our textbook, *Respiratory Diseases*, we had extensive chapters on tuberculosis, including a section on developing countries. The book was translated into Italian, Spanish and Russian and we issued two subsequent editions (1975 and 1981). We were still teaching many from developing countries. We had many visitors to the Department. Both I and my colleagues made a number of overseas trips, as I have mentioned above.

For several years our laboratory did all the drug resistance tests for Libya. After his retirement, our splendid bacteriologist, Archie Wallace, spent three years there setting up their own laboratory. He had an excellent effect on their standards of treatment. Norman Horne also twice visited Libya as did Andrew Douglas. Although invited on a number of occasions I was too occupied to accept.

In the 1950s Harley Williams, then Director of the National Association for the Prevention of Tuberculosis (later the Chest Heart and Stroke Association) asked me to write a short book on the chemotherapy of tuberculosis. At that time I was overwhelmed with work, clinical research, getting tuberculosis control programmes going in Edinburgh and of course much teaching, undergraduate and postgraduate. Accordingly I suggested he ask my colleague Ian Ross, who produced an excellent short book. In later editions he was joined by Norman Horne who continued with successive editions after Ian's death, with a total to date of some seven editions. The book was highly appreciated and used in many developing countries. It must have had a useful influence worldwide.

Later, in 1977, when I was about to retire, Ray Mills, then WHO representative in Nepal, asked me if I would be prepared to make a visit and advise on tuberculosis. Ray had previously been in the Department of Community Medicine in Edinburgh and I had known him well when, as Dean, I had been responsible for organising the joint medical educational project between Edinburgh and the Medical School of Baroda in Gujarat, India. The project was sponsored and financed by WHO. Ray had gone out as a member of one of the Edinburgh teams. He became enthusiastic about the work in the Third World and subsequently joined WHO.

As I was to retire in September 1977, I thought it would be entirely possible, and very interesting, to spend three months in Nepal in 1978. This would also give me the opportunity of completing the Indian part of my tour as President of the Edinburgh College, which had been interrupted in 1976 by a severe attack of gastroenteritis in Madras.

India 1978

Eileen and I had a very interesting tour, lecturing in Bombay and Delhi and combining, between Christmas and New Year, medical visits with lectures and sightseeing in Jaipur, Benares and Agra. We also paid a visit to Ludhiana Medical School in the Punjab. It is an excellent, mission-run school. We knew from contact with Dr Betty Cowan, a professor there and a Fellow of the Royal College of Physicians of Edinburgh, that they were doing excellent work in the community, both in the Ludhiana slums and in the surrounding villages. We were anxious to see this, especially from the tuberculosis and primary community medicine points of view. All medical schools in India were supposed to include such work in their curriculum, but in most we knew from previous visits that the component was symbolic rather than effective.

We were duly impressed with Ludhiana. I lectured and had much discussion on tuberculosis. Moreover an old postgraduate student, by that time the Professor of Tuberculosis in Amritsar, with whom I had had much correspondence but had not had time to visit, brought his entire Departmental staff down to meet me. All rather embarrassing. The Indians have an enormous traditional respect for their teachers – their gurus – and especially if he is senior and aging. To the young lecturers from Amritsar I was their guru's guru, and consequently only one step below the empyrean – and perhaps not even one step! I felt very phoney. I was conscious of the feet of clay positively crumbling as I held forth.

Over the years I have often felt India lying heavily on my conscience: so much medical misery, especially in tuberculosis, which should theoretically be remediable but which is so inadequately tackled on the ground. However, on this 1978 visit, at the All India Institute, I had one encouraging experience. Instead of unquestioning acceptance of anything I said, a young doctor actually argued with me, and argued very sensibly. At last, I felt, we are getting somewhere. But of course staff and students at that Institute were highly selected from all over India. I was meeting the young elite. But that elite would in due course lead the future.

Nepal

In mid-January 1978 we moved on to Nepal. Before 1951 it had been a closed country to which foreigners were not admitted. The exception was to accept a British Ambassador in connection with recruiting for the Ghurka regiments, a practice dating from the early nineteenth century and the appreciation by the British of the military virtues of the Ghurkas they had fought against.

The isolation of Nepal was facilitated not only by the mountains but also by a highly malarious jungle just inside the border with India, a thirty mile wide strip on the northern edge of the Ganges plain. The opening up of the country was facilitated by the effective, although somewhat temporary, clearance of malaria by the post-war WHO campaign. As a result much of the jungle was cut down and turned into productive farmland.

After 1951 a number of doctors were trained in India and gradually they tried to establish some medical services. By 1978 some administrative Districts had a District Hospital, usually with one or two doctors but perhaps only fifteen beds. They were just starting to establish rural Health Posts, manned by Health Assistants with a three-year training. These were intended to provide primary care and local preventive services. My visit in 1978 was the start of a fascinating association with Nepal. I had long held that one-off visits to Third World countries had only a very temporary effect. If you, and the relevant national colleagues, know you are returning things are much more likely to happen as a result of your visit. WHO SE Asia, and evidently the Nepal authorities, clearly agreed. I was asked back for another three months in 1981 and for some two months in 1985. I was invited again in 1989 but that same year I had been asked by WHO Western Pacific Region to run a workshop on Chronic Respiratory Disease at their headquarters in Manila. I had done a great deal of preliminary work, including designing the programme, producing two reports and preparing large numbers of lantern slides. But at the last moment the WHO's medical bureaucracy in Geneva refused to pass me medically because of my age (then 77). I could not blame them; clearly at that age I would be more of a medical risk. But if I couldn't be passed for the Western Pacific, obviously I would not be passed for Nepal and so had sadly to refuse that invitation.

During my first visit to Nepal I visited the Britain-Nepal Medical Trust (BNMT) which, on behalf of the Nepal Government, provided tuberculosis services (among other valuable contributions) in eight Districts in Eastern Nepal. As a result I was subsequently asked to become a "Patron" by the Trust and, somewhat informally, became their main technical advisor in tuberculosis. Being very impressed with the job the Trust was doing, through my contacts via the IUATLD I helped to obtain for the Trust a large annual grant from NORAD, the main Norwegian government sources of overseas aid. This involved two Norwegians, one of them Knut Ovreberg, the Norwegian government's chief advisor in tuberculosis and an old friend who had helped in raising the Norwegian funds, becoming Trustees of the BNMT. So BNMT set up a Tuberculosis Committee which then also included Wallace Fox and Janet Darbyshire of the Medical Research Council Tuberculosis and Chest Unit, who were also Trustees. I was made Chairman of this committee and conducted a fairly continuous correspondence with successive Directors in Nepal.

At the time of my first visit to Nepal, WHO had also invited as a tuberculosis consultant Dr H W Pereira of Sri Lanka. He proved an excellent and delightful colleague who had been involved in running the good tuberculosis service in Sri Lanka which had continued with high standards and developed further since our visit there in 1954. We ultimately wrote a joint report on Nepal for WHO.

There were at that time some 13 million people in a country about 500 miles by 150 in size varying from 300 feet above sea level in the Terai (the former jungle area in the northern strip of the Ganges plain, now largely farmland) to the 29,000 feet of Everest. Most lived in the intermediate hills from about 5,000 to 15,000 feet, though the narrow strip of the Terai was heavily populated. There was an, as yet incomplete, east-west road along the Terai, a road over an 8,000 feet pass from India to Kathmandu, a recent road built by the Chinese from Kathmandu to the Chinese border to the north. There were one or two other short roads between towns or from the Indian border to a southern small town in Nepal. But 90% of the population was rural and living in places only accessible on foot, days' or weeks' march from a road. With such divisive geography there were many tribes and castes. Thirty six languages are spoken, though most can also speak Nepali (which is closely related to Hindi).

Our job was to review the tuberculosis situation in Nepal and to make recommendations; also to help with the preparation and the conduct of their first National Conference on tuberculosis Originally there had been a sanatorium in Nepal, used, apparently, largely for longstay by a few patients with money or influence. This had been abolished on the recommendation of a previous WHO consultant. There was a busy "Chest Clinic" in Kathmandu with a number of doctors but their success rate in curing patients was very low. This was due to quite inadequate home supervision arrangements and the absence of staff to trace those who failed to come back for continuation of treatment. As the doctors were also engaged in part-time private practice there was perhaps a lack of motivation to make the clinic service too good; there would have been less incentive for patients to opt for private practice. We had little confidence in the activities of the doctors in the clinic and decided to concentrate on trying to initiate some sort of service in the rural areas.

Of course the great majority of patients were in the rural areas or in other small towns. In these almost the only service available was from a few mission hospitals to their surrounding communities – usually quite good – and from the Britain Nepal Medical Trust, the most effective body providing cover over a wide area.

The main national drive had been a country-wide effort to give BCG to children. This had been carried out by a series of teams who on the whole had done a good job in very difficult circumstances considering the terrain. The BNMT had played a very useful part in eastern Nepal in this drive. Moreover they had combined this with "active case finding". As a preliminary to a BCG campaign in a particular area, the team visited all homes to list and recruit children for vaccination. At the same time they enquired about anyone in the house who had symptoms that could have been due to tuberculosis and then arranged to test their sputum for tubercle bacilli.

This "active case finding" is contrasted with "passive case finding" when patients seek help from some medical professional or medical institution. Active case finding picked up more women (less likely than men to seek, or be allowed by their males to seek, help) and more chronic cases with mild symptoms. But these patients proved to be poor completers of treatment. Moreover such case finding is very expensive in terms of professional time. It was much more cost-effective to try to ensure that all patients presenting by passive case finding successfully completed their treatment. However active case finding provided information which helped us, with other methods, to make an estimate of the true prevalence of tuberculosis. As one might expect, this was highest in the Terai, where there was much contact with high prevalence India; there were no border controls; movement was free. Tuberculosis was lowest in the remote hills with less contact with the outside world. The "middle hills" were intermediate.

There was a central tuberculosis team with national responsibilities. They had done a good job on the BCG programme but not much else. They were supposed to provide drugs for treatment but had no system for sending them to where they were needed. The BNMT and the mission hospitals had to collect their supplies themselves from Kathmandu. Other District Hospitals etc might have drugs temporarily, for instance if the King was visiting the area or someone from the central unit was visiting, but there was none of the ensured continuous supply essential to successful treatment.

Clearly there was a long, long way to go before tuberculosis stood a chance of being integrated into a national medical service, itself only in the earliest stages of gestation even on paper.

Our own experience of a visit to some of the nearest units of BNMT's Districts indicated the logistical problems of producing a service in Nepal. I was anxious to see what it was like, so we[*] visited the BNMT tuberculosis clinic in Dhankuta and, from there, attended a tuberculosis session at a Health Post. These visits to some of the nearest BNMT places involved us in six days walking and 16,000 feet up and down. Our visit to Ankasella Health Post from Dhankuta involved a 22 mile walk with 4,000 feet up and down by my altimeter. Eileen and I crawled back to Dhankuta by moonlight. I had to get back that night as I'd promised to do a ward round in Dhankuta District Hospital next morning; some of the party were able to stop off at a Tibetan "hotel" a couple of hours earlier.

Many years later, BNMT introduced short-term chemotherapy and integrated the tuberculosis services with the developing, but still very inadequate, provisions for primary health care through Health Posts. Many parts of Nepal may still have few, or very poor, tuberculosis services, but undoubtedly there has been much improvement in health services which at one time were virtually non-existent outside Kathmandu.

Diagnosis of tuberculosis in the Third World

Having been Chairman of the IUAT's Tuberculosis Chemotherapy Committee from 1957 to 1963 I was asked in 1968 to become Chairman of their Diagnostic Committee and continued in office there till 1972. With the outstanding assistance of an excellent Danish statistician, we carried out a trial of the reliability of diagnosis of tuberculosis from chest X-rays, then relied on so intensively by chest physicians in many countries. We used a set of, if I remember, about 100 X-rays from the routine Norwegian national survey (which at that time was conducted every few years). These films included a wide range of abnormal shadows, as well as a number of normal X-rays. We had the same set of X-rays read by chest specialists in, if I remember, about twenty countries. We found an enormous variation in

---

[*] Eileen acted as an extremely effective colleague in all John's visits to Nepal.

interpretation, which could be described as "observer variation" or "observer error".

We then went on to conduct a similar trial with a set of smears of sputum stained for tubercle bacilli, again containing varying numbers of bacilli, or with none at all. These were examined by the technicians responsible for routine readings in a main centre, again in about twenty countries.

The survey revealed a very much smaller variation between observers than in the case of the X-ray trial. The main differences, as one might expect, occurred when very few bacilli were present. This confirmed the value, in the Third World, of relying primarily on the cheaper and more accurate sputum method than on diagnosis by the expensive and demonstrably unreliable X-ray method, which would be even more unreliable in the absence of advanced training.

Later experience through the International Union against Tuberculosis and Lung Disease

After my "retirement" I was appointed as Chairman of the new IUATLD Scientific Committee on Tobacco and Health (1984-88). In that capacity, I was asked to attend all the Union meetings, including Regional meetings in Tunis, Kuwait, Sudan, Kathmandu, Lahore and Istanbul, as well as their World Conferences (Singapore and Boston) and the annual meetings of the Scientific Committees, usually in Paris. At all these Annik Rouillon, the Executive Director of IUATLD, asked me to take an active part in the discussions of tuberculosis, formal and informal, as well as dealing with tobacco.

I was also asked to act as rapporteur, and summarise each day's proceedings, at a Regional Tuberculosis IUATLD/WHO meeting in Harare, Zimbabwe, in 1986. This involved invited participants not only from Zimbabwe but also from Kenya, Tanzania, Uganda, Mozambique, Botswana and Basutoland. This was a very useful conference and the first, I think, to advocate the new short-course chemotherapy for use as routine in Third World countries. We had quite a battle with the then WHO Tuberculosis Unit over this. WHO still regarded short-term chemotherapy as too expensive for the Third World. This caused considerable delay in the publication of the report, which I wrote jointly with Karel Styblo[*].

---

[*] Karel Styblo (1921-1998) who pioneered the Directly Observed Therapy-Short Course TB therapy in developing countries.

National tuberculosis control programmes in the Third World

The mention of Karel Styblo makes it appropriate here to summarise a major advance for which he was largely responsible. Karel was given a job as Director of the Tuberculosis Surveillance Research Unit sponsored by the Netherlands Tuberculosis Association in liaison with IUATLD. This international research unit on tuberculosis epidemiology worked particularly with the full and detailed national data from the Netherlands and Canada. It made many notable contributions.

With this background Karel was in due course asked to be part-time Scientific Director of IUATLD. A number of Third World countries had asked the Union for help in setting up a National Tuberculosis Control Programme. It was Karel's job, among others, to provide that help. He did so with astonishing success. He stimulated each government first of all to give tuberculosis the necessary priority commensurate with its local importance, and to recruit outstanding leaders for the programme. He cooperated with the leaders in designing, developing and monitoring the programme and in training the necessary personnel. Each programme was integrated with, and worked through, the national organisation for primary care and through District Hospitals, ie. the routine medical services such as they were. Through the Union, and with the enthusiastic help of Annik Rouillon the union's devoted Executive Director, Karel persuaded certain rich countries, notably Switzerland, Germany, Norway, the Netherlands and Sweden to provide financial help for drugs, visits, training and logistic support.

The World Bank investigated this work and concluded that, on a world basis, in terms of years of life saved, tuberculosis control programmes along the lines established by the Union could be the most cost-effective of all health interventions. As a result WHO, with the World Bank and others, launched a project to develop a World Tuberculosis Control Programme.

Clinical Tuberculosis

When I completed my term of office as Chairman of the Tobacco and Health Committee of the Union in 1988 I expected to make little more contribution to the tuberculosis problem. But there was a quite unexpected development. I think it was early in 1989 that I had a letter from David Morley asking me to write, with a paediatrician Fred Miller from Newcastle, a book on clinical aspects of tuberculosis. The book would be for non-specialist doctors in the Third World dealing with much tuberculosis in the course of their routine work in District Hospitals, Health Centres etc.

David Morley was Professor of Tropical Child Health at the Institute of Child Health at the famous Great Ormond Street Children's Hospital in London. I knew him by reputation as having done splendid work for children in the Third World. I also knew Fred Miller by reputation from my early tuberculosis days, but I had never met him personally. Before he retired he had been a distinguished paediatrician in Newcastle, a pioneer in the social and community aspects of child health. He had written an excellent book on childhood tuberculosis with which I was familiar. He had made many visits to India on behalf of WHO. He was mainly concerned there with teaching of paediatrics, but in India tuberculosis is an important component of this. He had written a further book on childhood tuberculosis with special reference to Third World problems.

At the time David approached me I was very heavily engaged with other commitments. I asked him if we could involve a third author and suggested Norman Horne. But, as the book would clearly involve a lot of work, I said I would first like to check with WHO and IUATLD that there was a real need for it. I wrote therefore to Dr Kochi, the Japanese Head of the WHO Tuberculosis Unit, and to Annik Rouillon, the Executive Director of IUATLD. Both replied that there was a real need for such a clinical book and encouraged us to proceed.

So began a very interesting project. For me it was quite a new type of writing. David Morley had supplemented his original approach by suggesting that the book ought also to be made appropriate for "Medical Assistants" or "Health Assistants" the names given in Africa and Asia to non-doctors with two or three years of medical training who, in many countries, carry much of the burden of routine clinical work. In such countries it was these who delivered primary care and simple prevention in local health posts or health centres. As they might not have a good grasp of English, the book must be written in very simple language, quite different from the usual medical textbook prose. The style should be direct and personal "You must avoid", "You should do". No passives to be used; short sentences; simple words. David also said that Africans found "stories" about patients very useful.

So we proceeded. I produced a draft of possible content headings which were approved by David and my co-authors. It was agreed that I should act as editor and coordinator. We divided out the work. I was to write the introduction on the epidemiology. As a clinician should cooperate in his own National Tuberculosis Control Programme, I would write a section on the components of this. Fred, of course, would write the section on children's tuberculosis and Norman the adult section.

After many intermediate drafts I eventually collated a first overall draft which was approved by my co-authors. I had suggested, and all agreed, that this should be sent for comment, not only to WHO and IUATLD but also to various doctors of our acquaintance with experience of tuberculosis in developing countries. These included Africa, India, Papua New Guinea and China. Our contacts were full of praise for the work. In addition most also provided useful and constructive suggestions.

I then had to check the approval of my colleagues on the suggestions from the consultants and once more I rewrote the text extensively, taking the opportunity of further simplifying the English, polishing up various sections, and providing a glossary on medical and more difficult English words.

The book was finally published in March 1992. The publishers and TALC[*] sent many free copies to a list we supplied of influential specialists working in, or with influence in, the Third World. We immediately had demands for 9,000 copies, even before any reviews appeared.

Subsequently, there was much demand for translations: French, Spanish, Chinese, Thai, Portuguese and others[#]. I must confess I find it very thrilling that the book has been and is being so warmly welcomed. I used to say, when I had many similar congratulations over our postgraduate textbook *Respiratory Diseases* that I felt like a first-time mother when people said her baby had beautiful blue eyes. It is a great boost to meet these experiences with the second baby!

Update in 2003: World Health Organisation

During the later years of my "retirement" I became extensively involved with WHO. In 1993 I spoke on drug resistance at an international seminar in the London School of Hygiene and Tropical Medicine in London. This was followed immediately by another WHO tuberculosis administrative meeting in London and a famous press conference there at which WHO declared tuberculosis a "Global Emergency" for the first time. This had a considerable political effect in alerting British governmental and public opinion to the vast and threatening problem. The declaration of the global problem was quite bold by Dr Kochi, the head of the WHO Tuberculosis Programme, because he had not cleared it beforehand with the top WHO bureaucracy. It had received great media coverage in UK and internationally and he got away with it. In 1994 at the International Union against Tuberculosis and Lung Disease's World Conference in Mainz, Germany, I

---

[*] Teaching Aids at Low Cost, an organisation founded by David Morley to provide free or inexpensive materials for medical schools in poor countries

[#] By the time of John's death in 2009, this book had gone to three editions and several reprints in 22 languages.

was asked to give the first Robert Koch Memorial Lecture. All this led up to the launch of WHO's DOTS global programme[¥].

Perhaps as a result, in 1995 WHO asked me to chair a Working Party in Geneva to produce Guidelines on Treatment. I was then closely involved in preparing the subsequent publication which became the standard throughout the world.

In 1996 the International Committee of the Red Cross asked me to review the tuberculosis work the Red Cross had been doing in prisons in Baku, Azerbaijan. I was asked to summarise the discussion and to produce a first draft of the report. There were many discrepancies in the data.. There were many delays. The report was finally effectively sorted out by a trained epidemiologist on the spot in Geneva. It did prove useful in the end. It notably demonstrated not only the high incidence of tuberculosis in prisons but also the high incidence of treatment failure due to multidrug resistance resulting from poor previous treatment. This was subsequently shown in many areas of the ex-USSR.

This made me interested in the vast problems of tuberculosis in prisons, especially those in countries of the ex-USSR. The USSR had regarded tuberculosis as a very important disease of the poor. This gave its control a high priority. They poured in money and staff. They had vast numbers of tuberculosis hospitals and beds, where a patient remained for one perhaps two years. They still did a great deal of surgery to prevent relapse, cutting out any significant residual shadow in the X-ray – practice that we and the rest had given up 40 years previously. They did lots of other odd things, like dripping an anti-tuberculosis drug through a tube into a lung cavity and passing an electric current through the lungs to dilate the blood vessels and hopefully allow more drug to reach the lesions. Yet both bacteriology and chemotherapy were ill-used.

MERLIN[*], a British charity, persuaded their Russian colleagues to agree to allot new patients every other week either to the old Russian system of hospital, surgery etc or to the WHO method of mostly outpatient treatment with standard drug combinations. The latter did just as well, even a little better, and at much lower cost.

Because of the misuse of drugs there was much drug resistance in Tomsk, especially in the prisons. The latter had a separate medical service and there was no liaison with the public service when prisoners were discharged. This has now also been remedied. Other Western bodies,

---

[¥] DOTS= Directly Observed Treatment, Short term

[*] Medical Emergency Relief International

especially from Scandinavia and America, tried to get pilot WHO projects going in various parts of ex-USSR. Effective reform is gradually starting both for the public and for the prison service.

India 1997

In the summer of 1997 I was asked by Fabio Luelmo of WHO Geneva to pay a visit to India. I replied to Fabio that, as I was now 85, I would again be turned down by the WHO Geneva bureaucracy. Fabio then said that they could get round this problem. I would be given a general contract to "lecture and advise", without saying where. I would have to arrange my own travel, accommodation and medical insurance and other expenses out of a block grant. There would be no reference to medical bureaucracy in Geneva.

India had had a theoretical National Tuberculosis Control Programme since the 1990s. In practice it hadn't worked effectively. I think they had had seven successive central Directors in a few years. However in the previous 18 months it had really taken off. There was an enthusiastic and dynamic Indian Director, Dr Khatri, helped by a small but able team and a young and equally dynamic (American) WHO representative, Tom Frieden. Tom had earned a high reputation by being moved into New York in the late 1980s to clean up a major tuberculosis epidemic, with much drug resistance, resulting from previous neglect of their tuberculosis service. This had been a great success. Now the pilot programmes were going well in India. But they were running into problems because of the objections to the programme among many of the highly prestigious academics in the medical schools.

Because of the British origin of the main Indian medical schools and the traditional respect for old age, it was thought that a very senior (ie aged) British academic might help to get them on side, especially as I had made frequent visits in the past. The other foreign consultant invited was Dr John Sbarbaro from Denver, USA, an academic with extensive practical administrative experience in tuberculosis control and considerable international experience and reputation in developing countries.

Originally it was suggested we should visit four centres in a week but it was finally decided to hold a "Consensus Conference" in Delhi. To this would be invited relevant academics and senior tuberculosis control staff from all over India. The only regional visit would be to the State of Kerala in southwest India, because it was Kerala which had sought help in the first place.

The Consensus Conference went very well. We ran into all the expected problems with the academics after the main initial Indian reports and the addresses by John Sbarbaro and myself. But the chairmen, both of the plenary sessions and the smaller sessions on particular aspects, did a wonderful job. Formal support for the national programme was agreed by consensus. Moreover important sessions and discussions were attended by Dr Agarwal, Director General of the Indian Health Services, and other senior civil servants who declared themselves converted. In later follow-up many of the medical schools had become involved in the programme. This has been most encouraging both for the programme's local prestige and for the teaching of the next generation of doctors.

I greatly enjoyed the later brief visit to Kerala, a State which was new to me. It is very beautiful with well-wooded hills rising steeply from a lovely coast. Education is much better than elsewhere, with a high literacy rate and much export of educated staff, for instance Christian nurses, to other parts of India. There is a good State welfare system by Indian standards and good local charities. The State has had communist governments elected in the past, sometimes with a resultant takeover by the central federal government. But Kerala remains relatively poor.

I was impressed by the quality and initiative of the people I met. Kerala had been one of the most successful of the pilot projects on tuberculosis with a very efficient and committed Director. Besides my contributions to the tuberculosis conference the chairman of the State Cancer Society asked me to give a talk on tobacco and cancer at the medical school. It had to be off the cuff as I had brought no materials on tobacco, but seemed to go down well.

Altogether a most enjoyable visit to India which I was assured had proved very useful. The National Programme has gone from strength to strength. By March 2003 nearly half the population (half a billion people) had access to free and good treatment, 80% or more of these being cured. But many problems remain. The remaining half of the population live in some of the more difficult and remote areas; the HIV and Multi Drug Resistance component have yet to be effectively tackled; maintaining standards will be more difficult when the projects move on from the exciting development phase to ordinary routine. But there is no doubt, thanks to all concerned, that it has been a massive achievement and an example to the world. One must particularly salute Dr Khatri and Tom Frieden, who really got it going.

Multi-Drug Resistance (MDR)

In April 1998 I was invited by Paul Farmer of Harvard University to attend a seminar there to discuss the problem of developing treatment services globally for patients with MDR. Originally WHO had decided that countries must first concentrate on treating new patients well. Most of these would have drug-sensitive bacilli. They would respond to standard drug combinations (four drugs as initial treatment). However as a result of our earlier memo on the importance of drug resistance, WHO had subsequently organised the first stage of an international survey of drug resistance in 35 countries, both in new and in previously treated patients. This survey was very well planned and conducted, with good standardisation of resistance tests to ensure comparability between countries. The survey showed that MDR was clearly a potential problem, higher of course in previously treated – mostly mistreated – patients but in some countries also with appreciable rates in new patients.

In 1995 in our WHO report on Standard Guidelines to Treatment, we recommended that patients with MDR should only be treated in specific, highly skilled national units. This was because of the lower effectiveness, very high cost, and frequent toxic complications of the few "reserve" drugs available to treat such patients.

Paul Farmer and his close colleague, Jin Kim (an American of Korean origin) had started, via the university, a charity called Partners for Health. Through this they had funded and themselves worked in a basic medical service for the very impoverished rural population in the plateau area of Haiti. They were subsequently approached by an American priest working in the slums of Lima, Peru. Peru, with strong backing from its President, had enthusiastically implemented a national tuberculosis control programme along the lines recommended by WHO, but this was basically for new patients. Paul and Jin liaised with local Peruvian colleagues. They successfully begged US manufacturers for reserve drugs. They arranged for resistance testing in a US laboratory. They trained, and raised money to pay poor neighbours to supervise the taking of every dose of the precious reserve drugs and to cope with their side effects. The patients were treated at home. At the time of our meeting this project had so far gone well, thanks to frequent visits by Paul and Jin with their outstanding capacity for tactful leadership and their excellent relationship with supporters in the US. These included the very influential ex-Dean of the Harvard Medical School – the sort of man who just took up a phone and rang up the Chairman of the World Bank! As a result, at our WHO/Harvard seminar there were representatives of all the relevant major US government research bodies, prominent medical advisors to the pharmaceutical industry, the main US experts in MDR tuberculosis, several Peruvian colleagues, and a group of top WHO tuberculosis officials.

I was the only one from the UK and was asked to do the final summing up with agreement on further action. I asked a small group of the most relevant contributors to meet me informally after the last evening's supper. We evolved a basis for agreement on future action. WHO agreed they would convene in Geneva a follow up working group to make detailed technical suggestions for international action. I had a tricky job chairing the main group the next day, with many and varied suggestions, but with final agreement along the lines our small group had worked out the night before. (I was flattered when, one of the main US government representatives, congratulated me afterwards informally on "a brilliant bit of chairing").

The WHO MDR technical committee took place in Geneva in July 1998 and proved very useful. It was agreed that there should be pilot projects both on individualised treatment and the standardised approach, depending on the level of technical sophistication and infrastructure in the country it concerned. International finance should be sought to enable bulk buying at reduced cost of the necessary drugs. Pilot studies should only take place in countries already running a successful DOTS programme along WHO lines so that new MDR cases ceased to be manufactured by bad treatment. The country's government would have to provide approved basics for the MDR unit and agree to on-going international monitoring to ensure standards. The government would have to accept international technical help and international monitoring of the programme.

Stop TB Partnership Meeting, Washington, October 2001

Following the Geneva WHO tuberculosis meetings described above, WHO had initiated a World Partnership to tackle the global tuberculosis emergency. The Partnership included not only governments from the 22 countries with the highest tuberculosis incidence, and others from interested richer countries, but international non-governmental bodies (such as the International Union against Tuberculosis and Lung Disease), national and international charities and particular bodies such as the Trusts set up by rich philanthropists, George Soros and Bill Gates. It also included, very significantly, the World Bank. A successful launch meeting had been held in Amsterdam, I think in 1998, which I had not been invited to attend.

A further global meeting of the Stop Tuberculosis Partnership, hosted by the World Bank, was to be held in Washington in October 2001. At 89, I was in the process of withdrawing from tuberculosis campaigning but agreed to give the introductory address and review the progress in controlling tuberculosis over the last 50 years! The Conference would then go on to plan how the world incidence might be halved in the next five years – an astonishingly bold ambition.

The Conference was opened by the Chairman of the World Bank with, to me, a surprisingly progressive speech emphasising world poverty as first priority, to which tuberculosis was very relevant. I was given a flatteringly glowing introduction as a near ninety-year-old whose group had many years ago pioneered modern methods of tuberculosis control.

I had only 20 minutes to cover 50 years of effort. I outlined the discovery of the three original anti-tuberculosis drugs: their initial successful clinical trials, especially by the British Medical Research Council; our own discovery that almost all failures of treatment were due to drug resistance, that these could be uniformly prevented by giving all three drugs initially to new patients, that 100% cure of pulmonary tuberculosis was therefore a reasonable aim (in contrast to the previous 50% mortality), that 12 to 18 months treatment prevented the previously high rate of relapse and made previously common lung surgery unnecessary, and that, astonishingly, good mass treatment in Edinburgh had converted a steadily rising incidence of tuberculosis to a fall of 59% within three years. I went on to outline the work of the British Medical Research Council in the Third World: the demonstration that sanatorium treatment was unnecessary, that cheaper drugs could now be used, that treatment could be tri-weekly instead of daily, and that, with the introduction of two new drugs (rifampicin and pyrazinamide) the treatment could be reduced to 6-9 months instead of 12-18 months. But only two countries (Hong Kong and Singapore) had applied this research in their national health services until the International Union against Tuberculosis and Lung Disease, through the work of Karel Styblo and Annik Rouillon, had demonstrated that, using simple methods of organisation and monitoring, 80% cure could be achieved in very poor African countries: Tanzania and Malawi and later others. The World Bank had assessed this work and reported that, for saving life, this was the most cost-effective of any global programme for any disease. Hence the WHO, with World Bank assistance, had launched the global DOTS programme of supervised treatment which we were here to spread to all high incidence countries.

Altogether it was a personally emotionally satisfying swansong to my tuberculosis career. I had long been in despair at so many poor countries having failed to prevent so much unnecessary misery and death from tuberculosis. But here at last was great hope for the future. It was good to have seen this before I died; to feel that there were now so many enthusiastic people pushing it forward. I could withdraw with a good conscience.

Envoi on tuberculosis

As I think my most important contributions have been to the control of tuberculosis, I will try to analyse what the "Battle with the Bug" has meant to me personally.

All of us are concerned with our own self-image. We want it to look as good as possible in our own eyes. This of course gives immense scope for self-deception! In many people competitiveness is a major incentive; they have to see themselves as more successful than others. In some this implies domination of others. Competitiveness can incite people to make very useful contributions in the professions, in science, art or business. It is a major driving force in the USA. I may be deceiving myself, but I do not recognise it as a major motivator in myself (though in the past I had a good deal of difficulty with a fellow professor who was so motivated and regarded me as a competitor to be done down!).

Though, again, I may be deceiving myself, I believe there were several elements in my own motivation. First of all there was a sense of my own inadequacy, so that I had to try to show to myself that I could do it, whatever difficult task "it" happened to be. As I gradually became established, my self-confidence increased, so that this incentive became less important, though it still comes over me at intervals.

Secondly I detect in myself a certain obsessionalism. Although I may be reluctant to start a job, I find it very difficult to stop or let go once I start.

Thirdly, there is the fascination of the job itself. This was an immensely motivating force for me in tuberculosis. Here was an age-old cruel disease which had cause misery and death for millennia. I have been reading *The Middle Ages* volume of the *Fontana Economic History of Europe* edited by C.M. Cipolla. Although the chapter on population points out that the great plagues in the late 6th and the 14th century more or less halved the populations of Europe, the author believes that in mediaeval times in Europe the major overall killer, especially in the productive period of life, was tuberculosis.

As one can learn from the many articulate victims among writers and artists, the disease was particularly cruel in its frequent "cat-and-mouse" course. The patient's spirits might be thrilled by apparent improvement, only all too often to be grimly shattered by successive relapses and ultimate death. Never was a dragon more worth slaying. These horrors were always at the back of my mind.

How fortunate I was that I was just about to launch on my postwar career when streptomycin, the first really effective treatment, came on the scene, followed later by other medicines. The contribution of our group was to learn how to use these medicines to maximum effect not only in curing virtually all patients but in preventing the disease.

I was equally fortunate to come to Edinburgh when the tuberculosis problem in Scotland was among the worst in Europe. Most countries had suffered increases, sometimes vast increases, during the war, but in virtually all except Scotland and Portugal the prevalence began to decline when the war finished. In Scotland, and Edinburgh, rates were still steadily increasing. There was a vast amount of misery and much public concern.

I soon saw that the services in Edinburgh were poor. We could set about improving these while we learnt how to deal with the disease effectively. With much public concern, the Regional Hospital Board was only too glad to let us get on with the job and to allow us the resources to do so. I was fortunate in recruiting enthusiastic consultant colleagues who worked desperately hard; in a succession of splendid junior doctors in training; in the exciting intellectual challenges of the disease; and in the exciting diplomatic challenges of getting the necessary resources. With success coming much more rapidly and much more completely than any of us dared to hope, these were indeed euphoric years. Of course one often thought that progress was slow. One might be depressed by some setback. But every now and then one looked back and was astonished at what had been achieved, especially when comparing it with the much slower progress elsewhere in the UK and abroad.

Of course, we had the secondary challenge that no-one believed our results. The thought of all those poor people suffering and dying unnecessarily was an immense incentive to try to persuade others that it could be done, though this took all too long. It was a great, and sometimes thwarting, challenge to select the right methods of persuasion without antagonising the leaders of medical opinion and so further delaying acceptance.

This chapter has been concerned with my own memoirs. Anyone interested in the whole picture of chemotherapy should read Frank Ryan's wonderful book, *Tuberculosis: the Greatest Story Never Told,* which gives not only a scholarly account of the discovery of the drugs but fascinating insights into the personalities involved and the intellectual climate in which they worked. A real thriller. Perhaps I am prejudiced. Sadly, as so often, the achievements are mainly attributed to me personally, whereas the strength of our group was that everyone made major contributions[*].

---

[*] This chapter was written mainly between 1989 and 1992, with additions in 2003.

Chapter 6
Non-Tuberculous Diseases

Organisation

I only accepted the Edinburgh post on condition that its title was Tuberculosis and Respiratory Diseases, and that I had beds for the latter. When I came to Edinburgh I was anxious to emphasise my broader interest in respiratory disease as well as tuberculosis. So I gave my Inaugural Lecture, the formal lecture which all new professors have to give in the university, on the subject of pneumonia. As I had to concentrate on tackling the enormous problem of tuberculosis, I handed two thirds of my thirty beds at the Northern General Hospital to Ian Grant when he was appointed consultant in the summer of 1952.

As tuberculosis rapidly decreased after we were given total charge in 1954, by 1960 it seemed logical to hand over the purely tuberculosis hospitals for the growing problems of geriatrics and concentrate our efforts in the City Hospital where we could keep the necessary beds for tuberculosis and develop those for chest diseases. Alec Welstead, the splendid administrator, converted one of the blocks of the City Hospital for my male and female non-tuberculosis wards. A similar change was made for Norman Horne's unit, soon to be joined by Ian Ross as the Royal Victoria Hospital was handed over for geriatrics. Ian Grant retained some tuberculosis beds at the City Hospital. As the tuberculosis went down, Jimmy Williamson looked for a new challenge with a major social component. He became a consultant geriatrician[*].

The other consultants in my new unit were Ross McHardy, who had joined us from the Royal Postgraduate Medical School in London, and Andrew Douglas who was appointed as Senior Lecturer soon after we moved to the City Hospital. We shared the beds of a male and female ward, each of 28 beds, in a single block, with steadily decreasing numbers of tuberculosis in other blocks.

---

[*] After a few years as Professor of Geriatrics in Liverpool, he was appointed to the newly-established Chair of Geriatrics at the University of Edinburgh.

Ross McHardy, a highly intelligent and skilled respiratory physiologist and a good clinician and teacher, steadily developed a first class respiratory physiology service, at that time the fashionable new field in respiratory diseases. We later achieved a new building and a much larger laboratory. Later still he became responsible for supervising all the respiratory physiology in Edinburgh[*] He was a man of great charm and a delightful colleague.

Andrew Douglas had a remarkable career. Son of a miner in Fife, he was the first child in his village to go to a university (Edinburgh). After postwar National Service he had a period in general practice. Following a severe attack of infectious hepatitis he spent a period as a bacteriologist before training in respiratory medicine with Ian Grant, Norman Horne and myself. As a fellow consultant he proved to be a marvellous colleague. He was a superb clinician, both in very acute and more chronic problems. Immensely caring, if anything hyperconscientious, he was deeply interested in patients' social problems. When he had been a relatively junior member of staff I had asked him to keep our register of patients with sarcoidosis. When I had arrived in Edinburgh I had been told that this disease was rare. I soon found otherwise. Before too long our group's sarcoidosis register amounted to more than 500 patients. Andrew continued this interest throughout his career, did a good deal of clinical research and attended many international meetings on the subject. He became my closest collaborator in many research projects as well as joint author of our textbook, *Respiratory Diseases*.

In due course we had a succession of Research Fellows for various projects, including several in association with the Research Committee of the British Thoracic Society. Successive BTS Research Fellows were responsible for various cooperative trials with units all over the UK. One of the most outstanding of these Fellows was Ian Campbell who coordinated with great skill several trials in tuberculosis treatment, and later in smoking cessation. He went on to become an outstanding consultant and teacher in Cardiff. We continued to collaborate in the international field, in problems both of tuberculosis and tobacco.

We also had a steady succession of foreign colleagues attached, the more senior at Research Fellow status who remained one to two years. Others, more junior, came primarily to learn clinical medicine. I felt that we could not give adequate personal attention to more than three or four at more senior level at any one time. We had to turn down many applications from many countries.

---

[*] He went on to become Chairman of the Lothian Division of Medicine

In addition we had an almost continuous stream of foreign visitors who stayed days or weeks. For a speech I had to make in 1965 about foreign collaboration I looked up the figures. I found that by that time we had already had visitors from twenty-seven countries. There were many, many more in later years but I never added them up.

Our junior posts were filled by young doctors from all over the UK, some also from abroad. Applications became even more numerous after our postgraduate textbook *Respiratory Diseases* was published in 1969. As a result of this we planted our trainees or consultants all over the UK and in a number of countries abroad.

At the City Hospital we had established our Respiratory Physiology Laboratory. This was started by James MacNamara, who, after a couple of years, went off to an independent consultant post in England. He was succeeded by Ross McHardy. Later, in close collaboration with Robert Cruikshank, the Professor of Bacteriology, a Regional Virus Laboratory was established at the hospital. There was already an excellent non-tuberculosis bacteriological laboratory, particularly serving the infectious diseases side of the hospital. We transferred the library from Southfield and further built it up. I started files for classified reprints, which stood Andrew Douglas and me in good stead when we began to write our postgraduate textbook.

There was already an excellent thoracic surgical unit at the City Hospital with two outstanding surgeons, Bobby Macormack and Philip Walbaum. We worked very closely with them. I and my unit usually attended their weekly problem sessions.

I continued my weekly outpatient clinic at the Royal Infirmary. The Royal Victoria Dispensary, founded by Sir Robert Philip, remained the chief chest clinic, but with progressively less tuberculosis and progressively more respiratory disease. I ran a Saturday morning clinic at the City Hospital for VIPs and working patients whose jobs might be at risk if they attended clinics on weekdays. I also continued a weekly clinic at the RVD.

Outstanding weekly commitments included a 5pm clinical meeting on Tuesdays where respiratory consultants from all over the Lothian Region took it in turn to organise the presentation of problems. Wednesday morning was the problem session in my own Unit. It was in many ways a teaching session. Patient problems were presented. I would often stop after the history and stimulate discussion about the possibilities, starting with students or junior staff. When all had been presented on that patient, I often first picked a student, undergraduate or postgraduate, to comment and then worked up the seniority. Neither I nor any of the consultants present were allowed to comment until the more junior had spoken. We did all this "blind", ie not knowing the true answer (if it was known at that stage).

We started with bacteriological or pathological problems, with those particular consultants present to discuss the case. The radiologist usually attended. I believe this was the best postgraduate teaching I did. The undergraduates also sat in, but were probably more benefited by bedside teaching with checking of their histories and physical signs.

Before each ward round we discussed each patient in a side room without the patient being there. Here I did more undergraduate teaching. One could discuss the patient's problems much more freely if he was not there to catch, and possibly misunderstand, snatches which might unjustifiably alarm him or her. The ward sister sat in on these sessions. We then went round and checked on each patient. I was already updated and could speak to the patient with full knowledge.

Another routine event in the week was the "Social Session". As already recounted, I had initiated these sessions while at the Postgraduate Medical School at Hammersmith Hospital in London and continued throughout my Edinburgh career. We went over all the patients from the social point of view. The junior doctors were expected to present the social aspects. All the Unit doctors attended as well as the ward sisters and senior nurses, the social worker, and a Health Visitor to liaise with Health Visitors in general practice. In later years we found it useful to have the physiotherapist and occupational therapist there also. They might have picked up the real problem from the patient. Of course most of the problems were the usual concerns, housing, finance, family problems, problems of the family carer or problems of inadequate care. Often we could do something about it, through social work, discussion with family etc. Of course you cannot totally change people's behaviour. You can often help, but there is a limit to how far you can live people's lives for them. And of course there were the basics. As soon as the patient came in we were discussing whether they would need help on discharge, such as changes for the house to enable a disabled patient to function or the provision of a home help. In some Units the problems would only be discovered when the patient was ready for discharge. Then it might take a week or two to make the relevant arrangements, with much waste of beds. Worse still, the problems might not be discovered at all.

Research

Although this is primarily an account of my personal involvement in non-tuberculosis research[*] I must pay tribute to the help of a succession of able junior colleagues undergoing training and above all to Andrew Douglas, who was very much my right-hand man from the 1960s. Quite apart from his own research on sarcoidosis and other problems, he was closely involved

---

[*] Only significant research relevant to these personal memoirs has been recorded here.

in our research on bronchial muscle function. During the years when I was Dean, Vice-Principal and President of the Royal College of Physicians, I obviously had very much less time for departmental duties and research. Andrew kept the research going ensuring in addition, with his own outstanding clinical skills, that the clinical work was of the highest order.

Pneumonia

Throughout much of my career I had been interested in infectious diseases. A group of us at the Postgraduate School, together with colleagues in neighbouring hospitals, had investigated what organisms, bacteria or viruses, caused pneumonia in West London. We published the results just before I moved to Edinburgh. I was then asked to act as secretary to a Medical Research Council committee to investigate the use of two of the newer antibiotics (aureomycin and chloramphenicol) in comparison with penicillin in the treatment of pneumonia. We found that penicillin was still more effective in severe cases.

Following the institution of the Regional Virus Laboratory at the City Hospital some ten years later, we carried out important surveys of the causes of pneumonia in patients admitted to our wards. As a consequence I stimulated the Research Committee of what is now the British Thoracic Society with which I was associated as Vice Chairman, Chairman or Member over a number of years, to expand such surveys on a cooperative basis in hospitals throughout the UK. We also did some controlled trials, with our colleagues, on other antibiotics in pneumonia.

Chronic Bronchitis.

For the ordinary person this diagnosis is much the simplest description of the disease, though, following the Americans, the fashion nowadays is to call it Chronic Obstructive Pulmonary Disease (COPD) or other synonyms. At the time I started working in Edinburgh this was an extremely common disease in the UK. The characteristic was chronic cough and sputum, worst in the winter, with frequent exacerbations of respiratory infections. The patient becomes more and more breathless over the years. Later he is often completely housebound, finally dying from respiratory failure, frequently in an exacerbation due to infection.

The great increase in mortality from this disease during the famous London smog in 1952 emphasised the importance of atmospheric pollution from coal smoke in its cause. The later studies on British doctors, which were originally made to study the effect of cigarette smoking on lung cancer, showed that the mortality from chronic bronchitis was also far higher in cigarette smokers than in non-smokers. The disasters from the London smog stimulated a great deal of cleaning up of atmospheric pollution through the

Clean Air Acts of Parliament. Similarly, the demonstrated effect of cigarettes in causing chronic bronchitis, lung cancer and many other diseases led to efforts to control tobacco smoking.

My wife Eileen and I became interested in the comparison of the chronic bronchitis mortalities in England and Wales and in Scotland. She had now become an unpaid epidemiological Research Assistant in the Department. We wondered whether mass cigarette smoking had started later in Scotland than in England as the mortality seemed to have increased later. As smoking had developed first in a big way in males in the First World War and in females massively only in the Second World War we looked at the male: female ratios of mortality for various diseases, including chronic bronchitis, from the beginning of the century. The results confirmed our original hypothesis that, with the surge of cigarette smoking in the First World War in males, the mortality from these smoking-related diseases, compared to the mortality in females, would increase as the male cohorts of the appropriate age who had started smoking heavily in the First World War grew older. Also in agreement with our original hypothesis, the increase tended to occur about ten years later, for each cohort, in Scotland than in England. No one had done similar studies in this field previously. It was also rather romantic to have a paper published listing "Crofton and Crofton" as the authors[*].

We also did a good deal of work on the causes of infectious exacerbations in chronic bronchitis, which were what usually brought the patients into hospital. We identified the common bacteria involved and investigated whether these might complicate an initial viral infection. We also did trials to identify the best antibiotics to use.

Much earlier in our work, being particularly interested in the social side of medicine, I had asked the then Chest and Heart Association of Scotland to support a social study of the effect of chronic bronchitis on the quality of patients' lives. A research worker, Miss Mary Nielson, using a standard questionnaire we prepared, interviewed 500 patients in Edinburgh and Glasgow. Miss Nielson was a social worker rather than a scientist and had some difficulty in analysing and writing up the results. My wife Eileen came to the rescue, did the analyses and wrote the report. The results and recommendations were published as a booklet by the Association under their joint authorship[#]. This showed the grim effects of the disease on patients' employment, finances, domestic life and social life.

---

[*] Crofton E, Crofton J. Influence of smoking on mortality from various diseases in Scotland and England: an analysis by cohorts. *British Medical Journal* 1963; 2: 1161-4

[#] Neilson MGC, Crofton E. The social effects of chronic bronchitis. The Chest and Heart Association, 1965.

We thought it possible that a number of these patients could be capable of part-time work. They would be happier and better off if they could have appropriate work. This might be possible if they could receive half sickness pay combined with half pay for their part-time work. One of my colleagues in Dundee, Robert Johnston, had access to money in a local Trust. They carried out a useful trial in association with social workers. They organised part-time work for patients who were thought fit for this and supplemented their pay to represent what they might have received in half-time sickness pay. Although of course a number of patients deteriorated and later had to come off work, it did improve the quality of life and income, at least temporarily.

Bronchiectasis

This used to be a very grim disease. It mostly arose from pneumonias in infancy, a very common cause of disease and death before the introduction of antibiotics. These infections might severely damage the bronchial tubes, particularly in the lower part of the lung. These then became dilated and failed to function properly. They frequently became chronically infected with large amounts of sputum, often foul and stinking, causing very considerable distress to the patient over many years. There was a high death rate. Before the discovery of antibiotics almost the only useful treatment was to tip the patient up several times a day to drain the infected sump at the bottom of his lungs. I remember when I first went to the Brompton Hospital after the war there was still a special room filled with aerosol disinfectant where the patients would sit and breathe in the disinfectant in a vain attempt to control the infection in their lungs.

When I moved to Edinburgh I had to resign as secretary of the Medical Research Council committee which had carried out the controlled trials on new antibiotics and pneumonia. But we cooperated with the committee's second trial of new antibiotics in bronchiectasis. They proved very effective. The disease became much easier to control, although one could not reverse the damage in the bronchi. Mortality became much lower. Moreover antibiotic treatment of pneumonia in infancy resulted in many fewer cases. The general impression was that the outlook had become very much better but nobody had carried out a systematic survey. Not long before I retired we did such a survey, reviewing the progress of patients who had been diagnosed ten years or more before by members of our group. We found, as we expected, that the outlook had become very much better for mortality, disability and social aspects of life. (Foul smelling sputum had of course miserably affected social contacts). Interestingly enough we were also able, at this follow-up, to test what had happened to the lung function. The lung function had badly deteriorated only in those who had continued smoking. Those who had given up smoking had only deteriorated at the rate expected with increasing age. On the whole both health and social life had greatly improved[*].

Lung Cancer

Of course we saw very large numbers of these patients. Once diagnosed the outlook was very poor. The only really effective treatment was surgery, the removal of the lung or the part of the lung concerned. However in a large number of patients, by the time they were diagnosed the cancer had spread too widely for surgery to be an effective option. Many other patients, because of their chronic smoking, had too poor lung function to permit operation. X-ray treatment might have a temporary palliative effect, as might anticancer drugs, though they could do no more than slightly improve the period of survival, often at the expense of unpleasant side effects. When I was compiling our postgraduate textbook editions between 1969 and 1981 I reviewed the literature over the previous thirty years and found that the survival rates had remained virtually unchanged. Only about 7% survived for five years after diagnosis.

Available treatments were clearly only of minor value but there was no apparent sign of anything more promising to research. The obvious need was to concentrate on tackling cigarette smoking, the overwhelming cause of the disease.

Pulmonary eosinophilia

Before I left London I became interested in a group of lung diseases characterised by a rise in eosinophils in the blood (usually associated with some form of allergy or with worm infestation) and various types of clinical illness. With a number of colleagues we described a range of conditions we had seen. They agreed that we might invent a new term "Pulmonary Eosinophilia" for the overall group. Our overall diagnostic label has been generally accepted in the British literature though the Americans tend to use different terms.

Communication with patients

Just before I retired I designed a trial in our Unit on another subject. I learnt that a public health doctor, D.M. Parkin, as part of his training, had done a study in Dundee on patients' knowledge of their diagnosis and treatment some months after they had left the teaching hospital. To everyone's surprise Dr Parkin had found that only 50% of the patients had a

---

[*] In fact, bronchiectasis is still a substantial problem in 21st century Edinburgh with over 500 patients attending the Royal Infirmary specialist clinic. However, only a small proportion of today's patients still smoke and their average age is over sixty years.

reasonable grasp even of the diagnosis of the disease from which they were suffering, much less a grasp of their main treatment. Like most doctors we thought that we were good communicators. Surely we should be very much better in our own Unit where we took a lot of time and trouble in informing patients. So we did a little pilot survey and were astonished to find that we were no better than Dundee! So we designed a controlled trial. When the patient was being discharged the doctor gave him or her detailed information about the diagnosis and the main treatment and any general advice to follow after leaving hospital. He wrote down exactly what he had told the patient. In every alternate week each patient was given a copy of what the doctor had written down. In the other week he only had the verbal communication (though of course a letter was sent to his GP).

The results were very interesting. When he had only been given verbal information, in spite of the fact that this was a research project and everybody was taking particular trouble, three months later his knowledge of the diagnosis and main treatment was no better than in our pilot study. But when he had also been given the information in writing, a reasonable knowledge of both diagnosis and main treatment went up from about 50% of patients to about 90%. However when he had been advised to change his habits in some way, such as change in diet or stopping smoking, only 12% of patients remembered what they had been told verbally and it only went up to 23% when they had had it in writing.

Thinking about it afterwards we were not very surprised at these results. When the patient is being talked to by the doctor he tends to be emotionally het up. The doctor is often talking to him in somewhat difficult language and probably in a different accent. But if he has a bit of paper in his pocket he can sit down at home when he is emotionally stable and read what he has been told at leisure. He is therefore much more likely to remember it. I know from discussion with non-medical friends that just the same sort of thing may happen even to the most educated. Later my friend, Professor Charles Fletcher, did a survey in the UK of communication with patients on behalf of the Nuffield Trust. He told me that ours was the only controlled trial on the subject he had come across[*].

This experience led me to become further interested in information for patients. I had long been on the Council of what is now Chest Heart and Stroke Scotland (the successor of the National Association for the Prevention of Tuberculosis founded in 1899). Clearly it would be difficult for every doctor to write out detailed information and advice for each patient. It would be useful to give him/her an appropriate printed sheet or

---

[*] Ellis DA, Hopkin JM, Leitch AG, Crofton J. "Doctor's orders": controlled trial of supplementary, written information for patients. *British Medical Journal* 1979; 1: 456

booklet, writing down more briefly any further advice particular to that patient.

Of course a large proportion of hospital patients are not highly educated. I looked through various publications, mostly from voluntary bodies. Most were excellent for the educated middle classes. I found that there was a special formula, based on length of sentences, simple words used etc, which enables one to calculate from any text what proportion of the population could read and understand it. Applying this formula confirmed my initial impression.

We set out to prepare more appropriate CHSS booklets, with relevant specialist and GP advice. We then commissioned the health group in the Department of Marketing in Strathclyde University to try out our drafts on "focus groups" of patients in Edinburgh and Glasgow. We knew that the Strathclyde group had done excellent work on testing out Health Education projects for the main government Health Education Group in Scotland. On the whole the draft booklets proved appropriate but we had one or two surprises. One of the booklets was for patients with stroke and in particular for their carers. The authors included a professor of General Practice and a professor of Geriatric Medicine. The patients greatly resented the word "Geriatric". So we altered it to "Professor of Medicine".

Illustrations are essential for more simple readers. In the tuberculosis booklet we had included what we thought was a comic caricature of the tubercle bacillus, but the patients found this too frightening. Less surprisingly, in the booklet on chronic bronchitis, patients resented our emphasis on the importance of giving up cigarette smoking, in fact the most vital step they could take to prevent further deterioration. We felt unable to backtrack on this essential advice.

Conclusions

Looking back I think all these various research projects were mostly useful contributions in their particular fields, though none of them could be regarded as a breakthrough. They did contribute to knowledge and they probably did contribute to better medical practice. In addition they provided a great deal of training for successive generations of young men and women both from the UK and overseas. Many of our trainees became consultants all over the UK and in many other countries, which further diffused our teaching. Over the years we also had on our staff several successive Research Fellows from the British Thoracic Society who coordinated from our Department cooperative trials and surveys of various kinds throughout the UK.

Chapter 7:
The War With The Weed

Personal history

I personally have never been a smoker, unusual in someone of my age. When I was young no-one realised the dangers. By the time I was born my father had become a non-smoker. When he was a student he had been a very heavy smoker; I gathered he chain-smoked continuously while studying. He then began to have pains across his upper chest. He consulted one of his teachers and as a result was sent to England to see the famous Sir William Osler. This must have been during the time when Osler was Regius Professor of Medicine in Oxford. Osler advised him to stop smoking. He did so. The pains disappeared. They never recurred. He ultimately lived to the age of 96!

When I was a teenage schoolboy my mother took up smoking Turkish cigarettes. They were rather glamorous, oval in cross-section and gave audible crackles with each inhalation. As a boy I found them rather fascinating. I presume smoking cigarettes, particularly this sort of exotic cigarette, was then rather "advanced" and fashionable among the wives of the professional elite in Dublin. Her habit did not last long. Retrospectively I have an idea that she gave up because she thought I disapproved. I don't remember either feeling or expressing disapproval. I may have conveyed some subconscious impression that smoking was inappropriate in beloved mums.

When I became a student I decided it might be manly to smoke a pipe. But it made me feel sick. I soon gave it up. Thereafter I smoked one or two cigarettes a year among my friends so as to emphasise, paradoxically in the present context, that my non-smoking was not a moral addiction.

During the war smoking in the Forces was almost universal. Everyone had a right to 50 free cigarettes a week. I sometimes drew my ration and gave it to friends. No-one of course then realised that the vast expansion of smoking was giving support (if somewhat dilatory support) to Hitler in his efforts to knock off the British. Ultimately tobacco may well have produced more death than he did, but fortunately too late to influence the outcome of the struggle.

The "enlightenment"

This was where things stood[*] for the first few years after the war. I knew that Richard Doll, who had been a fellow student at St Thomas's, was working under a Medical Research Council grant with the statistician, Bradford Hill, to try to find out the cause of the current steep and unexplained rise in deaths from lung cancer, formerly a rare disease. Their team was interviewing lung cancer patients and questioning them about exposure to various possible causes, such as car exhaust fumes, gas cookers, alcohol and, incidentally, tobacco. At the same time they interviewed control patients with other diseases but of the same age, sex and social class. The amount of previous exposure to each possible cause was compared in the two groups.

I suppose it was in 1950 that Richard and I both happened to be on the Members' Committee of the Royal College of Physicians of London. I remember one day as we walked along together to the College for a meeting asking him if anything was coming out of his research. He told me "Yes indeed" but that he was not yet at liberty to tell me what. A few weeks later their report came out. It showed the dramatic association of lung cancer with cigarette smoking. Their patients, of course, were reaping the whirlwind of the vast surge of smoking among troops in the First World War. They had now reached cancer age. Sadly, in due course many of the Second World War generation were to follow, this time also including women whose smoking had exploded during the war.

Doll and Hill followed with a prospective survey in which they asked British doctors, including me, to record their smoking habits. They then waited like a couple of vultures on the sidelines to record what we died from. Sadly, if fortunately for science and preventive medicine, many heavy smokers soon started to die far more quickly than non-smokers. And they died not only from lung cancer, but from certain other cancers, heart attacks, chronic bronchitis etc. Within three years or so the evidence had become so overwhelming that Doll and Hill published the results. About the same time similar studies in the USA had the same conclusions[#].

---

[*] This is not quite the context. As early as 1931, Angel Honorio Roffo had shown that tobacco tar can cause tumours on the skin of rabbits (*Zeitschrift für Krebsforschung* 33: 321-332), and Ernest Kennaway in the 1940s suggested cigarette smoking as a cause of the increase in deaths from lung cancer (British Empire Campaign, 24th Annual Report, 1947, 190)

[#] In fact, four papers demonstrated an association between lung cancer and smoking (Schrek et el, 1950, *Cancer Research* 10, 49-58; Levin et al 1950, *Journal of the American Medical Association* 143, 336-338; Mills & Porter 1950, *Cancer Research* 10, 539-542; Wynder & Graham 1950 *Journal of the American Medical Association*, 1143, 329-336) before Doll and Hill's first publication.

The implications for all of us were clear. We must try to get the message across and try to reverse the surging epidemic. This was not at all easy. For one thing in 1948 the smoking rate in male doctors in the UK (68%) was higher than in the general male population (65%). To reverse what had been a highly acceptable, highly social and enjoyable habit, previously carrying no opprobrium whatsoever, understandably proved to be a formidable task, a task still far from completed even in the UK nearly 50 years later.

The Doll and Hill publications received extensive publicity in the media. Male doctors' smoking rate dropped slightly and became a little lower than that of men in general which remained little changed. Women's rates continued to rise.

My friend Charles Fletcher had moved from the Medical Research Council Pneumoconiosis Unit at Cardiff into my job at the (Royal) Postgraduate Medical School at Hammersmith Hospital when I moved to Edinburgh in 1952. There he began work on the natural history and causes of chronic bronchitis. The vast prevalence of this disease and the extent of resultant disability and death had only just begun to be realised. This was largely as a result of the study of 1000 patients at the Brompton Hospital by Neville Oswald, later a consultant at St Bartholomew's Hospital. The great London smog in the winter of 1952 had been associated with a large excess of deaths from this disease. So attention at first became concentrated on coal smoke atmospheric pollution as the main cause. A year or two later the Doll/Hill results in doctors showed a great excess in smokers.

Charles had been liaising with the Department of Health about air pollution. One day he asked a visiting senior medical civil servant, Max Wilson, what the Department of Health was going to do about cigarette smoking. The reply was that the Department could not do much itself. Was not this a job for the Royal Medical Colleges? So Charles approached the then President of the Royal College of Physicians, Sir Russell Brain, through Sir Francis Avery Jones, suggesting the College should review the evidence about the ill effects of smoking and produce a report. They were turned down. In 1959, with a new President, Sir Robert Platt, he tried again, this time with success. So Charles acted as secretary to the College committee and personally wrote most of the report which was published in 1962. It received great publicity. But it only had a minor and temporary effect on general smoking rates, though the doctors' rates continued slowly downwards.

Up to this time my personal contribution was very minor, though I highlighted the problem in my postgraduate teaching in London and, after 1952 in both postgraduate and undergraduate teaching in Edinburgh, as well as during my trips abroad. There was one amusing anecdote which might have indicated a personal effect. An excellent New Zealand registrar of ours, who ultimately became President of the Royal Australian College of Physicians, thought it would be interesting one day to ask the technician who showed all the lantern slides in lectures at the Postgraduate School whether he got anything out of the many lectures he had to listen to. The reply was "Not much, but that Dr Crofton: I heard him once, I heard him twice, and the third time I had to give up". So I had achieved at least one triumph of preventive medicine!

Foundation of ASH (Action on Smoking and Health)

The Royal College of Physicians of London produced a second report in 1971. In view of the disappointingly little effect of the 1962 report on smoking rates, Charles suggested that the College should set up some body to keep the problem continuously before the media and the public. I was one of the people who supported him with a letter to the then President. So in 1972 ASH was founded, initially with accommodation within the College. Thereafter it went from strength to strength, especially under its outstanding second and third Directors, Mike Daube and David Simpson. Overall male smoking rates began to decrease impressively. The doctors' rates took a much steeper dive. Women's rates began to decrease for the first time.

After the foundation of ASH in London in 1972, we began to consider what we should do in Scotland. The first initiative came from Tom Hurst, then the chief administrator (I think the title was "Secretary") of the Royal Infirmary in Edinburgh. He was, and continued to be, a great, if sometimes eccentric, enthusiast in the field. He went on to become the Treasurer of UK ASH. But he was very much an individualist and often caused embarrassment by making public statements about ASH policy without discussing it with his colleagues. His public statements sometimes "went over the top". In due course he had to be eased out. Nevertheless some of his ideas proved valuable. Following an American example, it was he who really originated what is now the very successful annual National No Smoking Day. He later persuaded WHO to initiate the equally successful World No Smoking Day which leads to much publicity and initiative in many countries.

I had been on the Council of the Royal College of Physicians of Edinburgh for some years and was then Vice-President so he approached me in the first place. We decided to ask the Professor of Social Medicine (nowadays called "Public Health"), Stuart Morrison, and the then Director of the recently established Scottish Health Education Group, Alfred Yarrow, to join us for discussions. We had a series of meetings in the College. We decided that we should form a Scottish ASH. Yarrow very sensibly said that it must have some staff, perhaps initially with just two sessions a week. The media must always be able to contact someone by telephone. Who could we get? It struck me that Eileen, now that the children were growing up, might be interested. Our cohort study had intrigued her. My colleagues were enthusiastic. And so was she when I broached it. Having such a worthwhile mission she found immensely rewarding.

We decided to approach John Croom, the then President of the Royal College of Physicians of Edinburgh. He enthusiastically agreed. So did the Council of the College. The College provided an office. Eileen started with two sessions a week, raised money from the Scottish Local Authorities and was off. Its immensely successful later history is her story. Public appreciation of her splendid work was symbolised by the award of an MBE when she retired in 1987.

John Croom was about to demit office as President of the Royal College of Physicians. He agreed to chair the new organisation which worked closely with ASH in London, at least during Eileen's time.

I was a foundation member of Council both for UK ASH in London and for Scottish ASH. Later, in 1978, after completing busy years as President of the Royal College of Physicians of Edinburgh (1973-76), I persuaded ASH London to start a "Cessation Committee" which I chaired. The main aim was to bring together various groups who were exploring different methods of assisting people to quit smoking, either among the general public or in the workplace. I believe this provided a useful exchange of ideas and stimulated further research and further initiatives. At about the same time I also suggested that ASH should have a Research Committee. In this I worked closely with Charles Fletcher, who was then President of ASH. We asked Richard Doll to chair the Committee. Charles became the secretary and I became the vice-chairman. He and I, with Richard, organised its membership and agenda. Again we sought to bring together research workers and stimulate further research. Through Charles we persuaded the Medical Research Council to support the excellent work by Mike Russell and his colleagues on cessation at the Institute of Psychiatry in London. They pioneered the use of nicotine in various forms to help the addicts to quit.

We also raised the question of what biological mechanisms underlay tobacco as a cause of heart disease. There was little knowledge at that time. As a result the MRC financed a symposium which led to much productive research. We liaised with Professor James[*] of the Rowett Research Institute in Aberdeen over the metabolic effect of smoking, linked to the common weight gain after quitting. This is an unfortunate deterrent to quitting for many young women. Later, as Richard, Charles and I were now over

---

[*] W.P.T. (Philip) James was director of the Rowett Research Institute from 1982-99.

retirement age, we thought we should hand over to younger people. These were very distinguished but very much medico-biological research workers. They did not seem to have the campaigning stimulus or adequate knowledge of the community and epidemiological side which had motivated us. Not much happened and the committee fairly soon folded up.

As I was now getting older I resigned as chairman of the ASH Cessation Committee after some five years. Another chairman was appointed but I think thereafter there were only one or two more meetings.

We also started a research group for Scottish ASH, at first chaired by Sir John Brotherston after he had finished as Chief Medical Officer for Scotland and had succeeded John Croom as chairman of Scottish ASH. Our most useful success was to stimulate, via the Scottish Office and the Department of Health in London, a bi-annual UK sample survey of smoking rates in school children which has continued since. Unfortunately we did not succeed in persuading them to do similar surveys for relevant professionals – doctors, nurses and school teachers.

Later, when I succeeded John Brotherston as chairman of the committee, we tried to organise research on nurses, notoriously thought to have high smoking rates. We approached the Nursing Research Group in Edinburgh University. They agreed to take it on. Then the Scottish Office Nursing Department informed them that they were not funded or intended for such studies and must not take the lead.

Again, we organised, in excellent liaison with the Scottish Division of the Royal College of Obstetricians, a controlled trial of different methods of helping potential mothers attending ante-natal clinics to quit. There was a laboratory component written in to confirm that the women were smokers or non-smokers. Unfortunately the laboratories concerned thought it would be useful to build in a study on the importance of trace elements in pregnancy. This raised the cost immensely and we failed to get funding from the Chief Scientist's Office which controlled government medical research funding in Scotland. I suppose for both of these projects we were a bit ahead of medico-biological opinion on official research committees. So, apart from bringing various research workers together, we did not achieve a lot.

Scottish Health Education Coordinating Committee.

When in 1981 I was asked to chair a new Scottish Office committee (Scottish Health Education Coordinating Committee, SHECC), it was obvious that a top priority should be tobacco. We turned at once to ASH for a preliminary submission. Michael Daube, who had done a wonderful job in making ASH London the major organisation in England, was now a Senior Lecturer in Edinburgh University. Eileen, he and other colleagues gave us a splendid submission. I wrote most of the final report, very much based on theirs. After outlining the epidemiological background in Scotland we gave detailed specifications of what should be done by the Government, by the Scottish Office, by the NHS (Scottish Health Education Group, Health Boards and their officers and professionals, including consultants, GPs, Health Trade Unions etc), Education Services, Local Authorities, Health and Safety Executive, Employers' Associations, Trade Unions and voluntary organisations.

Two years later we monitored the report implementation by Health Boards. It proved pretty patchy. A few years later still (1990), after finishing as chairman of SHECC, I repeated this survey through the Scottish Tobacco Group, an informal group sponsored by ASH Scotland and the BMA. There had been appreciable improvement but still many deficiencies. Through the same mechanism we later surveyed action by Local Authorities: Regional and Island Councils in 1990, and District Councils in 1991.

The objective of these surveys was not only to monitor progress but also to stimulate further action. To achieve this we followed up the questionnaires by a draft report, which was sent to the authorities for comment and to ensure that we had not misinterpreted the information they had sent us. In the Local Authority report we produced a grading system and allocated marks for success. We listed the authorities and their grades in order to praise the leaders and stimulate the laggards to action.

British Thoracic Society Nicorette Trial

Mike Russell and his colleagues at the Institute of Psychiatry in London had published in the 1980s the result of a controlled trial of nicotine-containing chewing gum as an aid to quitting. They found that providing a chewing gum containing nicotine to help people get off cigarettes doubled the success rate; if I remember from about 15% to about 30%. The controls had the same gum without nicotine. On the Research Committee of the British Thoracic Society, on which I served for many years, we decided to do a large-scale collaborative trial in patients suffering from smoking-related diseases – mostly chronic bronchitis or heart disease. This was very effectively coordinated by Ian Campbell in Cardiff. Mike Russell and his colleagues were very cross because we could show no effect. The explanation was in fact clear – motivation. Mike's clinics were for individuals who wanted very much to quit. On the whole they were better educated than the average NHS patient with bronchitis or heart disease. Moreover the latter, ill enough to have been admitted to hospital, had probably been advised over and over again to quit, but had not done so. They were the hard core.

International Union Against Tuberculosis and Lung Disease: Tobacco and Health Committee

Since completing my stint as chairman of the Tuberculosis Diagnostic Committee of the International Union against Tuberculosis in 1963 I had had less contact with the Union. In Edinburgh we now had too little tuberculosis to do research on it but I was busy with other diseases and other jobs. Early in the 1980s the IUAT decided to extend its interest to other lung diseases and became the International Union against Tuberculosis and Lung Disease (IUATLD). The new Scientific Committee on Respiratory Diseases recommended that there should be a specific committee on smoking. I was invited to be its first chairman when it was set up in 1984. This started me on a very interesting few years in the international tobacco field.

Previously, on my various lecture tours abroad, I had tried to raise the tobacco question whenever appropriate. I was often asked to do a brief TV or radio broadcast. My routine was to raise two points. The first was to emphasise that tuberculosis was now an entirely curable disease, but only if patients took their complete treatment meticulously. The second was the lethal effect of smoking and the importance of campaigning against it.

In several countries, where Eileen was accompanying me, I emphasised to my local contacts her expertise as Medical Director of Scottish ASH and a member of a WHO Expert Committee on the subject. As a consequence in 1977 she gave what I think was the first public lecture on smoking in Brazil when I was a Visiting Professor there. Later in that year she repeated this in a lecture to the local Lions' Club in Ludhiana, India. This may not have been the first such lecture in India but I had not previously heard of any anti-smoking activity there.

During the 1980s Robert Pannier of Belgium, who had been largely responsible for founding what is now the very successful European Respiratory Society, almost annually asked me to speak at or chair a session on smoking at their meetings in various parts of Europe. It was perhaps symbolic that attendance was usually pretty sparse compared to that in the clinical sessions.

Influencing individual members of IUATLD

When our IUATLD Committee met we decided that we should first concentrate our efforts on impressing on individual members, mostly respiratory medicine specialists, their responsibility for helping to tackle the world-wide epidemic. As tobacco is primarily a health problem everyone looks to leadership from doctors.

Accordingly we decided to prepare a booklet, *The Smoking Epidemic: How You Can Help* to be distributed to all IUATLD members (thought at the time to be some 5,000) and to more than 120 national associations affiliated to IUATLD. Kjell Bjartveit from Norway, with a distinguished international reputation in the field and an old friend, served on the committee and suggested that we should also produce a single sheet leaflet on the subject which doctors and organisations could present to politicians. His wife had been a Minister in Norway and said that no politician would read more than one page!

I produced a draft of both these documents. They were reviewed by committee members. My memory is that there was little amendment. Kjell had done much of this sort of thing within Norway. He had a brilliant artist, an Englishman married to a Norwegian, who produced wonderful light-hearted colourful drawings and a striking cover.

I approached Halfdan Mahler, the Director General of WHO, for permission to put his photograph on the political leaflet. The booklet was produced in French and English, the leaflet in a number of languages, including Chinese.

IUATLD Conferences

In addition we ensured that the tobacco problem was given a prominent place at all the Union conferences. These included a World Conference every three to four years and Regional Conferences (Middle East, Far East, Africa, America) every two years. I participated in most of them during my term of office (1984-88). A particular success was a plenary session in the Union's World Conference in Singapore in 1986. Among the speakers was Peter Taylor, a brilliant media expert who had produced some fine campaigning programmes on the subject for the BBC. Preceding travel to the Conference he had visited Taiwan and Thailand. Both countries were trying to control the epidemic but having serious difficulties with US senators, tobacco financed, threatening retaliatory trade sanctions if governments resisted the free entry of US manufactured cigarettes.

We also had as speaker a recent Minister of Health from Western Australia who had lost that job by the political influence of the tobacco industry owing to his energetic efforts to control the tobacco epidemic. He told me privately that he believed the industry had informed the Prime Minister that if that man was reappointed Minister of Health after a subsequent election the industry would donate a million dollars to the opposition party funds. To his disappointment he had recently been moved to another Ministerial post.

We had an enormous turnout to our plenary session. This was followed by a most lively press conference which went on for two hours such was the media interest. Urgent phone calls went to activists in USA to give publicity to the nefarious activities of the tobacco industry and their tame senators in trying to bully Thailand and Taiwan.

Influencing medical students.

We also decided we must seek to influence the next generation of doctors. We developed a questionnaire to determine the smoking habits and test the knowledge and attitudes of medical students regarding tobacco. I modified the questionnaire which had been evolved for health professionals jointly by WHO and the International Union against Cancer.

The secretary of our committee was Professor Paul Freour of the University of Bordeaux. He offered to process the replies to the questionnaires through his Department in collaboration with the Statistical Department in their Faculty of Medicine. Paul was passionate about the smoking problem. He was, and is, a charming man, a poet and an artist. He was at that time professor of Respiratory Medicine which, in French universities, tended to be combined with Public Health. He treated me with great kindness and friendship, later successfully proposing me for an Honorary Degree at Bordeaux University. He himself was not a statistician and was less interested in epidemiological aspects. However his Lecturer, Jean-Francois Tessier, undertook most of the administrative work for the medical students research and did it with great devotion. He later became secretary and then chairman of the IUATLD Committee.

The major problem was the Statistical Department in Bordeaux, which kept on producing incompatible tables or figures that did not add up. I had to recheck all the calculations and frequently return tables for correction. I kept on suggesting that all figures and tables should be double checked. My relations with Paul and Jean-Francois remained excellent, though I continued to be very irritated with their statistical department.

Bordeaux felt that they could handle no more than 50 centres. We aimed at choosing one centre in each country except for the very large ones (USA, USSR, India, China) where we had three and Japan where we had two. I had friends or contacts in most of the countries, Paul in francophone Africa. In the end we were able to analyse results from 51 medical schools in 42 countries and all inhabited continents.

Of course we had our problems. Our questionnaire was intended to be filled up by all first year and final year students in order to test what they might have learnt in the medical school. It was reproduced in the national language where necessary and the translation checked by appropriate linguists in France.

For each year the absentees proved minimal. Colleagues from three medical schools in USA had agreed to take part. But one only produced replies from first year students, one only from final year students, and the third none at all. In South America two countries failed to produce results; finally we only had Chile as a representative. The one school that we had chosen in Canada also failed to produce results. On the other hand China, India, Japan and USSR did the job excellently as did most other countries, though we were defeated by postal problems in the Philippines and by civil war in the Sudan.

We managed to publish the results from fourteen European countries in time for a major WHO inter-governmental European summit in Madrid in 1988 in which I participated. (At that meeting, incidentally, I was presented with a WHO Medal for my work on tobacco). We published subsequent reports for Africa/Middle East and Asia; later from USSR, USA, Australia and Japan, with a final report summarising the lessons for medical education.

Jointly with Tapani Piha of WHO Europe we followed up the European survey by a questionnaire to Deans of all European medical schools, emphasising the many deficiencies in knowledge and attitudes we had found in medical schools and enquiring what action they would take. I guessed we would do well to get a 30% response. We achieved just about that. As expected there was a higher response rate in northern than in southern Europe.

Survey of action by IUATLD National Associations

I should add that we also did a survey of all the National Associations belonging to the Union to ask what they were doing about smoking. As one might expect this was very varied, with much more action in northern than in southern countries of Europe but quite enthusiastic work in some of the ex-USSR countries in eastern Europe.

International Co-ordination

During my chairmanship, with David Simpson (of the International Union against Cancer and his International Agency on Tobacco and Health) and Keith Ball of the International Society and Federation of Cardiologists, we made several attempts to initiate coordination between these international non-governmental organisations and others interested in the subject. The International Union against Cancer (usually known by its French initials UICC) had done much work in the field aided by a Norwegian grant. The International Agency on Tobacco and Health (IATH) was specifically founded by David Simpson as an information and campaigning resource for the Third World and eastern Europe. Although cardiologists in North America, and to some extent in the UK, had done a great deal in the field, in many other countries there had been little interest. Together with Keith Ball we tried to stimulate more activity. Although we got agreement from several international non-governmental organisations to exchange information and ideas and to share some campaigning efforts, the relevant honorary officers tended to change and the agreement was easily forgotten. Clearly we needed to have a paid coordinator with on-going responsibility to ensure continuity of action.

Michael Wood, in charge of the tobacco programme for the International Union against Cancer, was a very active leader in the field in northern Ireland and was now being equally active through the International Union which had previously done much excellent work in the Third World with the help of a grant from NORAD (Norway). Accordingly I asked him to chair a meeting at the World Conference on Tobacco and Health in Paris in 1996. It was well attended by representatives from twenty or so non-governmental organisations (NGOs), if I recall correctly. The International Unions of Cancer and of Tuberculosis and Lung Disease agreed to co-fund a part-time coordinator. We were fortunate to recruit Dr Karen Slama, subsequently based at IUATLD. This is now the "International Non-Governmental Coalition against Tobacco (INGCAT)". It has coordinated much international campaigning respecting smoke free air travel and the banning of advertising. It is now closely working with the presently very active WHO unit. I add that the IUATLD when I was chairman had almost annually written to Ministers of Health of the European Union countries urging a ban on tobacco advertising and promotion.

Since 1998, with Eileen's disability, owing to a bad back and increasing age, I have been unable to travel abroad. I have communicated with IUATLD mainly by mail and email. Karen Slama has obviously done a marvellous job. INGAT has been asked by WHO to be the main coordinator of international NGOs and has enthusiastically helped to campaign for an international convention on tobacco control. Its membership, at the end of 1999, was over a thousand NGOs in 100 countries as well as over 60 international NGOs. There is to be a new wholetime Director; Karen is moving wholetime to IUALTD. The original initiative has indeed come to fruition – thanks largely to Karen.

The World Health Organisation (WHO)

In September 1985 the then President of the American Cancer Society, Professor Le Maître, who was very interested in the tobacco problem, convened a meeting in Washington of what was flatteringly called "World Leaders". It was also attended briefly by the then Surgeon-General Koop, who had contributed considerable international leadership. There were fifty-six of us from twenty-five countries, including four from the UK (Alison Hillhouse, David Simpson, Michael Wood and myself), seventeen from the USA, but no one from WHO.

At the meeting, incidentally, there was considerable criticism of WHO for having done so little about this global threat to health. Its tobacco programme had only Roberto Masironi as its single WHO officer in Geneva. He did what he could, but with a small budget and little support.

I thought we should follow up by trying to get more urgent movement by WHO. I knew WHO's then Director-General, Halfstan Mahler, as he had been concerned previously with tuberculosis. He was an excellent man who had given splendid world leadership in many fields, though little on tobacco. Through the Scottish Health Education Group I now had very good relations with John Reid, the Chief Medical Officer in Scotland, and the longtime UK representative on the Executive Committee of WHO. I had some status as Chairman of IUALTD's Committee. I persuaded Charles Le Maître to lead a small group to Geneva to meet Mahler, and made all the arrangements. The group consisted of David Simpson representing UICC, myself representing IUATLD, Keith Ball representing the International Federation and Society of Cardiologists and one of the few cardiologists active in prevention, and, at David Simpson's suggestion a most impressive young Dutch woman, Atie Schipaanboord, representing IOCU (International Organisation of Consumer Unions) which had recently been very active regarding tobacco prevention in the Third World.

We met Mahler in May 1986 and I think made some impact. Privately he told me that he thought WHO was best at getting simple technology implemented in the Third World. Presumably he was referring, for instance, to various protective vaccines for children – and indeed to the success of vaccination against smallpox, with the triumphant abolition of the disease. He obviously had not given much priority to tobacco though WHO, initially pushed by George Godber, then Chief Medical Officer for England and Wales and John Reid's predecessor on WHO's Executive Committee, had produced a couple of excellent reports from Expert Committees. My wife, Eileen, had served on the second Expert Committee.

We thought we should further follow up this meeting. With the help of John Reid, a close friend of Mahler's, we persuaded him to meet a larger group in Tokyo at the 6th World Conference on Smoking and Health in 1987, when I was to report on IUATLD's tobacco activities. I had produced a memo as a basis for discussion, but was disturbed by rather offensive personal attacks on Mahler and WHO by some of the wider group of international activists.

However Mahler agreed to convene a WHO Advisory Group to prepare a Global Action Plan on Tobacco and Health. It met in Geneva in March 1988, chaired by John Reid; Judith Mackay was the rapporteur. The formal report on the proposed programme was submitted to the World Health Assembly in May 1988.

I had learnt that representatives of international NGOs were permitted to address the World Health Assembly. We thought it might help in persuading the Assembly to back the Action Plan. Accordingly it was arranged that David Simpson would address the Assembly on behalf of the UICC and myself on behalf of IUATLD. IOCU had now transferred its tobacco work for the Third World to an excellent group in Malaysia, one of whose members spoke for IOCU.

We had a fascinating day in Geneva. John Reid had worked with the Australian delegation to prepare a draft resolution. The tobacco industry had put up Malawi, very dependent on tobacco exports, to raise objections. The USSR had various misgivings. But John knew everyone, discussed and lobbied all day. With minor amendments the resolution requesting WHO to produce an Action Plan was ultimately passed unanimously. The WHO Programme for Tobacco and Health was to be strengthened. External funds were to be sought. Then followed further informal discussions.

It would be splendid if we could get a world leader in the field to head an extended WHO unit. I had discussions with an excellent American cancer and smoking expert (Joseph Cullen) who had funds he could pass on to WHO. This could be used as a carrot. He said he would hold it until I gave the word. I approached several excellent people, including Nigel Gray who had run a splendid programme on smoking in Australia, Judith Mackay who had done a wonderful job in Hong Kong and was extending her efforts to mainland China, and Kjell Bjartveit, a world leader from Norway. All were happy to help but not to move to Geneva for a long-term appointment.

Meantime Mahler had retired and been replaced by Nakajima from Japan. Claire Chollot-Traquet, who had been personal assistant to Mahler, was transferred to the Tobacco Programme as Acting Head. She proved full of energy and drive – but not of diplomacy! Roberto Masironi had been in post for many years. He understandably resented the resultant earthquakes and she did not make it any easier for him. Eventually he took early retirement (and incidentally went off with all the previous records). I remember I later had to provide Claire with a copy of the WHO questionnaire for health professionals on which I had based our IUATLD medical students' questionnaire.

I should add that Roberto, in retirement, founded the European Medical Association on Smoking and Health (EMASH) which has had important influence on European leaders, especially in Central and Eastern Europe. I was asked to speak at several of their meetings and to provide material for their Newsletter.

Dr Lopez, an excellent British epidemiologist, was also transferred from another WHO department and proved a great asset, working closely with Richard Peto in Oxford. An excellent Canadian civil servant (Neil Collishaw) who had guided the progressive Canadian legislation through their parliament, was seconded by the Canadian government.

I continued to have a lot of contact with Claire and served as secretary of an Advisory Group meeting in November 1989 where, at her request, I provided a checklist on appropriate medical school teaching which was issued with material for World No Smoking Day, I think about 1997.

China

In the autumn of 1986 I received a letter from Professor Julian Chu inviting both Eileen and me to participate in the first International Conference on Tobacco and Health to be held in China. I was asked to chair the meeting, jointly with the former Minister of Health in China. I was also asked to recommend the names of foreigners who might be invited to speak and to organise their participation.

This was an exciting challenge. For years I had been in close contact over tobacco issues with Judith Mackay in Hong Kong, a girl of great charm and personality, who had been a house physician with us in the 1960s. All the young men had been after her. But John Mackay, also an Edinburgh graduate, who had for several years been working in a large (British) general practice in Hong Kong, came home on study leave to take the membership examination of the Royal College of Physicians. He was attached to our department for part of his postgraduate study, met Judith and quietly carried her off back to Hong Kong. After having two children she first did part-time research on nutrition in local children. She got involved with the media on this and later extended this interest to include women's medical and social problems, and later still the ill effects of smoking (she says as a consequence of working with us).

However she then decided to further her training as a physician, arranged an unpaid attachment as a registrar in the Hong Kong medical school, came home on leave and, like her husband John, passed the MRCP examination at her first attempt. She returned to Hong Kong and was appointed a consultant physician at a mission hospital.

Over the next few years she became more and more interested in the tobacco problem. She initiated a Hong Kong campaigning organization which she led, unpaid. Eventually she found it was occupying more and more of her time and becoming more and more successful. She gave up clinical work and worked wholetime on tobacco. She spoke fluently the Cantonese version of Chinese and made a number of tourist visits to China and knew many Chinese.

Judith was therefore a top priority to be one of the foreign experts and an obvious source of advice. We very soon decided that we should spend a few days with her and John before proceeding to China.

A few words about my inviter, Professor Julian Chu. Just after I retired he and Professor Zhong Nan-Shan from Canton had spent a year in 1978-79 with my successor to the Chair of Respiratory Diseases, David Flenley. During that time I saw a good deal of them, professionally and socially. Julian Chu was from Shanghai. But during the Japanese occupation when he was a child, his parents moved to Hong Kong. As a result of his schooling there he spoke fluent English. After the war the family moved back to Shanghai.

Organising the foreign participation involved me in a vast amount of work, but we ended up with about twenty-five notable foreign experts, mostly from Europe and America. Judith had advised that one must be very diplomatic with the Chinese. One must never be seen to be telling them what to do. In consequence I could not be too pressing about the proposed programme, which was to be arranged locally. The conference was to be organized by a university department in Tianjin, a highly industrialized seaport serving Beijing. It had developed under German influence during the early 20th century imperialistic regimes in China.

We had a few days in Hong Kong together with other British delegates, in order to be briefed on China by Judith. Eileen and I stayed with Judith and John. We gave one or two lectures and saw something of the island. Then by air to Tianjin. There we met Professor Richard Peto from Oxford who had been doing much epidemiological research on behalf of the Chinese government. We also met the local Professor in charge of the conference who presented me with the proposed programme. We were rather horrified. It looked a pretty good shambles. How should we, especially me, handle it without offending the Chinese? Fortunately Peto already had great prestige in China and Judith's was growing. They borrowed computers and spent almost all night advising and consulting with the Chinese. To our surprise all the papers were to be given in English – I think with Chinese translation – except for the initial speech by the ex-Minister of Health. He made a speech about the great importance of the issue and then left, leaving me to chair the rest of the three-day conference.

We were astonished at how many of the Chinese spoke fluent English. A number of the older ones had been trained in missionary medical schools run by British or Americans, but many of the younger ones were also fluent.

Somewhat to our surprise, and greatly to the credit of Richard, Judith and their Chinese contacts, the conference was a great success. The Chinese had done some excellent research, including a "sample survey" of national smoking habits. The "random sample" was a mere half million! They had found very high rates in men, if I remember 63%, but only about 15% in women (though up to 23% in more sophisticated cities like Tianjin).

Both Eileen and I gave talks. I had the job of finally summing up the contribution and discussions. But I was asked not to enunciate publicly any recommendations of the conference. If I did, these recommendations would have to go through the local Communist bureaucracy and so up through successive bureaucratic levels towards the government. They might be blocked at any stage. Instead, after the conference a group of Chinese scientists would meet privately with a group of foreign scientists. We would agree recommendations. One of the Chinese knew the current Minister of Health and would ensure that they got to him.

And so it worked out. As a result a Chinese Association on Smoking and Health was established and proved very active. Judith and Richard continued close contact. They both in due course became official advisors to the Chinese Government. Later they were both presented with official medals in the Great Hall of the People in the presence of five Ministers. Judith, who had added Mandarin to her Cantonese, got to know the Prime Minister's wife quite well and once had a formal interview with the Prime Minister himself. She has very much become a world leader and incidentally was also later presented with a Congressional Medal in the USA! She also later founded the Asian Consultancy on Tobacco Control and has visited and advised in many countries in Asia and the Pacific.

So we certainly left our trail behind us. It was obviously better, considering my age and distance, that liaison should continue through Judith, on the doorstep and immensely active, and Richard Peto who regularly visited his research projects in the country.

British Council Tobacco Book

The British Council regularly produces a series of expert reviews on different medical subjects, issued in book form and known, curiously, as the *British Medical Bulletin*. They asked Richard Doll to edit one on tobacco but asked me to join a small informal advisory committee which would decide from whom to invite contributions. At that meeting Richard asked me to be a co-editor, as I was more familiar with the advocacy aspects. I also wrote a joint chapter with Judith Mackay on "Tobacco and the Developing World". The editing was a major job. We both read all the seventeen chapters from an equal number of authors. There was much correspondence. It ended as a very useful reference book. I gather it has had record sales for a Bulletin and is passed to editors of later reviews as a model of how it should be done.

Tobacco book for the Third World

Sometime about 1996 Professor David Morley, who had previously asked me and my colleagues to write *Clinical Tuberculosis* for Third World readers, suggested to me that I should organise a similar book on tobacco for a similar readership. I suggested that the best person to write it would be David Simpson. He had been for eleven years the immensely successful Director of ASH UK. In the course of this he began to appreciate what a vast threat tobacco was becoming to the Third World, as the ruthless multinational tobacco companies sought expanding markets there, partly to compensate for falling consumption in North America and some European countries. Accordingly he had founded his own charity, the International Agency on Tobacco and Health (IATH), and had invited me to be a Trustee. He had done a marvellous job, building up contacts in what are now over 100 countries in Central and ex-Communist Eastern Europe and the Third World. For these he provided a monthly Bulletin on scientific and campaigning aspects. He also acted as an advisory resource for those facing particular ruthless activities by the tobacco companies. He became a world leader with his advice sought by many international bodies.

David agreed to my suggestion. I produced a provisional list of chapter headings. We had an initial meeting between David Morley, David Simpson, Keith Ball (with long-term association with ASH and, internationally, with cardiologists), and Shirley Hamber representing TALC's[*] publishers, Macmillans. It was agreed that David should write the book with myself acting as advisor. In order to provide the book at a low price appropriate for poor countries, it would, like our tuberculosis book, require financial subsidies.

"The best laid plans...."[#]. Because of his high reputation, more and more was piled on to David's plate. To cut a long story short, there were many delays in David's starting owing to his innumerable commitments. I was embarrassed, as I had raised money internationally to subsidise the book. The only thing to do was to reverse our roles. I wrote the book with

---

[*] Teaching Aids at Low Cost

[#] "The best laid schemes o' mice an' men gang aft a-gley" (Robert Burns, *To a mouse*)

his advice and help*. Starting in July 1999 I finished in June 2000. It was backed financially by the Swedish Chest and Heart Association, the Danish Lung Association, and others and sponsored by TALC and IUATLD and the Swedish Association.

---

* John was 88 years old at this point.

Chapter 8:
On Being A Dean 1963-66

Background

In my time, the Dean was the academic head of a Faculty and its chief administrator. It was a formidable and very hectic job. When I arrived in Edinburgh in 1952 the then Dean, Sir Sydney Smith, had been in office for twenty-two years. Some time in the mid-fifties Sydney Smith retired. Professor Mackie, the Professor of Bacteriology, was elected Dean in his place. He died of a coronary in office a year or two later. Sir Derrick Dunlop, the Professor of Therapeutics, took over temporarily for a few months, and then George Montgomery, the Professor of Pathology, was elected. If I remember correctly, he served for several years and then felt he had done his stint in that burdensome office. There was obviously discussion among the senior members about his successor. I gathered that the choice had fallen on John Brotherston, the Professor of what was then called Community Medicine (now Public Health). There was some embarrassment at a subsequent Faculty Meeting when David Whitteridge, the Professor of Physiology, asked for the vote to be deferred to allow consideration of other candidates. David then suggested privately to me that, now that tuberculosis was going down very rapidly and I'd coped with my main initial challenge, I should take over the Deanship. I was flattered but refused. I was busy expanding the non-tuberculosis chest disease components of my Department; there was much to do. Even more important, I felt my candidacy would be very offensive and embarrassing for John Brotherston, who had clearly regarded the post as already his. He was duly elected and did the job very well.

Election

A few years later, in 1963, Brotherston was invited to become Chief Medical Officer for Scotland. The Deanship again became vacant. A good deal of pressure was put on me to accept the job. Apart from Dunlop's few months' occupation no previous Dean had been a clinician. I had no intention of giving up clinical work.

It was agreed therefore that Walter Perry, the Professor of Pharmacology, should become Pre-clinical Dean, taking some of the load off me. Walter was a strong character and an able and ambitious man, but we got on surprisingly well. We often had arguments, but they were always friendly arguments. To his great credit Walter always accepted that I was the Dean and therefore entitled to the final say.

When Pre-clinical Dean, Walter made a splendid job of anything in which he was interested, often a useful innovation of one kind or another. But he was less interested in the routine administrative work. Accumulating piles of unanswered letters used to exasperate Duncan Wood, the senior Faculty administrator. Nevertheless Walter did a very good job, especially in reorganising the admission system to make it as fair as possible and to try to ensure that, among the vast numbers of applications, we selected the most promising students. Undoubtedly Walter's activities on the pre-clinical side helped to reduce my own very heavy burdens.

The Administrative Life

My mainstay for the routine work was Duncan Wood. I do not think he had any academic qualifications, not even a university degree. But he knew a vast amount about every aspect of Faculty Office activities and a great deal about relevant general university administration. He knew all the academic staff in the Medical Faculty and was well aware of their idiosyncrasies. He soon got to know who were the leaders among each successive cohort of students. Above all he operated some sort of personal radar which identified the first whisperings of "trouble" wherever it came from. Sometimes this was a personality problem within a Department, or the first grumblings of a potential artillery barrage about to descend on the Dean's office, or the first broodings of paranoia within the bosom of some Departmental Head, or the first flickers of some emerging grievance among the students. Over and over again he would alert me, often in time to get things sorted out, cool the simmering lava and so prevent a major volcanic eruption.

My experience was that, with a very large Faculty staffed by independent-minded academics, in the clinical field often working with equally independent-minded non-academics, there was almost always a crisis in one Department or another. So often one Departmental Head or another would be nursing, or firmly expressing, one grievance or another, either against the Dean, or the university or some other Department. Of course he expected the Dean to sort it out. From one particular Head of Department I would expect regular five-page letters with problems for me to solve, sometimes every month or two, sometimes every week or two.

I certainly had plenty of opportunity to refine my technique for dealing with angry men. I had learnt way back in my army career that if you wanted something and wrote to the relevant administrator, you often received a negative reply, however good your case. If you telephoned it was a little better, but remained cool and evasive. But if you went to see the man personally he was usually charming and you got what you wanted. Now, in the senior administrative role myself, I applied this technique in reverse. With an angry man it was not usually very helpful to send back a soothing letter. The telephone was only marginally better. But if I immediately asked him to come and see me, I found I could nearly always rapidly defuse the situation, cope with the problem and restore good relations.

A Dean's life is a very hectic one. He automatically becomes chairman of innumerable Faculty committees, dealing with finance, appointments, the curriculum, honours etc. He has to serve as a Faculty representative on the Senatus, as well as on many university committees, including the Principal and Deans' Committee, the top administrative committee of the university. He has an enormous load of correspondence. The purely routine replies were handled very effectively by Duncan Wood and only required my signature, but many others needed much thought and diplomacy. There was correspondence with national bodies, other universities and the National Health Service as well as innumerable replies to letters from Departments and staff, old students etc. There was the occasional batty letter from some character who had discovered an infallible cure for cancer, or how to do without doctors, and demanded arrangements to address the assembled Faculty on the subject. Here Duncan Wood often advised "no reply". Others slightly less batty might be forwarded to the appropriate professor.

Then one was very much the ceremonial Head of the Faculty. One had to attend, and often speak, at innumerable dinners and to entertain visiting VIPs. Quite often I had to deputise in some such activity for the Principal, then Sir Edward Appleton.

For difficult relations with outside bodies I often found an informal working supper, with a glass of sherry and a glass of wine, an excellent technique for defusing paranoia and making things run smoothly. Hardworking colleagues could often only meet over lunch, so many committees were held over sandwiches. Working suppers were by no means infrequent. What with these and formal dinners I would often be out several evenings a week, sometimes more. I remember one period in September-October where I had to be out every evening, except Sundays, for six weeks running.

There was an official Faculty meeting once a month in term time, consisting of all Heads of Departments, perhaps about thirty in all. Faculty meetings were quite formidable affairs for the Dean. There was usually a mass of business to be got through, some routine, some controversial. Many needed careful preparation beforehand, especially over controversial items. The Dean had to give a lead. It was often wise to consult relevant professors in advance. One could almost guarantee that, with a bunch of academics, someone or other, often several, would object to almost any innovation or any new arrangement. If the Dean remained an impartial chairman, nothing would ever happen. Any change, any innovation, would be stymied. To try to get anything actually to happen one had to plot and plan, in short to use Machiavellian techniques. I have often said since, that when I became Dean, at the age of fifty-one, my character should have been fairly fixed. But in the event, after three years as Dean, I am sure I emerged a much nastier person. Otherwise we would have made no progress about anything.

Personality problems

Personalities were not always easy. The Professor of Medicine, Ken Donald, and the Professor of Surgery, John Bruce, were both very strong characters who could be very aggressive. Both were convinced that their own Departments were far the most important in the Faculty, which was at least to some extent true. They behaved accordingly.

Ken's specialty in medicine was respiratory and cardiovascular physiology, then at the height of its prestige. He had indeed a high and well-deserved reputation in that field, especially as regards respiratory failure from pneumonia, chronic bronchitis etc. When Ken arrived in Edinburgh, my own Department was already well established locally in the clinical respiratory field. Naturally other consultants and GPs tended to continue to refer problems to us. Ken understandably resented this and often made life awkward for me. This was sad, for I liked him personally and socially. I had one difficult incident about 1961-62 before I became Dean. This was just after the wonderful years when our group had really got tuberculosis under control in Edinburgh and were, I believe, justifiably proud of what we had done. We were already rapidly developing our interest and research in other respiratory diseases. At this time the Faculty sent a delegation, led by my predecessor as Dean, John Brotherston, to interview the Medical Subcommittee of the University Grants Committee responsible for university funding. The delegation, of course, included Ken as Professor of Medicine. At an immediately subsequent Faculty meeting John Brotherston read out the minute of that meeting prepared by the University Grants Committee secretary. In it the Faculty was said to have stated that "a Department of Tuberculosis was no longer appropriate in this day and age". This after we had just shown the world, for the first time in history, that 100% cure of pulmonary tuberculosis was a reasonable aim, but had yet to convince the world that our claims were true. I am afraid that event sent me into a quite severe depression for a number of months. It was the worst episode in my academic career.

The Professor of Surgery, John Bruce, had no sense of academic rivalry as far as I was concerned. He was a first class surgeon technically. He was a tough character but with very considerable charm and social skills which made him many friends in Scotland, the UK and internationally. His main sensitivity was to ensure that his Department was accorded the priority within the Faculty that was its due. It was amusing to contrast him with his fellow surgeon, Professor Michael Woodruff, Head of the Department of Surgical Science. Michael's strength was research. His main interest was in the immune system in which he had done, and continued to do, outstanding work. He became famous when he achieved the first successful kidney transplant in the UK. I gathered that he was a less accomplished technical surgeon than John Bruce but he and his Department were world class in research. I was often amused when each of these distinguished men, both of whom were given well deserved knighthoods in due course, seemed to want to be the other. John Bruce was pushing for research in his Department, Michael for more clinical work in his. Both, of course, achieved most when they stuck to the aspects for which they were endowed with outstanding talents.

My Own Department

As I also had to do my clinical work, teaching, supervising research, departmental administration, and coping with many visitors from home and abroad, it was a hectic life. I was always in my Departmental office by 8am and usually worked, at home or outside, until just before 11pm. I often worked before breakfast, starting usually at 6am, sometimes earlier. I remember at a working supper one of my colleagues started, about 11pm, boasting what long hours he had worked that day. I replied that I had started work at 6am and worked through every meal! With very full work days, I often had to do clinical consultations in various hospitals on Sunday mornings.

Consolations

There were, of course, many consolations. I got to know most of the senior people in the Medical School and made many new friends. I also had far more contact, through university commitments and administrative chores, with the general university administration and colleagues in other Faculties, especially my fellow Deans. As I have always taken a dilettante interest in a fairly wide range of subjects outside medicine, I greatly enjoyed these contacts and made many additional friends. I got on well with Sir Edward Appleton, the Principal (in Scotland equivalent to the Vice-Chancellor in England). Appleton, of course, was a very distinguished scientist. He had discovered the "Appleton layer" in the upper atmosphere, which was named after him. He was a very able, competent and distinguished Principal and easy to work with. In spite of all the recurrent crises, inevitable in a large university, which we had to deal with, he told me he never worried. I was not so blessed. From time to time I lost sleep over crises. Most of my life I have noticed occasional extra systoles, a harmless type of extra heartbeat which may produce a minor palpitation. These were often more frequent during one crisis or another I faced as Dean.

Challenges

Many of these difficulties and crises are now old hat. Indeed I cannot recall what most of them were. I will only recount some of what seemed to me now (in 1996) among the more interesting problems. They included a major medical educational link with the Medical School of Baroda (India) sponsored by the World Health Organisation; the establishment in the second main teaching hospital, the Western General, of an independent Department of Medicine; remedying previously very poor relations between the university and the National Health Service and helping to abolish the previously poor relations between NHS consultants and university academics. Among the more notable events was the Jubilee of the Polish Medical School which had been established in Edinburgh during the war.

Relations with the NHS

There were many interrelations with the NHS, in particular with the Regional Hospital Board. NHS consultants did much clinical teaching. Most laboratory services for patients were provided by the university. There were the usual arguments about money, squabbles over appointments and various tensions which I cannot now recall. There was a regular, formal University-Health Board "Standing Liaison Committee" which I gathered had been tense and ineffective. I began by cultivating the chairman of the Regional Hospital Board, Charles Gumley, whom I found a most pleasant man. We met first over an informal lunch. I went on to organise working suppers with the senior officials of University and Board. There the agenda of the coming formal committee could be discussed informally. There we came informally to agreed decisions which thereafter passed smoothly through the formal committee. We repeated this at each subsequent occasion and soon built up excellent relations. Many previously obstinate problems were solved by phone calls between officials who had got to know each other informally. In informal meetings, after a glass of sherry, you could say "Let's not get all paranoid about this", which you could not in a formal committee and you could not if you hadn't got to know one another. I was flattered at the end of the Deanship that the chairman of the Regional Hospital Board gave me a formal farewell dinner to thank me for what I had done to cement previously tattered relations.

Department of Medicine, Western General Hospital.

The WGH in Edinburgh was originally the old Poor Law Hospital. In those days, late nineteenth and early twentieth century, it was filled with the very old and disabled. The mother of my predecessor as Dean, John Brotherston, was one of the earlier women medical graduates in Edinburgh. She was a patient of mine in her nineties. She told me that when she graduated early in the century it was almost impossible for a young woman to get a job. The only one she personally could at first obtain was in Northern Ireland. This was as doctor to a home for alcoholics run by nuns! She then managed to find a job in Edinburgh, probably because no male doctor would take it. This was being the solitary doctor for the several hundred beds at the WGH. Theoretically they were under the care of the Medical Officer of Health (Dr Guy) to whom she would be responsible. But he had made it clear that he had no time to visit the hospital. She lived in the hospital. She was on duty twenty four hours a day, seven days a week! I did not enquire about holidays. I presume they would be regarded as an indecent luxury, quite inappropriate for a young doctor, particularly if she were a woman.

After the 1930s Act the hospital was transposed into a local authority general hospital under the City of Edinburgh. Sir Stanley Davidson, Professor of Medicine in the 1930s, had negotiated with the City about having it staffed by university appointed doctors and using it for teaching. The negotiations were interrupted by the prospects of war and, instead, attention was directed to the building of Emergency Medical Service Hospitals, away from large towns which were expected to be bombed. Stanley was largely responsible for advising the Scottish Office on these.

After the war the agreement between the City and the University was concluded. Stanley quite rightly decided that Edinburgh needed new blood. It had become very inbred and parochial in the interwar period, at least in medicine. (Surgery was better). Stanley and Derrick were the outstanding exceptions, so Stanley scoured England, largely London, for talent. He appointed an outstanding group of young doctors – Wilfred Card, Dick Turner, John Strong and Mike Matthews – to Senior Lectureships in the WGH. Others followed later. They built up an excellent clinical service with good teaching and research. But unfortunately Stanley's curious defect was that he was almost pathologically mean with money, in spite of being a relatively rich man himself and having married a rich wife. Once his staff were in place, he gave them very little support. And it was not only little support in finance. I believe he almost never visited the hospital, although it was supposed to be an extension of his own Department of Medicine.

Stanley's successor, Ken Donald, continued the pattern. He gave the WGH people little help or encouragement, concentrating on successfully building up his own part of the Department in the Royal Infirmary with new laboratories. Naturally his WGH staff were extremely dissatisfied. I knew them all very well. I frequently saw patients in consultation there and often went to their clinical meetings. The hospital standards were excellent and the nursing superb. I was very impressed with the set up and its potentials for future developments in the medical school. I agreed with the WGH staff that the only solution was to develop an independent Department of Medicine with its own budget.

Of course there was great opposition from Ken Donald and staff at the Royal Infirmary. The Royal had been the great teaching centre for 200 years and it was jealous of a possible rival. There were endless and inconclusive discussions at Faculty meetings. Finally I decided that the only thing to do was to take the Faculty members away for a weekend at Peebles Hydro and keep them there until I could get them to make up their minds. With great difficulty we at last got it through.

Wilfred Card was the leader of the WGH group. He was a gastroenterologist with a distinguished research record and a national and international reputation. He had resigned from his consultant post in St Thomas's Hospital in London to pursue a more academic career in Edinburgh. He had been much exasperated by lack of support from the Department of Medicine though he had, with his colleagues, obtained a number of facilities directly from the Regional Hospital Board. It seemed to me very appropriate that he should be appointed to a personal chair, a difficult thing to achieve in Edinburgh. I set up the preliminaries and it seemed to be going through very well. However I was most disappointed when Card came to see me and sought support to establish a separate Department of Gastroenterology at the WGH jointly with John Bruce, the Professor of Surgery, with whom he had already worked closely over the years. Having sweated blood to get the Department of Medicine through, the WGH staff having assured me that they were all anxious to work together in one Department, I was deeply shaken. I felt I could not put this to the Faculty with my personal support, but said that he and John Bruce were welcome to do so themselves. Wilfred then went off to Glasgow and sought a personal chair there to develop his pioneer interest in applying computers to clinical medicine. Glasgow wisely welcomed a good man and he left us. It was a disappointment to me to lose one of the main leaders of WGH who had so surprised me by his additional demands. However we remained on good personal terms and I later, after both of us retired, had discussions with him about applying computer technology to health education.

In due course I obtained a personal chair for John Strong, the most distinguished academically of the WGH group. When he retired a formal Chair of Medicine was established there. Their Department, with its independent budget, went from strength to strength, as did the hospital.

Rebuilding of the Royal Infirmary

Planning the academic component of the proposed new Royal Infirmary proved to be a lot of hard work, sadly ending up not with a bang or even with a whimper. The Royal Infirmary, the main teaching hospital of this internationally famous Medical School, had a long history. Starting in 1729 with accommodation for six patients at the head of Robertson's Close the main Infirmary, a new hospital, designed by William Adams, (father of the famous Robert), was opened in 1738. Some of it was briefly and partially, succeeded by a Surgical Hospital (1849-63) which soon proved unsatisfactory. Rebuilding on the Lauriston Place site, begun in 1872, was based on Florence Nightingale's design. The wards lay in a series of blocks connected by corridors. This gave maximum light and ventilation, which had been a serious defect in the two previous buildings.

In my time there had been much justified complaint of the deficiencies of a building now nearly a century old. At last the Scottish Office agreed to fund the new hospital. After much consideration, it was decided to rebuild on the same site. They would start at the western side of the "northern" Surgical Block of buildings and work east. This would then continue with the east end of the (southern) Medical block. I must say I felt the noise and disruption would make it extremely difficult to run the hospital during the building period.

My job was to ensure that all the academic Departments assessed their needs, within the limits that had been laid down. They had to provide the architect with full details about their future activities. This was a difficult job for everyone. There had been so little postwar hospital building in the UK that even the architects had little experience, much less the local doctors. It was no easy task to visualise academic activities ten years ahead. In addition we were asked to estimate the numbers of people and their daily movements along passages and between Departments, an exercise requiring positively psychic talents. Most of us, being ungifted with second sight, had to be content with semi-intelligent guesses.

My job was also to ensure that all the submissions were completed to time and were then coordinated into an overall academic plan. Incidentally I also had to plan my own Department as it had been decided that this should move into the new hospital. Fortunately I had the help of Malcolm Lowe, a relatively young medical academic, ex-Colonial Service. He was a very efficient part-time assistant to the Dean, his main remit being student affairs.

He did much of the work and was a wonderful support. Then came the problem of how we were going to pay for the academic component. This would have to come from the University Grants Committee. So, after careful preparation of our case, I led a Faculty delegation down to London to face the high-powered Committee. Of course I had to do most of the talking. There was much toing and froing but on the whole I think it went over very well. We came back with a promise of the £7 million that we had asked for. This was a lot of money in those days.

According to the planned timetable the new hospital should have been completed just before I was due to retire in 1977. But, with the usual fate of mice and men, the government soon ran into one of the cyclical financial crises that affects all governments. Cuts all round. The axe descended. Limbo returned. All our work disappeared down the drain. It was another thirty years before hope returned[*].

Now, 1997, more than thirty years later and twenty years after I retired, the planning is back. Thanks (if it is thanks) to "private" finance, the hospital is now to be rebuilt on a greenfield site to the south of Edinburgh. Perhaps I shall see the building at least beginning before my final "retirement" under the daisies[#]. I still resent having wasted so much time which I could have used more rewardingly. But I suppose it added to the patchwork of experience.

Baroda

The Faculty and University had been approached by the WHO Regional Office of South East Asia with a proposal that the Edinburgh Medical School should give an Indian medical school some six years of support. The aim was to raise standards of clinical work, teaching and research by two-way long-term exchanges. At any one time there were to be six senior members from Edinburgh attached to the Indian school. These members would each spend a year there. The most senior Edinburgh staff, such as professors, would pay shorter visits. Staff would continue to receive their Edinburgh salaries but would live in the normal staff quarters of the receiving school. WHO would pay for a locum in Edinburgh and all the expenses, including travel costs for families. Similarly, Indian staff would spend time in Edinburgh attached to the appropriate Department.

Before I became Dean, an Edinburgh delegation visited India to discuss details with Dr Mahni, the South East Asian Regional Director of WHO in

---

[*] This account is not quite true. Phase 1 of the proposed New Royal Infirmary (subsequently called the Lauriston Building) was built around 1980 and was in use in 1982.

[#] The present Royal Infirmary was opened in 2003. John actually became a surgical patient there.

Delhi. After their Indian tour the group provided a list of three or four schools which they thought appropriate. The final decision was to be made by the Indian Government. The decision in the event was along political lines routine in India. The wife of the relevant Minister was Vice-Chancellor of Baroda University, so Baroda was chosen.

Baroda had been a "Native State" with its own Maharaja. It was now part of Gujerat State, an area undergoing rapid industrialisation. The town of Baroda is in western India about two hundred miles from Bombay. The project was due to start in January 1964, within a month of my taking office as Dean. I had not been in any way involved in the previous planning nor negotiations. Now I had to make it all work. It was certainly a major administrative challenge. I had to negotiate with our own Faculty and its members, our own University, WHO in Delhi, the Indian Government, the Gujerat State Government (which ran the medical school as part of its medical service) and, in a minor way, Baroda University (whose function was mainly the conduct of examinations). Our planners had made no provision for any administrative help. The whole burden fell on me, assisted by the splendid Duncan Wood. It was a vast additional burden for both our loads.

Everyone has heard of Indian bureaucracy, which can far outpace (if that is the appropriate word!) our own. As an example, none of our staff was supposed to land in India until they had received final official authorisation both from WHO and from the Indian Government. Of course this was only after prior approval for each individual case by the Gujerat State Government etc. This final authorisation virtually never arrived before our man was due to travel and often only months after he had started work in Baroda. Fortunately at that time the immigration officials in India were pretty lax, and we always got away with it. A few years later, after my time, one of our paediatricians on a return official visit to Baroda, was put on the next plane home because he was not carrying the official authorisation. But this was during a somewhat xenophobic phase in Indian political attitudes as a reaction to some now forgotten tiff with Britain and the West.

Obviously our aim was to improve standards. Equally obviously we could not be expected in a six-year project, working entirely with current staff of the Indian school, to turn what we found was a third class school into a first class one. I have often summarised by claiming that, with much blood, sweat and tears, we probably managed to push what had been a third class school just into the second class.

The senior consultant staff worked a few hours a day in the hospital, with responsibility for teaching and some clinical care. They earned their main living by private practice, including treating their patients in local private hospitals. They were understandably not too keen on making the teaching hospital too good. Patients might then choose the hospital in preference to private consultation and private hospitals.

Apart from anything else, mere age carries a lot of weight in India. This was well illustrated by attitudes to two of our team members. One team was led by my close friend Norman Horne. I suppose he was then in his forties, but he looked twenty years older. For the Indians, he looked a "guru" (a traditional religious teacher with this sobriquet transferred to other disciplines). They treated him with enormous, and as it happened well-deserved, respect. In contrast Jerry Collee, a bacteriologist, was probably only a year or two younger than Norman. But he looked twenty years younger than his age. The Indians regarded him as a mere boy. They found difficulty in taking him seriously. His true quality was confirmed by his appointment a year or two later as Professor of Bacteriology in Edinburgh.

Prestige is very important in India, as elsewhere. When we started in Baroda the local surgeons were most anxious to start doing cardiac surgery. At that time this was very new and exciting in the West. But Bill Small, the surgeon in our first team, found that in Baroda surgical patients were frequently dying from post-operative infection, because theatre instruments etc were not being properly sterilised. He spent his year building up a routine system to ensure infection-free surgery.

Another achievement was reorganising the outpatient systems. Every morning hundreds of patients had turned up at the hospital and queued up, unsorted, to see the consultants on duty, and their junior staff. So the consultants saw vast amounts of trivia and had no time to deal properly with serious problems. Our staff reorganised the routine. They set up a series of teams of medical students, each team led by a junior staff member. The students, with their leader, sorted out the patients, dealt with the trivia, and identified the problem patients who would be seen by the consultant. There was initially much resistance from the consultants but they came to appreciate the change when they saw how much better it was both for them and for their patients. It was also splendid experience for the students who learnt a lot.

Yet another success was the teaching of clinical medicine by the bedside. In India the written word or the formal lecture is greatly respected. Students may thus acquire excellent theoretical knowledge. But unless there is good clinical teaching it will not do much good to patients. Many of our team members were very good at this practical teaching. They made students, under supervision, work things out for themselves. This encouraged at least the junior Indian staff to do the same. It was much appreciated by the students.

Our teams were often shaken by local conditions. Indian hospitals tended to be very dirty. Indian nurses, who should have been responsible for ensuring cleanliness, theoretically did this by supervising Grade IV cleaners. These (normally males) had a low level as regards caste, but had strong and bloody-minded unions. They had little intention of taking orders from mere women. The doctors did not seem to notice the dirt or at least did nothing to remedy it.

One of the things which struck our first and every subsequent team was that cattle wandered all over the hospital, depositing their customary visiting cards. Cattle were, of course, sacred and therefore immune from harrying officials.

The solution was obvious to our team members. Cattle grids were enthusiastically promoted. The requests disappeared into the thick fog of local bureaucracy, to be followed by a regular procession of reiterated proposals. Each succeeding team confronted the problem anew and once more perceived its inspired solution. And so on for six years. The cattle grids were finally installed just before the project ended. I wonder how long they survived our departure.

Recruiting staff for the project was one of my major headaches. My predecessor, who had made the agreement, had blithely undertaken to supply six senior staff, each to stay for a year. And this was to continue for six years. We managed always to keep some sort of team in Baroda but it did not always amount to the full complement. I had to recruit also from several other medical schools, mostly in Scotland.

Of course visits were a two-way affair. Our teams helped to select up-and-coming Indian staff who spent six to twelve months in Edinburgh, attached to the appropriate Department. A block of university flats was set aside for them and was dubbed "Baroda House".

Besides all the work on the project in Edinburgh, I paid two personal visits of a fortnight each to Baroda. Both were preceded and followed by "briefing" and "debriefing" at WHO in New Dehli. These tended to be day-long affairs in which one was scheduled to meet a series of officials. With most it was largely formal and really a waste of time. A number of the officials struck me then, and in my later contacts in WHO visits to Nepal and elsewhere, as "passengers". I came to the opinion that two thirds of the official WHO staff tended to be "passengers", a third really good and keen. A most notable exception was the (Indian) Regional Director himself, Dr Mahni. He was superb. He was pleasant, practical, efficient, enthusiastic and ready to cut through any red tape. He listened, and listened with intelligence. His attitude was "Let's see how we can do it" however difficult the proposal was. He was one of the best administrators I have ever met.

My two visits were in 1965, when the project had been going about 18 months, and in 1966, after 3 years, when I was introducing and handing over to Archie Duncan before demitting office myself. On both occasions it was a very busy non-stop fortnight. I met all the members of our own team, the Indian Dean (not a very powerful or effective figure), many of our Indian colleagues, and the Gujerat Director of Health Services. Almost every night there was some form of local hospitality. It was very hot, so it was an exacting and interesting period. (As far as I remember there was no air conditioning at that time. We subsisted on fans). The project had got under my own skin, just as it had with my colleagues. But they were whole time on it. For me it was a challenging and exacting fraction of my overall load.

What did I get out of it personally? I had already had a number of visits to India and to some other developing countries. I had some idea of the problems and not too exaggerated an idea of what could be achieved. I later used to say that in working in developing countries if you leave things 0.1% better than when you came you have done well. I also learnt the value of coming back. If you come as a consultant and make recommendations when you leave, they are much more likely to be carried out if everyone knows that you will return after a period. In addition you are able to help by correspondence in between your visits. I have often tried to persuade WHO, with at least some success, of the value of this approach.

So the project formed part of my education, especially on the diplomatic and administrative side, in a vast developing country. I made a number of friends among team members. I learnt more about WHO and governments. Fifteen years later, when I was chairman of the Postgraduate Board for Medicine in Edinburgh, we were asked to help medical education in Bangladesh. I had learnt not to advise our medical school to take over utopian obligations which it had little chance of fulfilling. We adopted more practicable objectives.

Was it all worthwhile from everybody's point of view, particularly the Indian? Yes, I believe it was – just!

Jubilee of the Polish Medical School

In 1966 we celebrated the 25th anniversary of the foundation of the Polish Medical School in Edinburgh. Quite a large body of the Polish army had escaped when the Nazis overran Poland. Other Polish refugees had later joined the exiled army. It emerged that the army contained many medical students as combatants. The army and the Polish exiles needed doctors. The idea of attaching a Polish Medical School to the Edinburgh School originated with Professor Frank Crew who later became Professor of Social Medicine in Edinburgh. With his capacity for taking new initiatives he approached the then Dean, Sydney (later Sir Sydney) Smith. And so the

Polish Medical School was born. There were a number of Polish medical academics available as teachers. The school had its own Dean. It gave its own degrees. The Edinburgh School provided facilities, also teaching in any disciplines which the Poles could not supply. Polish medical students were extracted from their combatant forces and enrolled in the school.

The school was a great success. It graduated several hundred doctors and continued for some years after the war so as to complete the graduation of the last wartime intake. With the Communist takeover in Poland, not so many returned there. Some stayed in Britain. Others emigrated to Australia, Canada or the USA.

The Jubilee celebrations were largely the brainchild of Dr Wiktor Tomaszewski. He had been a surgeon in Poland and then a teacher in the Medical School. He became a GP in Edinburgh after the war. He very much acted as a focal point for Edinburgh Polish graduates worldwide. He wrote a book about the school in the dark days of 1941[*] and another about the history of Polish-Scottish relations which included an account of the 25 year Jubilee[#]. He was a charming and enthusiastic man and, unjustifiably, appreciative of the relatively little help I personally gave to organising the Jubilee. He did most of the work himself. He only died in 1995.

For the Jubilee over 300 graduates came from all over the world, though, sadly, Communist bureaucracy permitted only four to come from Poland itself. The three outstanding figures connected with the School's foundation, the Polish Dean (Professor J Rostowski), Professor Frank Crew and Sir Sydney Smith were all then over eighty. Both Crew and the Dean made splendid speeches, though advancing age only allowed Sydney Smith to speak briefly.

There was an Honorary Degree Ceremony in the splendid hall of the Playfair Library in the University. I remember being deeply touched as they sang with moving fervour the splendid Latin academic hymn "Gaude mater polonia", commonly associated with major academic ceremonies in Europe. The Polish Dean, originally a surgeon, was a competent, if not startlingly original, sculptor. An exhibition of his work formed part of the celebrations, a charming gesture to general culture. Some of his work is permanently installed in the Polish Room in the Erskine Medical library[Ψ] which was installed as an ongoing memorial to the Polish School.

---

[*] *Fifty Years of the Polish School of Medicine, the University of Edinburgh:1941-1991: Jubilee Publication 1992*

[#] *The University of Edinburgh and Poland: an historical review,* 1968.

[Ψ] This relatively new library in George Square did not survive for long into the 21st century.

One of those who I think returned for that celebration, and certainly for the 50-year celebration later, was an old personal friend, Stefan Grysbowski. Stefan was and is a delightful man, with an outstanding personality and enormous enthusiasm. I had met him first while I was still in postwar London. He was then working in a children's tuberculosis hospital. Shortly afterwards he emigrated to Canada. He ended up as Professor of Respiratory diseases in Vancouver. He became a great expert on the epidemiology of tuberculosis. I once listened to him in Nepal giving the best and most entertaining lecture on the subject I have ever heard. Much of it was about Stefan's relations with his grandmother! Surprisingly he succeeded in making recurrent witty points which became instantly memorable by equally recurrent references to his grandmother.

After the war the Canadian Inuit (Eskimos) experienced a devastating epidemic of tuberculosis, having no racial resistance to the disease. Stefan was the main leader who helped the Canadian Government to do a splendid job in controlling the problem. Later he invited me to help run a postgraduate course in Vancouver, sandwiching the work between two splendid weekends in his home. In one we climbed the 5,000 foot Black Tooth mountain, the last 3,000 feet in snow, and in the other, with his family, we visited islands in his boat, digging on a beach for crabs and bathing in Vancouver Bay. On another occasion he visited Edinburgh and I drove him round Fife to see the places where he had been stationed in the army before being drafted to the medical school. One of these was Cupar, where he showed me the Town Hall where he had deposited his army cap on the summit tower.

In addition to the Polish room already mentioned there is also a permanent memorial in the Medical Quadrangle in the form of a bronze plaque.

Exchange visits with the University of Leiden.

Both the Royal College of Physicians of Edinburgh, dating from 1667, and the University Medical School, dating from 1726, were founded by doctors who had graduated from Leiden University in the Netherlands. This dated from the late sixteenth century. During the wars against the occupying Spanish, the town held out heroically against the besiegers, flooding the surrounding countryside and tolerating near starvation. When ultimately relieved they were offered either a year's freedom from taxation or a university. They chose the university (British public please note!). A Professorship of Medicine was one of the first Chairs to be established. In the second half of the seventeenth century Boerhaave[*] was appointed to the Chair of Medicine. Instead of the former scholastic teaching of medicine, based on classical texts such as those by the Roman doctor Galen[#], Boerhaave taught clinical medicine at the bedside. His school consequently attracted students from all over Europe, including Edinburgh.

Perhaps as a result of increased interest in medical history in Edinburgh, notably by Professor David Whitteridge and his wife Gwyneth who was an expert on Harvey[¥]; perhaps also coinciding with the 250th anniversary of the founding of the Edinburgh Faculty of Medicine, a feeling grew up that we should re-establish relations with Leiden. The upshot was that on one occasion I led a Faculty team of some twenty members to Leiden for a week of professional and social activities. A couple of years later, we invited a similar party for similar celebrations in Edinburgh. In addition there were a number of exchanges of research workers and others. Our own eldest son, Richard, who had done his clinical studies in Edinburgh after achieving first class honours at Cambridge, spent eighteen months in Leiden doing postgraduate research in immunology.

The death of the Principal

Sir Edward Appleton died suddenly. This was an academic crisis. In those days there were no Vice-Principals. Nowadays one of them would have taken over temporarily. In my day it would clearly have to be one of the Deans. I had been very impressed by Michael Swann who had been a friend since he had come from Cambridge to the Chair of Zoology. He had obviously proved an excellent Dean of Science introducing a number of innovations. The members of my Faculty whom I consulted agreed with me. But the Dean of Arts, Arthur Beattie, who was also a personal friend of mine, hated Michael. So there was a lot of rapid behind-the-scenes work with the other Deans. Finally we made a majority proposal to the University Court.

Michael took over as locum Principal. There he did such a superb job that after a few months he was given the permanent post. In due course he was knighted. After ten years or so he was invited to be Chairman of the BBC. He ended up as Lord Swann[§].

---

[*] Herman Boerhaave (1668-1738), Dutch physician, botanist and chemist. A founder of clinical teaching and of the modern academic hospital.

[#] Claudius Galenus (cAD 130-201), Greek physician and writer

[¥] William Harvey (1578-1657), English physician who first proposed the circulation of the blood.

[§] Strictly speaking he became Baron Swann.

Conclusion

How much did I enjoy being a Dean? I have often said since that the main reward was to *have been* Dean. It was certainly a wonderful experience, but it was extremely exacting. I had to make many sacrifices and so had Eileen. My time for family life was virtually reduced to Saturday and Sunday afternoons and a short annual holiday.

One of the sacrifices was to have had to refuse many invitations to various countries. The only one I accepted was a very brief visit to lecture in West Berlin. This was mainly to support the tuberculosis academic specialists in their struggles to expand into chest diseases in general. Apparently our Department in Edinburgh was regarded as a model. With local help I succeeded in giving my lecture in German.

A major sacrifice was having to refuse an immensely attractive invitation from Canada. To celebrate the centenary of the grant of Dominion status, they invited me for a month's visit in which I was to have lectured successively in each of the Provinces. As Dean I could not spare the time either for the trip or for preparation of the lectures.

Chapter 9:
Vice-Principal 1969-71

Background

At the end of 1966, Andrew Douglas and I concentrated on writing our postgraduate textbook, *Respiratory Diseases*. This had lain completely fallow during my Deanship. By 1969 the book was with the printers. We had dealt with the proofs. We were beginning to relax and look for the next challenge. It was then that Michael Swann, who had now been Principal (equivalent to the Vice-Chancellor in England) for about five years, asked me if I would succeed Walter Perry as Vice-Principal.

Soon after his appointment Michael had persuaded the Court of the University of the value of having two Vice-Principals to help him in some aspects of his immense load. Accordingly, Walter Perry and David Talbot-Rice had been appointed. The vacancy as Vice-Principal arose from Walter Perry's having been appointed Vice-Chancellor of the new Open University which he went on to launch with such outstanding success. I do not remember, if I ever knew, what his duties had been as Vice-Principal in Edinburgh. My own were clearly not to be the same.

David Talbot-Rice was Professor of Fine Art. He was very distinguished in his field. His particular specialty was Byzantine art. While on a lecture tour in Algeria and Tunisia in 1968 I had picked up a history of Islamic Art (in French) and had been delighted to find it was by David. He was probably ten years older than I and a charming man. We got on very well. He chaired a number of important university committees for Michael and also deputised on many ceremonial occasions. He obviously did these jobs very well. His warm and friendly personality and sensible approach made him very effective. But, unlike my future job, his job had no specific theme.

Michael said to me that the global wave of student unrest was beginning to hit Edinburgh. He thought that a clinician like myself might be the most effective person to handle these disturbed characters! He would like me, as Vice-Principal, to take a major responsibility for student affairs. They would give me a lecturer in my Department to take over some of the routine work and give me more time for the job.

Of course I was very flattered to be offered such a prestigious post. I liked and admired Michael. I had very much enjoyed my contacts with medical students. This would bring me contacts right across the university, both with students and staff, which appealed to my somewhat ecumenical tastes. It was, of course, not a financial lure. If I remember I received an extra £100 a year; it might have been £200; or even £400; it was mainly symbolic. However as an Honorary NHS consultant I already had an "A" Merit Award (and went on to the top A+ Award a year or two later after our book was published), so, for an academic, I was very well paid. One certainly did not do jobs for the money.

Now a little background about the wave of student militancy which swept the world at that time. One of my Polish colleagues, a Professor in Lodz, claimed that the movement first started in Poland in late 1967 or early 1968 as a protest against communist totalitarianism. There were many demonstrations in the universities there. Later these were crushed by the usual totalitarian methods. Student leaders were imprisoned or called up for military service. All university professors of philosophy, whose main job in Poland was to teach Marxist-Leninism, were considered to have failed and were sacked. All other professors had to go through intensive political screening before special committees. I gathered there was a nasty undercurrent of anti-Semitism among the investigators.

The West heard much more about the 1968 movement in France. It started in one of the new suburban universities in Paris, Nanterre, spread quickly to the others in the capital and then throughout the country, affecting also the schools. It seemed to have had two main stimuli. One was a reaction to the strong, somewhat dictatorial, government of General de Gaulle. He had done a wonderful job, not only in successfully maintaining the honour of France after the 1940 debacle, but also in unifying and directing the immediate post-war chaos towards very successful national recovery. Above all he had managed to extract France from the desperately unsuccessful Algerian civil war. But these achievements were now behind him. Many of the young were too young to remember them. They felt that de Gaulle was no longer the man for the times. Moreover they identified him with rigid and archaic features of their universities and schools, many dating from Napoleonic times. Anyone who passed the Baccalaureate could go to any university he wanted and study any subject he wanted. This resulted in enormous overcrowding, particularly in Paris and particularly at the Sorbonne. For instance I was told that there were 9,000 medical students at the Sorbonne – it was subsequently split into something like nine separate medical schools. As a result teaching was almost entirely by lectures. There was virtually no staff-student contact or small group teaching.

So they demonstrated and rioted on the campus. They demonstrated and rioted in the streets. Politicians cashed in. Others joined. The young felt free to do as they liked. Family constraints were rejected. The waves of revolt flowed higher and higher.

In the USA, about the same time, the main stimulus was the reaction against the Vietnam conflict and resistance to the call-up to serve in what many felt was an unjustified war – all the more so because it seemed to be becoming increasingly impossible to win. This spirit merged with the student reaction against university administrations and staff. These were thought to hold that only research was prestigious. Teaching was an unimportant chore. It was said that in Harvard a teacher was sacked because he had only written two books. The students thought he was a splendid teacher. They held a march through the university waving a banner "HOMER ONLY WROTE TWO BOOKS".

Sadly, things got particularly savage in the USA. In one state the National Guard were called out to quell a campus riot. They opened fire and several students were killed.

In both France and the USA there were long-term political effects. Later de Gaulle put his position at risk by calling a referendum, and saying he would resign if defeated. The referendum was overtly about proposed decentralisation of government. But it was treated as a confidence vote for de Gaulle. He lost it and resigned. In the USA the nation was devastated by the campus deaths. These undoubtedly led to seeking means to pull out of Vietnam, eventually rather shamingly achieved by retreat rather than diplomacy.

This was the background as the movement started in the UK, as in many other countries. The previous subservience of many Scottish students was disappearing. Students were demanding places on university committees, they were demanding more staff-student contact. They were getting increasingly militant. Daily they were seeing examples of student militancy on the TV, at home or abroad. Surely Edinburgh students couldn't be seen to lag behind in such an exciting international surge towards throwing off the yoke of the old and establishing new freedoms for the young.

The Start

To return to my own prospective duties, I had the advantage of having served as Dean. I knew a fair amount about how the University worked. I knew many of the Deans, though some had changed; they usually served for three years. I now knew many people in the other Faculties. I was used to the ways of the Senatus and knew many of its members. I had served as Dean on several of the important committees which I would now again attend. Deans did not serve on the University Court, the ruling body, but Vice-Principals did. I think it was formally *ex officio* and without a vote. But as we hardly ever had a vote that did not matter much.

Charles Stuart, the Secretary of the University, discussed with me how I might function. He had tended to write rather negative replies to written requests from me as Professor or Dean and was a bit of a stickler. But we got on pretty well. He was generally helpful. He was, understandably, conservative about students. He disapproved of my liberal attitude towards student aspirations.

Administratively we agreed that I should have a central office where I could talk with students or staff. This proved to be rather romantic. The entrance door was a false bookcase in the classical Upper Library (now called the Playfair Library after its architect). This is the most beautiful room in the University. My office was therefore near the main central administration with very easy access for students and staff. It looked out on the Old Quad. Later I obtained a charming Kandinsky picture out of the University collection to hang on the wall. For formal occasions I would have access to a University car and chauffeur. This included such things as representing the University at special dinners (usually deputising for the Principal) or attending Royal Garden Parties. Both as Dean and as Vice-Principal, Eileen and I were always invited to the latter with our unmarried daughters! It was worth going once or twice, especially when the girls were available to come*; it later palled.

If I remember I did most of my correspondence with my own splendid departmental secretary, May Corkey. But I had relatively little outside correspondence. I did most of my work by personal contact.

I got on very well with Michael Swann. He was enterprising, original and a man of ideas, but with a shrewd sense of what was possible. He was superb at handling staff. As he said, in a big university there is always a crisis in some Faculty or Department. He was adept at sorting these out with minimal trauma. But to my surprise he proved poor at handling students. I had remembered him as a 31 year-old Professor, when he first came to Edinburgh from Cambridge, riding to Medical Faculty meetings on a motorbike wearing a beret. I thought he would be very liberal. But in fact he tended to be pompous with students and resistant to their aspirations.

Although we never discussed it directly, I think he must have sensed this personal lack but, with his usual skill, had decided that I could help to correct the deficiency. Equally surprising, he proved very tolerant of me and my views. As I explored the problems I became sympathetic to admitting

---

* In fact, the daughters went only once.

students, as they increasingly demanded, on to University committees. I thought it would be very educational for them. After all, the more able of them would be doing this sort of thing all their lives. They might usefully learn to do it well. It might serve them better than obscure analyses of Shakespeare's sonnets! To my surprise only a minute fraction of staff colleagues agreed. I have often summarized my experience as Vice-Principal by saying I had far more trouble with conservative colleagues than with militant students.

Michael and I often argued, but in a very friendly manner. Much later, I think it was when I supported the formal demand from the Student Representative Council for student representation on the Senatus, and Michael strongly objected, that I suggested that as we could not agree, perhaps it would be better if I withdrew. But Michael, very creditably, said no. I should put the case to the Senatus in my own way and get it argued out.

Perhaps I might deviate here to describe the outcome. Of course I tried to raise support beforehand by contacting individuals. Then I made my own address. I felt it needed to be somewhat emotional. It would be an historic move. I thought it might stir them if I quoted Oliver Cromwell. In a letter to the very conservative Scottish Presbyterian Government[*], he wrote "I beseech you in the bowels of Christ, think it possible you may be mistaken" in resisting the proposal. Many spoke against my own proposal. I think I had two supporting speeches, one at least as a result of my own. But the silent majority, to my surprise and delight, voted it through.

I cannot give a detailed continuous account of my happy two years on the job. I can only pick out a few highlights which have stuck in my memory.

Formal Successes

I took charge of two rather formal advances, both of which emerged from discussions with Michael. I believe they were his ideas as least as much as mine. The first was to have a Student Welfare Committee. Students run into all sorts of problems – with work, with money, with accommodation, with their families, with their friends, with staff, and with fellow students. I knew there was an excellent woman in charge of student accommodation. She in fact did a good deal of student counselling outside her immediate remit. But there was no established counselling service. There was obviously an enormous unfilled gap. I got together a number of excellent people onto the committee, including James Blackie, the superb

---

[*] Actually to the General Assembly of the Church of Scotland (in 1650).

University Chaplain and, of course, student representatives. In due course we established a counselling service which thereafter went from strength to strength. I think in due course we also established student counsellors with a 24-hour telephone service like the Samaritans.

The other success was the Teaching and Learning Committee. In those days students had no formal instruction on how to learn in a university context where they are so much on their own, so much less disciplined and spoonfed than at school. Nor were staff, at that time in any university, given any training in teaching. I once passed the door of a law lecture theatre and heard the lecturer reading out his lecture at dictation speed. I believe a senior lecturer in surgery at that time read out his lectures from his own book.

I knew that the Faculty of Science had begun to address the problem. I discussed it at length with Peter Kennedy, a physicist, who had worked closely with Des Truman, a biologist. Peter became a very close friend till his death in 1995. We put many of our ideas to work across the Faculties. We held a series of residential seminars on teaching, examination methods, continuous assessment, etc. We judged it best to take people away to Middleton Hall, outside Edinburgh, then a conference centre. By making it residential we ensured continuous attendance. As so often, much of the useful discussions took place in the bar, over coffee or over dinner. People got to know one another across Faculties. The interest and the climate of opinion built up – rapidly in the young and more slowly in their seniors.

We established a 4-day course for all new lecturers, also residential at Middleton Hall. Among much else they had to give mini-lectures on their subject, which were criticised by their colleagues from other Faculties. We videoed them and played them back for their own criticism. When my daughter, Patricia, became a lecturer in Clinical Chemistry, she attended one of the induction courses and came away full of enthusiasm.

To begin with we had a good deal of resistance, especially from Deans and senior staff. But with full support from Michael Swann, with bucketfuls of diplomacy and probably the help of the infectious enthusiasm of those who had attended seminars, we gradually got the movement accepted. Years later Peter Kennedy, who succeeded me as Chairman, complained to me that it had now become too much "Establishment" and had lost some of the magic of a pioneering effort fighting against conservative odds.

Student Relations

Above all, the most attractive part of the job for me was the contact with the students themselves. The formal body to contact was the Students' Representative Council. It was elected by the students to represent them. I cannot remember whether its President was directly elected or elected by the Council members. My principal contacts were with the successive Presidents and officers of the SRC. I believed that informal contacts were best. The four successive Presidents in my time (Philip Mawer, John Allan, Ken Cargill, and Jonathan Wills) all proved very able, sensible and pleasant. I met them and their officers regularly and informally. This was often over a glass of sherry in my office, sometimes at an informal lunch at the cafeteria of the University Staff Club. Every now and then we invited them home.

In my first year the President was Philip Mawer who was in office during the height of the student unrest. I was impressed by his ability and good sense. I remember at one University committee, when Philip was submitting a formal SRC proposal for student representatives on certain University committees, Michael Swann said pompously did he really think that such young people could contribute.

"I'm an FRS* and very proud of it. Wait till you students achieve equal status", or words to that effect. I looked round the table and thought to myself "If I had to put my affairs in someone's hands here, I might well choose Philip". In fact, to Michael's creditable amusement, when some years later he became Chairman of the BBC and wanted to see his relevant Minister, he had to go through Philip who was by now the Minister's Personal Private Secretary! My colleagues used to get rather cross when I in supporting the students pointed out that Pitt was Prime Minister at 23 and Napoleon First Consul at 28.

Of course, we in the University Administration, and indeed Philip and his responsible colleagues, had plenty of trouble from the wilder students. One of Philip's problems was that SRC meetings, which occurred in the evening, at that time went on and on and on with vast numbers of speeches. The wild characters largely existed as nocturnal predators and slept during the day. Ordinary sensible students drifted away to bed. By the time the vote was taken in the early hours the nocturnal characters were liable to have a majority over the residuum of moderates.

I learnt from his experience and played it in reverse. When there were difficult wild students on a committee I had to chair, and there was a crucial problem, I arranged the meeting for 9am. The wildies would seldom turn up. This was their time for coma.

Of course there were lots of enormous student public meetings demanding the resignation of everyone in authority or complete abolition of all curricula – real Cultural Revolution stuff. Indeed some of them regarded

---

* Fellow of the Royal Society, the highest honour for a scientist in the UK.

themselves as Maoists, though they didn't wave little Red Books or overtly quote Mao.

I attended some of these meetings. Person after person would storm up to the stage, sometimes ranting *en route* on his or her particular form of extreme. In my memory, torn jerseys seemed to be *de rigeur*. They never addressed me directly. I was largely a spectator, but I did not seem to be suspected of espionage. It was sometimes difficult to keep one's face straight.

Charles Stuart, the University Secretary, told me later that he had gone into the backgrounds of some of the wilder students. They were often, like so many criminal delinquents, from broken families.

They could, of course, be very offensive. Michael – and even worse his wife Tessa, a sensitive musician – would get obscene telephone calls in the middle of the night. The student newspaper was often gratuitously unpleasant about individual staff, though I remember one delightful satirical article, along Alice in Wonderland lines, about the University Court which made even Michael and Charles Stuart smile. It was by a medical student, Colin Currie. I had known him when he was on the Medical Students' Council and I was Dean. He went on to be a distinguished novelist as well as a distinguished geriatrician. My contact with him at that time started a lifelong friendship[*].

The most dramatic episode occurred at the height of the UK and Edinburgh unrest. The students had gone into a surging paranoiac frenzy that the authorities had secret files on each of them. In such files the minutiae of their behaviour were recorded: revolutionary activities, suspected drug-taking, etc. Later the evidence would be used against them. Michael told me he had asked to see some student files. Of course all Faculties kept files on the students to record exam results etc. In the central office Michael found a file labelled "Jewish Students". He feared that this might be hot stuff. But it proved to contain letters from one or more rabbis complaining about holding examinations on Saturdays.

One afternoon Michael, Philip Mawer and I were meeting in Michael's office to discuss how we could defuse the Secret File myth. Suddenly we began to hear in the distance what I had read about but never heard before – the sound of an approaching mob! The sound grew louder and louder. Then a mob of some 400 students stormed into the Old Quad and charged up the stairs towards the Principal's office. Charles Stuart sent for the police. We came out. The students stopped on the stairs. Michael said he would receive a delegation of three or four students.

---

[*] Colin Currie (aka Colin Douglas) gave the major tribute at John's funeral.

Maurice Carstairs, the Professor of Psychiatry, a sensible, liberal person who later became Vice-Chancellor of York University, happened to be next to see Michael. He suggested that he and I should go out and talk to the students while Philip, I think, stayed to monitor the delegation. So I went out and chatted to a number on the stairs. One girl said to me "How is it that you are not more upset?" I replied that I was a clinician and used to dealing with disturbed patients and anyway I knew that basically they were very nice young people.

It was decided that we would all go to a lecture theatre across the Quad. There the students would voice their concerns. We went out into the Quad while someone went to get the key to the theatre. Meanwhile I addressed the crowd nearest to me from the raised balcony round the Quad. I said that as Vice-Principal I would expect to be hanged with a silken rope. I had no real reason to feel afraid. I knew that basically they *were* very nice young people who had just been carried away by rousing oratory – some of it from visiting student revolutionaries from across the border.

It was perhaps a commentary on a shaken administration that no one could find the key to the law lecture theatre in the Old Quad. In any case it could not accommodate 400 students. So it was agreed that Michael would have a session with the student delegation in his office. The rest of us would proceed to the large George Square Theatre where I would field questions or observations.

A few police had arrived some time before but stood individually and discreetly in the background. No one referred to them but it may have had a calming effect. I don't think they featured in the George Square Theatre.

So I stood up on the platform and fielded assertions and questions on files and drugs. Drugs were a problem at that time as elsewhere. No doubt other problems were also raised, but I have forgotten the details. I said that, as far as I knew, apart from purely academic Faculty files, the only secret files were in the University Health Service and they were only accessible to medical staff. I said the students seemed to dream up these airy Aunt Sallies and then waste vast amounts of indignation in shooting them down.

As far as I remember the emotion steadily settled down. A messenger eventually arrived with some promise agreed by Michael's group to consider any further file problems. This allowed a peaceful finish to the meeting. Thereafter we had no more riots or mobs.

Two comments. Perhaps it was my informal approaches to students. Perhaps I was known to sympathise with their more sensible objectives. But I never personally suffered any attack, either verbally or in writing.

The second comment is that I was prematurely reassuring about files. Not long afterwards the office of the University Appointments Officer was broken into and his files stolen. This Officer's job was to help graduating students to find jobs. It emerged that he had made a number of tactless and critical comments, including anti-Semitic ones, on individual students in some of their files. We were all very upset. I think that he was soon moved on.

This episode was the peak of the revolution, but of course things continued to simmer on, with ups and downs. I handled these various problems in close cooperation with Philip Mawer, his colleagues and their equally sensible successors. We slowly persuaded our conservative colleagues to concede the more sensible reforms. Things gradually eased down during 1970.

Nationally and internationally the pot continued to boil merrily. Excitement in the media about some stirring riot or protest obviously stimulated local emulation by the wild men (and a few wild women). One of the leaders was a rousing orator. It was he, I believe, with some visiting militants from other universities, who had set off the mob assault on the Old Quad.

In order to build up interfaculty rapport, from time to time I gave a dinner for selected staff from different Faculties, often including students. These were held in Abden House, originally a home for the Principal but now devoted to university functions. Eileen reminds me that to one of these I invited our showpiece Wild Man. He turned up an hour late in suitably shabby clothes. But I do not recall him otherwise behaving badly. I had probably invited staff members who were likely to prove reasonably tolerant.

The Malcolm Muggeridge Affair

Malcolm Muggeridge was at that time a very prominent public figure in the UK. He was a journalist and broadcaster with a genius for publicity. He seemed instinctively to know when to come out with some exciting challenge that would capture the headlines. These challenges varied, but he always hit the right one at the right time as far as boosting his persona was concerned. From talking to him before the present episode, I am not sure that the choice of the appropriate challenge was even fully conscious. His brain was just wired up in that way. It was indeed a sort of genius. Much of the fuel that exploded into personal publicity was derived from highly articulate moral fervour. The moral component varied according to the opportunity.

At that time, by tradition, students in Scottish universities annually elected a Rector. He was supposed to represent their interests in the University. He was usually a well known public figure, sometimes a politician (I think Gladstone and Churchill had featured in the past), more often an actor or a TV star, particularly popular with the young at the time. After election he had to give an address to a traditionally very rowdy student audience. Thereafter he usually appointed some appropriate local person in the University to act as Rector's Assessor. The Assessor did most of the work. Theoretically and legally the Rector was also Chairman of the University Court, the university's governing body. Rectors always delegated this privilege to the Principal, his Assessor only sitting in as a member.

It must have been in November 1969 that Malcolm Muggeridge was elected in Edinburgh. I cannot recall whether he had already given his election address when he was also invited to give an address from the pulpit of St Giles. The evening before, Michael Swann gave a dinner for him at Abden House with about twenty people.

I think Michael and I, and probably Jonathan Wills the then President of the Student Representative Council, had had some talk with him beforehand about student affairs. Certainly I sat beside him at the dinner.

I was astonished to find that all he could talk about was the wickedness of Edinburgh students, their primary interest in sex and drugs, their general absence of morality. Nothing about student militancy. It was all about marijuana, heroin and condoms. Of course I was deeply shocked at such misrepresentation. I came back as hard as I could on the students' side. If I remember there was general discussion after dinner, with Malcolm playing the same old record stuck in the same old groove. He was quite impervious to any other views. Was this genuine or was it a guileful plot to gain publicity? I suspect that it was, consciously or unconsciously, the latter. This then wired his conscious centres to believe it was genuine.

There was not a hint the night before, but he took the opportunity next day, from the pulpit of St Giles, to denounce the Edinburgh students as a wicked immoral crew, to say he could not dream of representing such monsters and to dramatically resign as Rector. It was a gift for the media. It was certainly a gift for Malcolm. There was enormous publicity.

In the long run it did not do the University much harm. The sophisticated recognised the well known Muggeridge hyperbole. The unsophisticated soon forgot it. It was so unjustified that it may have brought staff and students closer together. Paradoxically, Malcolm was said to have led a very loose life in his own university youth, defending his activities with equal fervour on his own contemporary moral grounds.

The University Court

Perhaps I should say a little about the Court which is the University's governing body. It has to approve major items of policy, discipline and finance though, if I remember, the Senatus has theoretically the last word on purely educational matters. It is normally chaired by the Principal, by courtesy of the legal Chairman, the Rector. The Chancellor of the University (the Duke of Edinburgh) appoints his own Assessor to the Court, in my time a very senior judge, Lord (Jock) Cameron; the Rector his; the Lord Provost his. The Senatus elects three members. The General Council (all graduates) one or two. There are several co-opted by the Court, usually distinguished Edinburgh people, such as financial or business experts or a headmaster of a major school. I suppose we were about twenty in all.

The Court normally met at 2pm on Monday afternoons in term-time. The meeting often went on till 6-7pm. There was usually an immense agenda, much of it formal. Fortunately the necessary action had usually been taken and it was largely a matter of reporting. From time to time, of course, the student crises intruded. The Court was severely conservative, as one might expect (in my time there was always at least one other judge besides Lord Cameron). The Rector's Assessor might be slightly liberal, together perhaps with one of the Senatus representatives. If the Court in general was conservative, the then Lord Provost's Assessor, a City councillor, was almost a caricature. He shocked us all one day by announcing that "these young people must learn how to behave to their betters!"

On my last Court before I demitted office, Michael Swann gave me a very heartening tribute. I felt rather sorry and embarrassed in one way, because he started by saying that David Talbot-Rice had done a useful job chairing many University committees but then adding that I had done superb and outstanding work on all aspects of student affairs. It sounded a bit of a contrast between the contributions of the two Vice-Principals and I felt it was unfair to David. But of course I was selfishly pleased that my own work was appreciated. I got a round of applause from the Court.

Although that was my last Court meeting as Vice-Principal, I might extrapolate into the future. Almost immediately after finishing as Vice-Principal I was elected as one of the three Senatus Assessors to the Court. With my then knowledge of student affairs, and the continuing if less violent student unrest, I thought I could be useful in contributing a mildly liberal slant to a deeply conservative body. Peter Kennedy, equally liberal, was elected at the same time. We were largely alone, with some support occasionally from the third Senatus Assessor.

Perhaps it was in 1970 or 1971 that a body of students had taken the unprecedented step of proposing a student candidate for election as Rector. Unfortunately for the Establishment there was nothing in the laws to prevent this. Their choice had fallen on a very bright PhD student in Geography. His name was Gordon Brown[*] who, a few weeks before I write this in June 1997, has become Chancellor of the Exchequer in the new Labour Government.

Not only was Gordon elected Rector but he also declared that he intended to assert his legal right to chair the Court. Of course this infuriated the elderly judges and, very understandably, Michael Swann and Charles Stuart (who as Secretary of the University was responsible for organising Court business and was its Secretary). However they could not demur. Charles creditably briefed Gordon well. As one can imagine from his future distinction, he did the job very efficiently, but in a pretty frigid atmosphere. I saw a certain amount of him off the Court. He obviously had grateful memories. In 1996 when he was invited to give a public lecture in the University he asked that Eileen and I should be invited to the Reception afterwards. I had a chat with him then. He said he had very happy memories of a dinner at our home, an event which both Eileen and I had forgotten. We did a good deal of that sort of thing at the time. That particular dinner must have merged in our memories with the rest. Few other staff seemed to entertain students at their homes.

Later, as a result of this "scandal" of a student as Rector and as Chairman of the Court, the University laws were changed. In future the Rector would be elected by the whole University staff, academic and non-academic, as well as by the students.

Final Period as Vice-Principal

Later in 1970 it became increasingly difficult to meet all my obligations to my clinical work and my own Department and also carry the burden of Vice-Principal. Michael was keen that I should continue if possible. One of my problems was that one departmental member at the time had a major family crisis, lasting many months. This involved me in much intensive counselling, happily ultimately successful. But unfortunately it also decreased, over many months, his own contributions to the work. I said I would need another lecturer for the Department if I were to continue as Vice-Principal. The then Dean (Kenneth Donald) said that this would not be possible. Thereafter Michael agreed that the worst of the student unrest seemed to have subsided. I was now less essential. So he consented to my terminating after two years. It had formally been a four-year appointment.

---

[*] James Gordon Brown (born 1951) was in fact a history student at the time and became Rector a little later (1972-75) than John recalls. He later became one of the longest serving Chancellors of the Exchequer (1997-2007) and briefly Prime Minister (2007-09).

In any case I was quite keen to be able to give more time to clinical academic work.

Conclusions on my Period as Vice-Principal

I regarded these two years as some of the happiest of my career. It was, of course, a very prestigious job. I was very happy in the company of academics. I was always interested in their academic interests and learnt a lot from them. The job gave me a much broader, if peripatetic, intellectual range. I felt very much on the same wavelength with colleagues – and indeed with students – across the Faculties. Coping with student militancy was an exciting new challenge. It was made very much easier by my close friendly relations with the student leaders. It was rewarding to have been able to help a good deal over the welfare and teaching and learning fields. As I demitted office I left welfare in the able hands, *de facto* if not *de jure*, of James Blackie, the University Chaplain, who sadly died prematurely a few years later. I left the teaching and learning in the equally able hands, both *de jure* and *de facto* of Peter Kennedy.

I had found it a vastly less stressful job than being Dean. Although I still worked very long hours, I did not so often start at 6am or have to work through so many meals. Moreover Eileen was much more involved, either in informal meetings at home or in more formal dinners, suppers etc to which she also was often invited. She also met many pleasant people in other Faculties. We were able to see more of each other. My problems were of far more interest than those I had had as Dean with their much narrower Faculty context.

During the period I was Vice-Principal our postgraduate book was published in 1969. Its enthusiastic reception, with a very laudatory review by Guy Scadding in the *British Medical Journal* and, later, excellent reviews round the world, was an additional boost to a sometimes shaky ego. We still had a steady stream of international visitors to the Department, requests for Fellowship attachments from all over the world (even more so as the book became well-known) and many bright young people from all over the UK applying for our junior jobs. Thanks to Andrew Douglas and my other outstanding consultant colleagues, the reputation of our group was very much in the ascendant and that in spite of the titular Professor spending some of his time fielding showers of metaphorical brickbats from non-medical student revolutionaries. I should remark that medical students were too hard-worked to do more than offer occasional and nominal support, often to very justified proposals for reform.

During my Deanship I felt I had to refuse most of the recurrent invitations to lecture or visit abroad. During my Vice-Principal period acceptance was easier, though the visits were usually brief. From my records I see that I gave a series of lectures in a postgraduate course in Vancouver, Canada, in 1969 and had a week as a Visiting Professor at the University of Tel Aviv in Israel. I think there were some other shorter visits. I remember a brief visit to Moscow with a research group when I was surprised to meet in the hotel lift my fellow Vice-Principal, David Talbot-Rice.

So overall it was not surprising that, as the student militancy caused me personally little stress, I found it a euphoric period, and indeed an exciting one to live through.

Postscript on Student Militancy

Only three or four years later, when I was no longer concerned with such problems, I happened to have a patient who was a lecturer in the Department of Politics. Their Department's students, of course, had been the powerhouse of student militancy. I asked him how student militancy was going. He said it had disappeared. As part of his job, he now taught a module on the international events in 1968. He was astonished to find that none of the students had even heard of them. When he went on to explain the issues they tended all to be on the side of the Establishment!

About the same time I happened to be President of the British Thoracic Society when we held a joint meeting with the corresponding Swedish Society in Uppsala, the Oxbridge of Sweden. It was in mid-May. The weather there was unusually warm and beautiful. This was the time of year when their students held a traditional Summer Festival. While we were there the students trooped down the steps of the University in the sunshine in full evening dress with white ties, student caps and student gowns, singing what we gathered were traditional jingoistic patriotic songs. Later I sat beside the Vice-Chancellor's wife at dinner. She told me that this was the first such celebration for seven or eight years. The students had previously rejected the Festival as they had rejected so much else. She said she and her husband had long had a habit of inviting groups of students to breakfast. For the last seven or eight years they had always turned up in disreputable old clothes. She and the Vice-Chancellor were determined not to bat an eyelid. But this year they all arrived in smart suits. Their hosts could scarcely conceal their astonishment. Revolutions can clearly move in both directions!

A Clinical Episode of Depression

Sadly there is still often a certain stigma attached to episodes of clinical depression. My personal experience convinced me that the underlying mechanism was basically physical and biochemical, though precipitated by an important and challenging administrative problem which, at the crucial time, I could see no way of resolving. I later remembered that there was in fact a straightforward solution which I could and later did use. But the biochemical damage had been done. It took me more than two years to return to my normal psyche.

Although, in a highly active and challenging career, there were naturally recurrent anxieties when things were difficult, I don't remember any other period in which I had any trace of clinical depression. Indeed when I came largely to run my own show I sometimes had a rewarding sense of euphoria, which I think was entirely normal and natural, certainly not a symptom of being hypomanic.

My attack of depression was very sudden. It occurred one Saturday morning just about midday in late September 1971. I had recently completed my term as Vice-Principal. However, I was glad to get back to more clinical work and research. Moreover I had been elected by the Senatus to the University Court and so kept in touch with wider University affairs. Looking back I do not think that my ceasing to be Vice-Principal contributed to my depression.

The basic reason was this. A few years before, one of our house physicians, Barry Kay, became very attached to my Department. So much so that he asked to be allowed to repeat another year in the same job. As he was very bright I agreed. In due course he became very interested in immunology. Later we took him on as a lecturer. We both thought it would be good for his scientific development and career for him to spend a year as a Research Fellow with a Cambridge University immunologist. This was then followed by a similar year in Harvard University in Boston, USA.

Barry was then, at the time of the onset of my depression, just about to complete his year in Harvard and return to Edinburgh. Our excellent hospital administrator, with his usual skill, had prepared a personal laboratory for him. But I suddenly realised that he would need quite a pile of expensive technical equipment. I had no money for this and could think of no way of financing it in the immediate future.

Paradoxically, in spite of my depression, I remembered a week or two later that, when I was Dean, there had been a specific fund just for this, equipment for any new laboratory developed for a Department. I had already missed the statutory date for applying. The relevant committee was irritated but I did in due course get the money. Barry and I had excellent personal and professional relationships. Even when he later moved to a job in the Department of Pathology in Edinburgh we lunched together about once a fortnight. He clearly enjoyed discussing his, usually very original, ideas with me. Barry later went on to a brilliant career as Professor of Clinical Immunology in London.

Now back to my affliction. On that grim Saturday morning I felt as if there had been a sudden biochemical explosion inside my head. I remember visualising it as centred on the pituitary. But I suppose it was more likely to have been in the amygdala, now thought to be the major emotional centre in the brain. It was an absolutely sudden feeling of overwhelming and utter despair, irrational but overpowering.

Soon I had the classical symptoms of waking at 3am soaked with sweat. I was able to continue all my routine clinical, teaching and administrative work but felt as if I was doing it in a sort of gloomy shade rather than with my usual enthusiasm. Everything was an effort.

The solution of the precipitating financial problem, which I achieved in a week or two, had little effect in relieving my deep depression, however great a relief it gave to the intellectual part of my brain. I became much less chatty than was my usual wont, more silent. Friends noticed there was something wrong. Because of the stigma involved at that time I did not talk to them about it. One of them however, Andrew Douglas, a close collaborator in the Department, did diagnose the problem. I followed his advice to seek the help of one of the Professors of Psychiatry, Henry Walton. I visited him regularly at his home. He put me on an anti-depressant drug. This helped me to sleep and to lose my 3am sweat baths. It probably gradually, over many months, somewhat ameliorated my gloom.

Understandably the difference in my personality affected Eileen. It gave her, poor girl, a bit of a depression also, if fortunately less severe. Of course Henry Walton asked me the expected question, whether I at all contemplated suicide. Perhaps because I had soon solved the intellectual aspect of my problem, fortunately this never entered my thoughts, which gave some reassurance to Eileen.

It was just about two years before I felt I was beginning to come out of the shadow. I probably seemed so to others as, in December 1973, I was elected President of the Royal College of Physicians of Edinburgh; I had been elected Vice-President the year before. This was a major emotional boost. I at last knew I was coming out of the depression. By the end of January 1974 I was back to normal as, thank goodness, I have remained emotionally so ever since.

I have written down this account as it may help some of my readers to learn something of the clinical problem involved from the patient's perspective. Perhaps some readers may in turn be able to help others who become afflicted as I was.

Chapter 10
President of the Royal College of Physicians of Edinburgh 1973-76

A Little History *

The Medical and Surgical Royal Colleges in the UK are an important component of the medical "establishment". They are not government bodies but, because of their prestige, are frequently consulted by governments and indeed often seek to influence government policy, particularly on medical standards. Historically the oldest Colleges, dating from the 16th and 17th centuries, were originally founded to ensure, before there were national standards of qualification, that local medical practitioners could be seen by the public to be suitably qualified if they had become Members or Fellows of the College. After formal university undergraduate medical schools were established in the 18th and 19th centuries, the Colleges jointly, both in England and Scotland, also examined for an extramural qualifying medical degree, usually regarded as a slightly lower standard than the university degree. When I was a clinical student at St Thomas's Hospital in London it was common first to sit the joint Colleges' extramural examination and later the university. The advantage was that you could take the Colleges' examination 6 months before the university one and so fully qualify 6 months earlier. It could also be a useful rehearsal for the somewhat more challenging university test.

In Edinburgh some undergraduate teaching had been undertaken under the aegis of the Royal College of Surgeons from its foundation in 1505. This during the 19th century evolved into the extramural School of Medicine, with much teaching and coaching by up and coming young surgeons and physicians. As medical income at that time came almost entirely from private practice, paid teaching was a useful supplement in the early stages of their careers. From 1895 this teaching also became formally associated with the Royal College of Physicians of Edinburgh (RCPE). The Extramural (non-university) School was abolished by the UK government in 1948, as

---

* The Royal College of Physicians of Edinburgh (RCPE) was founded in 1681 (despite strong opposition from surgeons) to promote the establishment of professional standards comparable with those in Holland at the time.

was the London conjoint examination. The College Licentiate was continued; it was mostly taken by doctors qualified overseas who needed a UK degree to be recognised to practise in the UK.

The Modern Colleges

The modern Colleges are mainly concerned with standards in postgraduate medicine, the Royal College of Physicians primarily with standards for hospital consultants but also including consultants in Public Health by incorporating in the Colleges the Faculty of Public Health Medicine. The three UK Colleges of Physicians (Edinburgh, Glasgow and London) jointly run an advanced postgraduate examination "The Membership" which has to be passed to be accepted for higher specialist training.

Since the Second World War the Royal College of Physicians of Edinburgh has become more and more involved in such training, both on the theoretical side and in the regulation of the practical clinical side. The latter is mainly carried out through the trainee working in a hospital job under the supervision of consultants.

The membership examination has very high status internationally, especially in the Commonwealth. It is taken by large numbers from Asia and the Middle East. When I was President we initiated arrangements for taking the first theoretical stage of the examination overseas, for instance in Hong Kong, Malaysia and, rather unsuccessfully, in Egypt. Subsequently the full examination has been held in a number of places overseas.

The Colleges have long been concerned with ongoing education throughout physicians' careers via conferences, seminars etc. In recent years, and since my time as President, this has been formalised and made legally compulsory.

Election to the Fellowship of the College is obtained by established consultants on the basis of the quality of their work and on the recommendations of senior colleagues. Most of these will have already become Members by examination but a few non-College Members with particularly distinguished records, especially from overseas, can be elected Fellows. As a result of all this I think about half of all Fellows work overseas. The Royal College of Physicians of Edinburgh regards itself as an International College.

Personal

Some years before I was elected President, a previous President, Rae Gilchrist, suggested to me that I should allow my name to be proposed for election to the Council of the College. The Council meets regularly and conducts, under the chairmanship of the President, most of the ongoing business of the College. I served for some years, got to know most of the routine business, and in 1972 was elected Vice-President. At that time the Vice-President's major, but very important, job was to do a preliminary sort of the large numbers of Members, and a few distinguished non-Members from the UK and abroad, who were annually proposed for election to the Fellowship. As the latter was very prestigious, it was important to ensure that the candidates were fully up to standard. Particularly for those abroad, this might involve correspondence for confirmation by well-known senior Fellows in the relevant country or region. (Later the College appointed Regional Advisors for this purpose among others). As Presidents also had to do much travelling in the UK, and increasingly overseas, the Vice-President carried out his functions when the President was away.

I greatly enjoyed my time on the Council and as Vice-President. Administratively it was less exacting than the frequent personality crises I had to deal with as Dean of the Faculty of Medicine and the recurrent staff-student crises during my time as Vice-Principal of the University. It was mainly committee work rather than direct personal responsibility. Apart from the Fellowship problem, implementation of committee decisions devolved on the President, Secretary or Treasurer. I had more time for the clinical, teaching and research work in my own university department; more time to build up material for the second edition of our postgraduate textbook (1975); and more time to accept invitations to lecture abroad (Egypt in 1972; The Argentine, Uruguay and Peru in 1973).

I had the happiest relations with the two Presidents, Christopher Clayson and John Halliday Croom, under whom I served. Christopher, as a chest physician, was an old friend. He was in his last years as Director of a large sanatorium at Lochmaben in Galloway. When a student in Edinburgh he had had a large haemoptysis* just before taking his final examination. He did not go sick. He took the examination but, understandably, failed. Again he did not report sick but was allowed to resit. He passed three months later. He then did report sick, was diagnosed as having tuberculosis, and was flat on his back in Southfield Sanatorium under Sir Robert Philip for two years. Later he was gradually rehabilitated to take increasing responsibility for Southfield, particularly in the early years of the Second World War and after the death of Sir Robert. From there, during the war, he was appointed to head Lochmaben. As the revolution in the cure of tuberculosis in the 1950s and 60s started to empty sanatoria, Christopher began to use his great administrative, diplomatic, oratorical and initiating skills in medical politics, at first mainly through the British Medical Association. As a result of these

---

* Bleeding from inside the lungs.

obvious talents, he was later elected first to the Council of the College and later still as President, the first in history from a non-teaching hospital. He soon became highly regarded not only in Scotland but throughout the UK.

John Croom had a more conventional background. His father had been a distinguished obstetrician. He himself had qualified in Edinburgh and had been appointed a consultant at the Royal Infirmary of Edinburgh just before the Second World War. He had served like me in the RAMC. His army hospital had moved on from Malta to Italy on the day I myself arrived in Malta from Egypt in 1944, so I had just missed meeting him there.

He was a very charming man, an excellent physician, and proved an efficient and very popular administrator, a pleasure to work with. Both he and Christopher became my close friends.

In December 1973 I was elected President. In those days the actual election process was largely formal. The routine was that the Treasurer, or a senior Fellow, informally sought the opinion of former Presidents and perhaps one or two other senior Fellows. Only one name was then submitted to the annual meeting of Fellows. I myself felt it was wrong that the decision should always be made by old men. I thought there should be a genuine election. Later, as President, I put this to the Fellows. They turned it down at the time, but the reform did come later.

For my own nomination, a senior retired Fellow and previous College Secretary, Henry Matthews, approached me informally and asked me if I was willing to stand. The only condition was that I would have to resign from the University Court, to which I had been elected by the Senatus when I finished my term as University Vice-Principal. Of course I readily agreed.

There followed an extremely busy and very enjoyable three years. Everyone connected with the College, in Edinburgh, in Scotland, in London and abroad, was both friendly and supportive. The Royal College of Physicians of Edinburgh had immense local, national, and international prestige – and this rubbed off on the President. In contrast with my experiences as Dean, when I had to become expert in recurrent dealings with angry men, in my whole three years as President, I only had one cross letter. This was from a diabetes consultant who felt he had been insufficiently consulted concerning our initiative to launch a pilot project on "Shared Care" (see below), with consultants and GPs collaborating for the longterm care of diabetic patients. I immediately asked him to come and see me, as I had learned to do with angry men, and all was well.

I was aged 61 when I was elected in December 1973. I was not due to retire from my University post until the end of the academic year when I should become 65. So I continued to do as much as possible of my departmental work: clinics, teaching, supervision of research etc.

Fortunately Andrew Douglas had all the talents, all the energy and all the devotion to cope when I was not available.

The job of course involved almost daily visits to the College, and many meetings there, regular meetings in Edinburgh or Glasgow with the Presidents of other Scottish Colleges, with the Presidents of the English Colleges in London, and from time to time, with the President of the Royal College of Physicians of Ireland in Dublin.

President's Report

At that time there were regular quarterly meetings of the College open to all Fellows. At these all business that statutorily required the approval of Fellows was voted on. Most of the items were purely formal. There was seldom comment or debate from the floor; most complex business had already been fully discussed by the Council. The President usually gave a brief report of Council business. But because most of the business was formal and most Fellows were busy clinicians, the attendance level was usually low and, anyway, confined to those living in Edinburgh. I thought therefore that the large number of Fellows elsewhere in the UK and overseas were ill informed on the numerous very important subjects discussed and decided by the Council. As a result, I was the first President to initiate a regular President's Report in the then *College Chronicle* which went out to all Fellows wherever they were. Many years later a subsequent President, John Cash, was astonished to hear about one of the projects I had initiated. He asked me to write him a memo on the more important initiatives in my Presidency. I was able to do this after the Librarian provided me with copies of all my Reports. The resultant memo has formed a useful basis for this section of my memoirs.

One important initiative was a College Committee on Education for Health, set up at the suggestion of a future President, Michael Oliver. David Player, the then Director of the government Scottish Health Education Group served on it as did my wife Eileen as the first Medical Director of Scottish ASH (Action on Smoking and Health). To give it prestige, the immediate past President, Sir John Croom, agreed to be its first chairman. I later joined it myself. It did an excellent job over a number of years, notably in producing *The Book of the Child* which was issued to all mothers in antenatal clinics in Scotland. Later it proved difficult to recruit an appropriate chairman or secretary, at least one of whom is essential to give such a committee drive. It ceased to function in spite of my own efforts to persuade several succeeding Presidents to resuscitate it.

During my time as President, W.S. Craig's *History of the Royal College of Physicians of Edinburgh* was published. It had originally been commissioned during Christopher Clayson's Presidency in anticipation of the coming tercentenary of the College. Craig was an enthusiastic and meticulous retired paediatrician who did a devoted job. He produced a useful reference book but, I am afraid, a rather unexciting text. Sadly, one day when the book was almost completed, he developed severe chest pain while working in the library. I telephoned the Coronary Unit at the Royal Infirmary and drove him there in my car. Sadly that illness killed him. Derrick Dunlop agreed to see the book through the press. I obtained a supporting grant from the Carnegie Foundation and wrote a foreword.

At the celebration of the bicentenary of the University Faculty of Medicine I had learnt that the grave of Robert Sibbald[*], the most important founder of the College, its first Secretary and second President, was unmarked. I approached the minister of Greyfriars' Kirk, who agreed that the College could erect a monument. This was formally unveiled at the later Tercentenary celebrations of the College; I was asked to give the address.

Sibbald had also initiated, with Balfour, later the first Professor of Botany at Edinburgh University, a Physic Garden for medicinal plants at Holyrood Abbey. This had, later in the 17th century, been transferred to the grounds of Trinity College, the site of the future Waverley Station. I negotiated with British Rail, the Royal Botanic Gardens, and the University to erect a plaque opposite No. 10 platform at the station. This was unveiled by my successor, Ronnie Robertson, in 1977. (Later still a Physic Garden has been set up, with the aid of the Royal Botanic Gardens in one of the College courtyards).

The Membership Examination

The Membership Examination, passing which grants the higher degree essential to acceptance for training as a consultant, had previously been separately awarded, after separate examinations, by the Edinburgh, Glasgow, London and Irish Colleges. In the Presidency of Christopher Clayson the three UK Colleges of Physicians had first recognised reciprocity and recognition of each others' examinations. They had then agreed to aim at a common examination, the MRCP(UK). It would be planned by inter-College Committees and held in all three Colleges. Those passing the examination could then choose to become a formal Member of the College of their choice.

All this had gone forward in John Croom's time. In the RCPE a successful Members' Committee had been formed. Much inter-College negotiations still continued during my own Presidency. It had the great advantage that the relevant Presidents and Fellows of the different Colleges

---

[*] Sir Robert Sibbald (1641-1722), Edinburgh-born physician and naturalist.

got to know each other well. During my time a previously informal conference of English Colleges became formal. Initially the Scottish Colleges were allowed to attend as observers but we negotiated full membership in 1976.

Higher Medical Training

There had been much discussion in the General Medical Council and with the Government on Higher Medical Training. The MRCP was, in the UK, an examination to determine fitness for training as a consultant. It was followed by five to ten years in successive junior training posts, perhaps in different hospitals, before the trainee was judged fit to compete for a consultant post with full responsibility.

It was now decided that standards must be centrally laid down for the quality of practical hospital training posts. The training hospitals must be regularly monitored to maintain these standards. A joint committee on Higher Medical Training was set up. Statutorily it would cover both the UK and the Republic of Ireland. It would be chaired for a year at a time successively by the current Presidents of each of the three Colleges of Physicians. I thought it tactful to suggest that the President of the London College, Cyril Clarke, who had become a close friend, should be the first chairman. I became the second and had to conduct some tricky negotiations with the General Medical Council which now had overall statutory responsibility.

All this usually took me to London at least every two weeks, sometimes more often. I always went and came back by railway night sleeper usually on successive nights. I occasionally spent a night in London if I had more than one day's commitment. Much inter-college work was involved in setting up the central committee; working out the details of committees to establish appropriate standards of training in each speciality; and the formidable job of organising hospital visits by external assessors to monitor implementation. If training facilities were judged inadequate the hospital would be unable to recruit junior staff. This proved a useful sanction, for instance ensuring that all more peripheral hospitals had adequate libraries and that, in a few highly academic institutions, junior NHS staff had adequate clinical training. For instance when I later chaired my own specialty committee, we found in one London teaching hospital a Senior Registrar, theoretically in the advanced stages of training, was doing only two outpatient sessions a week and had no in-patient responsibility; nearly all his time was spent on research. There was much discussion how, with particularly bright young trainees, the valuable research experience should be balanced by adequate and essential clinical experience.

UK Joint Consultants' Committee

This met two or three times a year in London. It was supposed to be concerned exclusively with standards in the NHS, particularly in hospitals. It consisted of the Presidents of the English and Scottish Royal Medical Colleges and an equal number representing the British Medical Association. We met in the morning. We discussed various proposals put to us mainly by the Department of Health for England and Wales. In the afternoon we were joined by the Chief Medical Officer for England and Wales (and perhaps sometimes the CMO for Scotland) and civil servants.

I was highly critical of its work. The BMA representatives were primarily medical politicians who seemed to be concerned mainly with the conditions and pay of doctors, not with the welfare of patients, which was supposed to be the committee's main purpose. I began to realise that one of the BMA's priorities, or at least these representatives of the BMA, was private practice in England. For instance, any government proposals to deal with the notorious waiting lists were usually strongly opposed by the BMA; long hospital waiting lists meant more demand on private practice. The BMA representatives were experienced long-term medical politicians. Most Presidents were normally in office for about three years and far less politically skilled. So the committee's recommendations usually went the BMA's way. When I came to demit office as President I wrote a critical letter to the Chairman about this. As a result a group was set up to consider how to make the committee's activities more appropriate to its statutory purpose. I could not later find out whether it succeeded.

"Shared Care"

It seemed to me that the long-term care of patients with chronic diseases was not satisfactory. GPs did not seem to have any agreed method of monitoring patients' care. At that time I was surprised to find that such patients were not given routine follow-up appointments; it seemed to be up to the patient to make an appointment when he thought fit. In consequence much of the necessary supervision of the treatment was often conducted only by a concerned specialised hospital department eg. for diabetes. It might be much more convenient for the patient if most of the routine supervision of his treatment was done in his General Practice Unit with reference to a hospital specialist only when there was a problem. Perhaps one GP in a practice might have had part of his training in a hospital specialty or might do a regular assistant session in a hospital department to keep in touch and get to know the local hospital specialist in that subject.

We initiated a project to explore this subject by a working supper in the College, with representatives of the three Scottish Royal Colleges, the Scottish Committee of the Royal College of General Practitioners and the

Faculty of Community Medicine (now Public Health) with observers from the Scottish Home and Health Department. This resulted in the setting up of Working Parties on Stroke, Diabetes, Peptic Ulcer, Hypertension; later on Geriatrics and Care of the Mentally Handicapped Child. Reports from these Working Parties were circulated to all Scottish Health Regions for discussion, followed by a two-day Colloquium in the college in 1976, edited by the late James Syme and published as *Conference on the Integration of Patient Care.*

Other Health Professions

I thought that physicians had much to learn about the great potential value of other health professions and that there was a case for much closer cooperation with them. Consequently, in October 1975 we held a working supper with representatives of the Royal Colleges of Nursing and Midwives, the British Association of Social Workers, the Institute of Laboratory Medical Science, the Society of Radiographers, the College of Speech Therapists, the Society of Chiropodists, the Medical Microbiological Scientific Group, the British Association of Occupational Therapists, the British Diabetic Association and the Chartered Society of Physiotherapy, together with the Chairmen of the National Medical Consultative Committee, the Scottish Committee for Hospital Medical Services and the Scottish Council of the British Medical Association, as well as the Scottish Secretary of the British Medical Association.

A series of Working Groups were set up for particular disciplines. Each had representatives of the relevant profession, together with Fellows or Members of the Royal Colleges, including GPs where appropriate. A very successful Symposium on Social Work and the Health Services was held in the College in May 1976.

Two series of Reports were finally published: *Cooperation between Medical and Other Health Professions* (1976), covering Chiropody, Dietetics, Medical Use of Laboratories, Occupational Therapy, Physiotherapy, and Speech Therapy and (1978) covering Nursing, Pharmacy, Radiography and Social Work.

Crisis in the NHS

At the time there was considerable conflict between the profession and the government. The BMA was very militant and even suggested doctors' strikes. The Royal Colleges were very much against such action. At one joint meeting between the Colleges and the BMA, when the Colleges were urging that patients must not be harmed, a BMA representative (an obstetrician) stated "There are bound to be casualties in War"! I was several times involved with the media on the subject and used much pressure to prevent strikes. I think in the end none occurred.

At one stage all the College Presidents and representatives of all the medical school Deans met the Minister of Health (Barbara Castle) urging the problem of resources for medical education. I think we made some progress. There is always a crisis in the NHS!

Celebration of the UK's Entry to the EEC*

During the UK's application to join the EEC followed by the confirmatory referendum, I suggested that the College might celebrate by electing to our Fellowship a distinguished physician from each of the other EEC countries. After wide consultation we did so and invited them all to a very successful ceremony and dinner in the College.

EEC Specialist Training

As doctors were to be the first profession to be allowed to work anywhere in the EEC, there would have to be EEC-wide standards of training. Initially the only rule for qualification was that medical students must have had 5,000 hours of teaching! In my time international discussion began to try to agree standardised qualifications more precisely. Similar efforts began for specialist training. But it took a number of years to achieve uniform European standards both for undergraduate and postgraduate education.

International Action Regarding Imprisoned Doctors

Following the revolution in Chile in 1973 many doctors were imprisoned. I had particular knowledge of one of these who had been active in the International Union against Tuberculosis and Lung Disease. After high-powered training in respiratory physiology in the USA he had returned to Chile. There he realised that the major neglected problem was tuberculosis. He did a wonderful job organising a good service for the whole population. His service to the poor put him under suspicion by the new extreme right wing dictatorship. He was imprisoned. Together with a number of organisations I wrote on behalf of the College, with the agreement of the Council, and in consultation with Amnesty International and the International Union against Tuberculosis and Lung Disease, to relevant Ministers in Chile. We were assured in due course that all the doctors had been released but I think it was some time before this was completely fulfilled.

---

* European Economic Community, later superceded by the European Union.

I took similar steps concerning a Jewish doctor in the USSR who had been imprisoned on completely false charges of poisoning his child patients. Many prominent physicians and academics in the UK took similar action and the man was released. It was interesting that I was informed that the best action was to send cables to the Minister of Health and the President of the Academy of Medicine in Moscow because both of these would be seen by the KGB.

International Trips

It had been the custom for the American College of Physicians, the Royal Australasian College of Physicians and the Canadian Royal College of Physicians and Surgeons to invite the Presidents of each of the three UK Colleges of Physicians (Edinburgh, London and Glasgow) to their annual conferences. The UK Presidents usually took it in turn to attend, representing all three UK Colleges at each attendance. After I was elected in December 1973 I decided not to travel abroad for my first year. I concentrated on working myself into the job.

Canada

In January 1975 I accepted the invitation from the Canadian College and decided to extend the trip to meet our Fellows and lecture in Hong Kong, India, Bangladesh, Sri Lanka and Pakistan. In Canada I was expected to wear the full paraphernalia of heavy gold embroidered gown and academic hat. (The Edinburgh president doesn't have a formal hat; I substituted my Cambridge MD one). The Canadian meeting was in Winnipeg, where the winter temperature at night could be -30°C, whereas in Hong Kong, South India and Sri Lanka I would need tropical kit. So my luggage was very bulky. Fortunately the College sends its Presidents first class.

In Winnipeg it was in fact -30°C when I arrived. The meeting was in the large hotel where I was also accommodated, so I did not have to brave the weather. A day or two after my arrival we had a blizzard, with vast deposits of snow. Roads were blocked. The airport was blocked for 48 hours. Then the sun came out. The wind dropped and I had a pleasant walk in the sunshine. The efficient and experienced local services soon cleared the roads.

The conference was professionally good and I had a very pleasant week. Then away by air across to Vancouver, where there was a little green grass to be seen down by the sea. A night there, followed by a wonderful flight north along the wintry coast and westward along the south coast of Alaska, with conifer forests, snowy mountains and long fjords. And so away in darkness across the Pacific to Hong Kong.

Hong Kong

I had taught many postgraduates from Hong Kong. I had been most impressed by their knowledge and by their ability to use that knowledge in clinical practice.

Socially I had felt very much on the same wavelength. One of my British friends who had worked long years in Hong Kong had the highest regard for the Chinese. For instance he admired, when one of the not uncommon typhoons had caused much damage to their houses, how little fuss they made and how they immediately and efficiently set to put things right. He said you had only to attend a joint British-Chinese banquet to realise which was the civilised race!

I was put up in a charming university postgraduate hostel in modern Chinese style and with a fine view down over the crowded harbour. The climate at that time of the year was a little drizzly and the temperature comfortable. I gave one or two lectures. I was entertained by the local Fellows of the College at a delightful Chinese banquet. I saw something of the excellent medical school. Judith Mackay, who was now married to a British GP in a large private medical firm which served many of the local businesses, took me out to lunch at the golf club across the bay in Kowloon.

I had time one day to walk up to "The Peak", a semi-wild park, bare of buildings, from which one can gaze down on the massed but disciplined skyscrapers of what must be one of the most densely populated areas in the world, and over the equally densely ship-populated bay to the mountains of the mainland. It was a weekday. I was alone. The path was deserted. What a counterpoint to the millions busy at their hectic lives down there below me.

Someone drove me, via the car ferry, over to Kowloon and the Chinese border. It was heavily built-up on the Kowloon side. We looked over to an apparently deserted countryside in China proper. I gather it has since become just as crowded as Kowloon.

Bangkok

I had planned to follow my intense social and professional programme in Canada and Hong Kong with a weekend in Bangkok in Thailand where, at that time, I had no contacts and no responsibilities. I booked into an old and famous classical hotel (since that time rebuilt). It had a relaxing swimming pool. My memory is of the pool surrounded by fat, middle-aged, German males pinkly lazing in the sun, as they rested between bouts of what I, possibly unfairly, suspected were bouts of sex-tourism. My suspicions on this had been aroused when I booked a couple of tours to see the sights and was pestered by the guides to visit nightclubs, no doubt high class brothels.

My own tourism was confined to the lovely old temples and palaces in central Bangkok and a wonderful early morning trip on the canals, bordered with water-borne houses and markets, so peaceful compared with the busy noisy traffic in the streets.

I had an interesting talk with one of the head guides about his own career. He had been born in the very poor northeast part of Thailand, overpopulated but too dry for successful farming. He had decided to walk to Bangkok. His local Buddhist priest had arranged for him to be taken into a monastery in the big city where, as adolescents, they had subsisted on the food left over from the meals of the senior monks. He had learnt English and become literate both in Thai and English. This enabled him later to get a junior post in a tourist company. He sent money back to his parents, saved hard and in due course started his own company. He seemed to be doing very well. Apparently the Buddhist church commonly provided this career pathway for able children of poor families.

India and Bangladesh

From Bangkok I flew to Calcutta where I was very well received by local Fellows. I gave several lectures, was taken sightseeing, contrasting the classical architecture of the early 18th to 19th century British government buildings and a country club with the appalling poverty of the slums, probably the worst in the world. Modern Western medical education for Indians started in Calcutta. I was horrified to visit several teaching hospitals, pretty filthy and with their walls covered with graffiti by militant medical students. One of the College Fellows, a Parsee, took me to lunch in the Calcutta Club, once exclusively for the British but with Indian members for many years and now only a small minority of British. I had expressed an interest in Mogul painting and was taken on a visit to the vast house of a rich merchant family with many lovely paintings in that charming 16th to 18th century style.

There was much interest in the College among the local Fellows. As a result of my visit a local Royal College of Physicians of Edinburgh Club was set up, meeting regularly for social and professional discussions. I believe it has continued to meet. The subsequent similar one in Madras ran enthusiastically for some years but faded when its initiators retired or died.

One of the Calcutta Fellows had a small evening reception for me. A fellow guest was the editor of one of the English language newspapers. The British General Medical Council had recently ceased to recognise for medical registration in Britain qualifications from Indian Medical Schools. The editor attacked me about this. I diplomatically replied that of course a long-established Medical School like Calcutta had no doubt maintained its standards, but that after independence the previous 18 Indian Schools had been rapidly expanded to more than 100, so it had been difficult to staff all these with high standard teachers. After the editor had left I was shaken to be told by other Fellows that in Calcutta no final examinations had been held for two years. The students had firmly said that they were not yet fully prepared. Previously examiners who failed a student had been threatened with serious violence. I began to appreciate the misgivings of the British General Medical Council.

From Calcutta I flew to Bangladesh which no President had visited for ten years. I think we then had only three Fellows there. My main host was Professor Nural Islam, now Director of the National Postgraduate Medical School in Dakha. The School had been initiated and developed by Sir James Cameron, a previous President of the College. After he retired he had spent several years in Bangladesh as the Postgraduate School's first Director, shadowed by Nural Islam who succeeded him when he left. Nural was obviously immensely influential both with his own profession and with successive governments. Indeed he had been personal physician to each successive national President until each was assassinated and replaced! Nural had also, following the war of independence from Pakistan, founded a Bangladesh College of Physicians and Surgeons and was anxious to build up relations with the Edinburgh College. I had taught him when he was a postgraduate in the UK and we had met and corresponded ever since. He was very anxious to propose that several other local Members of the Royal College of Physicians should be promoted to our Fellowship. He and the Director of Medical Services, a physiologist with a British PhD, were also anxious that Bangladeshi medical degrees should be re-recognised by the British General Medical Council so that Bangladeshi doctors could receive postgraduate training in the UK. Recognition had been withdrawn owing to the local medical schools' disruption during the war of independence from Pakistan. This led to a later six-year liaison project between Edinburgh and Bangladesh medical schools.

I was only in Bangladesh for five days but I was impressed by the postgraduate school and by the local enthusiasm for progress. I suggested that Nural Islam should put forward appropriate names for election to the Edinburgh Fellowship. Again I gave a couple of lectures.

I flew back to Calcutta. There I was to change planes and fly on to Madras where I was due to lecture next day. I landed in Calcutta airport. But when I came to go through Customs I was stopped.

"You do not have a visa for India in your passport" I was told. "But", I said, "I have been to India a number of times, indeed last time only five days ago, and was never told I needed a visa". It appeared that in my passport, having transferred from a previous Irish passport to a British with appropriate formality after the war, I was a "British Subject" not a "Citizen of the United Kingdom". Since the mass expulsion of Asians, who had "British Subject" passports from Uganda, India had introduced visas for them to prevent an influx. They said that my unobstructed entry at Calcutta five days before was due to a mistake by the Passport Officer.

I asked where I could get a visa. They said only in Delhi and it would take a fortnight. So I had to play the VIP card. I said I was President of the Royal College of Physicians of Edinburgh. I was due to give an important lecture in Madras next day and meet senior Fellows of my College. Fortunately I had a four hour wait for my Madras plane. They said I would have to go in to their head office in Calcutta. They sent me in a taxi with a policeman (I paid for the taxi there and back). In Calcutta they gave me a 24-hour pass and said I would have to get a visa from the Chief Immigration Officer in Madras.

All proved well. Of course, as I was just passing through, no one had been meeting me in Calcutta. But a large delegation of Fellows met me in Madras. One of them had the Chief Immigration Officer as a patient. He gave me a three-week visa which would cover my Indian stay; I was later due to go on to Delhi and Bombay. In the event, as you will see, my stay was over three weeks and my visa had to be renewed.

I think it was my second large lecture in the medical school that proved my undoing. Surprisingly I was still unsophisticated enough to have fallen for an attractive iced pudding in the hotel. Subsequently my interior fell even further with a severe tummy upset. By the time of my main lecture the following afternoon I had hoped it was subsiding. It was very hot. The large lecture theatre was absolutely crammed. Halfway through my lecture, as I turned to the slide screen, my entire body water cascaded to my bowels, draining my brain. This time I truly did fall down in a dramatic faint.

Everyone of course thought I must have had a heart attack. I came to relatively quickly. My soaking filthy trousers convinced me of the correct diagnosis. But my kind and attentive hosts were taking no chances. I was rushed to the private cardiac ward in the hospital. My cardiac electrocardiogram showed a temporary minor abnormality (attributed by Michael Oliver when I returned to Edinburgh as due to the electrolyte abnormality in my blood from the diarrhoea). But my cautious and attentive Madras cardiologist was still taking no chances. He insisted on three weeks of bed rest, followed by delicate convalescence.

It was an interesting, fairly exacting, three weeks. All the politicians were aware that they might have a heart attack some time in their lives. In consequence the private cardiac ward had a staff of nine of the brightest young doctors and there were plenty of nurses.

Now I should turn to poor Eileen's story. Although our children had grown up, we had her widowed father living with us. Eileen could only get away for a limited time. She would meet me in Delhi and then accompany me to Sri Lanka, Bombay and Pakistan.

In Delhi, instead of me she was met by a group from the British High Commission and the wife of Ray Mills, who was then working for WHO in Delhi. The poor thing was told that I had had a heart attack and was in hospital in Madras. They looked after her very well, fed her, rested her, and put her on an afternoon plane for Madras. What a let down!

She was only partly reassured when she came to see me as my physician was understandably cautious about the future. But as I was to be in hospital for some weeks, it was suggested that it would be much better to stay with one of the Fellows' families than be stuck in a hotel. This was a great success. Her host, Dr Selvaraj, had spent seven years in Britain. He was a distinguished physician at the Medical School with an extensive private practice. His wife was also a doctor. They had no children. They lived in a house on the estate of his father, a retired high court judge and a devoted Hindu. Eileen fed with her host, often on European food, arranged by his wife who did not eat with them.

Eileen then, as I convalesced, had a far more interesting time than if she had had merely to accompany me to many receptions, entertainments and lectures. She joined her host on his medical rounds, including visits to schools. She went with the whole family on a Hindu pilgrimage. She travelled to Madurai to represent me at a meeting of the Fellows in a famous old city.

Her host very kindly sent European food in for me. Mostly I had two nurses to look after me. The Minister of Health decided that, as a VIP, my hospital stay would be free – and what a contrast in my clean, quiet, well-staffed ward to the grossly overcrowded general wards of the hospital.

But as a VIP I had endless visitors and this was rather exhausting. These included the Minister and other political VIPs and numerous Fellows with wives. They mostly seemed to have no small talk so I had to make all the effort. But I did have books to read and Eileen to tell me about her fascinating local experiences. It was also heart warming to receive vast numbers of letters from all over the world wishing me well. Apparently there was a journalist at my fatal lecture. My attack got into the newspapers. The first my children knew about it was when Eileen's father spotted a small news item in the Guardian reporting that the President of the Royal College of Physicians of Edinburgh had had a heart attack in Madras! My letters, naturally, said kind things. It was as good as being alive for your own obituary. Of course I had a busy time answering them all.

They sent me to convalesce for ten days or so at a charming country hotel down by a beach thirty miles south of Madras. I requested that there should be no visitors. We had a separate cottage in the grounds of the hotel. We sat and read. We borrowed a beautifully written bird book, the best I have ever read, about Indian birds and tried to identify those we saw. I was allowed a gentle float and swim in the hotel pool. We strolled slowly along the beach to a famous series of ancient Hindu temples running down to the sea.

My physician cut down my subsequent trip to a purely hotel stay in Colombo, where the Fellows came to me; no social reception or lectures. Bombay and Delhi were to be omitted. In Pakistan I was only to visit Karachi, instead of several other cities on my original schedule. Regarding India I later made up for my omissions by a further tour in 1978 funded by the British Council.

Sri Lanka

We flew on to Sri Lanka. My physician had decided I should work mainly from our hotel. Fellows would come to see me. I had had many friends in the country since my official visit in 1954, though some had since died and most whom we had trained in Edinburgh had by now retired. The beautiful country was of course new to Eileen. She managed a delightful railway tour to the famous ancient cities, once lost in the jungle, Polonnaruwa and Anuradhapura. Our hosts were charming.

Much of my business, besides meeting our Fellows, was concerned with the proposed Sri Lankan College of Physicians and Surgeons. The government was anxious that local qualification for higher medical training and consultants should be through the Membership examination in their own College rather than the UK Royal Medical Colleges. Our Sri Lankan Fellows were anxious that standards should be maintained by close liaison with UK Colleges, perhaps including visiting UK examiners.

One of our Fellows was involved in a new hotel which had just opened in a lovely beach area south of Colombo. He arranged a delightful weekend there at a cheap rate! Architecturally, and in every other way, it was superb with a great wide window opening over a lovely bathing pool and views to the beach and ocean beyond. No other buildings. Lovely palms and sunshine but not too hot. We relaxed and bathed and had a pleasant visit from some of our Sri Lankan friends.

Pakistan

Again, I had been advised to confine my tour to a few days in Karachi. Receptions for Fellows; a couple of lectures. Much discussion on medical education.

Fortunately my travel insurance covered the risks of illness. These included provision for a "carer" to accompany me on my flights, also first class. The very efficient Cook's travel man in Madras had fixed it all up. (I subsequently wrote to Cook's headquarters in the UK praising his efficiency. They wrote back to say how delightful it was to receive a praising letter; usually correspondence was concerned with complaints!)

So we had a lovely flight home, much of it in daylight. First along the hill-backed desert north coast of the India Ocean where Alexander the Great had marched his thirsty troops back from India to Greece. Then several hours across the Arabian Desert to the sudden green of Damascus and the Lebanese mountains; in the fading light over the Taurus Range of southern Turkey; a glimpse of Istanbul and the Bosphorus; finally in the darkness to London. An eventful but rewarding tour. Many new friends. Much useful work for the College.

Presidential Tour in 1976

This tour was primarily to represent the three UK Colleges of Physicians at the annual meeting of the Royal Australasian College of Physicians, that year in Auckland, New Zealand. Family arrangements allowed Eileen to accompany me everywhere except to Western Australia. Her ticket did not admit that deviation. Instead she later flew directly from Sydney to join me in Singapore. In view of my Madras experience I decided that on this tour I would not give lectures, though I was happy to take part in seminars etc.

It was a perfect time of year in Auckland, warm but not too hot. At the major reception we were greeted by a Maori War Dance in the open air. I was introduced to the Governor General, I think the first local New Zealander to have been appointed. I told him about my happy experiences with New Zealanders during the War, including my stormy voyage from Alexandria to Greece as the only British officer, acting as Medical Officer on a ship carrying a New Zealand Battalion. He turned out to have been a junior officer in that Battalion and shared our experiences in the storm.

At a few hours notice I was asked to give the main speech for the guests at the formal dinner. On a free conference afternoon we had a delightful expedition to one of the lovely islands in the Bay, with a picnic supper cooked Maori-fashion buried with hot ashes in the ground.

I had arranged that we would have the weekend off before continuing our official business. For this we took the local bus to the famous volcanic tourist centre at Rotorua, in central North Island. There we did the tourist round of pools of hot bubbling mud, geysers suddenly erupting to a precise eerie timetable, heroic algae growing over flat shelves of sedentary rock in steaming hot water and then flowing down to a lake, and a modern electric plant, powered by exploding steam from the nether regions below. We gazed with appropriate wonder at the great lateral gap in the snow-topped local volcano. The gap had been blown out of it in a sudden vast and disastrous eruption many years before.

Then again by local bus south to Wellington for meetings with local Fellows. We had an amusing incident when we came to fly by New Zealand Airlines down to my next assignment in Christchurch in the South Island. Eileen was at this time still Medical Director of Scottish ASH. So of course we asked for non-smoking seats. Only to be told that New Zealand Airlines had no non-smoking seats. Eileen, of course, exploded. "We have flown all over the world and this is the first airline which does not provide non-smoking seats". The reply from the nice young man at the counter was typical of New Zealand leg pulling. "If I were you, madam, the best thing to do when you get up there, is just open the window!"

I had a somewhat similar experience during my previous New Zealand visit in 1963 to run a postgraduate course. While I was there the British Royal College of Physicians published its first report on smoking and health. This received a lot of publicity in the New Zealand media. I was invited to appear on television. During the interview I was asked about the problems of stopping smoking. I speculated that perhaps New Zealand needed a "Smokers Anonymous" to parallel "Alcoholics Anonymous". A few days later there was a letter in the local newspaper. The writer said that he had been very interested in my talk. In turn I would be interested to learn that in New Zealand they had a "Smokers Anonymous". He belonged to it. Every time he felt an overwhelming desire to smoke, he rang up a fellow member and they both went out and got drunk together!

In Christchurch we stayed with our friends John and Shirley Macleod. John, then recently married, had been my first House Physician in Edinburgh in 1952. We had got to know them very well and had taken them sightseeing in Scotland before they had a car. He was now a senior consultant. They were splendid hosts. After the normal social and medical meetings with Fellows they drove us for a weekend in the New Zealand Alps. We saw lovely snow-capped mountains, forests of the New Zealand beech (quite different from the European). We spent the night in a tourist bungalow. At our picnic breakfast the next morning kea birds*, looking like black crows with red tails, tried to rob us of our food.

Then away to Sydney, Australia. Again delightful dinners and medical occasions with Fellows, at one of which I met the senior Australian Medical Officer, under whom my Casualty Clearing Station in Greece had come

---

* Actually, keas (mountain parrots) are olive green with scarlet underwings and rump

during the retreat. To our relief, in contrast to his previous British equivalent, he had both visited us and given us precise orders in writing. He was quite touched when I told him, nearly thirty-five years later, how much he had been appreciated.

We stayed with Malcolm and Margaret Schonell. Malcolm had been a lecturer with us for five years. He was now a consultant in a teaching hospital. They were both great friends. On a wonderful evening they took us out to dinner at the famous Sydney Opera House and then on to the opera. We saw the lovely building, first in the afternoon sunshine and later, after dark, with a full moon demonstrating all its glory.

As Eileen's ticket did not cover it, I flew on alone to Perth in West Australia for further meetings and also to visit my old friend Denis Keall. We had been students at Cambridge together and then close partners as clinical students at St Thomas's Hospital.

My flight from Sydney to Perth was first along the coast of the vast southern desert, then north over the inner desert. Eileen later flew direct to Singapore where we joined up again. I had been there several times before. I had taught many of the local doctors as postgraduates. Many were Fellows of the College. Their friendship and hospitality was delightful and included a Chinese banquet.

Then on to Kuala Lumpur, which again I had visited before. Here our host was the senior physician of the government health service. He had arranged an excellent social and medical programme. As his own work was both intensive and extensive, he had arranged for a friend, a Chinese millionairess, to take us sightseeing. This she did charmingly and effectively. Her own family background and career were even more interesting. Her father had come from a poor peasant family in China. In the early 1900s he and many others had been imported by British firms to work in the tin mines in Malaysia. He proved very hard-working and efficient. He steadily progressed from manual to more and more managerial posts. He became very good friends with the British managers. Later on his British friends said "As you are very able why don't you set up your own mining business?" I presume that his pay was by then quite high. He was not married and had savings. His British friends probably provided some capital. He continued to work full time for the same British firm, started his own mining firm and before long was a millionaire. He did all his own business in his own "spare time". He provided all his own lorries etc. He never used the British firm's transport.

Because of all this intensive application he did not marry until he was forty-one. Our hostess was his first child. Of course she was sent to school. But her father made her leave at age twelve to help him run his business.

Her job was as a very busy supervisor of all aspects of the work. But she received no pay. After a few years his British friends said to her father what a wonderful manager she had become. He really must pay her, and properly. Later she repeated her father's career pattern. In her own "spare time" she started her own business. In due course she also became really rich. Again, she was never allowed to use her father's lorries in her own business.

At some stage in all this Malaysia was overrun by the Japanese and their cruel rule. Thousands of the local population were killed. Every time a local passed a Japanese sentry he or she had to bow. She and her father always walked a long way round to avoid having to do this.

As the Japanese approached, Australian troops had blown up all the pithead buildings and machines at the mines. Some way into the occupation she and her father were summoned before a Japanese officer. He ordered her father to get the mines going again. Her father raised various difficulties. The officer drew his sword and told him just what would happen if he did not obey his orders to the letter. Over protests by her father, she intervened. She said to the officer "Is this the way to behave? Would you do this to your father?" The sword was re-sheathed but her father had to resuscitate the mines.

Later the local Resistance against the Japanese got going. They began to threaten her and her father for starting up the mines. But they said "We had no alternative. They would have killed us. Use your energies against the Japanese, not your own people". Which they did. A fascinating glimpse into two fascinating lives.

Conclusion

This was an extremely happy, if extremely busy, three years. Because of so much support it was much less exacting than being a Dean. It gave me wide experience of national medical politics at a time when many new things were happening and of the early stages of international medical politics in Europe when things were just beginning to happen. I completed my term of office just a year before I reached retirement age, both for my university job and my honorary clinical job in the NHS.

Chapter 11
"Retirement"

Invitations

Looking back, it is amusing to remember my thoughts on prospective retirement in the final year or two of my formal professional career. I did not expect to do any more professional work, apart from producing with Andrew Douglas a third edition of our textbook, *Respiratory Diseases*. My intention for some years had been to try to write a history of humanitarianism (but hopefully not under such a stuffy title). I had always been interested in history. I thought it might be intriguing to try to trace how some societies became more caring. I had asked my historian friends. They did not think that anyone had tackled the subject previously.

For about ten years I had represented the University as a Trustee of the Scottish National Library. I visualised myself as a quiet scholar working there and in the University library. I had started a card index and had already done some reading. On a very wet 1977 final holiday before I retired – in Southern France (two fine days in three weeks!) – I had even drafted the first chapter featuring a surprisingly humanitarian ruler in one of the third millennial BC Mesopotamian city states.

End of effort! As things unfolded I found myself successively involved in much else. First of all I was yet again invited to advise on chest services in Libya*. Then I was invited to lecture in Bergen, Norway. That would give me an opportunity of accepting a standing invitation to visit the Medical School in Tromsø, the most northern medical school in the world. Then Ray Mills, the WHO representative in Nepal, asked me to visit and advise on tuberculosis. About the same time I was asked to be a Visiting Professor to Denver and Stanford Medical Schools in USA followed by a further invitation from the University of California in Sacramento. Some time I would have to fit in an operation for a left hip replacement owing to

---

* John had had several invitations to visit Libya when he was too busy to accept. On retirement, he agreed to go there. However, the Libyan Embassy failed to provide visas in time. Then the Embassy held on to their passports for about three months despite the involvement of the Foreign Office. John never visited Libya.

progressive osteoarthritis and increasing pain and disability. And of course I had to get along with the promised third edition of our book.

A few retirement jobs!

In the end it worked out time-wise as follows. Retirement at the end of September 1977: Bergen and Tromsø in October; depart to India in mid-December for a month's lecture tour on behalf of the British Council; Nepal for WHO mid-January to mid-April 1978; return to write the 3rd edition of our postgraduate textbook and prepare for the American trip. It was a busy start to retirement.

I had had recurrent professional contacts with Norway ever since the early 1950s when I invited Hans Jacob Ustvedt to lecture in Scotland. Later Hans arranged for the Norwegian Medical Society to invite me to lecture on controlled trials, then a novelty; Eileen was also invited. Our initial visit to Norway was the start of a lifetime's happy relationship with that country and its people. I found many friends among a delightfully caring, egalitarian, friendly society. Eileen and I had another delightful trip to Norway in 1974 when I was asked to give the Hansen Memorial Lecture[*] at Bergen University. My lecture was a general one on infections and chemotherapy and as the Hansen Lecturer I had a large audience.

In 1977 my lecture in Bergen was a more specialist one to the local respiratory medicine doctors. As I had retired, I had decided to take four days to travel to Tromsø by the regular coastal ship. It was a beautiful trip, mostly inside the islands and with wonderful views of mountains and fjords. And Tromsø proved to be a beautiful place.

My assignments in Nepal as a WHO consultant in 1978[#] would bring me through India (described in Chapter 5). After those visits, I got down to preparing the third edition of our postgraduate textbook *Respiratory Diseases*; this was to be my main occupation for the rest of the year and all of 1979. However, during 1979 I had two major hiatuses in my writing, my left hip surgical replacement in May and my visiting professorship, preceded by a holiday, in USA in September/October. By May I could only walk for about a quarter of an hour before pain stopped me. I had the operation by my old friend Jimmy Scott, whom I had got to know when he was with one of our teams in Baroda at the time when I was Dean[¥]. After the operation I

---

[*] Armauer Hansen (1841-1912), Norwegian physician and bacteriologist, is best known for his work on lepsosy (Hansen's disease).

[#] John and Eileen made two more follow-up trips to Nepal in 1981 and 1985 under the auspices of WHO. They were to remain involved with the Britain-Nepal Medical Trust for many years thereafter.

[¥] John had two further replacements of this hip at approximately 10-year intervals.

worked hard on my muscles as advised by the physiotherapists. Before long I was walking normally. I was soon down to preparing material for my coming Visiting Professorships in the USA and completing work with Andrew Douglas on the third edition of our book. Toward the end of 1979 I was working every evening and throughout the weekends. With the usual publication delays, our textbook finally appeared in 1981.

My visits to Denver and Stanford were endowed by a very anglophile American chest physician who had inherited a considerable private fortune. His aim was to provide a sum which would also pay for a good holiday in the USA. I had visited there many times but always just rushing from one medical school to another. I had seen little of the country. Eileen had never previously been able to come with me. She, very sensibly, said she would prefer to visit the National Parks in the West and skip the art galleries and tourist centres in the East.

My professional work would start in early October. The September weather was said to be good and not too hot. We flew directly to Seattle on the first Monday in September. We hired a small car, stayed in motels and moved from National Park to National Park, south through Washington State and Oregon (including the Mount Rainier[*] and Olympic Temperate Rain Forest Parks[#]) to San Francisco. Then to Yosemite and on through the Sierra Nevada across the hot desert of Death Valley to Nevada. There was nowhere to stay but the notorious Sin City (Las Vegas). And so on to the Grand Canyon, the only place where we encountered many tourists. On again by lovely and quite lonely drives across northern Arizona and southern Colorado. We just caught the glories of the autumn aspens before a sudden cold snap and troublesome cold fog stripped them of their leaves. Finally, we by-passed Denver for a final three days in the lovely Rocky Mountain National Park.

After our holiday, we drove down to Denver for lectures, seminars and the usual generous and friendly American hospitality, followed by Stanford University, a brief professional visit to the teaching hospital in San Francisco and on to my final assignment in the University of California at Sacramento.

Bangladesh 1981

In 1981, Eileen and I spent an intensive three weeks in Bangladesh. After the Indian/Pakistan war of 1971, which resulted in Bangladesh becoming independent of Pakistan, the disruption of the medical schools

---

[*] Mt Rainier in Washington State is the highest mountain in the Cascades (>14,400 feet; 4,390m)

[#] Presumably Olympic National Park in Washington State.

there led to the de-recognition by the UK General Medical Council of all Bangladeshi medical degrees. As a result a high powered government and academic group was despatched in about 1980 to the UK to seek for help. I was still chairman of the Edinburgh Postgraduate Board for Medicine and therefore I had discussions with the group from Bangladesh and subsequently with the British Council. Our Bangladeshi colleagues had suggested that the British Council should pay for UK examiners to participate in Bangladesh exams to ensure standards. The British Council suggested to me, very reasonably, that it would be better to sponsor two-way exchanges and raise standards in that way, as well perhaps as participating in examinations. I felt that we should not commit ourselves to any such scheme unless we were convinced that both the Bangladesh Ministry of Health and the academics were really serious in their desire to raise standards. It was finally agreed that, after my 1981 WHO assignment in Nepal, I should pay a 3-week visit to Bangladesh to explore how serious they were.

During our visit, we visited six of the eight medical schools. I had long sessions with the Director of Health Services, who proved to be an excellent and enthusiastic man, a physiologist with a PhD from Newcastle. I also met the Minister of Health. In spite of my repeated denials, everyone seemed convinced that I personally would ensure immediate re-recognition of the degrees, (essential if their graduates wished to undertake any postgraduate training in the UK). I believe the hospitals were literally whitewashed before my arrival. They looked surprisingly clean compared to those in India or Nepal, which were normally filthy. Even with the whitewashing we felt those in Bangladesh must ordinarily have been better kept.

Of course we were given super-VIP treatment. In Dhaka we were invited out formally every evening, usually to meet the same people wearing different hats – university, medical school, government, College of Physicians and Surgeons etc. In a Moslem country it was strictly non-alcoholic; we did it all on "7-Up". In one northern medical school near the Assam border we were greeted by an enormous floral notice "WELCOME SIR CROFTON" and of course garlanded with flowers. The enthusiasm there was perhaps understandable. I was the first formal visitor the medical school had ever had. They had not previously even had a visit by an academic from Dhaka.

I probed libraries. I looked at the ward notes. In Dhaka Medical School they appeared quite good. So I went down to the Records Department and looked at the notes for the month before. It became clear that the current notes had also been specially prepared. The past ones were of a much lower standard.

As in India, only lip service was paid to community aspects of medicine. For instance obstetric and gynaecological wards were filled with obstetric disasters which could have been avoided if there had been any form of community maternity service. Paediatrics was still a lowly handmaiden of internal medicine. There was no Professor of Paediatrics in the country.

Incidentally, the Director of Health Services did ask me to spend a day giving a national seminar on tuberculosis. There was a theoretical national programme. But I discovered, by a little probing in depth at what was supposed to be an outstanding rural clinic outside Chittagong in the south that, as in India, the programme was mainly on paper. It was not working in practice.

In the event we in Edinburgh decided that government and academics were sufficiently serious to justify an effort on our part. The British Council funded a scheme, in which Edinburgh specialists visited and advised, and Bangladesh teaching staff spent periods in appropriate departments in Edinburgh. Eventually, the two Dhaka Medical Schools were recognised as was that in Chittagong.

Societies and Associations

We returned from Nepal and Bangladesh at the end of 1981*. In mid March, I was due to give a major lecture at an Italian radiological conference in Brescia. It was basically a conference for Italians. I was one of three foreign speakers; the others were American and Swiss. I had spoken medical Italian fairly fluently during the war, but it was now very rusty. I only gave a brief introductory passage in Italian; the rest was done by simultaneous translation.

I was also around this time asked to chair the liaison committee between the two previous respiratory societies, the Thoracic Society (which had been a select largely academic society with a very limited membership) and the much larger British Thoracic Association. I had been a previous President of each Society and a previous chairman and long-time member of the British Thoracic Association Research Committee. The climate of opinion had moved on. Objectors to the union were now fewer. With a bit of tact and diplomacy a joint British Thoracic Society was born and, thanks to others, has gone from strength to strength.

Ever since I came to Edinburgh I had been on the Council of what had originally been the Scottish branch of the National Association for the Prevention of Tuberculosis, but which, with the major decrease of tuberculosis in the UK, had now become the Chest, Heart and Stroke

---

* This was, of course, John and Eileen's second visit to Nepal.

Association, Scotland. This charity was concerned with welfare matters for patients and relevant diseases, with education both for the public and professionals, and with supporting research. It had been agreed that when I retired from clinical work, I would take over the chairmanship in a year or two.

But now, with my new international and national work, I really could not give that important job enough time. After some discussion we all agreed that Norman Horne, who had a superb record as a clinician, an administrator, and a handler of people, would be ideal. But he had never served on the Council and was not very familiar with the work. It was therefore suggested that I should become Vice-Chairman for a year or two and help Norman to work his way into the job. When Norman had settled in to his outstanding period as Chairman, I retired from the Vice-Chairmanship, though I remained on the Council until 2001, mainly to ensure that tuberculosis was not neglected. In fact CHSS continued to support tuberculosis through the International Union against Tuberculosis and Lung Disease and incidentally by supporting our Third World book, *Clinical Tuberculosis*.

Scottish Health Education Coordinating Committee

The busiest new job I was asked to undertake in 1981 was to become Chairman of the new Scottish Health Education Coordinating Committee of the Scottish Home and Health Department, which I continued until I resigned in 1986, when I had given nearly six years to it, mostly taking up about half of my time.

When I started it was made clear to me that I was expected to provide both the agenda and the remit for the work. The membership was quite prestigious. It included the Chief Medical Officer, the Chief Nursing Officer, the Chief Dental Officer, the Chief Social Work Advisor, the Chief Inspector of Schools, the Head of the Scottish Health Education Group (the central group with a budget to carry out health education); two Chairmen of Health Boards, and a Health Board Treasurer. There were also several Heads of Local Authority Departments, and a couple of Heads of voluntary bodies (Disability and the Brooke Advisory Centre).

I had certain initial problems with bodies such as the Pharmacists and Local Health Councils, who thought, as too many others did, that they ought to be represented, but I managed to smooth things over. I had one particularly negative member of the main committee, the Health Board Treasurer who I suppose was used to blocking any new initiative by saying there was no money. After one of the earlier meetings, when he objected to almost every item I put forward, I wrote him a letter. I said that, seeing that he objected to every item I had proposed for the committee to address, would he please write me a memo giving his own proposals for its work. Of course he failed to produce anything and thereafter caused me little trouble.

Before retirement I had been the only clinician on the Scottish Office Committee to produce proposals for the priority activities of the Scottish National Health Service in the 1980s. This had given me some insight into the needs on the Health Education side. I proposed therefore that our main work over the next year or two should be to produce successive reports on three outstanding health problems – smoking, alcohol, and areas of multiple deprivation.

We started by setting up subcommittees the first two of which I chaired. Our report (*Health Education and the Prevention of Alcohol-related Problems*, 1983) and its subsequent publication got me gradually involved in many aspects of the alcohol problem. I also personally wrote the tobacco report (*Health Education in the Prevention of Smoking-related Diseases*, 1983), extensively utilising the submission we had requested from ASH.

In both these reports we started by outlining the ill-health in Scotland resulting from the substance, and in the case of alcohol, social and legal consequences also. We then detailed, mostly in simple note form, what everyone should be doing about it. For ease of reference there was an executive summary and each section was on a different coloured page so that the relevant professionals could readily turn to their own sections.

Both reports were published by the Scottish Office in 1983. Both were very well received. The *British Medical Journal* wrote a most laudatory editorial entitled *Scotland Leads the Way on Alcohol*. These two reports, and other business of the committee, took up a good half of my time, often having to start work at 6am or even earlier. But it was great fun.

Community Development

The third report *Health Education in Areas of Multiple Deprivation* was published in 1984. It was a pioneer effort in a somewhat new field. I had served as the only clinician in a group set up by the Scottish Health Service Planning Council, to produce a report *Scottish Health Authorities Priorities for the 80s*. We had reported that health education (eg. on smoking) had been far more successful in the richer and more educated classes and had had relatively little effect in the poorer and less educated. Moreover, in 1978 the World Health Organisation had broadened the definition of health to consist not just of absence of disease but as a state of "complete physical, mental, and social wellbeing". Clearly this could only be achieved with favourable social and environmental conditions. Long-term, achieving these would involve major national political and economic advances in alleviating poverty and environmental improvement.

Experience in the Third World had shown the value of involving local communities, especially in very poor areas. This had come to be called "The Community Development" approach. I had learnt something about this from some of the more enlightened workers in the World Bank whom I had met in Nepal. They told us that if they wanted to develop some new technique to benefit a community (eg a much higher yielding crop or new irrigation methods), it was relatively easy to do so via big landowners. But it was very difficult to get the new ideas adopted by poorer peasants. You had to start by finding out what the peasants' own concerns were and then encourage them to cooperate with each other in doing something about those concerns. Local leaders would emerge. Something would be achieved to improve things. Gradually the local community might come round to itself cooperating in trying out the new techniques. It had to be a local initiative by the local community, not something imposed from above. Otherwise it either didn't start at all or soon faded out of use. Community workers consisted of people who developed the skills of helping poor communities to appreciate, first that they indeed had local problems (which they usually denied initially), and then that they could do something about them. The professionals could advise whom to approach and what might be realistic help to request. Once the community had had some success, it often developed the capacity to make things happen in a wider field and might eventually try out the "establishment's" new technique. Our report covered some of the principles. We took evidence from people in various areas who had pioneered such initiatives and had an Appendix covering these examples.

The two examples that most influenced my own thinking were John Hubley's research in a very poor area of Paisley looking at, from the health point of view, the problem of initiating community development, the role of professionals, and the role of community workers. This research was initiated by David Player, at that time Director of the Scottish Health Education Group. Hubley's persistent enquiries in the community elicited, after initial denial that they had any health problems, bitter complaints that they had cold damp housing. Indeed many of the damp walls were black with fungi. Hubley provided cameras. Local people took pictures. They then formed a Tenants' Group. They showed local councillors how awful things were. Some action began to be taken by the authorities. Hubley compared Health Visitor reports for the local area with those from other areas and showed the locals that their children were, by comparison, less healthy. Out of all this came a Mothers and Toddlers Group and gradually things began to happen.

Hubley also found that there was little coordination between professionals, general practitioners, health visitors, social workers etc – a general pattern which I soon saw in many other areas. Besides cold, damp housing, when they began to think about it, other major local concerns proved to be glue sniffing and youth problems of drink and sexual behaviour. It all resulted in increasing public and professional interest in health problems. Professionals began to realise the differences between professional conceptions of "real health needs" and local perceptions of "felt health needs". Clearly one of the needs was for more Health Education both for the local public and for the local professionals.

The other very important witness was Jane Jones. She had trained as a radiographer but had become interested in deprived areas after her marriage to a lecturer in the University Department of Public Health. She had provided video cameras to groups of parents which she had helped to form in two deprived areas of Edinburgh, Wester Hailes and Pilton. She showed us the film that the women had made. There they were, surrounded by their children, smoking away and taking hell out of the primary health care services. Problems that had emerged were: local services were not available at suitable times; physical distances to cart children to health centres; health centres large and unfriendly; patronising attitudes of some GPs; GP receptionists' primary concern with not bothering the doctor; personal feelings of isolation, or living in high-rise flats with growing children and few childcare facilities. I was extremely impressed by this film. I thought it important that decision makers should see it. So I arranged a special showing by Jane Jones one evening at the then Scottish Health Education Group. I invited the Chief Medical Officer, the Chief Nursing Officer, the Chief Social Work Advisor, several social workers whom I knew would be interested, and several Health Visitors. I also invited two GPs from the extensive general practice in West Pilton.

To return to our report on Health Education in Areas of Multiple Deprivation, it was greatly welcomed by many of those throughout the UK who were concerned with poverty (even the existence of poverty in the UK was at that time denied by the Tories).

I myself had had initial doubts about the community development approach. But David Player, the then Director of the Scottish Health Education Group and soon to become Director of the equivalent body for England and Wales in London, persuaded me to read John Hubley's report in detail. I was also soon persuaded by the other evidence we had collected. As a result of our report I became more and more persuaded of the community development approach to improving health in impoverished areas. It was only when the initiative came from local people that local leaders might gradually influence the local climate of opinion and help people on their own terms to take action to achieve better health. You had to let them decide their own priorities and hopefully gradually come round to recognising the importance of the professional priorities such as lifestyle (smoking, alcohol, diet etc). It seemed that people like Hubley and Jane Jones had the sort of genius which could catalyse this process.

How could we carry things forward? Clearly we could not yet do it through normal statutory funding. It would have to be a research project and funded as such.

So over a year or so I convened a series of evening meetings at the Scottish Health Education Group of a small group to see if we could design a research project which would have some hope of successful funding. I can't remember the precise members but they included the two GPs mentioned above from the West Pilton practice (Drs Bernard Kuenssberg and Malcolm Morrison), Jane Jones, John Cormack and Angus Skinner, social workers from Pilton. Later we involved Willa Carr, a principal social worker from the Western General Hospital, Martin Vallely of the Scottish Council for Research in Education, and others.

We finally decided that the best way forward was to involve a Community Development worker (Jane Jones) covering the Royston/Wardieburn area of the large local general practice. This had about 5,000 inhabitants. I knew that Dr Alistair Donald from a neighbouring general practice, had a high reputation among his colleagues and the Scottish Office and was very socially orientated. I suggested that a formal proposal for support should be made by him and Dr Malcolm Morrison of the West Pilton practice, to the Chief Scientist's Department of the Home and Health Department of the Scottish Office. The Chief Scientist's Department controlled the endowment funds for research. In fact I wrote the application, but in the name of the two GPs. I based the application on WHO's 1975 declaration of the wide definition of health, including all social aspects and involving local communities. I also quoted the Black Report (1980: largely suppressed by the incoming conservative government) which had demonstrated the major inequalities of health associated with poverty. The main objectives of the project were:

1. To initiate and explore cooperation in promotion of health between general practice overall, local GPs and local professionals.
2. To explore with GPs, Health Visitors and patients the potential of working with patients, especially those with particular health needs.
3. To assess by interview and discussion the main health concerns of the local community and local professionals.
4. To work towards establishing a local management committee, representing both local professionals and the local community, to run the project, to determine objectives of a proposed second phase and to define extent of success.

To my great relief we got a grant for two years. We formed an initial Management Committee, chaired by Alistair Donald and consisting of local professionals who had been involved (plus myself). To this we gradually added leaders of the local community as they emerged. Later also, and outstandingly, we added Sonja Hunt, an academic (non-medical) who had joined the University Research Unit on Health and Behavioural Change, and who would advise on research. She turned out to be highly acceptable to the local health and social work professionals, to Jane Jones, and to the local community. So later we made her chairman of a new Executive Committee of locals, professional and community, managing day-to-day affairs of the project.

It soon emerged that the major local concern was, as in Paisley, cold damp housing. This had been a recurrent theme for patients in many areas over the years. As there had been no real scientific evidence, doctors tended to assume that patients' objectives were to obtain a medical certificate that might help them to move to a better house. Sonja decided to do a scientific investigation. In our project area her team did a medical survey on illness in families and arranged that the local authority Environmental Department did a separate survey on dampness in the houses. Each survey was done not knowing the result of the other and both results were later compared in the final analysis. For the first time good evidence was found that various illnesses were significantly more common in the cold damp houses. After considerable resistance from the general UK establishment these results were finally accepted, especially after they were later confirmed by similar surveys in Glasgow and London.

Out of all this came a vast range of activities, for example, women's health groups; self-help groups (including a "tranquilliser group" who all got off the drugs through mutual support); stress groups; an elderly forum (and a Pensioners' Swimming Club); health courses on subjects chosen by the community; a healthy food forum and healthy food cooperative; a survey of problems in high-rise buildings; a house study; as well as upgrading and adapting many services: health, social, educational, to local felt needs. There was immense improvement in community morale. Social and community workers learned far more about health. Health workers learned far more about the effects of other disciplines on health. Members of the community learned far more about both. I myself learned as much as anyone. Though of course I was more an initiator and facilitator and entrepreneur of the project rather than an active worker, for which I would have had much less skill.

Finally, after many successes and great local appreciation, at the end of the second research phase, the project (nowadays called the Pilton Health Project) was taken over jointly by the NHS Health Board and the Local

Authority (at first Regional, later Edinburgh District). It budded off a separate Stress Centre (employing local people) which also served patients discharged from mental hospitals; an old people's centre; and a well-established health food cooperative.

Moreover it shortly led to a joint NHS/Local Authority Community Development Health Project in Craigmillar, another deprived area. I was asked to join the initial management committee. But this time we were able to hand over to the local community within a year. Two years later I was asked to get involved when financial support was threatened with withdrawal. Apparently this was because GPs and others were now referring patients for help to local community support groups instead of, as previously, to overworked social workers. Help from people of the same social group and with the same sort of problems was often more effective. The Social Work Department felt neglected. I wrote to various top brass in the Local Authority and fortunately support was restored.

All this had a ripple effect. I think there are now about nine such projects in Lothian. Some of these get visited by medical and social work students as part of their education. Jane Jones later moved on to teach in this field at the College of Education. I myself got involved in many relevant conferences, seminars etc both in Scotland and England. A very time-consuming resultant task was consulting and personally writing for the Public Health Alliance (Scottish and UK) a Report on Housing and Health in Scotland (1993) which was very well received. I also was asked one year to give a lecture on Poverty and Health in Birmingham at the annual meeting of the Public Health Alliance UK. In addition one of the sections of the public lecture which I had to give for the award of the Edinburgh Medal for Science and Society was on poverty and health. The other sections were on tuberculosis, tobacco, and crime. I also emphasized this aspect in a lecture I was asked to give as part of the Lothian Health Board celebration of 50 years of the NHS.

One of the problems we had when we started, as we had partly expected, was the relationship among the different professionals and disciplines concerned. They had mostly been ignorant of each other's work – and where there is ignorance there is often suspicion and mistrust. I learned that social and community workers tended to have been educated to regard the medical profession as arrogant, patronising and merely self-serving of its own interests. The doctors in turn tended to regard the social and community side as impractical longhaired lefties. When the community start realising that something can be done, they tend to make demands that are financially impossible and to criticise strongly the inadequacies of what are often grossly overworked professionals. One of my jobs in Scotland has proved to be getting these groups together to develop achievable, even if modest, aims and in the process, build up mutual respect and confidence.

Royal College of Physicians appeal: 1982 – 1985

In 1982 Professor John Strong, then President, asked me to chair an Appeal Committee to raise £1 million to construct a Lecture Theatre and Conference Centre behind one of the College buildings in an area where the original house garden had been long replaced by a dim warehouse. The College bought the ground and used it for building the Centre.

I had had virtually no experience of raising money. I had recently agreed to chair a Scottish Office Committee to coordinate health education in Scotland and had a number of international commitments. I was not at all keen. "We only need your name" said John. It proved much otherwise.

But I did think the Centre was needed and decided I ought to accept. We agreed to ask Dale Falconer to be the Director. He was a charming man who had been the Scottish Secretary of the BMA and seemed to know every doctor in Scotland. We agreed a good committee, including Andrew Russell who had recently retired as Treasurer of the Bank of Scotland. We were given a temporary staff of an administrator and a secretary.

I thought we must start with our own Fellows. A positive response from them would make it much easier to go on to appeal to banks, industry, trusts etc. I composed an appropriate letter. After some discussion we decided that we would subsequently publicise the names of Fellows who had donated but not the amount each contributed. It happened that I was about to reach the age of seventy and would then begin to receive my Old Age Pension, deferred because of previous receipts of royalties from our textbook. I felt it was not essential and committed it to the Appeal in an annual covenant for ten years.

By the time we were ready to start John Strong had demitted office and had been replaced by Ronnie Girdwood. Always the pessimist, he was very gloomy that any Fellow or Member would subscribe. They were all too poor! I had been away to some meeting and came back to receive an official visit from the Treasurer, Ian Campbell, to say that the Council of the College thought my letter unsuitable and would not agree to its being sent out. I was sure that the initiative for this refusal came from the President.

I replied that I would be delighted to resign and hand over the Appeal to the Council if they wished to take it on. But if I was to be in charge of the Appeal my letter must go out unaltered. And so it did.

Of course a large number of copies were made but I inserted the "Dear Blank" in manuscript and tried to add a personal message in manuscript to each letter. I knew many of the Fellows personally and could compose an appropriate message. For the others I consulted the Medical Directory about their interests and added an appropriate note. Some of my colleagues on the Committee, and I myself, did the same for overseas Fellows they knew personally. Ronnie Robertson, another ex-President, was particularly helpful as he had made recent visits on behalf of the College.

We later went back twice to Fellows (and later Members) who had not so far subscribed. We reinforced the Appeal through College parties for Fellows and Members in various centres throughout the UK. These were organised by the local College Advisors, and attended by myself and occasionally by the President. It included one organised for London Fellows and Members at the House of Lords by (Lord) John Richardson. We were not allowed to raise the problem of filthy lucre in that sacred House, but it helped to create a "giving climate".

A successful ploy was to encourage donors to endow one or more seats in the future Lecture Theatre in the names of themselves or others. Each seat was then given a plaque with the name. I endowed several, including one in memory of my late friend Professor Derrick Dunlop and my late colleague Dick Borthwick, later from Tromsø, Norway, who died tragically from cancer in his early forties.

Then our administrators checked through the lists of Trusts in appropriate publications. We approached those we thought appropriate. We sought Fellows with personal knowledge of Trustees and I tried to write letters appropriate to each Trust, including a manuscript note. Many were fruitless but every now and then we received a major donation. Andrew Russell arranged for me to visit the Chairmen of the four major Scottish Banks who usually collude in deciding about charity donations. I was terrified but they all proved charming and gave us £5,000 apiece.

One might expect medical insurance companies, with their major health component and with some of our Fellows as medical advisors, to be sympathetic. But we got very little from them. We were also not all that successful with industry.

Over the two and a half years or so of the Appeal I estimated I signed, and mostly added manuscript messages, to some 28,000 letters. I often took boxes of 500-600 home at weekends. I notice Ronnie Girdwood in his autobiography says he himself signed 28,000 letters. I cannot remember his signing one but he may have signed one or two. One can see how written historical records may give a fuzzy measure of reality! He remained uniformly pessimistic almost to the end.

All this work took up about half my time over the period. I was distressed when the cost of the project was later recalculated and the target was raised from £1 million to £1.3 million. But we made it in the end, though the sum included receipts from a sale of one College portrait to the National Portrait Gallery next door.

This experience gave me insight into the enticement of proving a successful financial entrepreneur. The figures for takings moving steadily up the graph were a simple and rewarding measure of success much clearer than most measurements of clinical success. I met many nice people and received virtually no brickbats.

The Conference Centre was really the concept of John Strong as President and much of the detailed supervision of it was by James Syme, a previous College Secretary and chairman of the project Committee. It was formally opened by, and named after, the Queen Mother. It has proved a great success and is used intensively both by the College and by others. Blood, sweat but not many tears. It was worth it.

Of course I have concentrated above, as this is an autobiography, on my own part in the effort. Dale Falconer, the members of the Appeal Committee and our splendid administrative team did a wonderful job and much of the work, but I felt, as Chairman, I must set an example of hard work. And it was hard work!

Lothian Health Challenge

About 1991, I was telephoned by the Convenor of the then Lothian Region to ask if I would agree to be the medical member of the proposed Lothian Health Challenge Group. My first reaction was to ask whether they had consulted the Lothian Health Board. They had not. I suggested they should but agreed to come to a working lunch to discuss how they should proceed. At the subsequent rather indecently luxurious and well-wined lunch I was presented with the new Lothian Region tie glowing in politically appropriate red.

There followed what for me was a very busy few years. It involved a lot of local work in Region and District. Soon after the Labour Government was elected in 1997, the sort of interdisciplinary and professional/community activities which, with limited success, we had tried to initiate were taken over and made statutory. As a non-statutory and independent member, and well on in my late eighties, it seemed an appropriate time to disengage.

During this period I discovered that politicians' interest only lasts for a year or two, while they can get publicity for their efforts. If anything was to happen thereafter the initiative would have to come from the amateurs and independents. Initially the councillors' interest resulted in excellent initiatives from the highly enthusiastic and intelligent Council officers. But as the interest of the politicians gradually waned the administrators were able to give us less help.

I cannot go into details of what was done and what was achieved. I think I can summarize by saying that all this activity contributed to the gradual evolution of a climate of opinion, among the numerous different professionals and among the mosaic of communities, towards the maintenance of a very broad view of health and what affected it. Various initiatives in healthy food, transport, poverty, alcohol, crime and much else contributed to this. None was very dramatic but they amounted to a cumulative effect. With a vast amount of work, often frustrating, I think we all did leave things a little better than we found them. We laid the basis for others to carry things forward, hopefully with increasing effect. We trust that the successor of more statutory groups will achieve this.

Alcohol Abuse

My personal major professional concern with alcohol and its social ill effects dates from being asked to chair a new Scottish Home and Health Department Committee, the Scottish Health Education Coordinating Committee (SHECC) in 1981 after my retirement from clinical medicine. Just before my retirement I had been the only clinician on a committee to advise the government on priorities for the Scottish NHS in the 1980s. From the data that emerged from that committee it seemed clear that there were three high priorities for Scottish Health Education: tobacco, alcohol, and the problems of poverty and multiple deprivation. We had to defer Health Education about food as at that time the UK experts had not come to an agreement about recommendations. In the event these were only becoming clear about 1986 when I handed over the chairmanship to my successor John Strong. I became involved later through my work with multiple deprivation.

Personal Background

I never heard of any particular alcohol problems within my own family. As an adolescent I was very sensibly introduced to alcohol with an occasional glass of wine when my parents had people to dinner. At my boarding school, Tonbridge, as a school prefect I remember being asked to dinner by the headmaster; we were all served with a glass of white wine. When I was about to go up to Cambridge I knew that undergraduates drank beer, so I gave myself a mild introductory course to get over what I first regarded as the revolting taste so that I could accommodate to university norms of student behaviour. At school in my day, as far as I knew there was no trouble with secret drinking (or at that time with other drugs). Of course at Cambridge there was from time to time a good deal of drunken behaviour, mostly at club dinners. I myself overdid it once after one of these. But I normally began to feel physically uncomfortable when I was beginning to have too much and learned to stop before I reached that stage. It was forbidden for undergraduates to go into pubs. You still had to wear gowns after dark and could be arrested and fined by the Bullers if they spotted you. The two Bullers, dressed in tall hats and tail coats, were the minions of the senior academic, the Proctor, responsible for undergraduate discipline. After dark they stalked the streets, accosting and fining any undergraduate not wearing a gown or breaking other rules, such as drinking in pubs. If the victim fled, he was chased and arrested by the fleet-footed Bullers. This was known as being "Progged". I imagine "Buller" was derived from "Bull-dog".

The most noisy and destructive drunks in the streets were the young men from the landed classes, often members of the snobbish "Pitt Club", sent to Cambridge to be "finished". The classical sound of Evelyn Waugh's "English county families baying for broken glass" was a recurrent evening reminder of their communal social life. I don't think by that time, the 1930s, that their fathers were very excessive drinkers in middle age. In the past, certainly in the 18th and early 19th centuries, I believe country house parties were pretty drunken affairs, as was certainly witnessed by Lord Cockburn in his judicial travels in Scotland in the 1840s. My mother told me that when her father was a young curate in rural Ireland he would be invited to dinner parties at the nearby "Big Houses". At the end of dinner the ladies would retire to the drawing-room leaving the men to their drinks and cigars. At ten o'clock the gentlemen's carriages would drive up to the front door and the gentlemen's footmen would carry the gentlemen into their carriages. The gentlemen would all be expected to be dead drunk by that time.

Of course, early in my professional career alcohol was bound to cross my path. Alcoholics were common in the more down-and-out patients in Edinburgh – often drifting to doss houses and with tuberculosis as a result. Faced with these I sometimes expressed the exaggerated view that few middle-aged working class men in Edinburgh were still living with their wives. Most had been booted out by their wives because of alcohol or had drifted away. It was only later that I realized just how much cryptic misery was caused to wives (and children) by alcoholic domestic violence and other disruption. It has only recently been appreciated how much "wife-battering", often alcohol-related, occurs also in middle and upper class homes.

At one time, in dealing with tuberculosis, we agreed with the hospital administration that alcoholic men with advanced disease could be prescribed a daily small dose of whisky if that induced them to remain in hospital and complete treatment – a service to themselves and to the public whom they might infect if they discharged themselves prematurely.

I had one intriguing case of cryptic alcoholism in a middle-aged middle class woman. She was admitted with very far advanced pulmonary tuberculosis. She improved dramatically and was sent back to her good home to continue treatment. But she kept on coming back with a relapse, often admitted filthy dirty and uncared for. It was her GP who eventually found a cupboard full of empty bottles and thus diagnosed her secret drinking, a well-known affliction of middle-aged women. Her husband eventually threw her out and divorced her. We got her a job in a nursing home run by nuns. Then she started handing whisky round to other staff and was dismissed. She drifted down to a basic hostel run by the Salvation Army and had to be rescued again.

But her story had a happy ending. One of the hospital porters was a recovered alcoholic. He took her in hand, got her off the alcohol, and eventually married her. We cured her tuberculosis. He cured her alcohol problem. I learned several important lessons, especially to remember the potential problem of secret drinking and the potential value in extending training in simple aspects of preventive medicine to non-professional NHS staff who can often influence patients through informal contact.

Report by the Scottish Health Education Coordinating Committee (1985)

The SHECC decided that alcohol should be one of our major concerns. We had relatively little personal expertise in the alcohol field but I knew there was considerable expertise in the Edinburgh University Department of Psychiatry. I started by consulting Professor Robert Kendall, Norman Kreitman, head of the Medical Research Council Unit for Studies in Psychiatry, and Bruce Ritson, the main clinical expert in the field. These gave me many other names of experts to consult elsewhere in Scotland. We started off with a working supper at St Andrews House attended by about 12 experts. We then set up a Working Group which met regularly. In between meetings I arranged to visit a number of other experts throughout Scotland.

We early decided the plan of our report. We should give an initial outline of the adverse effects, physical, mental, and social, of alcohol in Scotland with relevant statistics about trends and costs. We had to balance this, in contradistinction to tobacco for which we could only advise total abstinence as the smallest dose was dangerous, with the traditional pleasurable and social catalytic effects of mild or very modest drinking and the enormous export and tax income from the alcohol industry, especially from Scottish whisky[*].

We should then go on to give an account of the present background of alcohol in Scotland. We should follow with detailed recommendations for UK Government action, over which we could have only limited influence; and actions by the Scottish Office, Scottish Home and Health Department, Scottish Education Department, the NHS (including detailed recommendations for Health Boards and for individuals and groups within the NHS), Local Authorities (including Social Work), educational services, Health and Safety Executive, voluntary bodies, trade unions, employers' associations, the media and the Courts.

UK consumption had doubled between 1950 and 1980, during which the price in real terms had more than halved. Scots spent £3.5 million daily on alcohol, 7.4% of their consumer spending. In any one week 80% of men and 50% of women in Scotland would drink alcohol. At the age of 15-16 years, 45% of boys and 32% of girls were regular drinkers; and 50% of boys and 30% of girls had had some degree of intoxication in the last 6 months.

We divided the resultant personal problems into those related to intoxication, to excessive use, and to dependence. Intoxication effects included attempted suicide, fire deaths, homicide, head injuries and fatal road accidents; also domestic accidents, pedestrian accidents, drowning and deaths in young people. It was an important problem in prisons and prisoners. Excessive use gave rise to medical, social, and legal problems. There was evidence of high rates of such problems in general practice and hospital admission. A high proportion of cirrhosis of the liver is alcohol-related; in 1970-81 this had increased in Scotland by 104% in men and 73% in women. Maternal drinking could cause damage to the unborn child. Family problems included loss of work, domestic problems, and child abuse. Dependence was the most familiar long-term effect, which also gave rise to medical, social, and legal problems. Alcohol-related psychiatric hospital admissions had increased importantly in men and dramatically in women.

Besides a fairly full executive summary, we went on to detail, as already indicated, what a wide range of individuals and groups should do about it. As a convenience to busy readers, action by each general group was summarized and detailed on different coloured paper.

---

[*] At that time, UK revenue from the alcohol industry exceeded £5,200 million and exports exceeded £900 million; by 2002 the Scottish whisky industry exports alone had reached just under £1,000 million. UK costs of abuse were calculated at greater than £1,000 million.

Various members of the committee had produced individual drafts. I acted as general editor, wrote much of it myself, and produced the final draft. We were struck with the lack of knowledge about alcohol and the lack of training in dealing with it, not only within the alcohol industry (including pub-owners and staff), but within the NHS, and within educational and social work departments. The Police College at that time had only one afternoon's session on the subject.

Besides the widespread need for training in alcohol problems there was a similar need in all the various bodies for a formal policy regarding alcohol and work and related problems among staff. Although there were limited but helpful statistics on alcohol problems in general practice and hospital there was at that time surprisingly little from social work departments; social workers seemed reluctant to enquire into what they tended to consider their clients' private lives. There were isolated findings of high rates related to social problems in children and family social work but little general collection of statistics. At that time there was little alcohol education in the training of social workers and no systematic postgraduate training of any kind. We strongly advocated strengthening this field.

In the NHS we advised further development of pilot remedies in general practice and the value of far more in-depth enquiries in hospitals and remedial action by specialist nurses. The latter proved very effective in one or two pilot schemes. We also recommended each Health Board should set up an expert "Alcohol Reference Group", including social workers, to advise broadly within the NHS and liaise relevantly with local authorities and police; this was subsequently implemented but still rather patchily and inadequately.

Alcohol and Work

Alcohol is a major cause of inefficiency, accidents and absenteeism at work. I was asked by Alcohol Concern UK to write an editorial on alcohol problems in employment and spoke on this at a number of seminars in England and several in Scotland.

I found that most managements considered only the problems of employees who came into the "addicted" category, the very grim end stage of excessive use often leading to unemployment and not uncommonly to suicide. From the employer's point of view, statistical research had revealed that this was a relatively small component of the inefficiency, accidents and loss of work resulting from alcohol. Norman Kreitman had demonstrated the epidemiological paradox that, though heavy drinkers had a much higher incidence of alcohol-related work problems, really heavy drinkers were only a small minority of the workforce. The actual incidence of problems in moderate or light drinkers was much less but these were much the majority of the workforce so they gave rise to much the largest total of incidents, through occasional hangover, accidents etc.

Of course the problems were not only in the lower ranks. Alcohol often featured heavily in Directors' lunches. An officer from the Health and Safety Executive told me that after one inspection he was asked to stay to lunch with the Directors. Before lunch he observed the Chief Safety Officer drinking three double gins! How well thought through are many decisions made after well-oiled lunches?

I increasingly realized and supported a policy of not mixing alcohol and work. At that time there was a long way to go even in the medical profession. At scientific meetings in the Royal College of Physicians of Edinburgh the only drinks provided at the statutory lunch were wine together with a postprandial coffee. Not even water was on the tables. A year or two later the press picked up the programme of a symposium on alcohol at the Royal College of Physicians of London at which "Bar Open" was indicated before lunch.

I am glad to say that these errors have since been corrected at least in the Colleges of Physicians, and increasingly in industries. In some industries nowadays no alcohol, even for Directors, is allowed on the premises, though I think there is a long way to go before there is no drinking among workers lunching away from their workplace.

Alcohol Concern's seminars in England for employers were designed to encourage preventive alcohol policies, particularly concerning the handling of employees who had demonstrated problems. I was asked to contribute to a number of these in various cities. Schemes seemed to work out best if they were based on general counselling schemes for employees. These were more likely to avoid stigma and encourage more ready reference by supervisors, colleagues and individuals themselves.

I was particularly impressed by a talk in Birmingham from one company. This was a large local computer company which had been taken over by an American firm. The American Directors asked whether the British firm had a counselling service for its employees. The British replied that, with the NHS, social services etc, this was not needed in the UK. The Americans then asked their British colleagues to issue a survey questionnaire to their employees asking each if in the last year he/she had had a personal problem which had an effect on his/her work and who or what they had consulted as a result. It turned out that about 40% had had a problem and many had not known whom to turn to.

The British firm then called in consultants to design them a counselling service. This was independent of the firm's management. It provided counsellors to serve both the employees and their families. The counsellors had access to alcohol experts, but also to experts who could give advice on other medical problems, on legal problems, on family problems, on mortgages etc. Employees could seek advice by telephone or personally. This was extremely successful in improving work efficiency. Moreover an employee might initially consult over some relatively minor matter, perhaps over the telephone. Having been helped and reassured he might then go on to consult on his real and more serious problem, perhaps alcohol or drugs. One of the difficulties with these schemes is the responsibility of the counsellor. It is generally agreed that his counselling is confidential to the employee. Any report to management must only be on the employee's fitness for his current work or to advise any necessary change in the work allotted to him.

When I was asked to review the influence of alcohol on workplace accidents I found it very difficult to get a true statistical picture. The causer or the victim of the accident would not want to reveal the alcohol component. Often the management would not wish to emphasise it because of insurance complications. I managed to get some British data but it seemed widely agreed that most available statistics were probably gross underestimates.

My committee was enthusiastic and readily approved and finalized the report. It received a glowing leading article in the *British Medical Journal* and much favourable review from alcohol control organizations throughout the UK. As a result I was invited to lecture, write articles, or participate in conferences in many places in England and Scotland.

Follow-up Activities

Most of the activities were in the first few years after the publication of the report. I believed that such reports would only have a real impact if they were followed up and resulting action monitored. While I was still chairman we carried out a monitoring survey of resultant action on our tobacco report with the Scottish Health Boards. I emphasized to senior Civil Servants the importance of carrying out monitoring on the implementation of all three of the SHECC reports – tobacco, alcohol, and multiple deprivation. I said that after my retirement as chairman I would be prepared to supervise that monitoring, but that I would need a Research Fellow and secretarial help. They advised that I should apply for the necessary support to the Chief Scientific Officer's Research Fund. Their administrative officer was strongly supportive but suggested it should be attached to a university department. The then Professor of Public Health in Edinburgh University was enthusiastic. I had strong backing from the Chief Medical Officer, Chief Nursing Officer and Chief Social Work Advisor. I recruited provisionally an excellent possible Research Fellow who had already done good work in the University Public Health Department. But to the surprise and dismay of all of us we were turned down. Our report became forgotten except for one or two enthusiasts. Later the new Executive of the Scottish Parliament established a committee that produced a draft report in 2002 on a Scottish Strategy on Alcohol. The governments of England and Wales have done virtually nothing except making placatory noises.

Action on Alcohol Abuse

A year or two before this the UK government had set up a committee to review the several charities concerned with the prevention of alcohol abuse, all of which were receiving government financial support. The committee sensibly recommended that the various charities should be combined into one large one in each of England, Scotland and Wales. This would be concerned with the training of alcohol counsellors to help individuals with alcohol problems, coordinating preventive work etc. The resulting body in England was Alcohol Concern and in Scotland the Scottish Council on Alcohol. The committee also recommended that another alcohol NGO should be established with the primary duty of advocacy, as with ASH for tobacco. It would keep the alcohol problem before the public through contact with the media and push for effective alcohol control measures to be implemented by the NHS, Local Authorities and the government.

At that time it was a Conservative government. Although the committee had recommended that all these bodies should be at least partly subsidized by the government, the government agreed to support Alcohol Concern and the Scottish Council but not the advocacy body. The tobacco advocacy body, ASH, had been initiated in the early 1970s by the Royal Colleges of Physicians in London and Edinburgh. On this occasion these and several other medical Royal Colleges agreed to launch AAA (Action on Alcohol Abuse). I think much of the initiative came from Edinburgh through Mike Daube, then a Senior Lecturer there, and David Player in London who had recently been appointed Executive Director of the English Health Education Council. Of course I gave the proposal enthusiastic support. So more directly, did Professor John Strong, the then President of the Royal College of Physicians of Edinburgh, who became its first chairman. But to have a whole time Medical Director and his assistant and to provide running costs would need considerable financial support. The government would not provide support and nor could the Colleges.

David Player has told me that he persuaded the King's Fund in London (an independently funded Trust to support health measures) to provide the first three years funding. Thanks to a superb Executive Director, Don Steele, AAA was an astonishing success during its short 3-year life. Don Steele well knew both the subject and the relevant people. He and his assistant were enthusiastic, very hard working, and highly effective. He helped to set up a Parliamentary Cross-party Committee on alcohol. He established excellent relations with the media, as had ASH, and supplied them with relevant and publishable material. He kept the problem continuously before the public, and consequently before the politicians. Alcohol came away up the political agenda. The government even set up a parliamentary alcohol committee which published reports.

But three years later all came tumbling down. The new chairman, a previous President of the Royal College of Psychiatrists, took it on. I had the impression that he put little enthusiasm into the job. He certainly failed to obtain further funding. The superb Don Steele had to go away to a far less prestigious job in preventive cardiology. John Strong and I went to see the Executive Director of Alcohol Concern. We tried to persuade him to take Don Steele on for the advocacy component of Alcohol Concern but he refused. He claimed that Alcohol Concern was already being an effective advocate, which it was not.

National Alcohol Forum

I was very flattered when I was approached in about 1985 by the UK Department of Health and Social Services (as it was at that time) to ask if I would become the independent chairman of a new body, the National Alcohol Forum, to explore mutual action between the alcohol industry and the various bodies concerned with public and personal alcohol problems. David Player, then Executive Director of the Health Education Council in London, warned me that his own experience with the industry was that they had made many friendly approaches, given him lots of entertainment, and made encouraging noises, but that nothing ever actually happened as a result.

As I did not want to waste my time chairing a mere cosmetic talking shop, I agreed in the first place to a purely exploratory role in which I would probe the commitment of those concerned and then make proposals. In the following five months I negotiated in depth, both by correspondence and individual interview, with five bodies and finally made my proposals for constitution, remit and initial subjects for discussion. The breakdown came over specific tests of commitment, and perhaps because I made it clear that I was only interested in discussion if discussion would result in action.

It was agreed that the core of the Forum should be kept as small as possible. As it was to be a UK body, it was essential to include the Councils on Alcohol in Scotland and Northern Ireland and also the Scottish Health Education Group. It was also agreed to invite Action on Alcohol Abuse (AAA) and an organization representing the retail trade. In addition I proposed four "independent" members, who might provide balance and act as chairmen of working groups. We agreed on a short list of distinguished people for these places. Including the chairman, secretary and DHSS observer, there would have been a core group of seventeen.

I suggested starting with less controversial subjects of mutual interest and going on to more difficult fields later. It was agreed that initial subjects might include training of managers and employees from the alcohol and catering industries in the physical, psychological, medical, social and legal aspects of alcohol; drink and driving; underage drinking and alcohol education for the young; and employee alcohol problems. Others listed were research and development; general education of the public; more effective implementation of the alcohol advertising code; alcohol content of drink and alternatives to alcohol; licensing laws and their implementation; services for alcohol-related problems; education and training of professional groups; alcohol and women. Subjects thought particularly difficult by the industry included increasing taxation of alcohol; restriction on advertising and promotion; a levy on advertising; health warning labels on alcohol containers; and restriction on licensing hours.

All seemed to have been verbally agreed, though perhaps slightly nervously, in direct discussions. But before finally agreeing to accept the chairmanship I had to have some commitment to action. I first proposed a Research and Development Fund of £10 million a year for five years (not so extravagant a sum in view of an estimated £100 to 200 million a year spent in alcohol promotion. When that was rejected without counter-proposals I asked for some commitment to funding projects which had been proposed by the Forum; the counter-proposal was that we should press the government to fund the projects out of current alcohol taxation. (It had been agreed that the cost of the Forum administration would be divided equally between the industry and the other bodies).

When it was suggested to me that it might be unfair to ask hard-headed businessmen for such a commitment in advance, I tried a test of intent which should have been simple if there had indeed been serious intent. I asked each of the three industry groups to produce a brief memo on how they would ensure that future training proposals for the alcohol and catering industries would be implemented in practice, how that implementation could be monitored, and how we might hope to finance the training of the trainers and the provision of training materials. This was apparently the break point. I received a tactful letter from the DHSS suggesting that, as my perceptions of the Forum clearly differed from those of the group, this was the time to part.

In his tactful letter of dismissal, the Permanent Secretary of DHSS said that he would be delighted to see me and discuss the matter. They obviously wanted minimum publicity. I did have a friendly chat with him and in that chat said that I would have to consider whether it was in the interests of alcohol control to stimulate some publicity on my dismissal.

I did not want to be motivated by pique. On the other hand, publicity would draw attention to the major alcohol problem and the nervousness of the industry in doing anything really effective about it. I took advice from one or two people, as I had warned the Permanent Secretary, and decided I should go public. David Player put me in touch with the Guardian's health correspondent, then Andrew Veitch. The result was the headline "ALCOHOL CHAIRMAN SACKED". A further result was that no-one else would take on the chairmanship. The industry set up its own "Portman Group", initially chaired by an ex-public school headmaster. I asked him and his wife to dinner at the Royal Society of Medicine and gave him some background. I was unimpressed with him or with later action by the Portman Group with which I had no personal connection. One of their more disreputable actions was to write round to a number of alcohol experts in the UK and offer them £2,000 to write articles rubbishing a recent very progressive WHO paper on alcohol control. One of the recipients of the offer leaked this to the press, causing a considerable scandal.

Chapter 12:
Reflections on Life and Death

Saving lives and preventing misery

Having lived an active and busy life, like most of us I have been mainly involved with trying to cope with the day-to-day problems I faced. From time to time I would consider longer term aims. Although medicine's immediate concerns are to save lives and prevent or ameliorate misery, I had to be aware of related longer term aims such as relieving poverty, more closely at home, more remotely internationally.

If I occasionally thought even more remotely, I would face the disturbing question of how far advances in medicine might be partly responsible for the threat to the planet from the present Malthusian population explosion. Historically the logarithmic explosion had been partly controlled by the disasters of plague, famine or war, often working together. I might ease my minute paradoxical sense of guilt with the hope that the spread of techniques for modern population control might gradually provide the answer. I might take comfort from one or two recent speculations by experts that in due course they might become sufficiently global to do so. But one has to be only too well aware of the powerful contrary influences of ignorance or religion, even in advanced technological countries such as USA.

I remember in my youth one of my close friends, Donough, drawing my attention to the "Charm of Near Horizons", as distinct from the beauties of distant views. I have since found many delights in gazing at landscapes in this sense. In my working life it was equally comfortable to turn from disturbing misgivings about long term objectives to the "Near Horizons" of more immediate short term ends which seemed practicable, achievable, moral and rewarding.

Religion

From time to time, like most societies in history and many individuals, I came to speculate on "Why and How Are We Here?" Such of course has been the subject of religions, certainly in all historical periods. Archaeological evidence suggests that the universal experience of death, in families and societies, evoked emotional reactions, religious speculation and perhaps symbolic or magical ceremonies, certainly among early *Homo sapiens*, perhaps even in Neanderthal man who seems to have used red ochre in possible burial ceremonies.

The evolutionary development of the brain probably enlarged the capacity to plan ahead, for instance leading to cooperation in hunting and food gathering. A sense of responsibility to others must have started with parental care of children and later children's care of elderly parents. Cooperation and responsibility must then have extended to other members of the hunter gatherer groups. Such groups, of course, have been the basis of human society for most of its existence, perhaps even among groups of their hominid predecessors.

This capacity to "put yourself in his place" must have given rise to the second, moral, element, in religion, the sense of duty to your fellow men, leading to personal and tribal loyalty. But hunter gatherer groups, in anthropological studies, often consist only of about a hundred individuals. The size of the group is limited by the size of the land area sufficient for the group's subsistence. This will vary both seasonally and geographically. The area has to be covered on foot, with the women carrying the young children. It must provide sufficient animals to hunt and food to gather.

There may well have been competition for productive subsistence areas between rival groups. So loyalty to members of one's own group would tend to be accompanied by antagonism and aggression against members of other groups, the seed of mankind's perennial drift to violence and war.

After the Neolithic farming revolution, of course, groups became more localised and could support much bigger populations. Hence we move on to tribes. Tribes give rise to wider loyalties. Their individual members identify with each other. But we all know how aggressive tribes can be to members of other tribes.

In due course, first in Mesopotamia, later in Egypt, China etc, increase in food supply allowed the development of cities and nations supporting non-farming specialists, artisans, priests, rulers and so on. These evolved into nations whose members could to a considerable extent identify and empathise with each other. Patriotism was born, with all its mosaic of good and evil.

The educated elite in some nations could later begin to identify and empathise with members of other nations, even those with different coloured skins, different cultures and different languages. The global extension and interactions of this moral trend perhaps gives the best hope for the future of the planet. The disastrous backlash of the Nazis, and the current Middle East, warn us how much effort will be needed and how provisional is the hope.

The third stimulus to religious development was of course seeking to account for the vagaries of the natural world. All societies had to eat and breed. Accounting for the changes in the seasons, in the stars and in the planets gave rise to speculations and various claims of different religions.

Someone once said that all religions are initiated by highly creative individuals but are soon taken over by the most conservative elements in the society. They become frozen in long term rigidity. Even the dramatic developments of reasoned thinking by the Greeks occurred against a traditional background of a ridiculous and all too human mixed team of gods. The outcome of this conservative backlash was shown by the Athenian jury's condemnation to death of Socrates, one of history's most original thinkers. More notorious still has been the later freezing of the early scientific speculations on cosmology by the rigidity of the mediaeval Christian church, to say nothing of its modern residua of religious creationism attacking Darwin's science of evolution.

Most religions therefore are concerned with three main components: explaining the infinite vagaries of nature and the world in which we live; morality in its widest sense, personal morals and group morals; and death and its possible successor of an afterlife.

The Natural World

The evolution of more accurate observations through the development of technology has led to confirmable scientific theory explaining most of the more immediate phenomena which must have puzzled hunter gatherers and their successors. But the vast advances of science in the last couple of centuries have also revealed the counter-intuitive worlds of space-time and particle physics which can still leave us puzzled. The difficulties in explaining very complex phenomena initially led to these being expressed by the title "Chaos Theory". As our astonished intuitions had shaken down a bit and become used to surprises, the term has progressed to the more reassuring "Complexity Theory". We now realise that this applies to many phenomena, including biology, in which vast numbers of components interact often in very unexpected ways. As an amateur I read about these in simplified versions, written by specialists for the general public, without being able to do more than achieve a shadowy comprehension. But it is enough to give me great emotional excitement as I contemplate these vast and personally unachievable Brave New Worlds. From their infinite and unattainable horizons I can always retreat to the more comfortable near horizons to which I have drawn attention earlier.

Among these unattainable horizons must also be included the precise nature of the cosmos. Although astronomers have been achieving more knowledge about the details they are still confronted with many more puzzles not yet explicable by adequate evidence. Was the Big Bang the beginning of everything or just of our own little Universe? Is that universe indeed just our own? Is there intelligent life in some other applicable planet, or many planets, revolving round some of the almost infinite numbers of stars? What about Dark Matter or even Dark Energy waiting to enlighten our ignorance?

But how dull it would be if mankind knew everything and there was nothing left to learn! I can at least enjoy some of the scraps of emerging knowledge which titillate my ignorance.

Morals

The all too obvious maelstrom of "good" and "evil", not only in human societies but in nature has always puzzled the best thinkers in most religions. In polytheistic religions "evil" in the form of disasters to individual people, or to human groups, whether inflicted by other human groups or by individuals, has often been interpreted as due to the all-too-human squabbles between rival gods seeking to do down their rivals' human favourites. Monotheistic religions believing in a single benign God find it difficult to believe that if He is so creative and so powerful, He permits so much obvious evil. From Manichaeism onwards a rival Devil had to be supposed in some religions as an explanation. How can those in a modern puzzled "enlightenment" explain all this?

Science nowadays can explain, if not yet prevent, the unexpected evils of great natural disasters. But much of evil is man-to-man, among individuals, all too often man to woman. Within most societies crime is perennial. Between societies recurrent war, often with its evil companions of famine and plague, is equally perennial. Can we explain all these? Could explanation lead to prevention?

Let us start with evil committed by individuals. During my long life I have become more and more struck with the vast range of human personalities. That should be no surprise. It is the main work-stuff of novelists. In the more benign central range of personality, among the majority in society, there are simple competing interests about work, love etc. that have to be handled in the context of the sort of family, group or tribal loyalty which I have discussed earlier. Most do reasonably well. Most have at least occasional selfish lapses at the expense of others. Most have sometimes to choose between rival goods. Most fail to do as much good as they could in responsibilities to others. Most manage to avoid doing anything which could be classed as positively evil.

But at the lowest level of personality there are individuals, often referred to as psychopaths, whom it seems at present impossible to reform. We do not know whether this derives from some mischance in the genes depriving their brains of capacity to remedy their behaviour. At present societies are faced with the difficult moral possibilities of long term or permanent incarceration to protect others at the cost of the individual's general right to ultimate liberty.

A little further up the range is evil done by personalities afflicted by early nurture. Factors may be bad parenting, including parental poverty, resulting in lack of development in the child of the norms of behaviour. The sad sequence of poor, uneducated parents not talking to their children results in poor vocabulary, resulting in backwardness in primary schooling, resulting in truancy and illiteracy, resulting in crime, is sadly all too evident in our prisons. At last the present UK government has started to try to remedy this. Efforts are being made to educate parents. Nursery schools are set up to foster the basic vocabulary essential to benefit from primary education. Such nursery schools also lay the foundations for social behaviour. The hoped-for benefits will mostly be long term as these initial cohorts of children grow into adolescents and adults. We must wait and see.

Remedies at the adolescent stage when many children with these early deprivations drift into crime, are much more difficult. Rehabilitation of these deprived youngsters can be done but requires highly motivated and well-trained remedial staff. In the UK much of the public, encouraged by the tabloid press, thinks only of crime in terms of police, punishment and prison. Politicians who have to seek election are nervous of providing the necessary resources for enlightened experiment, towards developing enlightened policies which actually work.

Happily at the middle and upper range of personalities there are those who spend large parts of their lives helping others and society in general. As always, older people often complain that the contemporary young are uncaring. Having been concerned through part of my career with areas of multiple deprivation I have been immensely impressed by the numbers of devoted well-educated young people working, often at low salaries, in such areas. Although not formally religious myself, I am particularly impressed by the immense motivation that formal religion can provide. I have particularly admired some of the medical missionaries I have met working so devotedly, with much self sacrifice, in Third World countries. Naturally, not sharing their formal religious views, I am most admiring of those to whom it provides personal motivation but who do not splash it about.

Perhaps this is an opportunity for a slight deviation on "Saints". Naturally my inclination is to admire those who have made immense self-sacrifice to serve the poor and afflicted. Naturally I am much less sympathetic to those, such as the Desert Fathers, who were primarily concerned with saving their own souls. I still have to withhold my sympathy if they claim they are helping others by praying to God for the wider world, without doing anything about it themselves.

Of course I can only condemn Sainthood for those whose fame consists largely in leading national or religious groups against others. Joan of Arc was a great leader but basically phoney as a "Saint". One can set her against the Indian emperor Ashoka. After a highly successful career as a conqueror he was converted to Buddhism and embarked on a second career of non-violent caring for the subjects of the empire he had conquered.

In a modern context, though he would never tolerate it I am sure, Mandela of South Africa has all the elements of the genuine sainthood I could admire. Jesus' preaching of the social value of forgiveness is the element of Christianity least often practised. In our own officially Christian society look at the perennial calls for "Justice", meaning revenge and punishment for wrongs done against us.

Ever since mankind, after the Neolithic farming revolution, formed big enough groups to become tribes, society has been at least partly motivated by the herd instinct. This has its good and bad elements. The good includes extending the caring role for the family to other members of the tribe. It includes actions to benefit the tribe as a whole. The bad include antagonism towards other herds and those who are not members of one's own tribe.

National and International Morals

Herds require leaders. In quiet times these may be older members of the tribe, often making decisions by discussing amongst themselves. But when faced with major challenges or danger, a single leader with capacity, charisma and self-confidence tends to take charge, usually with the acclamation of the herd. The classical case is the Roman Republic where, in such an emergency, the elders (the Senate) would appoint a Dictator – theoretically only for three months at a time. "All power corrupts. Absolute power corrupts absolutely"[*]. As was indeed shown when Julius Caesar appointed himself Dictator for Life, as so many other leaders have done up to our own time. Caesar, in consequence, was killed by his peers in the Senate. Many other dictators elsewhere were killed or exiled when they lost a subsequent war. Strong central power usually at least ensures law and order rather than anarchy. Its obverse may be giving privilege to the ruling elite and its leader at the expense of the rights and welfare of the non-elite.

Power feeds on itself. It overblows self-confidence. The Dictator takes the salute from his vast army. He becomes confident that, with this powerful

---

[*] John is slightly misquoting Lord Acton (1832-1902) who wrote "Power tends to corrupt, and absolute power corrupts absolutely" in his *Historical Essays and Studies*.

force, he can defeat his enemies, perhaps rule the world. He launches his war, or successive wars. Too often it leads to disaster and misery not only for his enemies but also for his own people and even for himself. It is not necessarily only dictators that power corrupts. In the Peloponnesian War the Athenian democracy developed the hubris which ultimately destroyed it.

Where are we now? The Austrian and German empires crumbled in the First World War. The British, French and Portuguese empires were persuaded to resign after the Second World War. That left the gainers as the empires of the two rival super-powers, the USSR with much of Central Asia and its puppet states in Eastern Europe, the USA with its bases and dependent client states all over the world.

The victorious Allies created the United Nations to encourage international cooperation and resolve international quarrels, so far with only limited success. Led by enlightened international experts, such as Monet and brave politicians, France and Germany set about founding long term cooperation in Western Europe. The resultant European Union now has inherited the successors to the Communist puppet states. Hopefully it will ultimately incorporate the notorious war-basket of the Balkans.

We have, of course, the contemporary backlash of oil-rich Muslim states fuelling a ruthless fundamentalist minority displaying all the worst horrors of the blind and selfish herd. Much of Africa is still chaotic. But there is some hope of remedy through mitigation of gross corruption and military greed. The present trends in the future great powers of India and China may give us some shaky hope for the future.

Death, Permanent or Transfigured?

In due course we know that death eventually comes to all of us personally and to all those whom we love. It is understandable that individuals have felt that their own and these loved personalities could not just disappear. They must move on to some conscious afterlife. Hopefully this would be a sort of heaven where we would again meet those whom we have loved. Whether these, or our own souls, would reflect the vigorous personalities of our youth or the benign or doddering personalities of old age was usually not considered. In some societies the ancestors played a major part. They might be worshipped. They might influence our own current lives, usually for good, perhaps sometimes for evil.

In many religions the nature of your afterlife would depend on your behaviour in this life. Hence mediaeval Christianity's concepts of heaven, purgatory and hell. Hindus and Buddhists believe in reincarnation as a mean animal, a potential saint, or a merger with the eternal.

Since the eighteenth century's Western "Enlightenment" many Western thinkers have found such concepts highly unlikely. I have to share their doubts. Emotionally I like to feel that my own personality and those that I love will have been left, after my death, as a pattern in time. That pattern may linger in some people's memories, family or other. Or, if one's achievements have been sufficiently notable or sufficiently notorious, in some sort of written deposit in history. In Western medicine Osler is perhaps the best recent example of a great personality with an ongoing historical influence. The most I myself could hope for would be an odd footnote, perhaps in a later history of the control or, hopefully, elimination, of tuberculosis. Meantime my working life and marvellous loves have been their own reward. They have brought me so much happiness in my old age, when the inevitable past struggles and anxieties have faded from my emotional present.

For me, ultimately, death is permanent slumber which carries no fear. Our many loved ones will continue to live in our thoughts, our timeless memories. My hope is that the actual process of dying proves not too uncomfortable!

Conclusion

There is probably nothing much original in this outline of my *personal* philosophy. I am sure I must be the child of what I hope is the more enlightened opinion of the present age, with its increased insight into basic knowledge and its residual shackles of human evolution. I hope my descendants can do better!